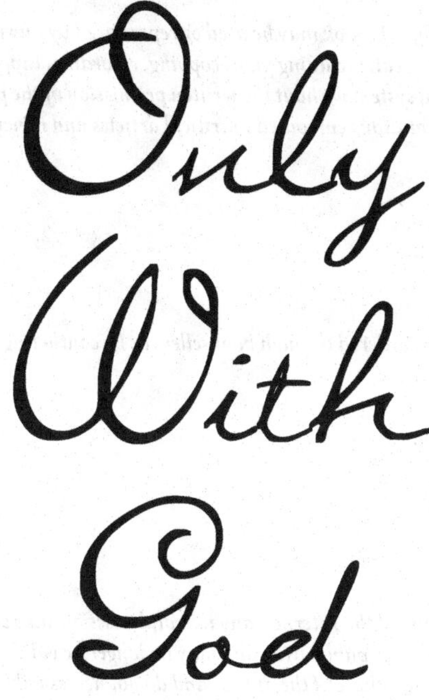

Only With God

One Families Cancer Journey

Dione Campbell

WestBow Press
A Division of Thomas Nelson

WestBow Press books may be ordered through booksellers or by contacting:

WestBow Press
A Division of Thomas Nelson
1663 Liberty Drive
Bloomington, IN 47403
www.westbowpress.com
1-(866) 928-1240

ISBN: 978-1-4497-6139-4 (sc)
ISBN: 978-1-4497-6140-0 (hc)
ISBN: 978-1-4497-6138-7 (e)

Library of Congress Control Number: 2012913667

Printed in the United States of America

WestBow Press rev. date: 07/26/2012

Chapter 1

My name is Dione Campbell, and this book is about my husband, Bill Campbell, affectionately known as Billy. This story chronicles his battle with cancer and how the Lord carried us through it.

To start with, allow me to give you a little background on Billy, myself, and our kids. Billy was born on January 2, 1972, in Missouri and grew up on his family farm near Russellville. I was born in Denver, Colorado, on February 14, 1971. I lived in Colorado for only a few months before moving to Nebraska to my grandparents' farm near Hershey. My family moved to the Russellville area shortly before I turned sixteen. We did not wish to leave the farm in Nebraska, but it became necessary to sell the farm. God was good because He knew we would not be happy no matter where we moved when we first left the farm, so He gave us a nine-month layover in Wichita, Kansas, before we moved on to Missouri.

My parents, Ron and Bobbie, my brother, Tyler, and my sister, Dru, were pleased to be able to move to the country again when we found a farm house to rent outside of Russellville. We were just a quarter mile from Mt. Olive Baptist Church, and although I didn't know it at the time, we lived less than two miles away from my future husband. Neither Billy's parents nor my parents attended church, so Billy's mom would drop him and his sister, Brenda, off. After I got my driver's license, I would take Billy and Brenda home from church quite often.

Tyler, Dru, and I began attending Mt. Olive in early 1987, just before I turned sixteen. Billy was one of the young men in the Sunday school class I attended. It didn't take me long to decide he was the guy for me; however, first I had to get him to realize it. With my heart settled on this boy, I worked at sending Billy the idea I liked him. I sat next to him in choir practice and church and often offered him a ride home from church. After a while, I even sat next to him during Sunday school, which was a bold move because the girls sat on a pew along one wall and the boys sat on a second pew along another wall.

Billy eventually got the hint, and it wasn't long before we were a couple. We felt the Lord brought us together. Even still we believe God's plan was pretty obvious because I traveled from Denver, Colorado, spent most of my growing-up years in Nebraska, took a short detour through Kansas, and then headed on to Russellville via a layover in Jefferson City. Only God could have brought our paths together.

Billy and I were both committed to remaining pure until our wedding night, and although it wasn't always easy, we did wait. Billy and I both believe this is one reason our marriage has always been so strong. Billy and I were married on August 15, 1992, at Mt. Olive Baptist Church by Rev. Ferry Cole. It was a small ceremony, with only our grandparents, parents, sisters, and brothers at the actual wedding. We then had a large reception following the ceremony, which all our other family members, church family, and friends attended.

After our wedding, Billy and I were living in my apartment in Jefferson City, but neither of us liked living in town very much. In April of 1993, we were able to rent a house out by Russellville that was not far from my parents and Billy's parents. We were very happy to be out of town.

Before we even married, we decided that when our first child was born, I would quit working and be a stay-at-home mom. Our firstborn, Kaylyn Santana Campbell, was born on June 12, 1993, and while I was still on maternity leave, I sent in my letter of resignation to my employer and became a stay-at-home mom. While I was pregnant with Kaylyn, we made the decision to homeschool our kids. We have never regretted that decision, and I felt blessed to be able to do it.

Our second child, James Max, was born on July 18, 1994. We knew what our first son's name would be before we even married. In Billy's family, the first boy on the Campbell side was named James, and as long as I can remember, I had said that my first son would be named Max after my

Grandpa Max. Billy and I agreed that our son's first name could be James but we would call him Max.

We purchased a mobile home and placed it on Billy's parents' property in July of 1995, and that is where we remain. We love living in the country, and the kids really enjoy it. After a miscarriage in November of 1995, our second daughter, Cassandra Renee, was born on September 8, 1996. We gave her the nickname Cassy, and it stuck, although sometimes Sassy would be more fitting.

Justin Allen came along on September 6, 1997, just over three weeks early. He gave us quite a surprise when he arrived. Justin was born on a Saturday morning at about 5:35. On the Friday evening before Justin was born, we had our friends Dee and Lee and their little one over to our house. Lee needed Billy's help to replace a water pump on their vehicle. I had been having some contractions most of the day, but they were far enough apart that I wasn't too concerned about it. I told Billy about the contractions just before Dee and Lee came over and called my mom. My mom and dad were going to be keeping the rest of our kids when Justin was born, and I wanted to give her a heads-up that we could be showing up during the night.

While Billy and Lee worked on the vehicle through the evening, Dee and I visited and played with the kids, discussing whether we thought the baby was a boy or a girl. I had pretty much decided it was a boy. In fact, I was sure he was a boy. As the evening went on, the contractions progressed, and I began to wonder if the guys would finish on the car before we needed to head for the hospital.

Once the vehicle was finished, Dee and Lee headed home around midnight. About forty-five minutes later, Billy and I loaded up the kids and headed for the hospital. We dropped the kids off at Mom and Dad's and arrived at the hospital around 1:30.

At around 7:30 that morning, I called Dee and said, "We were right—it is a boy." She sounded puzzled and said something about how we had decided that the night before. I told her that he was definitely a boy because he was here. That was quite a surprise for her since she had just left our house about seven hours before.

I was induced on October 18, 1999, with Levi Emanuel. He was our biggest baby at nine pounds, ten ounces, and he gave the doctor a bit of a scare when his shoulder got stuck briefly.

On May 16, 2001, I was induced with Faith Elizabeth. She made her appearance pretty quickly in only about three hours from start to arrival. Kaylyn was eight years old when Faith was born and had asked me to make this baby smaller than Levi. She loved holding and taking care of the babies, but Levi had been a bit much for her to handle. She was pleased with Faith's weight of eight pounds, four ounces.

Life is not boring with six kids. Although our kids are generally pretty healthy, we have dealt with occasional health issues or childhood illnesses. One such event occurred when Max was two. He was really sick, and doctors suspected that he had meningitis. After a spinal tap, the doctors determined Max had a virus that was causing multiple bacterial infections. He was put on four different medications, mainly strong antibiotics. He continued to run fevers as high as 104 for more than forty-eight hours after beginning the medications. His doctors decided the virus had come from a tick bite.

Another health issue came up during the summer when Cassy was two years old. She got a very nasty urinary tract/kidney infection that put her in the hospital for five days due to dehydration and her need for IV antibiotics. She was released with an IV in her hand because she still needed three more days of IV antibiotics before going to seven days of oral antibiotics. Within a few days of finishing her antibiotics, her infection had returned. She fought UTIs and kidney infections for a few years. Quite a bit of testing was done trying to figure out why she kept getting these infections. Since the antibiotics were making her sick and causing other problems, we looked into ways to prevent the infections. With the help of an employee at a health food store, we came up with a plan to help keep her infection free. It worked well, and she has only had a few infections since then. She seems to have outgrown the problem because she has not had an infection for a long time.

Like most families, we have had our share of common illnesses that have affected our children. One such time was on Easter Sunday, which I believe was the first Sunday of April 2006. Chicken pox began making its way through our house, starting with Max. Levi was the last to get the chicken pox, and although he had the least amount of pox, it seemed to take the longest for him to recover. He continued to be very tired and had dark circles under his eyes for a long time.

We went to Silver Dollar City for a couple of days during the week before Memorial Day. While we were there, Levi was not himself. While he was drinking and eating okay, he was also going to the bathroom a lot, was very tired, and just didn't seem to feel very good. We thought it could be a combination of getting over the chicken pox and being overtired from our two-day trip. By Memorial Day, Levi was so tired all the time that if he did get off the couch, it was only for a few minutes. He was not eating, and he was running a low grade fever.

I called the doctor on call at the hospital and explained how Levi had been behaving and that he now had a fever. We were concerned that Levi was having some complications from the chicken pox he had recently recovered from. The doctor on call felt Levi was most likely suffering from a virus or something along that line and told us to take him to our regular doctor the next day.

When we described Levi's various symptoms and lack of appetite to our regular doctor, he ordered some blood work, including a CBC and a mono test. I called the doctor's office the following day, and Levi's blood work was all fine. I told the nurse that Levi was not any better and was actually more fatigued. She asked if he was still drinking okay, which he was, so she was not concerned about dehydration. She said that the doctor felt it was a virus, and it just needed to run its course. She told me call back if he got worse.

The next day, Thursday, June 1, I called the doctor's office again because Levi was becoming more lethargic and was throwing up. The nurse called back about 4:00 p.m. and again said that the doctor felt it was a virus but made an appointment for Levi for 8:30 the next morning, just to be sure there wasn't something more going on. I needed to go grocery shopping, and it was Max's turn to go with me, so we headed out.

Billy and I had agreed before I left that if Levi seemed to get any worse, Billy would call me and head for the ER. Billy called me about 6:30 and said he was taking Levi to the ER because Levi was crying about his stomach hurting, and he was so weak he couldn't lift his head off the pillow.

Max and I arrived at the ER first, and I had the paperwork filled out when Billy arrived with Levi. Billy brought Levi in and put him in my arms. I could not believe he was the same kid I had left just a couple of hours before! Since I was with him all the time, I had not noticed before how much his condition had deteriorated. He was so weak that he could barely open his eyes. His speech was slurred and very quiet, his color was ashen, and he had obviously lost weight. The ER staff took him back immediately, even before some others who had been waiting for a while. That along with the speed with which the nurses were working told me they also felt Levi was very sick.

It didn't take them long to determine what was wrong. One of the nurses said Levi was presenting with textbook symptoms of type 1 diabetes. It took almost an hour to get the final reading on his blood glucose, which was 990; normal is 120 or below. The ER doctor said Levi needed to be in a pediatric intensive care unit (PICU) immediately. He gave us the choice of going to Columbia, St. Louis, or Kansas City. We chose Columbia because it was closest to us. I believe the Lord guided us in that decision because it turned out that the University of Missouri Children's Hospital in Columbia, Missouri, has one of the best pediatric diabetic teams in the country.

Levi spent that night and most of the next day in the PICU. He stayed in the hospital for a total of five days while they worked on getting things under control, and the medical staff taught Billy and I how to do finger sticks, give shots, and manage his diet. Levi has done very well since his diagnosis.

In September of 2006, Cassy also spent five days in the University of Missouri Children's Hospital with a broken femur. It was a beautiful Tuesday afternoon, and the kids and I headed out for a walk. Several of the kids were riding bikes, including Cassy and Levi. As we walked along, Levi rode in front of Cassy and cut her off. When she hit her brakes, her bike slid on some gravel on top of the pavement, and she put her left foot out to catch herself. The bike continued to scoot on the gravel, which caused her left leg to be pulled and twisted as she fell. I was behind her and saw her fall. As I watched the way her leg twisted as she went down, I thought she could have dislocated her hip.

Cassy was obviously hurt, but we needed to get her out of the road. We had our wagon with us, so Max and Kaylyn helped me get Cassy up and into the wagon. However, it hurt her too much when we tried to pull it. I decided she needed to go to the ER and ran to the house to call Billy and get our Suburban. Billy was just getting off work, so he met us at the ER. Billy's Mom was headed by on her way home from work and helped me get Cassy into the Suburban. When we got to the ER, it was pretty obvious Cassy's leg was broken because her left leg was four to six inches shorter than her right and very swollen. X-rays showed the femur was broken in two places, which left the bone in three pieces. The doctors in Jefferson City were not comfortable treating Cassy, so they sent her by ambulance to the University Children's Hospital, where they have a pediatric orthopedic surgeon who could do the needed surgery.

It was a very painful and sleepless night for Cassy. The doctor was unable to do the surgery until the next day and had to put Cassy in traction. The staff members were giving her as much morphine as they could every hour. However, the traction had been done incorrectly, and the meds were not touching her pain. The doctor who did rounds the next day saw the problem as soon as he walked into the room, and he fixed the traction immediately. It really helped Cassy's pain management once the traction was done correctly. This was a blessing since it was after 9:00 p.m. before they were able to do her surgery.

Because it was a really ugly break, it took quite some time for Cassy to recover. She was in a wheelchair for six weeks and then on crutches for another eight weeks. A rod and screws were used to repair her leg, and those were removed the following April. The Lord was very good; He healed Cassy's leg up beautifully, and she doesn't even have a slight limp.

After Cassy recovered from her broken femur, everyone stayed pretty healthy. We had occasional bouts with colds and flus, but as a general rule, everyone was healthy. We had no reason to suspect any major health issues would come our way. Little did we know how quickly things would change.

Chapter 2

In November of 2008, Billy's lower back began to bother him. He thought his kidneys needed to be flushed and began drinking more water. This did seem to help a little, but then he was doing some work at church and was carrying a toilet by himself when his lower back and right shoulder began to bother him. After that he made an appointment with his chiropractor. The chiropractor's adjustments seemed to help Billy's shoulder a little at first, but they were not helping his back. By the end of December, Billy's back was hurting him so much that he was having trouble getting around. I was helping him get dressed because he couldn't manage it on his own. Showering had also become too difficult for Billy, so I was giving him sponge baths. Billy would go to bed at around 6:30 in the evening because he was so exhausted, and the only way he could avoid being in pain was by lying on his back in bed.

He continued to go to the chiropractor, but things were not improving. The chiropractor recommended that Billy see his regular doctor because he was having muscle spasms in his back that almost put him on the floor.

Billy finally had me call our doctor one morning at the end of January when he could not make it up and get to work. Our doctor was not there, so Billy had to see the nurse practitioner. She checked him out and felt it was probably a muscle strain, but she sent him for X-rays to make sure she wasn't missing anything. The X-rays really didn't show anything, so she decided to send him for physical therapy.

Billy was to have his first physical therapy session on February 4. However, that morning the muscle spasms in his back were so severe he could not stand up. The pain was incredible, and I hated to see him hurting so much.

I called the physical therapist to let him know Billy wouldn't be there and why. He said we needed to call our doctor. I was not sure how we would get Billy in to see the doctor because he couldn't stand up, but I did call. The doctor could not see him until the next day, which worked out for the best.

It was still hard to get Billy to the doctor, but the spasms had calmed down. Billy could stand up and take just a few steps, but it was very painful and quite difficult. In order to get him from the house to the Suburban, I stood in front of him and he held on to my shoulders. We then moved forward very slowly, with Kaylyn and Max following behind him with the office chair in case he needed to sit down. At the doctor's office, Billy again held on to my shoulders, and we moved slowly. Because there was no indication nerves were being affected, our insurance would not pay for an MRI. Once again, the cause of his pain was determined to be chronic muscle strain. The doctor suggested Billy try sleeping on a hard surface, like the floor, because that can sometimes help. He also gave Billy a prescription for muscle relaxers and pain medication.

Billy decided that he would try sleeping on the floor. We took an old twin mattress and put it on our living room floor. Because it was very painful and difficult for him to get up, I slept on the couch in case he needed something. We did this for a week or more. We then used some of our tax return money to get a new, firmer mattress for our bed. While Billy slept okay on the floor, getting up and down was very hard on him. Getting up each morning was almost more than he could do.

I picked up a back brace, and that did help a little. We got the new bed, and Billy was happy to be off the floor again. He continued going to work as much as he possibly could and was in bed by 7:00 or earlier each night. Getting Billy ready for work each morning became quite a process. He would sit up on the edge of the bed, and I rubbed his back for about fifteen minutes. He would then move to the office chair (the only chair in the house he could sit in), where he sat with his back on the heating pad for thirty minutes or more. While he was on the heating pad, I brought him what he needed to brush his teeth, shave, and comb his hair and such. I would then help him get dressed and put the back brace on him, and he would head for work. I took him to work and picked him up quite often.

Billy went to physical therapy two to three days a week through February and into March. Thankfully the therapists were very concerned with the amount of pain Billy was in. They had him doing exercises in the pool. This worked well for Billy because the water helped support his weight and he was able to do the exercises with less pain. I always went with him because he needed help changing into and out of his bathing suit. There were a few days when we thought there might be some improvement, but it didn't last.

Billy continued to work as much as he could possibly handle. On Wednesdays, since the kids and I helped cook at church, Billy would come home just before the kids and I had to leave. I would get him settled in bed with a portable DVD player, a couple of movies, something to drink, and the phone. I would help get the meal at church ready. Then I would bring Levi and Faith home with me, and someone else would bring the other kids home.

On March 2, Billy went to the chiropractor because his neck was really bothering him. While he was there, they found that his blood pressure was rather high, and even more concerning was his heart rate. At rest his heart rate was running between 120 and 130. The chiropractor told Billy he needed to see his regular doctor. We checked Billy's heart rate through the evening, and it continued to run around 120. I called the doctor's office the next day and made appointment for Wednesday, March 4. Since the doctor's appointment was at 10:00 a.m., we expected to be able to make his physical therapy appointment at 1:00 as well.

The doctor's concern with the elevated blood pressure and heart rate was that Billy might have a blood clot in his lung. An EKG was done in the office, but apparently it really didn't tell the doctor anything. The doctor said that there was a specific blood test they could do to try and determine if Billy had a blood clot somewhere. Since the doctor was sending us over to the lab at St. Mary's for the blood test, I asked about doing other blood work as well and mentioned that the chiropractor felt a full panel of blood work would be a good idea. The doctor said that he would order a full blood workup since Billy was having blood drawn anyway. We were told to stay at the lab and wait for the results of the blood test for the blood clot to see if Billy should have a CT scan.

I had to call and cancel the physical therapy appointment because we were still waiting to hear something from the blood tests at 12:30. When we did finally hear something, we were sent for Billy to have a CT of his lungs. Again we were to wait there until we heard the results. It didn't take them long to get Billy back for the CT, but it took a little while to hear from the doctor. Our doctor was off that afternoon, so we knew one of his colleagues would be calling us. When the doctor did call, I took the call since we had to leave the waiting room and go around the corner to the phone, and Billy was just hurting too much to move more than he had to.

I knew as soon as I heard the doctor's voice that it was not good news because he was hesitant to speak to me over the phone, and his voice just sounded odd. He said that while there were no blood clots, the CT did show spots on several of Billy's bones, and they appeared to be cancerous. The areas with the spots included both shoulder blades, the middle of his back, the breast bone, and the ribs on both sides. The worst areas were the right shoulder blade, middle of his back, and his breast bone. The doctor then said that they would know more once all of the blood work came back and we would be hearing from our doctor. He said that due to Billy's age, they suspected the cancer originated someplace other than his bones. I asked him if this explained Billy's back pain, and he said that it did. I then said, "Good, at least we have an answer to that." He seemed rather surprised at that response.

Billy and I decided not to mention the cancer to anyone that evening. We did not really know anything for sure, so we decided to just let everyone know there was no blood clot and wait for the results from all of the blood work before saying any more.

You know it isn't good news when the doctor's office calls and says they are setting up an appointment for the doctor to discuss test results with you. Good news can be given over the phone. When we met with the doctor, he told us that it was cancer, but they didn't know what kind. The doctor ordered a biopsy of Billy's shoulder blade, and we set up an appointment with an oncologist.

When we got home from the appointment with the doctor, we gathered the kids in the living room and explained what we knew so far. The kids handled it very well, and like us, they were glad to have an answer for Billy's back pain. After talking with the kids, I started making phone calls and sent out a mass e-mail explaining what we had learned and asking for prayer. The kids agreed with Billy and I that we must trust God in everything, good or bad, and we would continue to do so no matter what the future might hold.

On Monday, March 9, we had our first appointment with the oncologist. He spent fifteen or twenty minutes with us. They drew more blood, scheduled several tests for Tuesday, March 10, and told us they needed to find out what kind of cancer it was and where it started.

On Tuesday, March 10, we had to be at Jefferson City Medical Group (JCMG) first thing in the morning to begin Billy's tests for that day. It was a miserable and very long day for Billy. He had to drink the nasty stuff for a CT scan of his mid-section. He was also injected with radioactive (at least that was what we were told) dye for a two-hour bone scan that required him to lie on a very hard table. He also had one other test of some kind. We had to be there to get started about 8:00 a.m., and it was after 3:00 before they were done with Billy.

The biopsy on Billy's right shoulder blade was done on Wednesday, March 11. Because of the pain Billy was in, this was hard on him. However, God was looking out for him. Those doing the biopsy were very concerned for Billy and the pain he was in. They treated him very well. We learned later that the bone biopsy was not necessary for Billy's diagnosis and was actually quite dangerous. It is amazing that Billy's shoulder blade was not shattered or otherwise damaged because of the condition of his bones. God is in control.

On St. Patrick's Day, March 17, 2009, we met with the oncologist to go over Billy's test results and get the official diagnosis. The oncologist gave us the diagnosis of multiple myeloma, a cancer of the plasma cells. He told us that it was treatable, wrote out a bunch of prescriptions, and ordered a twenty-four-hour urine capture for some more tests. This was all done in about fifteen minutes. While he was writing out prescriptions, I asked if he could give Billy something else for pain because what he was already on really wasn't doing him any good. The oncologist added prescriptions for a 25 mg fentanyl patch and 100 mg three times a day of gabapentin (for nerve pain).

The oncologist wanted to do a bone marrow biopsy in his office that afternoon but had other appointments before he could get to it. Since he also wanted Billy to have an IV infusion of a bone builder, he had the nurses hook Billy up for that first. I went to the pharmacy and picked up all of the prescriptions while Billy was getting the bone builder.

Shortly after I got back, they put Billy in a room to do the bone marrow biopsy. That was just plain torture for Billy! He was really hurting bad, and they required him to get up on a table, laying on his stomach for the biopsy. The oncologist stuck a very long needle into Billy to deaden the area. I watched as long as I could but started getting a little dizzy and turned away. The oncologist said the bone was a little solid to start with but then felt like cheese. Myeloma weakens bones by causing calcium to leave the bones. The calcium is not replaced, so the bones become soft and even have holes in them. This was another very difficult day for Billy, and it was the last day he worked. That's right—Billy was still working as much as he possibly could. Our appointment with the oncologist wasn't until 1:00, so I took Billy into work that morning when I went in to help with the grocery shopping for the Wednesday-evening meal at church. I then went back and picked him up for the doctor's appointment.

When we left the oncologist's office that day, the plan was to get a port placed the following week and begin chemo after that. I was supposed to call and get the surgery for the port placement set up for the following week. After this things moved and changed very quickly. I was living it and almost needed a program to keep up.

That evening we first explained everything the best we could to the kids and then again made some phone calls. I also went through the bag of prescriptions, put the pain patch on Billy, and discovered two things I did not know about. The oncologist had not mentioned them when he told us the prescriptions he was writing (or we didn't hear him because we were in a bit of a daze), and I did not know what they were for. I called the pharmacist about one of them and found information online about the other one. We started all of the Billy's prescriptions on Wednesday, March 18, 2009, and began the twenty-four-hour urine capture. One of the prescriptions was for the steroid prednisone.

My dad came out that day to replace our ceiling fan for us because Billy was sweating a lot. At the time we thought it was because of his pain and his use of the heating pad. We would learn otherwise later on. Dad could not get over the amount of pain Billy was in and still mentions it occasionally. He says doesn't want to ever see anyone in that much pain again.

Unfortunately, the prednisone really upset Billy's stomach. Because he could not bend in most ways because of the pain in his back and neck, he would go out on our deck and lean over the rail as best he could. When he threw up, it felt like his back was being torn apart, and it was not something he could continue to tolerate.

The pain patch was not helping at all, so when I took the urine capture back in on the morning of Thursday, March 19, I stopped in at the oncologist's office after talking to a pharmacist to see about something more for pain. The oncologist told me to put on two of the 25 mg fentanyl patches.

Billy's parents contacted Cancer Treatment Centers of America (CTCA) in Tulsa, Oklahoma, on that day. They then called us with the information they had been able to get. After talking to them, I called Sharon at CTCA, and once again we saw God's hand at work as He opened doors and made things happen.

Sharon was very concerned about the amount of pain Billy was in and how long he had been hurting. She said that the body can only handle that kind of pain for so long before a person begins to give up and the body starts shutting down. Sharon thought the biggest obstacle could be our insurance. When I told her the insurance we had, she was excited and then asked me to look for a specific emblem on the card. Sure enough, it was on the back of our card. She was sure our insurance would approve us going to CTCA, but they still had to get approval before we could go. She said that we would hear for sure by Friday afternoon, March20.

Since Billy was still having trouble with an upset stomach from the steroid, I called the oncologists on Friday morning. I wanted to see if they could give him something to help his stomach. Instead I was told that Billy could just quit taking the steroid, which really pleased him.

We heard back from Sharon on Friday afternoon, and our insurance did approve us going to CTCA, so we talked to a scheduler. He made us an appointment for Billy with pain management on Tuesday, March 24, and then with the oncologist on Wednesday, March 25. They usually schedule the appointment with the oncologist first, but because of the severity of Billy's pain, they wanted to get him into see the pain management team right away. The scheduler even bumped another person's appointment. He said that was okay because the guy lived fifteen minutes away from the center, and he was okay with it.

We decided to go down to Tulsa on Monday, March 23, instead of leaving early enough on the March 24 to make the appointment with pain management. We were also given cell phone numbers for two people at CTCA, who instructed me to call them if Billy had trouble tolerating the trip and they would send someone to get Billy.

We had a family meeting on the Saturday before Billy and I left for Tulsa. Arrangements were made for the kids to stay with their grandparents, my sister, and a couple from our church as needed. We didn't know for sure how long we would be gone. We had been told to plan for at least three days, but if we decided to begin treatment, it could be longer. Our families said they would make sure the kids were taken care of and we were to stay as long as we needed to. They were true to their word, and the kids were well taken care of. None of us had any idea how long we would be gone, but I am pretty sure none of us imagined it would be as long as it was.

Chapter 3

On March 23, Billy drove the five hours to Tulsa. I really don't know how he did it because he was really hurting. I kept an eye on traffic in his blind spots and helped as much as I could since he could not turn his head very far due to the pain in his neck.

We went to CTCA first, and they gave us a big binder of stuff and explained a lot to us. We were also given a voucher so we could stay at the Radisson at a reduced rate. We got checked in, and then I found us something to eat. After eating a bite, Billy lay down. Billy did not sleep very well that night because of his neck and shoulder pain as well as nerve pain going down his right arm and into his hand.

On Thursday, March 24, we took CTCA's shuttle from the hotel over to the Cancer Treatment Center. The ride was hard on Billy. It was their older shuttle, and the ride was pretty rough. Billy decided to use a wheelchair because it just hurt too much for him to walk. As I mentioned earlier, Billy was sweating a lot. In fact, at times he was pouring sweat, and I would mop his head with a napkin, paper towel, or handkerchief. Everyone was concerned with the amount of pain Billy was in. The first thing Dr. A the pain doctor, did was remove Billy's two 25 mg pain patches and put on a 100 mg and 50 mg pain patch. He had Billy continue the other two pain medications he was already on.

Dr. A explained that it was very important to get Billy's pain under control. When a person is in pain, that is all his or her body can focus on; it can't fight the cancer, heal, or anything else when in it is pain. Also, after the body has dealt with severe pain for a long time, it will give up. Severe pain over a long period of time also affects people mentally, and they often give up and quit fighting.

Dr. A sent Billy to the infusion center for some morphine, hoping it would help to get on top of the pain and allow the other pain medications to take hold. The infusion center is where all CTCA patients go for any kind of medications, chemo, or anything else that is administered by IV or through a port. They also give patients all blood products and draw blood from the port at the infusion center. The infusion center also acts as an emergency room for CTCA patients.

When we went to get the morphine, the staff started by giving him a small dose to make sure he wasn't allergic. After about fifteen minutes, it really hadn't helped, so they gave him more and then fifteen minutes later a little more. The morphine helped a little with some of Billy's back pain, but it did nothing to help with his shoulder and arm pain (nerve pain).

While they were giving the morphine, they checked Billy's vital signs frequently. He was running a low-grade temperature, but they weren't too concerned. They thought it could be from the pain. However, when it reached 102.1, they began their fever protocol, and we were not allowed to leave until they decided it was okay for Billy to go back to the hotel. The fever protocol included Tylenol, IV fluids, a chest X-ray, blood cultures being drawn, and peeing in a cup. The staff members ran several blood tests in addition to the cultures being drawn. After a few hours, Billy's temperature was down, the X-rays looked okay, and the blood work was okay. The infusion doctor agreed to let us go back to the hotel as long as I promised to bring Billy back in if I had any concerns or if his fever came back.

By the time we were released from the infusion center, it was 11:00 p.m. The shuttle quit running at 8:00, but there was a driver who took us back to the hotel in a Lincoln. The driver was very nice and helped get Billy in and out of the vehicle, as well as getting a wheelchair for Billy at the hotel. He even offered to help me get Billy to our room.

This was a pretty late night for Billy since he had been going to bed around 6:30. It ended up being a very rough night, with little sleep. I used pillows and found various positions for Billy's right arm trying to get him some relief from the nerve pain. I was able to find a position that helped and he would fall asleep, but within ten to fifteen minutes, he would wake up in pain. I did various adjustments all night, giving him ten to fifteen minutes of relief at a time all night long.

I was a little worried about how things would go getting Billy up and ready for the appointment with the oncologist, but it didn't go too bad. The new pain management plan was helping some, but there was still a long way to go. We took the Suburban to CTCA since Billy had been in so much pain on the shuttle the day before.

When we arrived at CTCA, Billy again rode in a wheelchair, and I pushed him around. I have to tell you, I think they should put you through some kind of training with an obstacle course or something and make you get a license to drive those things! Thankfully, Billy did survive my driving.

We really liked the oncologist, who was named Dr. R. He is an older man, and he lays it all out there. Dr. R spent more than an hour and a half with us, and we were on information overload when we left his office. He was very concerned about Billy's condition. He had received the test results from Jefferson City, and wanted to know what we had done that we weren't currently doing. According to the blood work comparison between what had been run in Jefferson City and what they had done so far in Tulsa, Dr. R knew something had really helped Billy's kidneys. I told him about Billy's two days of prednisone, and he said that would do it. What we had not been told in Jefferson City was that Billy's white blood cell count was almost nothing, and his kidneys were failing. Dr. R could not get over how much difference those two days of prednisone had made. He believed that without them, Billy would have needed dialysis by the time we arrived in Tulsa. God can use anything, even just two days of medication.

Dr. R told us that Billy had a very bad cancer. He said that if we looked at it from a pessimistic point of view, it was a very bad deal. However, looking at it from an optimistic point of view, Dr. R had treated many people with this cancer, and many of them were in remission. He said it would not be easy, and it would take time. He said Billy would be treated for a minimum of six months, but we should plan for longer. Dr. R would treat it very aggressively, with a combination of chemo drugs as well as some radiation of the bones. There are several combinations that could be very effective, and Dr. R said he had recently learned about some new treatments. He also mentioned possibly doing a stem cell rescue at some point using Billy's own stem cells. Since they don't do stem cell transplants in Tulsa, Dr. R planned to talk with the transplant doctors at CTCA in Zion, Illinois, to find out what chemo protocol they preferred.

Dr. R was also very concerned about the condition of Billy's bones and the possibility of a bone being broken. He leaned forward in his chair, looked Billy right in the eyes, and said, "I am very concerned about you! We have to take care of those bones. I do not want a broken bone!" He then made it very clear that Billy was to continue using the wheelchair and be very careful about moving around. We were to move from the hotel to a room on the CTCA property, and Billy was to use a hospital bed.

Dr. R scheduled multiple MRIs for Saturday and Sunday. He wanted a good look at Billy's bones. His staff would then schedule radiation to treat the worst areas of the bones to help keep them from breaking.

As Dr. R was about to leave the room, Billy asked, "So, Doc, am I going to make it?"

Dr. R said, "We will get you in remission; we just don't yet know what it is going to take."

That gave Billy the hope he needed. (We learned later that Dr. R really didn't know at that time if Billy would make it, but if he didn't give Billy some hope, he knew he wouldn't make it.)

We met with Dr. A again, and since Billy was still in a lot of pain, they bumped his pain patches up to 250 mg, took away the Percocet, per Dr. R's orders (because it's bad for bones), added oxycodone for breakthrough pain, and then added methadone because it helps with all pain, including nerve pain.

After the appointments were over for the day, we needed to get moved into our new room on the CTCA property. I took Billy to the room, and he waited there (in his wheelchair) for the guy who was bringing the hospital bed. Since we had driven the Suburban over, I had to take it back to the hotel, get everything packed, and get checked out by 6:00 p.m. I left CTCA at 5:15, and thankfully the hotel was only ten to fifteen minutes away. I followed the shuttle over. I packed up and loaded our things quickly and was able to check out at 5:45.

Chapter 4

At this point in our journey, I started a daily journal in order to keep family and friends updated on Billy. I will let the entries tell the story of what happened next.

Thursday, March 26, 2009

We only had an appointment or two today, so Billy was able to rest more. One of the appointments was with the mind and body medicine department. This is part of CTCA's whole-person treatment philosophy, as they want to make sure the patients are in a good place mentally. We met with a psychologist, and he mainly just asked a lot of questions. He then gave us some information about a few things and prayed with us.

Billy's back and neck are doing quite a bit better today, and I removed one 50 mg pain patch because he was getting too much. (The nurse told me how to tell if he was.) The nerve pain in his right shoulder, arm, and hand is a little better but not much. It will take a little time for the pain to ease. He sees the pain doctor again tomorrow.

Friday, March 27, 2009

We met with Dr. A today. He has raised Billy's gabapentin (for nerve pain) dose and is working on getting another breakthrough pain medication for Billy. When we saw Dr. Axness this morning, Billy's pain level was a seven. Barbara, Dr. A's nurse, said that was not acceptable, and she gave

Billy a Fentora. Fentora is a breakthrough pain medication to knock the pain down so Billy's other pain medication can take hold. The Fentora worked great for Billy! In twenty minutes, his pain went from a seven all the way down to a one! Dr. A said they will get Billy a prescription of Fentora since it worked so well for him. However, it may take them a few days since insurance companies don't like to pay for Fentora, and they will have to fight to get it. He said to give them about three days or so and they would get it. We will see Dr. A again Monday or Tuesday after he sees the MRIs.

We met with both the nutritionist and the naturopath as well today. Billy needs to eat plenty of protein, fruits, and vegetables. Billy is not big on eating vegetables, but the V8 V-Fusion juice is acceptable to get him his vegetable intake.

The naturopath will work with us a lot more when the plan for Billy's treatment is actually put together, but he did give us some information to look over. We found it interesting that the psychologist and naturopath are free services to us. Our insurance does not pay for them, and neither do we. They are paid a salary by CTCA to be here and provide their services. The patients are not charged in any way since insurance companies do not recognize these services as being necessary in the treatment of cancer.

It is amazing how much time each person will spend with you! Most doctors generally allow about fifteen minutes with a patient. We have yet to spend just fifteen minutes with any of the doctors or others that we have seen. They are all very thorough and make sure you understand everything or at least that you understand the best you can at the time. They also make sure they have answered all of your questions before they send you off to the next appointment. God is good, and He is blessing us every day.

Tomorrow Billy has three MRIs scheduled, and then Sunday he has two more. We asked our care manager about MRIs today because we really know nothing about them. We discovered that they will not take as long as we expected. It will take a couple of hours to do the MRIs, but we were thinking they would take most of the day.

I gave the short-term disability papers to the person here who handles those things. I also talked to the human resources department at Billy's work. They suggested asking them if they would back date the paperwork to the first day that Billy couldn't work, which would be March 18. Our care manager didn't think there would be a problem with that, and she is making sure the right person has the information.

They also said that the board of directors met, and even though Billy had not contributed to the sick bank at work, they revised the policy, and Billy will be getting paid for four weeks of sick leave. He just has to donate eight of the sixteen hours of paid time off (PTO) he will be getting on April 1. There will be some paperwork to take care of, and they will call me and we will take care of it together. This will give Billy four weeks of pay that he wouldn't otherwise be getting. God is amazing! The company president and the executive director have also both called to let Billy know that the entire company is thinking about him and praying for him and our family. Missouri Farm Bureau is a wonderful company to work for! They really treat you like family.

Billy continues to sweat a great deal and seems to be very tired. He dozes off a lot, and his memory is not very good right now. I am thankful he is not in nearly as much pain.

Saturday, March 28, 2009

Billy had his first set of MRIs today. It took about two hours altogether and was pretty hard on him. I gave him oxycodone before he went in for the MRIs, but he had to lay on a hard metal surface.

It was hard for me to wait for him. The nurses were very nice. Billy did not look good when they finished, and it was obvious he was in pain; so I gave him some more oxycodone. Billy was completely exhausted after the MRIs, and since it was a Saturday, there was nothing else scheduled, so I took him back to the room to lie down.

It ended up being a long evening because I took Billy to the infusion center at about 9:00 this evening. He felt warm to me when I woke him up from his nap for supper. I picked up a thermometer at the pharmacy the other day, so I checked his temperature. It was a little elevated but not bad, so we waited until he had eaten some supper and checked it again. It had gone up, so I decided (even though he wanted to go back to bed) that we needed to get him checked out. They did fever protocol on him again, which means a chest X-ray, blood draw, and fluids. Since he slept all afternoon, the fluids were a good thing because he was a little dehydrated. He needs to drink plenty of fluids to keep his kidneys flushed.

The nurses and I are not sure if the cancer has Billy's internal thermostat off or what. As I have mentioned, he has been doing a lot of sweating, but this evening while he was running a fever, the sweating seemed to be worse. The nurse seemed quite concerned about Billy not being able to stay awake for very long. He is dozing off even if you are talking to him, and the sweating seems to be concerning the nurse as well. However, the X-ray seems to be okay, his liver enzymes are good, and his white cell count is normal. After he got Tylenol and fluids, his temperature stayed down, and we were able to go back to our room at about 1:00 a.m., with instructions from the nurse to bring him back if his fever returned or if I was otherwise concerned.

Sunday, March 29, 2010

I took Billy back to the infusion center early this morning. He has become less responsive, and his breathing was not right. He seemed to be taking a long time between breaths. He needed to pee but could not stay awake long enough to do so. We have been using a urinal because he is so weak, and it just works out better for now.

I did not take Billy's temperature, but he did feel warm. I got him up and dressed, and he was sitting in the wheelchair while I was getting dressed in the bathroom. I am really not sure how I got him up and ready. He was very out of it and did not stay lucid enough for any length of time to remember what I was telling him. While I was putting my contacts in and getting ready, all of a sudden he said, "Where are we going?" I told him I was taking him back to the infusion center, but before I could finish explaining, he was basically unconscious again.

I wheeled him into the waiting room of the infusion center and was signing him in when he looked up and said, "What are we doing here?"

I replied, "I told you that I was taking you to the infusion center."

Again before I finished, he was unconscious. The nurse behind the desk heard this exchange and looked over at Billy. She immediately told me to bring him back and called for another nurse to help.

Two nurses helped get Billy into one of their recliners, and they started doing vital signs and drawing blood right away. Because Billy was mentally altered and had an oxygen saturation of around eighty, they were very concerned and worked quickly. Their thought was that he had been overmedicated in the process of trying to get his pain under control, and they removed his pain patches. (While too much pain medication was part of the problem, we learned later that the cancer had a lot to do with Billy's condition.) They found that Billy had pneumonia. When I told the nurse Billy was supposed to have MRIs later in the morning, she said, "Oh honey, he is in no shape for MRIs today."

Because they suspected the pain medications were part of the problem, they took off his pain patches and withheld his methadone. He was admitted to the special care unit (their ICU), where they started IV fluids, antibiotics, and breathing treatments every eight hours, and they would give IV pain meds as needed. He was put on three liters of oxygen to start with, and they began giving him a medication for his tremors and twitching because they were pretty bad.

Billy has been put on complete bed rest, and they have placed a catheter. The condition of Billy's bones in combination with his weakness, disorientation, and tremors make it unsafe for Billy to be up and around at all.

Later in the evening, Sunday, March 29, 2009

The nurses have ordered Billy a special air mattress that circulates the air and helps prevent pressure points and sores. Billy's oxygen requirement has lessened through the day, and his fever is staying down. The tremors are still pretty bad, and he is very weak and still not staying awake for very long at a time. The nurses have told me Billy will be inpatient for at least a couple of days.

Even though Billy is quite out of it, he is still so very sweet. The nurse was asking him his name, date of birth, and such, and then she asked him, referring to me, "And who is this lady?"

He said, "This is my God-given wife." He is so sweet.

By the end of the day, Billy was doing a little bit better. He is still on oxygen but not very much, and he is a little more alert.

Chapter 5

I began a Caringbridge page for Billy on Sunday, March 29, 2009, and updated it almost every day. Following are the entries from the Caringbridge journal. This journal's purpose was to keep our family and friends updated. They are being entered here as they were written, minus some grammar and spelling errors.

Monday, March 30, 2009

Things are improving. Billy was taken off of the oxygen during the night last night, and his breathing treatments are going well. He is no longer sedated by too much pain medication, but they are still keeping his pain down. He did get two units of blood today to help with the anemia and hopefully his high heart rate. He is having some trouble with spasms today, and they are quite annoying to him. They are nothing like the tremors and spasms he was having yesterday, but they do wake him up from time to time when he is napping. The nurses do have some medication they can give him that makes a difference, but you can really tell when it is wearing off.

Dr. R came in this morning. He was surprised to find Billy was an inpatient but understood what happened and said that it does happen from time to time. He wants Billy to just stay put for now, which means complete bed rest. He did have a bit of good news. Billy's disease is light chain rather than large chain, which makes a difference in treatment because the light chain responds quicker and better to the treatment. Dr. R has come up with two different aggressive chemo treatments, and they each involve three different drugs. They have both been proven equally effective, with a 95 percent remission rate. He called the CTCA in Zion, Illinois, and talked to a doctor there who does stem cell rescue. If the chemo regimen were to fail then stem cell rescue would be the next step. Dr. R wanted to check with them on which treatment they would prefer to give Billy the best chance at a stem cell rescue if it is needed. The regimens that Dr. R came up with are equally acceptable to the doctors at Zion, so he was going to check with insurance today and see which one they would approve.

The MRIs were put off for now because Dr. R did not want Billy moved around. He ordered some bone-building medication and steroids for Billy to get through the IV. The radiation oncologist also came to talk to us today, at the request of Dr. R, and he will be doing radiation treatment on Billy's right shoulder, the middle of his back, and possibly his left hip. They did X-rays of Billy's entire body the other day, so even without the MRIs of the spine, they have a pretty good idea of what is going on. The radiation oncologist was going to take another look at Billy's hip because he was not sure it would need the radiation treatment. We asked him about the purpose of the radiation, and he said it was to kill the cancer in that specific location. The radiation should help to relieve the pain in those areas and also will allow the bone to heal itself. The radiation treatments will take ten days, about twenty minutes a day. It sounded like Dr. R was also trying to get the chemo drugs approved so he could get that started right away as well.

Billy is a bit frustrated and down because he is weak in his shoulders and arms and can do very little for himself. His right hand and arm are especially weak and don't quite work as they should because of the nerve issues in that arm. The doctors do have the nerve pain well under control, but Billy's hand feels rather numb and the arm is very weak. The radiation oncologist could not guarantee it, but he felt doing the radiation on Billy's right shoulder might help some of that, or at least it will help it to get better a little faster.

Dr. R said he will be in to see us in the morning, and if he doesn't come in, I am supposed to go downstairs and get him. He said I know where he is and he wants me come get him if he doesn't show up in Billy's room. I don't really expect to have to go get him, but I will if need be.

God is good, all the time!

—Dione

Tuesday, March 31, 2009

Billy is feeling a little better today. He is doing really well with the pain medication they are using. Dr. A's nurse came up this morning to go over a few things, and they are making some changes. They are changing Billy's long-acting pain medication and his breakthrough pain medication as well. They are going to work at getting things just right while he is an inpatient so we will have a good handle on things when he becomes an outpatient again. Billy even says he feels a little better today, and Vicki (his nurse yesterday and today) thinks he is looking and acting much better today. They have now taken off the oxygen sensor because his oxygen level has stayed very high for almost twenty-four hours. The breathing treatments are continuing and are working. The pulmonary doctor is very pleased with how his lungs are sounding.

Dr. R was in this morning, and he is getting the chemo regimen approved and will get it started as soon as he can get the drugs. Billy did start part of his treatment today. He is still getting the bone builder daily, but he is now getting Decadron as well. Decadron is a steroid along the line of prednisone, but it is much, much stronger. The radiation oncologist has not made it in today and may not be in until tomorrow, but Dr. R gave the go ahead on the radiation treatments, so they will start as soon as the radiation oncologist gets it lined up. We don't know yet when that will be, but it looks like it will begin sometime this week.

Dr. T (the surgeon) also came in and told us that Billy will be getting his port placed sometime in the morning. It is about a twenty-minute procedure, and they will be able to start using the port the same day.

I think that is about it for now. C. B. stopped by for a few minutes on his way to Dallas today. Thank you for the short visit and prayer.

Thank you to everyone for your prayers, notes, help with the kids, and just being there if we need you.

God is good, all the time!

—Dione

Wednesday, April 1, 2009

This morning Billy got his port placed. As the doctor told us, it was about a twenty-minute surgery, and it went very well. They are already using it, so he will have no more IV hanging off his arm. Billy was glad to get the IV out of his arm because it was placed right next to his elbow.

They moved Billy out of special care and into a regular room today. The radiation oncologist is planning to start radiation on either Friday or Monday. The radiation treatments will be twenty minutes a day for ten days, Monday through Friday. Dr. R is getting the chemo drugs approved by our insurance and is hoping to get chemo started within the next five to seven days. Once they get radiation and chemo started, the doctor said Billy should start feeling better and improving in two to three days. I will need to ask him how long we can expect Billy to stay on bed rest. I plan to track down Dr. R tomorrow if we don't hear from him so I can ask my questions.

They are doing a good job of staying on top of Billy's pain. From a scale of zero to ten, they are doing their best to keep him no higher than a two. When his pain starts reaching a three, they want him to tell them so they can give him something and bring it back down. For the most part he does, but sometimes I have to remind him to ask when I can see it is creeping up. They are making some changes in his meds, so when he is ready to go back to being an outpatient, they will have things well under control.

Have a good night!

God is good, all the time!

—Dione

Late in the day, Wednesday, April 1, 2009

Since most of what I have updated the last few days has been medical, I thought everyone might like to know how Billy is doing mentally. His faith is strong, and his spirits are up. He has already been earning the respect of many of the people he has encountered here, and they are very impressed with his faith and understanding that this is all in God's plan. Billy is just praying that God will use him through all of this. (We are both looking forward to seeing the kids this weekend! (Thank you, Steve, Linda, and Dru!)

Billy is getting back to himself after having too many drugs in his system, and he is giving the nurses a hard time (all in fun, of course). There were three nurses who came to transport him for his port placement surgery this morning. Since he is on a special air mattress and they had to unplug it for transport, it deflated, which was rather uncomfortable for him. He gave them a hard time for "letting him down" and being so mean to him. It was all lighthearted, and they took it that way and gave it right back to him. He was just being himself, and that was good.

Later in the day, two nurses from the special care unit transported him to the regular hospital side. (We can't wait to see the kids this weekend!) Again they had to let his bed deflate, and he started giving them lip before they even got started. It was still all in fun, and they gave it right back. Everyone was smiling and laughing. The nurses from the special care side said they hated to see him go but were glad he was getting better. They told him that his new nurses would love him, and so far they seem to be getting a kick out of him too. (It will be so good to see the kids!)

It is so good to see Billy in very little to no pain and feeling good enough that his quick wit and personality are returning. Praise God! Thank you all for your prayers, notes, cards, and everything else you are all doing for our family.

Did I mention we are excited about seeing the kids this weekend! Thanks again, Steve, Linda, and Dru.

God is good, all the time!

—Dione

Thursday, April 2, 2009

The information just keeps coming. Dr. R was in this morning, and he is still working on getting the chemo drugs he wants approved. However, there are many different drugs, and he has talked to the doctor in Zion about the different possibilities depending on what our insurance will approve. They are all acceptable. We also learned a bit more about the chemo and stem cell rescue stuff. At this point in treating multiple myeloma, they do some high-dose chemo to put the patient in remission and then do the stem cell rescue as a way to keep him or her there. It is now our understanding that the high-dose chemo will be used to achieve remission, and then a stem cell rescue will be done at either Zion, which is in Illinois, or if we choose, there are some other places that do it. Since Dr. R has been talking to a doctor at Zion and that doctor is already aware of Billy's case, we are thinking that might be the best choice, but we will see.

The Decadron is a high-dose steroid Billy has received that is a big part of his treatment. We have not heard back from the radiation oncologist, so we are not sure if they will be starting radiation tomorrow or Monday.

Dr. R gave the okay, as long as Dr. K, the radiation oncologist, and the doctor here on the floor agree, then Billy will be able to go back to being an outpatient in two to three days. We have not heard from the other doctors on this, but we do know there is a lunch meeting with all the doctors today and Billy's case will be discussed, so maybe we will hear more this afternoon.

Pulmonary is very happy with how Billy's lungs are doing. They are good and clear, and the doctors are even skipping the nighttime treatment when Billy is asleep.

From what Dr. R said, they will have someone form the physical therapy (PT) department come up and help get Billy up in a chair and will do a few things to see how things go with his pain. Pain management will also be involved to stay on top of the pain as PT starts getting Billy up. He will still be required to use a wheelchair and not be up walking any more than he has to.

Have a great day! God is good, all the time!

—Dione

FRIDAY, APRIL 3, 2009, 9:16 A.M.

Good morning to all!

God is good, all the time! We have heard from the company that makes one of the chemo drugs Dr. R really wanted to get Billy on, and they will be sending it FedEx. It will be here Monday. Billy also will be getting another dose of the Decadron. Dr. R was in first thing this morning, and again he said that it is fine with him for Billy to go back to being an outpatient, but other doctors have to sign off on that. It sounds like Dr. R is about to get the last of the chemo drugs approved by our insurance company.

As always, God continues to bless, as the one breakthrough pain medication Dr. A really wanted to get for Billy but had to fight the insurance for was approved yesterday, and I picked it up. They have been giving it to him when he needs it while he is an inpatient, but now we will have it when he goes back to being an outpatient again. Also, while

Billy has had really good nurses, the one we had this morning is great! She came in, introduced herself, asked some questions, and then prayed with us. She is also checking into getting PT to come up and helping to get Billy up in the room and see how he does. Hopefully he can be back in the outpatient room when the kids come tomorrow, but we will have to see how he does. Yeah! The kids are going to be here tomorrow! Billy is getting really excited about seeing them too. He just doesn't want them to see him in the hospital.

The nurses will come get Billy for his first radiation treatment in about an hour. They were hoping to get him on the schedule for today, and they did it. Dr. K said that after a couple of treatments, it should be easier to keep Billy's pain under control.

I stayed in the room with Billy last night as they took his catheter out, and he is using a urinal. I helped him with it all day because he was just not very comfortable with having a nurse help him. He woke up about three times during the night, but a couple of those were when they took his vitals.

Have a great day!

—Dione

God is good, all the time!

Friday, April 3, 2009, 9:15 p.m.

Guess what! I keep telling you all that God is good, all the time! *The kids will be here tomorrow!* And Billy was released from the hospital today and is back in the outpatient room. Plus, he has no appointments scheduled for the weekend. He is a very weak from spending almost a week in bed, but he is doing pretty well. Physical therapy came into the room today to help Billy get up and into the wheelchair if needed. The physical therapist was very pleased because Billy was able to get out of the bed and into the wheelchair all on his own. The physical therapist said that Billy really hadn't lost any muscle but has lost endurance. It sounds like we will be seeing PT on a regular basis as an outpatient. Billy will need to see Dr. A again about Tuesday since they raised his long-acting pain medication a little because he was getting released. He may need to back off on it some as they get the radiation done.

Billy was so glad to get released before the kids came to see us. It will make the visit more enjoyable because we can wheel him around and he won't have to just stay in bed, although I am sure he will need to come back to the room to rest a time or two.

I may not update tomorrow since the kids will be here. Thank you for the continued prayers, support, encouragement, and cards. Billy has gotten a bunch of cards in the last couple of days, and it is great! When I picked them up today, the gal said they were going to have to bring Billy's cards in his own mailbag, and if it keeps up he may need his own mail truck. I thought that was really neat. She thought it was great and was sure it would put a smile on Billy's face, which it did. She knew he had been an inpatient.

God is good, all the time!

Love you all.

—Dione

Saturday, April 4, 2009, 4:26 p.m.

Oh, it's so good to see the kids! They arrived just after 1:00. We took them on a tour and visited until almost 3:00. Then Steve and Linda took them to check into the hotel. Linda was taking the kids swimming, and Steve was going to take a nap. Billy is napping as well. It is doing him a world of good to see the kids, but we will have to be careful he doesn't get completely worn out.

My poor sister, Dru, had planned to come along, but she has a very bad case of the stomach flu and was left at home feeling rotten. We missed you, Dru. Get better soon!

Thank you to Susan for making the really cool Scripture quilt and to our church family for signing it. It is beautiful, and we will read every Scripture and signature on it. We love you all and miss you so very much. Thank you to Grandma Doris, Grandpa Jim, Grandma Bobbie, and Grandpa Ron, as well as Dru, for keeping our kids and running them here and there to activities and to take care of animals. We love you all and miss you very much. Thank you to everyone who is sending cards and signing the guest book on here. We read them all and treasure every one.

The kids all look great! Max's haircut looks really good on him, even if he isn't very happy with it. I told Levi he needs a haircut too, and he disagreed with me. It is so good to see them, and the hugs are *wonderful*! Steve and Linda will bring them back over later, and I think they are going to come eat breakfast with us since they have biscuits, gravy, eggs, waffles, breakfast burritos, omelets, and other things here each morning. The kids weren't impressed with the menu for this evening, so they are planning to get something else but may bring it over and eat in the dining room with us. We will see how that works out. I'm not sure Billy is going to be ready for supper when they are, so we may just have them come over after they eat. He is sleeping pretty well.

Have a good weekend!

God is good, all the time!

—Dione

Sunday, April 5, 2009, 10:45 a.m.

Steve and Linda brought the kids over for breakfast, and we enjoyed a nice visit with them. They came over at about 8:30 and left about 10:00. They were thinking about swimming for about thirty to forty-five minutes, and then they will get checked out of the hotel. They will be back around 12:30, and they are bringing lunch from the outside world. The food here is good, but lunch is not something Billy cares for, although they will fix him a sandwich or something else. However, since Steve and Linda offered, we took them up on it.

We are all really enjoying the visit. The kids all look great, and it is wonderful to visit with them and hug them and hug them again! They are a little tired today from the swimming yesterday. I think Steve will get a much quieter drive home.

Billy is taking a nap. I read all of the Scriptures and the messages on the quilt to him before he dozed off, or as he was dozing off. It looks like the higher dose of methadone they started him on Friday may be a bit much, so we are going to cut it back a little and see the pain doctor about it tomorrow. It is nothing like it was last Sunday when I took him to the infusion center, but he is much drowsier today. Since we now know what to watch for, we can keep it from going too far like it did last time. I will just put him back on the dose they had him on while he was in the hospital, and we will talk to Dr. A tomorrow. Thankfully, Dr. A's nurse who saw Billy while he was an inpatient did a good job of explaining how methadone works so we can better understand how to use it correctly.

Billy will have radiation treatments Monday through Friday this week at 10:00 a.m. I will talk to Dr. R tomorrow about one of the medications Billy was on while he was an inpatient but was not given a prescription for as an outpatient. It was my understanding that Dr. R wanted him to stay on that medication because it protects his kidneys from clogging up with all of the dead cancer cells as they do the radiation and start chemo. I think it was just overlooked since Dr. R was not the one who released him from the hospital. I also need to talk to Dr. R about whether they are going to do radiation on Billy's left hip. Dr. R talked like he wanted them to, but Dr. K didn't seem to think it was needed. At this time they are not doing it on the hip. However, yesterday Billy was saying that hip was hurting him some with getting up from the bed and to the wheelchair. That is a pretty good indication that they at least need to take another look at it. Most likely Dr. R is correct and it needs to be treated with radiation as well. Anyway, I will be tracking him down tomorrow to find out about the medication and the hip, and we will make an appointment with Dr. A to discuss the methadone dose. At least we know the methadone works well. It works better than the patches and doesn't require as high of a dose.

Other than being sleepy from the medication and being weak, Billy is in a very good mood and holding strong. He is really enjoying the visit with the kids.

Thank you all again for everything you are doing. We love and miss everyone!

God is good, all the time!

—Dione

Sunday, April 5, 2009, 7:50 p.m.

The kids headed back home around 2:00. It was hard to say good-bye, but we are so very proud of them! While the kids were very glad to see us, it was also a tough visit for them. This was the first time they had seen Billy in a wheel chair, and he is still very weak. Billy is unable to use his right hand, and for the most part I have to feed him. Billy just doesn't look very good right now, and I know it was hard for the kids to see him so sick and weak. There were lots of tears when it was time for the kids to leave. I know they are a little worried about how Billy will do and if they well see him again. I hate to admit that I am a little worried about that myself. We have decided Billy may have just needed a morning nap because he did much better at keeping his eyes open during lunch with the kids. He took another nap this afternoon, but I think he probably needs the extra rest. With all that is going on with his body, it is tired. We will continue to watch for signs of too much medication, but he is doing pretty well and has only used breakthrough pain medication three times today. He took an afternoon nap and is doing well sitting up and staying awake this evening.

Have a good night, and take care.

God is good, all the time!

—Dione

Monday, April 6, 2009, 9:27 p.m.

Good evening, everyone. I want to start by asking that you all remember to pray for Bill and Kay. Bill was diagnosed with pancreatic cancer and will be going to see a surgeon in St. Louis, I think next week. Kay says that Bill is currently feeling good and eating well, so we need to pray for wisdom for the doctors as well as praying for Bill and Kay. I also ask that you would pray for Margaret, a little girl who was in a very bad car accident.

Billy only had two appointments today. First he had radiation at 10:00. It only takes about twenty minutes, and he says he doesn't feel anything. The only side effect he has had so far is a very short-lived bought of nausea. Then he had an appointment with Dr. A at 11:00. Since the pain medication Billy is currently on is doing a good job, Dr. A didn't change anything today. Billy will see him again next Monday.

Billy has been pretty tired today. We are watching for signs of too much pain medication, but he seems to be okay that way, at least for now. He was up all morning with getting up for breakfast, getting a new outpatient bracelet, and then his appointments. He lay down a little after noon after eating a little. He then slept off and on all afternoon and got up a little after 6:00 to go down for supper. He went back to bed between 8:30 and 9:00 and is sleeping for the most part. We were watching a movie, and he will open his eyes and watch for a few minutes now and then. I think with everything his body has going on, it just needs to rest a lot.

The chemo drug Revlimid arrived today. It is a pill Billy will take once a day. He will be able to take it at home when we get there. It is once a day every day, two weeks on and one week off. I do not know yet how many rounds he will need to do. I talked to Libby, our care manager, today and let her know that we have the Revlimid. I also let her know that when they released Billy as an inpatient, they did not give him a prescription for the allopurinol that Dr. R had him on. She said he needed to be on that, which I told her I knew. As I mentioned before, allopurinol is to help protect his kidneys from getting clogged by the dead cancer cells as the radiation and chemo kill them. Dr. R said he wanted Billy on the allopurinol for two days before starting the Revlimid. Dr. R also wanted Billy to make an appointment after some blood work was done, so tomorrow Billy will have his radiation and then have some blood drawn. He needs to have blood drawn at least once a week while he is on radiation anyway, so tomorrow's blood work will take care of that as well. I also mentioned to Libby that Billy's hip was hurting him a little over the weekend as he got into and out of the wheelchair. That will need to be addressed by Dr. K, so she said she would talk to him about it.

Some specific ways you can pray with us are

- That Billy remains fever free;
- That all of the pain medication and other meds don't make him too sleepy;
- That the radiation treatments will give him back the use of his right hand. It is currently numb and he cannot grip with it due to a nerve issue believed to be caused by the deterioration of the bone in his right shoulder; and
- That he has a bowel movement, preferably tomorrow. All of the medication is very constipating, and he is taking stuff to help with that.

Have a good night!

God is good, all the time!

—Dione

Chapter 6

Tuesday, April 7, 2009, 9:08 p.m.

> My brethren count it all joy when you fall into various trials, knowing that the testing of your faith produces patience. But let patience have its perfect work, that you may be perfect and complete, lacking nothing.
>
> —James 1:2-4

Well, today was fairly uneventful. Billy had radiation at 10:00 and then a blood draw. When he is doing radiation, they will draw blood every Tuesday to check his counts. While the radiation kills cancer cells, it also kills some of the good cells, so he may need blood or blood products while he is having radiation done. Dr. R also ordered some other blood tests, so the technician drew blood for those as well. We are pleased that we are seeing some improvement in Billy's right shoulder. He has more range of motion without so much pain. His right hand is still numb and of little use, but we are hoping that will improve as well.

He did a lot of resting today, but I think that is good for him. He also had a bowel movement so that is one prayer answered. Some may find that an odd prayer request, but it is important to keep those things working. Since he is taking multiple medications that can cause constipation, it is something we really have to watch. I have said all of that to say thank you for the prayers. They worked!

We will meet with Dr. R tomorrow after radiation and find out if he was able to get the second chemo drug that he wanted and what kind of chemo regimen he wants Billy on. We have the first chemo drug, and it is a pill

Billy will take once a day at bedtime for two weeks on and one week off. I don't know yet how many rounds will be needed or how the other drug will be administered (IV, pill, etc.). We should get a better idea of these things tomorrow.

I talked to the kids this evening, and they seem to be doing well, although Faith is sick this evening. She is running a fever, and Kaylyn said that she had some goop in her eye. Cassy is pretty stuffy yet from having a cold, and her ear was hurting a lot in the night last night. If they come to mind, you might pray that the kids get over whatever bug is going around (Max had it mid-week last week) and that they will stay healthy. Healthy kids will make it easier on grandparents (and Mom, who can't be there to take care of them).

If you think about it, you might also pray for Levi. The stress of Dad being sick and Mom and Dad being so far away is really messing with his sugar readings. I talk to Kaylyn every day, and we make adjustments to his insulin, but he is still having some pretty high readings. Kaylyn and Max are doing a great job taking care of him, with instructions from me daily. They are amazing. We are very proud of all the kids!

Thank you for the continued prayers, cards, messages, and encouragement.

Have a good night, and sleep well, everyone.

God is good, all the time!

—Dione

Thursday, April 9, 2009, 11:10 a.m.

> The salvation of the righteous is from the Lord; He is their strength in the times of trouble.
>
> —Psalm 37:39

Hi, everyone. I'm sorry there were no updates yesterday. I just didn't get to it. Things are moving forward as we met with Dr. R yesterday. He is really neat because he comes in the room, sits down, gets comfortable, goes over everything, and makes sure there are no questions he needs to answer before he leaves the room. He did get the Velcade (the second chemo drug) approved. We already received the Revlimid, so everything is set to begin chemo. Billy will take the Revlimid just before bed each night. The Velcade is given by IV, and this protocol includes the steroid, Decadron. Dr. R was going to write a prescription for Billy to take the Decadron by mouth, but I asked if he could get it by IV to avoid upsetting his stomach. Dr. Ri agreed that was a good idea.

Chemo began yesterday. The regimens are fourteen days on and seven days off. The Revlimid is taken each day on the fourteen days while the Velcade and Decadron are given on days one, four, eight, and eleven. There will be eight rounds of chemo total. Blood will need to be drawn on Monday and Thursday at least. Dr. R told Billy to be a wimp while doing chemo. If he has chills with or without a fever, has a fever of 100.4 or higher, doesn't feel quite right, is overly tired, or feels anything out of the ordinary, then he is to go to the infusion center.

There is a chance we can go home on the weeks off of chemo depending on what is going on as far as radiation and Billy's health. Dr. R also said it is possible Billy could do some of the treatments at home, as long as we have a doctor who will agree. I will need to do some checking with our family care doctor and the oncologist we saw in Jefferson City. However, the first two to three rounds must be done here so Dr. R can see how Billy is tolerating it and how it is working. However, there is a chance we will be home on Billy's weeks off. We are still working on that.

Dr. R told us that the blood draw done on Tuesday showed that Billy's white cell count was good, his calcium was low, and there is no kidney failure! God is good!

Specific prayer requests are that the chemo does not cause any nasty side effects, and that Billy will regain some strength and stamina, as well as regaining the use of his right hand. A big need right now is that he will get an appetite. He was doing better for a couple of days, but for the last two to three days, he has been back to having little to no appetite, and that is a concern. We were told yesterday that if he does not regain his appetite soon, we need to let our care manager know, and they can give him something that will make him hungry. He would rather not do that if he can avoid it, but he continues to lose weight and that needs to stop. In the just over two weeks that we have been here, he has gone from 223 to 205. He really needs to be eating and feeding his body to keep it strong. He tries, but he is not having much luck. Thankfully he is not sick to his stomach; he just has no desire to eat.

The kids are doing well. Faith recovered quickly from her little illness, so thank you for the prayers. Kaylyn and I think a big part of it was that Faith needed to catch up on some sleep.

Thank you for all the prayers, cards, encouragement, and everything you are all doing for the kids and us! We love and miss you all!

God is good, all the time!

—Dione

Friday, April 10, 2009, 12:42 p.m.

> And we know that all things work together for good to those who love God, to those who are the called according to His purpose.
>
> —Romans 8:28

Billy had radiation this morning, and then we met with Dr. K's nurse practitioner. I asked her about Billy's left hip and upper leg hurting him part of the time. We will have an appointment with Dr. K either Wednesday or Thursday next week, so she suggested we talk to him about it then. Billy would not be able to do radiation on his hip or leg at the same time he is doing the back and shoulder anyway.

Billy did eat better yesterday and is eating better today as well. He just needs to keep eating more, and hopefully that will come. He will get his IV chemo and steroid in the morning, and then he has four more days of radiation next week, as well as his IV chemo and steroid on Wednesday and Saturday.

We saw Dr. R in the hall after radiation today. He thought Billy was looking better. He said he is convinced they can get the multiple myeloma under control. He is just not sure how well Billy's bones are going to recover. He did give Billy some high-powered bone builder when Billy was an inpatient, and Billy is taking three things recommended by the naturopath that are for bone building and bone health, so we will just keep praying that the bones will recover and he will regain the use of his right hand. Apparently those doing the radiation are a little concerned that he still has no strength and very little use of his right hand. Again, we will just have to pray and leave it in the Lord's hands.

The kids are doing well. Thank you to everyone who is doing things for them and taking care of them. They have a big weekend planed with Max and Justin helping at the church work day on Saturday. Kaylyn and Cassy will be going shopping with Dru and Linda while Levi and Faith will be staying with Bill and Kay. They will get to go to the donkey basketball game, and they are looking forward to it. They are also all looking forward to Easter at church.

Our prayer requests remain much the same as the last few days: little to no side effects from chemo and radiation; that his appetite, strength, and endurance improve; that his bones would heal and he would regain the use of his right hand; and also that he would continue to avoid infections and stay fever free.

Thank you all for your prayers and everything else everyone is doing for us.

God is good, all the time!

—Dione

Saturday, April 11, 2009, 7:02 p.m.

He is risen! Happy Easter!

Billy's appetite is getting better! Keep the prayers coming. He has eaten better the last couple of days and continued to eat more today as well.

He had his IV chemo and steroid this morning. The nurses remember him from two weeks ago on Sunday when I took him to the infusion center and he had pneumonia and was sedated by all of his pain meds. They were very happy to see him doing so much better and told him so several times. One told him that he was one very sick young man and she was so glad to see him doing so much better so soon.

I have to tell something kind of funny about when Billy was being released as an outpatient. When the nurse told us he was being released, I said I would go back to our room and get his clothes because he had just been wearing a hospital gown. All of a sudden he looked very worried and asked, "What did I have on when you brought me in here?" Of course, he didn't remember that Sunday at all, and all of a sudden he wondered if I had gotten him dressed or just taken him in the shorts he sleeps in. I told him I had gotten him dressed but I had taken the clothes to wash. He asked if I was sure. He was funny! The nurse didn't help much because she said that I had just thrown a blanket over him and wheeled him in. He was very glad to learn that he was dressed when I took him to the infusion center.

There are no appointments tomorrow, so it will be a very quiet day. On Monday he has radiation, a follow up with the pain doctor, a blood draw, and an appointment with Dr. R. We are going to ask Dr. R if he should be seeing physical therapy to work on getting up and walking, because he has only been going from the bed to the wheelchair and back. He has been pulling himself around in his wheelchair with his legs, so that gets him some exercise. We will have an appointment with Dr. K either Wednesday or Thursday, so Dr. R may want to wait and see what he says about the hip and leg before he decides on physical therapy.

I know the kids have all had a big day, and I will talk to them a little later. Max is staying with Steve and Linda tonight so he can help cook breakfast at church in the morning.

We really miss the kids and everyone else and would love to come home for a little while. However, we will have to wait and see what Dr. K says about the hip and leg as well as a few other things before we can make the decision about whether we can come home for a week or so. We will just have to play it by ear.

Our prayers continue to be that his appetite will continue to increase and stay there; that he will continue to regain strength; that the radiation will do its job; that he would regain the use of his right hand; that his bones will be able to recover; that the kids will stay healthy and continue to do well; and that we will all be together (even if just for a few days) soon.

Remember to praise the Lord for the incredible gift of His Son, our beloved Savior and Lord!

God is good, all the time!

—Dione

SUNDAY, APRIL 12, 2009, 8:48 P.M.

Father, thank You for the incredible gift You have given us by sending Your Son to die on the cross and rise on the third day. We are so thankful for the incredible gift of our salvation. Amen

Today was a quiet, cloudy day. We slept in a bit this morning since there were no appointments to get to or anything. Billy was still eating pretty well today. He isn't eating as much as he needs to yet, but he is doing better than he did for a little while. They had prime rib for lunch today and chicken fried steak for supper. Billy ate both pretty well.

Tomorrow Billy has radiation, a follow-up appointment with Dr. A, a blood draw, and an appointment with Dr. R.

Billy does seem to be developing a rash from the chemo. We were told this was a strong possibility. The nurse who did the chemo education with us told him not to suffer with it for more than twenty-four to forty-eight hours at the very most. She told us he could go to the infusion center or talk to his care manager and they could do something for it. It is not bothering him in any way. It doesn't itch or hurt or anything. He didn't even know he had it until I was getting him ready for bed. I had him look in the mirror since he could see it that way. He doesn't want to go to the infusion center tonight. He will have blood drawn there tomorrow, and he sees Dr. R tomorrow as well, so I will mention it and have it checked out.

Thank you for all of the prayers and everything everyone is doing. We love and miss you all.

God is good, all the time!

—Dione

Monday, April 13, 2009, 7:43 p.m.

> My mouth shall tell of Your righteousness and Your salvation all the day, For I do not know their limits. I will go in the strength of the Lord God; I will make mention of Your righteousness, of Yours only.
>
> —Psalm 71:15-16

Today was a rather long day. Billy didn't sleep as good last night, and the rash covered a much bigger area and looked really red this morning. He says it doesn't itch or hurt. He had a follow-up appointment with the pain doctor at 11:00. His nurses were concerned about the rash, and Billy was running a fever of 101.5. He was supposed to have blood drawn in the infusion center at 12:30, but they sent him straight up to get checked out. They really didn't find anything other than that it is probably a reaction to one of the chemo drugs. They did put him on an antibiotic as a precaution and gave him some fluids. He is still sweating quite a bit at times, and apparently he will need to drink more than he has been to make sure he keeps well hydrated. He has been drinking enough for normal circumstances, but with the sweating and running a low fever, he needs to drink more.

He is doing better with his eating and has even gained a pound and a half since last Wednesday. That is a good sign because every time he had been weighed recently he had lost weight.

We asked Dr. R about physical therapy, and he thought it was a good idea because they could show Billy some exercises that will help him even while he is in the wheelchair. Dr. R was showing Billy a couple he knew of, and Billy showed him how he pulls himself around with his feet and legs in the wheelchair. Dr. R laughed and said that was great! Billy was asking him about his right hand because it is still numb and he has no strength or grip in it. Dr. R said he still thinks it is from a pinched nerve but does not know if Billy will get part or any of the use of it back. He said he thought physical therapy might be able to at least work with him and maybe they could help. None of the doctors can guarantee Billy will get the use of his hand back, but they are trying their best to find things that might help.

We will meet with Dr. K on Thursday and can then bring up the issues of Billy's hip and upper legs hurting him part of the time. Billy says they don't hurt him too much except when he is first getting up in the morning, but we need to talk to Dr. K about it. They may need to take a closer look.

Billy and I have discussed it, and as much as we really want to go home for a visit, we feel that Billy needs to be stronger and getting around a little better. It is possible that physical therapy is all he needs to help with his hip and legs since he has been using a wheelchair for so long, but at this point we don't know. We also feel we need to stay here until we know the full extent of any reactions to chemo. We talked about it for a while on Sunday morning, and although we would really like to be home with the kids and everyone for a few days, we also need to be comfortable and confident in Billy making the trip and being okay.

I have been homesick and missing the kids over the weekend, and we are hoping they can come visit soon. We are looking forward to my parents visiting this coming weekend, and hopefully Billy's parents and sister will be able to visit soon too. Billy has said that visitors would be nice now that he is feeling better and up and around more, so anyone who wants to visit is welcome. He has a few days here and there with several things scheduled, but as a general rule, his schedule each day at this point isn't too bad at all. He has quite a bit of free time.

Our prayer requests are much the same—that he will continue to eat more and gain strength; that his right hand would recover; that he stays fever free; that this rash will go away with no complications; and that he will have little to no other side effects.

Oh, that reminds me—his blood counts were all good today, so at least the chemo is not knocking them out, at least not yet. We were reminded that can change, but we like to recognize a blessing when we see one.

God is good, all the time!

—Dione

Tuesday, April 14, 2009, 8:40 p.m.

> For my thoughts are not your thoughts, Nor are your ways My ways, says the Lord. For as the heavens are higher than the earth, So are My ways higher than your ways, And My thoughts than your thoughts.
>
> —Isaiah 55:8-9

I forgot to mention last night that when we met with Dr. R yesterday, he said not to get too excited or worked up about the stem cell rescue just yet. There is a big medical conference at about the end of May, and quite often new treatments and breakthroughs come out of this conference. He said that he doesn't go because it is such a madhouse, but he checks out all of the new treatments and things. Just since the mid-1990s they been able to successfully treat multiple myeloma (MM), and they have made big strides in treating it since then. They keep coming up with better stuff, so he is hoping something new and effective will come out of this conference.

Billy just had radiation today; he only has two days left. We will then meet with Dr. K Thursday afternoon and talk to him about Billy's left hip and upper legs that hurt him part of the time. We will see what he says and go from there.

Tomorrow Billy will see physical therapy, have radiation. and then get his IV chemo. Since we will be in the infusion center for the IV chemo, I am going to have them look at Billy's rash again. It looked better this morning because it was not as red or raised, but it is really red again tonight and I think it has spread a little more. Billy says it doesn't hurt or itch. From what Dr. R said yesterday, it looks like it was most likely caused by one of the chemo drugs. One of them does list a rash as a side effect. Since it doesn't hurt or itch and does not seem to be causing any problems, Dr. R said it may just have to be put up with. We will see how it goes.

I talked to the kids today, and Levi and Faith have a cold or allergy something going on. Levi had a pretty nasty-sounding cough, so if you think about them, you might say a prayer for them too. It makes it much easier on everyone if the kids are able to stay healthy. It also stresses the kids out when any of them have a cold or anything going on because they want to stay healthy so they can come visit as soon as they get a chance. I really don't think a cold or allergies will be enough to keep them from visiting, but they are worrying about it. The kids and I would all be less stressed if they could stay healthy. It is hard for me not to be able to be there and take care of them, and it causes them to worry.

Thank you to the IT department at Farm Bureau for the gifts for the kids and us. That was very kind of you, and I know the kids are excited and making big plans to use theirs.

Tonight's prayer requests are: no fever; that the rash will go away; that he will continue to eat well (he ate chicken twice in the last two days and has started trying a few new things here and there since he was told they are good for him); that his bones will heal and recover; and that he will be strong enough and we will be comfortable enough to visit home before too much longer.

Thank you for your continued prayers and support. We are so very blessed to have such wonderful family and friends; we love you and miss you all.

God is good, all the time!

—Dione

Wednesday, April 15, 2009, 9:32 p.m.

> And He said to me, "My grace is sufficient for you, for My strength is made perfect in weakness." Therefore most gladly I will rather boast in my infirmities, that the power of Christ may rest upon me. Therefore I take pleasure in infirmities, in reproaches, in needs, in persecutions, in distresses, for Christ's sake. For when I am weak, then I am strong.
>
> —2 Corinthians 12: 9-10

Thank you for the prayer; Billy's rash is going away! He is still eating pretty well, and he even stayed up longer this evening.

He met with physical therapy this morning. They were really pleased with how he pulls himself around in the wheelchair, and like Dr. R, they agreed that is good exercise. She also showed him a few more exercises that will work other muscle groups and help keep things in shape. He will be meeting with physical therapy some more, and they are going to see about getting him some appointments with occupational therapy because the physical therapist thought they would be able to do more to help with the hand. It may just take a while for his hand to recover. Brenda, Billy's sister, called this evening and said to remind Billy how long it took for his dad's arm to recover after the combine fell on him years ago. Billy remembers, and he said he didn't figure the hand would recover right away.

He has his last radiation treatment on his right shoulder and the middle of his back tomorrow. We will then meet with Dr. K late tomorrow afternoon, and we plan to talk to him about the hip and upper femurs. We will see where we go from there. Billy also has had his blood drawn to check counts, and Dr. R ordered some other blood tests as well to see what the chemo is doing so far.

My parents and my brother, John, are coming to visit this weekend, and then the kids will be down on Monday and Tuesday! We are looking forward to the visits.

The kids with colds are starting to recover, so thank you for the prayers in that area. I would just ask that when it comes to mind, please pray for the kids' health. I know when the weather gets its act together and truly acts like spring, it will help things.

Thank you for checking in, and thank you again for all the prayers and everything you are all doing.

God is good, all the time!

—Dione

Friday, April 17, 2009, 9:24 p.m.

> Finally, my brethren, be strong in the Lord and in the power of His might.
>
> —Ephesians 6:10

Oops, I missed a day. Sorry about that. We had a surprise visit yesterday from Billy's parents. It was pretty neat; as we left our room and headed down the hall for his first appointment, they were coming down the hall. We did not know they were coming, so it was really cool! We enjoyed the visit. Seeing someone from home is so nice!

My parents and brother are at the hotel. They just got in, and we will see them in the morning. Then the kids will be here Monday!

We did meet with Dr. K yesterday and talked to him about Billy's hips and upper legs hurting. He pulled up the X-rays that had been done the first week we were here and saw that there was quite a bit of bone thinning in his left hip and some in the right. He is going to go ahead and do radiation on both hips. The mapping appointment to get Billy marked for the radiation will be Tuesday, and then radiation will probably begin Thursday. However, we don't know for sure yet. We did learn yesterday that radiation treatment causes quite a bit of fatigue, and the fatigue can last for six weeks or so after the radiation treatments are over. That was good to know because it explains why Billy doesn't have much energy and needs his naps. He was told not to push himself. He is supposed to rest when he needs it, and they told him not to be hard on himself for not feeling like doing things he thinks he should do.

He will be meeting with physical therapy probably twice a week, and they are working on keeping all of his muscle groups strong. The stronger the muscle groups in the legs are, the more work they do, and that takes pressure off of the bones. Billy had blood drawn yesterday morning, and his hemoglobin was low. It was 9.1, and for a man it should be between 13.8 and 17.2, so he needed blood. He got his blood transfusion this afternoon. He needed two units, so it took about six hours. The nurses made him nice and comfortable, and he got a good nap in. He will have his last IV chemo for this round tomorrow and will finish the oral chemo on Tuesday.

Billy ate very little today, but I think some of that had to do with how low he was on blood. He just didn't feel very good this morning. Although they would have gotten him something to eat during the transfusion, he just wasn't hungry and had no desire to eat. Hopefully tomorrow will be better that way. They weighed him again yesterday, and he is maintaining his weight, which is good.

Our prayer requests for tonight are once again for him to have an increased appetite. He also really needs to have a bowel movement again. He had been doing pretty good, but I think the antibiotic they put him on this week has messed things up. He also needs to gain strength and stamina.

I hope everyone has a great weekend!

God is good, all the time!

—Dione

SATURDAY, APRIL 18, 2009, 9:40 P.M.

> You must grow in the grace and knowledge of our Lord and Savior Jesus Christ. All glory to Him now and forever!
>
> —2 Peter 3:18

Today was another rainy, cloudy day, but we enjoyed a very nice visit with my parents and brother. It is really nice to have company, and the visits are great! *(The kids will be here on Monday!)*

This morning Billy had his last dose of IV chemo for this round. He will finish the oral chemo on Tuesday. Our care manger, Libby (she is also an RN), did Billy's chemo this morning, so I said something to her about finding out that radiation causes fatigue. She said that fatigue from radiation is worse than chemo, and it last longer. That is actually good to know because we understand better why Billy continues to be so fatigued and needs so much rest. As far as we know, the only other radiation he will need is on his hips. After that is over, we are hoping some of his energy will begin to return. Libby also felt that once the radiation is done on his hips we should be able to start working on getting him up and walking some. We will just have to start out slow. We will find out Tuesday when the radiation on his hips will begin. It will be ten days' worth.

Oh, I almost forgot—the constipation problem is once again being corrected, and things are moving again. Thank you for the prayers for this issue.

For tonight the prayer requests are that his appetite will begin to return again, because in the last few days, it is becoming an issue again. He is having some trouble with certain foods' textures causing him to gag really badly, which hurts his back and makes it hard to eat. We will be having his throat looked at on Monday to make sure there isn't something going on there. I also ask for prayer that this issue will simply correct itself; that the fatigue with this next round of radiation will not be too hard on him; and that the radiation will go well with no real complications. The only real side effect from the last round was the fatigue, so we are very grateful for that.

Thank you for all of the cards, comments, and everything else so many people are doing for us. Continue to remember the Brown family as well as Bill and Kay in your prayers.

Have a very blessed Sunday, and remember, God is good, all the time!

—Dione

Sunday, April 19, 2009, 1:44 p.m.

I thought I would start today by telling you the story of a miracle. Last night we met Dan. Dan and his wife are from Alaska, and his wife had a cancer of the lungs that has never been cured. They have been battling this cancer for several years and have been coming here for twenty-nine months. Over a year ago, Dan's wife had nineteen tumors in her lungs. They had been doing treatments and were at a point where they were able to go home for three weeks.

While they were at home, Dan began anointing his wife with healing Scripture verses every morning, and she was careful not to cheat on her diet. When they returned and the CT scans were done, the doctors found that there were only nine tumors. They asked Dan what they had been doing, and he told them. The doctors then allowed Dan and his wife (he didn't tell us her name, and she was resting in her room) to go home for twelve weeks with instructions for Dan to continue anointing her with Scripture every day. She was also to follow her diet and not chase bears with brooms. They gave them this instruction because while they were home, a 450-pound black bear was trying to steal a fifty-pound sack of grain, and she had chased it with a broom trying to get the grain back. (Dan is quite a character, and we loved visiting with him.)

They returned twelve weeks later, and she had only three tumors left. Again they were able to go home for twelve weeks and were told to continue the anointing with healing Scriptures. Dan's wife was also not supposed to cheat on the diet or chase bears with brooms. When they returned, the tumors were gone, and she has now been completely cancer from for one year and two weeks. If all her scans are clean this time, she will be considered cured. There is still a chance it could return, but this is truly a miracle. The doctors here have said that they have never seen this kind of cancer cured or even totally in remission. Dan's attitude is that someone has to be first for everything, and his wife is the first in this case. God is the ultimate healer!

Billy slept really well last night and even slept in this morning. He is now napping after visiting with Mom, Dad, and John until they left just after lunch. He is still not eating very well, so we really need to work on his appetite again. He will have blood drawn in the morning, so we are going to see about having someone look at his throat to make sure there isn't something going on there. We have really enjoyed our visits with our parents and my brother this week and are looking forward to seeing the kids and my sister tomorrow.

Our prayer requests are for his appetite and that he will stay healthy (no fevers or anything like that). We also pray that he will be able to drink enough because he is required to drink a lot, but he doesn't care for the water here. The bottled water tends to taste at least a little like the bottle, and he is getting tired of juice, Gatorade, and lemonade. If he doesn't drink enough then I will have to take him to the infusion center and get him fluids by IV. Of course, we also want his bowels to keep working (and currently things are good in that department).

There is not much else going on. Enjoy the rest of the day. Thank you for all everyone is doing and especially for the prayers.

God is good, all the time!

—Dione

Monday, April 20, 2009, 8:00 p.m.

> For I know the thoughts that I think toward you, says the Lord, thoughts of peace and not of evil, to give you a future and a hope.
>
> —Jeremiah 29:11

The kids look great! It is so good to see them! Dru and the kids made it around 1:30. They admitted that they got lost, but they would have been fine if Kaylyn hadn't second guessed herself and asked the other kids what they thought. Dru said that Kaylyn was right about where to go, but then second guessed herself and they ended up missing the exit. However, it wasn't a very big deal to get back were they needed to be. Dru was very pleased when they checked in to find that they have adjoining rooms. She had requested them when she made the reservation, but they could not guarantee them to her. I think everyone found their sleep number when they took the luggage to the hotel and checked in. (All of the beds are sleep number beds.) From what they said, it sounds like all of them chose very soft beds, so we will see what they think in the morning. Everyone will be able to sleep on a bed, with Max getting a bed to himself. They came back over for a little while this evening, but Billy was getting pretty tired and needed to get ready for bed, so they headed back to the hotel to swim and hang out in the hot tub for a little while before calling it a night.

Billy had blood drawn this morning, and Debbie, Dr. R's nurse, called this afternoon to tell us his white cell count and ANC are down. I don't know a lot about this other than that means his immunity is low. Debbie will call tomorrow and let us know if Dr. R wants Billy on an antibiotic or not.

Billy has eaten almost nothing today, and although he didn't do too badly with his drinking, because he is still sweating quite a bit, I am afraid he is not taking in enough. I think we will go to the infusion center tomorrow afternoon after Dru and the kids leave and have them see if he needs some extra fluids. He doesn't really want to go and is trying to drink enough, but with the sweating, it is hard for him to keep up.

Our prayer requests are that Billy's appetite will come back; that he will be able to drink enough; and that he will have more energy and just plain feel a little better. I think his lack of appetite and trouble drinking enough have a lot to do with his fatigue and that he just doesn't feel very good. Thankfully his pain is still well controlled, and we are very grateful for that.

I would ask that you continue to remember Bill and Kay in your prayers. Bill is in the hospital in Columbia, Missouri. His pancreatic cancer has been found to be of a fast-growing nature, and he will be starting treatments as soon as possible.

Thank you!

God is good, all the time!

—Dione

Tuesday, April 21, 2009, 9:30 p.m.

> But sanctify the Lord God in your hearts, and always be ready to give a defense to everyone who asks you a reason for the hope that is in you, with meekness and

> fear; having a good conscience, that when they defame you as evildoers, those who revile your good conduct in Christ may be ashamed. For it is better, if it is the will of God, to suffer for doing good than for doing evil.
>
> —1 Peter 3:15-17

We really enjoyed seeing the kids, and it was hard to see them go. Thank you for bringing them down, Dru! We had a good visit with Dru too.

Billy will start the radiation on his hips on Thursday. He will have ten days like he did on his shoulder and back, but they only do radiation on Mondays through Fridays.

Dr. R started Billy on an antibiotic today since his ANC and white cell counts are basically zero. We saw Libby (our care manager) in the hall today, and we asked her if that is normal with chemo. She said that it can be a little different with each person, but yes, it is fairly normal. The multiple myeloma also affects the bone marrow anyway, and the bone marrow is where the white blood cells are produced. Billy will have blood drawn again on Thursday, so hopefully his counts will be starting to recover.

Billy did eat a little bit today, but he needs to be eating a lot better than he did today. When we saw Libby, I mentioned that he has no appetite. Libby said if that does not improve in the next day or two to let her know. She told Billy it is very important for him to eat well because his body really needs the nutrition.

Billy did try to drink well today, but he did not drink enough to get caught up. I tried to talk him into going and getting fluids without being bossy or pushy, but he just didn't want to go today. He doesn't have anything scheduled for tomorrow, so he said he will go tomorrow and see if he needs fluids. I can pretty much guarantee that he does. It isn't that he is completely dehydrated or anything, because he has been drinking around sixty ounces a day, but because of the amount of sweating he does, he needs to drink quite a bit more than that to keep his kidneys flushed good like the doctor wants. I guess I will just have to remind him tomorrow how important those fluids are for his kidneys.

Our prayer requests remain for his appetite, fluid intake, and fatigue and that this next round of chemo will go well, with no issues.

Thank you for all of your prayers.

God is good, all the time!

—Dione

WEDNESDAY, APRIL 22, 2009, 8:40 P.M.

> These things I have spoken to you, that in Me you may have peace. In the world you will have tribulation; but be of good cheer, I have overcome the world.
>
> —John 16:33

It was a beautiful day! It was eighty-four degrees this afternoon, and we sat outside for a little while and enjoyed the very pretty afternoon. We met another couple from Missouri while we were outside. They were headed home this afternoon. They are a very nice older couple. They were asking about the kids because they had seen them here yesterday. Several people have commented that we have the most visitors. They thought the kids were great and very well behaved.

Billy didn't have any appointments scheduled today, so we went to the infusion center at about 9:30 to see about some fluids. They agreed that he could probably use some and hooked him up. He napped for most of the two hours it took for the fluids to run and said that he did feel some better when they were done. He has been drinking pretty well the rest of the day. He still really doesn't have an appetite, but he did try to eat a little more today.

Because of all the sweating Billy does he can drink quite a bit, but he just can't always keep up. He has not been sweating as badly the last couple of days, so maybe whatever has been causing the problem is being corrected. No one is sure exactly what the problem is, but they figure it has something to do with the cancer, although chemo can mess up peoples' internal thermostat too. However, he had this problem before the chemo.

He will start radiation on his hips tomorrow. I think this is none too soon because his left hip has been hurting more the last couple of days but especially today. He will also have a blood draw tomorrow to check his counts.

We are very thankful that he has not had a fever or any sign of any infection of any kind. With his counts being so low, this is a real concern, because it would be very easy for him to catch about anything. The Lord is keeping an eye on him, and so far all is well.

Our prayer requests for tonight continue to be for his appetite to improve, that he can drink enough to prevent dehydration, that the sweating will quit, that the radiation will do what it needs to for his hips so he can begin walking again, that he will stay healthy and his counts will recover quickly, and also that the fatigue will not get any worse with this next round of radiation. This is his week of chemo. He will begin again next Wednesday as long as his counts are not too low.

Thank you for your prayers and support!

God is good, all the time!

—Dione

Thursday, April 23, 2009, 8:50 p.m.

> And He said to me, "My grace is sufficient for you, for My strength is made perfect in weakness." Therefore most

> gladly I will rather boast in my infirmities, that the power of Christ may rest upon me.
>
> —2 Corinthians 12:9

Because Billy's white count is so low, he was not able to start his radiation today. He had a blood draw this morning. He does not need a transfusion, but because his counts are so low, they are giving him a shot for three days, beginning today. The shot is to help boost his white cells. They will not do radiation tomorrow either since he will be getting the shot tomorrow and Saturday. They are going to wait until after his blood draw on Monday and see how his counts are doing. If they have come up enough then they will start the radiation on his hips.

Since we were at the infusion center today anyway, we got him some more fluids. He still has almost no appetite, although he is trying. He tried several different things today to see if something would taste good. After a couple of bites of each, he was just done. He said that it is hard to explain. It isn't that his stomach is upset; he just doesn't really have a desire to eat. After a couple of bites of something, he just doesn't want anymore. He has almost decided we need to talk to Libby about it because he has to get to eating to help keep his strength up. We are also wondering if part of the problem with trying to eat is because he has not eaten much of anything for most of the week and his tummy just doesn't really know what to do with the food when he tries to eat. That isn't exactly what the deal is, but it is the best way we can come up with to explain it. If he will agree to it in the morning, we will give Libby a call and see what she might be able to do to help him out with his appetite.

The sun was shining, and it was a really pretty day, although windy. We sat outside a couple of times today and just enjoyed the sunshine and fresh air.

It looks like it will be a pretty quiet weekend. We will be praying for our church family and the lay renewal this weekend. We would love to be there and are sure that God will be working in a big way. Speaking of our church family, *thank you* for everything you are doing for us. You are all amazing!

Hopefully you are all having pretty weather too. If so, enjoy it.

God is good, all the time!

—Dione

FRIDAY, APRIL 24, 2009, 9:05 P.M.

> Let your conduct be without covetousness; be content with such things as you have. For He Himself has said, "I will never leave you nor forsake you."
>
> —Hebrews 13:5

Today Billy got his second shot to help boost his white cell count. The nurse who gave it was looking at his lab results from yesterday and commented that he basically had no white cells. The normal white cell count would be 8,000 to 10,000; his was .05. Hopefully these shots will work like they are supposed to and he will be able to start his radiation on his hips Monday.

It was a beautiful day here today, and we enjoyed sitting outside a couple of times. Billy said he felt pretty good today. Some days are better than others. He is still not eating much, but he is trying different things and is at least eating something. We will just have to keep praying.

Our thoughts and prayers are with our church family and their lay renewal weekend. We know the Lord has big plans, and we will be excited to hear how He works this weekend.

We also continue to pray for Bill and Kay. It is our understanding that Bill will be starting chemo today. Bill, as always, is using every opportunity to witness. *Go Bill!*

Have a great weekend, and take care! Thank you for all of your prayers and support in so many ways. We can't thank our church family enough for all they are doing for us and the kids. You all are amazing! We love and miss you all!

We also want to thank everyone at Billy's work because they have been praying and supportive in so many ways too. Billy misses you all and would really like to join you at the office each day.

We will continue to take one day at a time. We know it is all in God's hands, and we will trust Him in whatever may come.

God is good, all the time!

—Dione

Saturday, April 25, 2009, 8:12 p.m.

> The Lord is my rock and my fortress and my deliverer; My God, my strength, in whom I will trust; My shield and the horn of my salvation, my stronghold.
>
> —Psalm 18:2

It was very quiet around here today because many patients go home for the weekends. Billy got his last Neupogen shot today and will have blood work done on Monday. We are praying that his white cell count will be up so he can begin the radiation on his hips. He still isn't eating that much, but he is trying. He is eating just a little more each day.

We have heard from a few people today about our church's lay renewal weekend. They are having an amazing weekend, and God is working in a big way! While Billy and I are thrilled to hear how well the weekend is going and how God is working, at the same time, we really miss being there. Just know that you all have been in our thoughts and prayers, and it is exciting to hear how the Lord is using this weekend.

The main prayer requests tonight are that Billy's white count will come up, so he can get started with the radiation and keep his chemo on schedule, that he will continue to eat more each day, and that he will begin to regain some strength.

Thank you all for your prayers and support. We are very blessed to have such wonderful family and friends.

God is good, all the time!

—Dione

Sunday, April 26, 2009, 8:15 p.m.

> Finally, brethren, whatever things are true, whatever things are noble, whatever things are just, whatever things are pure, whatever things are lovely, whatever things are of good report, if there is any virtue and if there is anything praiseworthy—meditate on these things. The things which you learned and received and heard and saw in me, these do, and the God of peace will be with you.
>
> —Philippians 4:8-9

It was a very quiet day. Billy didn't eat much today. He said he just wasn't hungry. He will have blood work tomorrow to see if his white count is up enough to start his radiation.

This has been a pretty hard weekend for Billy (and me too). This is our lay renewal weekend at church, which is where we were supposed to be. We are hearing wonderful reports of the weekend being *amazing and wonderful* and that God was felt in a big way. My youngest nephew accepted Jesus as his Savior and wants to be baptized as soon as Billy and I can be there to watch him. My sister and oldest nephew joined the church and just had an incredible weekend of growing in the Lord as well as growing in relationships with others. We have heard other reports of how this weekend was full of the Lord and how it touched everyone. This is all wonderful to hear, and we are thrilled because we knew the Lord would use this weekend in an amazing way—*but* we were supposed to be there. At least in our minds we were supposed to be there; obviously God had other plans.

We were both struggling a bit yesterday with not being able to be there. Today it really hit Billy hard and was pretty rough for him for a little while. He said he was thinking about the weekends he has done at other churches and how he felt bad for the kids whose parents didn't attend. Here was our weekend at our church, and our kids were there without us. He knows it isn't quite the same, but he was still having a hard time with it. He knows how the Saturday evenings go and how families come together at the end and pray for each other. Not being there with our kids was very hard. We are so very proud of the kids and how well they are doing even though it is hard for them. The Lord has blessed us with six very special kids.

We are very excited for our church family and will continue to pray that the Lord will continue what He has started this weekend.

I found this in my *Blackaby Study Bible* when I was reading earlier today, and it really grabbed me. It is so very true:

> *He is Enough*—The test of pure Christianity, the evidence of a personal relationship with Christ, is contentment in all circumstances. He is enough, for when you have Him, you have everything.[1]

God is good, all the time!

—Dione

[1] Ibid., pg. 1419.

Monday, April 27, 2009, 3:30 p.m.

> Be merciful to me, O God, be merciful to me! For my soul trusts in You; And in the shadow of Your wings I will make my refuge, Until these calamities have passed by.
>
> —Psalm 57:1

Thank you all for your kind words and support. It means a lot to know there are so many prayers going up for us. I have to say I never really thought of this site as being something that witnesses to others, lifts others up, or anything like that. I just knew it would be a good way to keep all of our friends and family up on what is going on. I also like doing things on the computer. It gives me something to do when Billy takes a nap or goes to bed early. It is pretty neat to see how God can use something as simple as this. We serve an *awesome God!*

Billy had blood counts done this morning, along with a few other tests. We got a call at about 11:30 from Dr. R's nurse. Billy's white cell count is still 0.5 and his ANC was 0 (normal is 1,800 to 7000). Dr. R wanted to see Billy, so they had him in there by noon. Dr. R's first thought was to admit Billy to the hospital for three or four days for IV antibiotics. However, he asked Billy some questions about how he is feeling and discovered that he has not been running a fever. Dr. R decided to give Billy three more shots of Neupogen (to help his bone marrow produce white cells). He got one today and will have one on Tuesday and on Wednesday. He also prescribed a few more days of oral antibiotic because Billy will be finishing the current one tomorrow. He said that while Billy is doing fine right now, that could change in a matter of thirty minutes. If Billy begins running a fever, has chills or shakes, or just plain doesn't feel good, then I am to take him to the infusion center right that minute, no matter what time of day or night.

Dr. R said he knew there was a chance of this happening with the high-dose chemo he threw at Billy, along with radiation. However, he felt he had to do it to take control of the cancer and keep it from killing Billy. He also said that he feels the bone marrow tests that were done were not right. He doesn't think they had enough bone marrow because according to the test results on the marrow (done in Jefferson City), Billy's bone marrow should be doing a better job of replacing the white cells than it is. He said he is not apologizing for what the treatment has done as far as the ANC and white cell counts; he is just saying that he knows it is his doing because of the treatment he put Billy on. It basically comes down to the fact that he knew this could happen, but he also knew if he didn't do something drastic, the cancer would kill Billy, so we will now deal with this.

Billy has another appointment with Dr. R on Wednesday afternoon, and we will see whether he can start his next round of chemo yet. He is supposed to start it Wednesday, but Dr. R doesn't really think he will be able to start it this week, so we shall see. Starting the radiation on Billy's hips is pretty questionable for Wednesday, but we know that God can do anything, so we will just put it in His hands.

As far as the rest of Billy's blood work today, it looked pretty good. His hemoglobin was rather low, but Dr. R said that was to be expected. It was not low enough to need a transfusion. His kidney function is normal, and everything else looks really good.

Billy still has no appetite, but he is trying to eat at least a little several times a day. He has tried Ensure, and he says that it is very heavy. Someone suggested adding a little milk to thin it, but I haven't gotten him to agree to try it that way yet. He was weighed today, and he has lost another ten pounds in the last two weeks. I may have to call our care manager when Billy is napping or something since he keeps telling me to just give him another day or two to see how it goes.

The kids are supposed to come visit Thursday and Friday, but we will have to play that by ear with Billy's counts being so low. We will see how things are Wednesday when he has blood work and sees Dr. R again.

Prayers needed are for Billy's counts to come up so he can begin radiation and the next round of chemo and the kids can visit. Please also pray that he will begin eating better and quit losing weight and that he will not catch anything while his counts are so low.

Thank you again for all of your prayers and encouragement. We love you all!

God is good, all the time!

—Dione

Chapter 7

Tuesday, April 28, 2009, 8:38 p.m.

> Great is our Lord, and mighty is power; His understanding is infinite.
>
> —Psalm 147:5

Blessed! That is how Billy and I are feeling tonight. We had a wonderful visit with Dan. (I always forget his title, so Billy just tells me that he is second in command at Farm Bureau.) Thanks for driving all the way down here, Dan. It was very nice to meet you, and Billy really enjoyed the visit. Thank you to everyone at Farm Bureau for all of your prayers, the goodies you sent along with Dan, and everything else you have all been doing. You all are wonderful, and we are very blessed to know all of you.

I talked to Bro. Brian for a little while this evening, and I have to say, our church family is *amazing*! Thank you all for your prayers and everything else you are doing for us and the kids.

We are also very grateful for our families and all they are doing by keeping the kids and running them here and there and just everything you all do. Thank you! We are truly blessed by all of our family and friends, and we love you all!

Now for how Billy is doing today. He is still feeling okay and has no fever. God is good. He had a follow-up appointment with Dr. A, the pain doctor, today, and since everything is working well for him, no changes were made. Dr. A was concerned about Billy's lack of appetite and said that he could prescribe a pill that would give him an appetite.

Billy really didn't want to take another pill, so Dr. A decided to get him an appointment with nutrition. If that doesn't help, Billy will need to take the pill. Billy has agreed to that, and we will meet with nutrition on Thursday morning.

Billy will have blood work again in the morning, so pray for those white cells. If his counts are okay then he will begin the radiation on his hips tomorrow. We also have an appointment with Dr. R tomorrow. Whether he begins radiation or chemo will all depend on those counts. Also pray for Billy's appetite. Thank you all for your prayers and support. We are very blessed to have such wonderful friends and family, and we love all of you!

God is good, all the time!

—Dione

Wednesday, April 29, 2009, 7:45 p.m.

> Know that the Lord, He is God; It is He who has made us, and not we ourselves; We are His people and the sheep of His pasture.
>
> —Psalm 100:3

Billy tried Boost today, and he likes it much better than Ensure. They also have Boost with extra protein, and protein is something he is supposed to be eating a lot of. We will meet with the nutritionist in the morning to see where to go from there.

Billy had blood drawn today, and his white cell count is now 0.8, up from 0.5, and the ANC is up from 0 to 0.2. Billy has quite a way to go to get it where it needs to be. He will continue the Neupogen shots for four more days and he will be getting the Decadron for the next two days, as well as Zometa, which is a high-powered bone builder. The Decadron is a steroid that has been very good for Billy the last few times he had it, and it did help his white count once before.

While Billy's white count and ANC are still way too low, all of the other blood tests look very good, which pleased Dr. R. We will be doing another twenty-four-hour urine capture tomorrow. Dr. River has several tests he wants to run on the urine. He also had some blood drawn for a blood test that, along with the tests on the urine, is supposed to give Dr. R an idea of how much good the chemo did.

We learn a little something every time we meet with Dr. R. Today after he looked at the blood test results and commented that the kidney function was normal, he then looked at Billy and said he was one very lucky sucker. He went on to say that Billy should have been in kidney failure and a coma. He told us that the prednisone that he only took for two days saved his life. According to the test results Dr. R looked at before and then after Billy had the prednisone, he feels that there was a very good chance Billy would have died if he had not had those two days of prednisone. He feels that at the very least Billy would have been in kidney failure, on dialysis, and in a coma. God is so good!

The kids are coming to visit tomorrow! My dad is going to bring them down to visit. We are looking forward to it!

Our prayer requests are

- that Billy's white count and ANC really climb over the weekend so he can get back on track with his treatment;
- that we would learn something from the nutritionist that will really help Billy's appetite;
- that Billy will continue to feel pretty good and remain fever free (thank the Lord he is still doing good that way); and
- that Dad and the kids will have a safe trip.

Thank you all for your prayers. We are very thankful for every one of you!

God is good, all the time!

—Dione

Thursday, April 30, 2009, 8:56 p.m.

> Cause me to hear Your lovingkindness in the morning, for in You do I trust; Cause me to know the way in which I should walk, for I lift up my soul to You. Teach me to do Your will, For You are my God; Your Spirit is good. Lead me in the land of uprightness.
>
> —Psalm 143:8, 10
>
> Cause Me to Know—We can acquire knowledge, but only God can give wisdom. Only He knows the best paths for us. Only He can guide us unerringly.[2]

My dad and the kids arrived a few minutes after 1:00! They look great, and we spent the afternoon and part of the evening just visiting and hanging out. It is great to see them! They are going to stay until just after supper tomorrow, so we plan to enjoy the day with them.

We met with the nutritionist this morning, and she was very helpful. She also apologized that they had not gotten to us sooner because according to Billy's record, he has lost fifty pounds in just over a month. (Actually, he has lost just over fifty pounds since January, but he has lost around twenty-five pounds in the last month.) She said she would give him some tips on how to increase his appetite and give him about a week or so to

2 Ibid., pg. 734.

start eating better. If that didn't work, then they would have to give him something to help his appetite.

She told us a few things to do to help moisten his mouth and help get things to start tasting better. She also told him that for now, he can eat anything that he wants to, and he needs to eat every two to three hours. He doesn't have to eat a lot each time, but he needs to eat at least a small snack every two to three hours to help stimulate his appetite. He does like the Boost, and the kids brought some Carnation Instant Breakfast. We can also get a special kind of Carnation Instant Breakfast from the cafeteria. We just have to ask for it. It is much higher in calories and protein then the regular kind.

The nutritionist made many suggestions on things Billy can eat for snacks that will be high in calories and protein. She also told him that once we get his appetite back, then she will go over guidelines on things he will have to cut back on as well as things he shouldn't eat, but for now he is to eat anything that he wants. Her suggestions are already helping because he has eaten more today than he had been eating in two days. Thank you to everyone who suggested the Boost. He likes it much better than the Ensure.

The only other thing Billy had to do today was get his Decadron, Zometa, and Neupogen. We spent about an hour and a half in the infusion center getting all of those, and then he was done for the day. He will get the Neupogen for each of the next three days, and he will get the Decadron tomorrow. The Decadron only takes about thirty minutes to get, so we shouldn't be in the infusion center more than about forty-five minutes tomorrow. That is all he has scheduled for tomorrow. We will spend the rest of the day with the kids and Dad. The kids and Dad are going to play pool or watch the big-screen TV in one of the family rooms while Billy is in the infusion center. If it is nice tomorrow, we plan to go for a walk on the walking path, but we will have to see how the weather is.

Thank you for all of your prayers. Billy is still doing well as far as no fever or other issues (thank the Lord!) and he seems to be getting a good start on getting back to eating. The kids also brought a different brand of bottled water, and it does taste much better. Billy has already enjoyed a pretty decent amount of water since it doesn't taste like the bottle.

Drinking more water will help restore the moisture in his mouth, which will help with his eating (at least the nutritionist seems to think it will make a difference, and Billy seemed to agree).

Prayers for tonight are

- that Billy's counts come up over the weekend;
- that his appetite continues to grow;
- that he continues to remain fever free (he finishes his antibiotic tomorrow);
- that the kids and Dad have a safe trip home and the kids remain healthy. A couple of them are dealing with some allergies, which is no big deal, other than it annoys them.

Thank you again for all of your prayers and support.

God is good, all the time!

—Dione

Friday, May 1, 2009, 8:15 p.m.

> Lord, what is man, that You take knowledge of him? Or the son of man, that You are mindful of him?
>
> —Psalm 144:3

> What is Man?—It is incomprehensible that God concerns Himself with us. In truth, we are nothing compared to His greatness, yet He loves us and cares about the smallest details of our existence. This is so true and I have always loved Psalm 8, take a few minutes and read it.[3]

3 Ibid., pg. 734.

What a great day! We spent a wonderful day just hanging out and visiting with the kids and Dad! We talked, laughed, and had lots of hugs and smiles. It was just great to spend time together.

While Billy got his Decadron and Neupogen, the kids and Dad played a little pool and then went to the library, where a couple of them got on computers. Faith discovered some kids' books, and she was having a big time reading some of them.

Billy has let his whiskers grow, so he has a bit of a mustache and beard. He asked the kids what they thought, and they all like it, so it will stay for at least awhile. Kaylyn, he did shave the scraggly whiskers up high on his cheeks like you suggested, and it does look better.

Billy is feeling pretty good, and he ate a little better today than he did yesterday. He didn't take a nap today or yesterday, but he did very well without getting too worn out. Although he needs the radiation on his hips and he needs to get his next round of chemo going, I think the break has allowed him to get a little energy back.

Prayers remain the same: that his counts come up, that his appetite continues to increase, and that he continues to stay fever free and feeling good. Something I need to add is that he still has little to no use of his right hand, so I think it would be good to pray for that hand because no one knows if he will regain the use of it or not. Also pray for his bones. I have not mentioned it for a while, but the doctor does not know if his bones will recover from the damage that has been done to them, so that is something we need to pray for too.

Thank you again for all of your prayers and everything. We love and miss everyone, but we are confident that we are where God wants us.

God is good, all the time!

—Dione

Saturday, May 2, 2009, 8:22 p.m.

> Enter into His gates with thanksgiving, and into His courts with praise. Be thankful to Him, and bless His name.
>
> —Psalm 100:4

It was another rainy day, although most of the afternoon it was just very cloudy and didn't rain. We slept in some this morning and then went to the infusion center for Billy's shot of Neupogen. He is still feeling pretty good, and he ate a little better today than he did yesterday. Any and all improvement is good.

This afternoon Billy laid down for a nap, and I went to Target for a little while and picked a few things up. The transportation department will take you pretty much anywhere you want to go, and they have trips to Target, as well as the mall and Wal-Mart, scheduled every day. They have the shuttles that run back and forth to the hotel, but they also have several Lincolns and a limousine they use to pick people up at the airport, as well as their runs to several places. I rode in a Lincoln today, but when they have several people going, they use the limousine.

There is not much going on tomorrow, just the Neupogen shot. If it is warm enough, we may spend some time outside, and if not, we may just watch some movies.

Our prayer requests are pretty much the same as last night. When you think about it, you might continue to add that the kids stay healthy. We really enjoyed their visit, and I think they did too. We are thinking of some things we might do when they visit next time if Billy is feeling up to it.

Have a good night, and remember, God is good, all the time!

—Dione

Monday, May 4, 2009, 3:23 p.m.

> The name of the Lord is a strong tower; The righteous run to it and are safe.
>
> —Proverbs 18:10

> God Our Fortress—Sometimes the righteous need protection, they must seek a place of safety from danger. The Lord Himself is not intimidated by our greatest fears. He remains unshaken in our worst calamity. We experience incredible peace and security when we abide in Him.[4]

It is still cloudy and rainy, and everyone would like to see some sunshine. From what we have seen of the weather, there are many areas with the same problem. It has been too cool the last few days to sit outside and enjoy the fresh air. It looks like it will be cool tomorrow as well, but the rest of the week should be warm enough.

Billy got his last Neupogen shot yesterday, and he had nothing scheduled for today. Tomorrow they will do blood work, and if all is well, he will be able to start the radiation on his hips.

We will see the nutritionist again tomorrow, and she plans to weigh him to see how he has done for the last several days. He has not been eating anything like he used to, but he has eaten pretty well for the last several days. He has not eaten very much yet today, but part of that is because we were in the dining area earlier today and they were cooking cabbage in the kitchen. Billy has never been able to stand the smell of cabbage cooking, and that did in his appetite for lunch. For supper I will go down and get our supper, and he will stay in the room so he doesn't have to smell the cabbage. It might not smell like cabbage anymore, but they have a cabbage soup today that they will have out with supper too, so we just aren't going to take the chance.

---

4 Ibid., pg. 760.

He has been pretty tired today too, but he just woke up from a long nap and is eating a good snack.

We will meet with Dr. R again on Wednesday, and that is when we will find out if Billy can begin his next round of chemo. However, we will have a pretty good idea after the blood draw tomorrow. If his counts are not up enough for radiation to begin tomorrow, then they won't be up enough for chemo. We will just have to see how it goes.

Prayer requests are

- That his counts will be up so radiation and chemo can begin again;
- That his appetite will continue to get better;
- That there is no fever or other issues and;
- That the kids stay healthy.

Thank you for your continued prayers and support.

For those of you who might have specific questions or just want to contact us personally, our e-mail address is at the right of this page.

God is good, all the time!

—Dione

Chapter 8

Tuesday, May 5, 2009, 2:14 p.m.

> O Lord my God, I cried out to You, and You healed me.
>
> —Psalm 30:2

> In you, O Lord, I put my trust: Let me never be put to shame. Deliver me in Your righteousness, and cause me to escape; Incline Your ear to me, and save me. Be my strong refuge, to which I may resort continually; You have given the commandment to save me, for You are my rock and my fortress.
>
> —Psalm 71:1-3

Thank you so much for all the prayers! Two prayers have been answered. Billy's counts are up enough that he had his first radiation treatment on his hips today. We will see Dr. River tomorrow, and most likely Billy will begin his next round of chemo. We also saw the nutritionist this morning, and she was thrilled. Billy has gained just over three pounds since Thursday. She said that she would be okay with him maintaining his current weight, but she does not want him losing weight. All in all, it was a pretty good day.

Now we will pray that he does not have any bad reactions to the chemo and radiation this time and that he will not become too fatigued. We also want to pray that he will be able to continue eating well.

Thank you again for all of the prayers and support. We enjoy reading the posts in the guestbook. You are welcome to ask questions and things in the guestbook or e-mail us personally. I can't guarantee that I will remember to answer the questions left in the guest book, but I will try.

Have a great week, and I hope the sun shines where you are. We are getting rain again, and it looks like it will continue to rain for the next few days.

God is good, all the time!

—Dione

Wednesday, May 6, 2009, 8:14 p.m.

> You will guide me with Your counsel, and afterward receive me to glory.
>
> —Psalm 73:23

> Guidance—God loves us too much to leave us to our own wisdom. He takes us by the hand and skillfully guides us through life's pathways.[5]

Billy started his chemo today, at least the oral one. He will begin his IV chemo and Decadron on Monday. Dr. R told us Billy's white count is up to normal and his platelets are good, but his hemoglobin is low and he will probably need blood before the weekend is over. They will do labs again on Friday, so if he needs it, he will get it Friday or Saturday.

Dr. R is not going to give him as much of the Velcade (IV chemo) this time, as he does not want to drop his counts and postpone any more treatments if we can avoid it. He feels the Revlimid (oral chemo) and the Decadron are the most important things for Billy and the Velcade

[5] Ibid., pg,684

is a bonus, so he is going to drop the dose a little and only give it twice during the fourteen days instead of four times. He is also going to give Billy one shot of something (I didn't get it written down) that is equal to ten days' worth of the Neupogen. That is to help keep his counts from dropping with this round of treatment. He is going to try his best to keep Billy's treatments on track. He doesn't like the extra time off between treatments.

Billy will also start back with physical therapy to try and work with his right hand. Dr. R thought they were already doing that, but there were some lines crossed somewhere and Billy didn't get scheduled. It looks like we should have asked a few more questions about it. Regardless, Billy will see PT tomorrow, and then we will go from there.

Billy has had two days of radiation on his hips now, so only there are eight left to go. Everyone he saw today (radiation and Dr. R's staff) thought Billy was looking good. They are all very glad to see him looking and acting so much better than was for a while. He is still eating pretty well and is keeping up with the amount that he needs to drink, so things are looking pretty good that way.

Our prayer requests are that he will continue to eat and drink well (starting chemo again can make a difference); that the side effects will be minimal; that the chemo will do its job and take this cancer out; that his right hand will improve; and that the radiation will do the job so we can get him up walking again.

Thank you for all the prayers and support.

Oh, we had sunshine and temperatures in the mid-seventies today. It was beautiful, and we enjoyed sitting outside and getting some fresh air for a little while today. It sounds like the rain may return tomorrow.

God is good, all the time!

—Dione

Thursday, May 7, 2009, 8:10 p.m.

> But let all those rejoice who put their trust in You; let them ever shout for joy, because You defend them; Let those also who love Your name be joyful in You.
>
> —Psalm 5:11

> Joy in God—Pure joy comes from our love relationship with God. The greater our love for God, the greater will be our joy in Him.[6]

Billy had occupational therapy this morning. This morning was his evaluation. The therapist thinks they can do quite a bit to help him get the use back in his right hand, as well as help him get the strength back in both hands. His left hand just doesn't have the strength it used to, so they will work on it as well as the right. They set him up with appointments every day (Monday through Friday) for the next four weeks. If he does not need that many appointments, they will take some off, but they wanted to make sure they had him on the schedule if he needs them.

We had a nice surprise this morning. When we went down to the clinic for occupational therapy, Billy's Parents and his sister, Brenda, were waiting for us. They had not been there long. Today was the only day Brenda could come down, so they left early this morning. We had a very nice visit, and it was good to see them. They headed home around 2:30 when Billy was getting tired and ready for his afternoon nap.

Billy has a blood draw in the morning to see if he needs some blood, and then occupational therapy, and then he will have his radiation at 1:15. That will be it for tomorrow. He doesn't have anything over the weekend unless he needs blood. If he needs some, then he will probably get it Saturday, but we will see.

---

[6] Ibid., pg. 637.

We did have sunshine and warm temperatures today, so we sat outside for quite a bit while we visited. It was so nice!

God is good, all the time!

—Dione

Friday, May 8, 2009, 10:38 p.m.

> The Lord also will be a refuge for the oppressed, a refuge in times of trouble.
>
> —Psalm 9:9

> God Our Refuge—God's children can encounter Him in whatever capacity they need Him. If we desperately need a refuge, that is how we will experience Him.[7]

Billy had a blood draw this morning that included a type and match since Dr. R was pretty sure he would need blood. On Wednesday his hemoglobin was 9.1 (normal is 13.8 to 17.2), today it was 8.6, so he will get blood tomorrow. Because they are planning to do a stem cell rescue after he finishes his eight rounds of chemo, he has to get special blood products that take about six hours to get ready. Since they didn't get the blood test results back until about 12:30, that would mean the blood wouldn't be ready until about 6:30 or so, and it takes six hours for the transfusion, so he will get it tomorrow.

He had occupational therapy at 11:30, and that went well. The therapist worked with him on some exercises for his hands and shoulders, and he will do them twice a day. During the week the OT will do them with him, and then he will do them one other time. Or some days she will do something different with him and he will do them on his own twice.

---

7 Ibid., pg. 639

We met with Dr. K's nurse practitioner after radiation today, and things seem to be looking good. Billy is not having as much pain in his hips when he gets up of a morning, so it looks like the radiation is helping. Billy is still eating pretty well. He was weighed today, and so far he is maintaining his weight.

We want to continue to pray that his counts will hold out with this round of chemo and radiation so he can stay on track with his treatment; that he will continue to eat well and feel pretty good; that the OT will really help with his hands; and that he will be up walking again before long.

Thank you all for your prayers, continued support, and love. We feel very blessed to know you and have so many friends and family.

God is good, all the time!

—Dione

Saturday, May 9, 2009, 8:50 p.m.

> For My thoughts are not your thoughts, nor your ways My ways, says the Lord. For as the heavens are higher than the earth, so are My ways higher than your ways, and My thoughts than your thoughts.
>
> —Isaiah 55:8-9

> God's Thoughts—We should not try to reduce God's Word to a level that makes sense to us. Rather we should ask God to raise our thinking so we have His perspective on the world around us.[8]

I have to say amen to this. God knows all. He knows how things are going to turn out. He understands what we are going through when we don't,

[8] Ibid., pg. 865.

and He is always there to see us through. Our human minds just can't understand it all, so we just have to *trust God,* give ourselves to Him, and do the best we can. I don't think God wants anything more from us.

The sun did peak out a little today, but the high was only in the upper sixties. We didn't get a chance to go outside because we were in the infusion center from 10:30 this morning until about 6:15 this evening. Billy got his two units of blood. He had one of the nurses who took care of him on the Sunday I took him in with pneumonia and he was so out of it. Her name is Sharon, and she was thrilled to see him doing so much better, and they gave each other a hard time all day. It was very quiet in the infusion center today because many people have gone home for the weekend, so Billy kept Sharon entertained today, and she seemed to enjoy it. Billy may give her a hard time, but she gives it right back. Let's just say there were a lot of smiles and laughter in the infusion center today.

Billy is still feeling pretty well, and he is still eating okay. He has had four radiation treatments on his hips, and they are already doing better. They are not hurting him when he gets up in the morning, and he has not had to take breakthrough pain medication for two or three days now. He will see pain management again on Tuesday; if he continues to go without needing the breakthrough medication, they will most likely lower the dose of some of his long-acting pain medication. We will have to see, but I am pretty sure they will.

Thank you for your continued prayers and support! We really appreciate all that everyone is doing and are very blessed by you.

Have a great Mother's Day, and remember, God is good, all the time!

—Dione

Sunday, May 10, 2009, 9:00 p.m.

> Blessed be the God and Father of our Lord Jesus Christ, the Father of mercies and God of all comfort, who

> comforts us in all our tribulation that we may be able to comfort those who are in any trouble, with the comfort with which we ourselves are comforted by God.
>
> —2 Corinthians 1:3-4

We just had a quiet day today. We slept in and went outside for a few minutes, but it was a bit chilly. The sun peaked out for just a few minutes today.

I talked to the kids today. We have such sweet kids! We are so very proud of them! They will be visiting again late in the week, and we are counting down and looking forward to it.

Thank you for all of your prayers and support, and Happy Mother's Day to all of you moms out there!

If the Lord leads you to do so, I would ask that you pray for a couple from west Texas we met this week. Their names are Marty and Dotty. They have twelve grandchildren and are a very nice couple. Billy got started talking to Dotty when he noticed she had on a Harley Davidson jacket. Billy asked if she rides, and sure enough, she and Marty ride Fat Boys (a kind of Harley). Marty was having radiation at the time.

Marty has cancer of the esophagus, and they have been here one week longer than we have. When we were in the infusion center yesterday, they were there too, only Marty was admitted for observation. We saw Dotty today, and things are not going well. They gave Marty two units of blood yesterday, and he has thrown up at least two units since then. He was in quite a bit of pain, and although they have been trying, they have not been able to get the bleeding stopped. They were doing a scope sometime this afternoon to see if they could figure out exactly where the bleeding is coming from and how to stop it. We really haven't had a chance to talk to Marty, but Dotty is very sweet. We prayed for them when we saw Dotty today and have prayed for them since then. Thank you!

God is good, all the time!

—Dione

Monday, May 11, 2009, 9:12 p.m.

> Fear not, for I am with you; Be not dismayed, for I am your God. I will strengthen you, Yes, I will help you, I will uphold you with My righteous right hand.
>
> —Isaiah 41:10

It was a busy day. Billy had radiation, a blood draw, and occupational therapy this morning. Then Billy took a nap while I went to Target. After I got back, Billy had an appointment with Dr. R. Then we had to go over to the scheduler to get some blood draws, IV chemo, and other things scheduled. Then this evening he got his IV chemo and Decadron.

All of Billy's blood work looks good. We went over how well the first round of chemo did. It is a bit hard to explain and make sense, especially typing it, but the long and the short of it is the first round did a pretty good job of knocking the cancer down, but there is still quite a ways to go. Dr. R just can't get over how good Billy is looking and how well he is doing, so that is very good. He looked at Billy today, shook his head, and said, "You know the saying 'a wing and a prayer'? That is why you are still here." Thank you again for the prayers! God answers!

Dr. R also asked if Billy was seeing occupational therapy now and we told him that he is. We also told him that Billy is scheduled to start seeing physical therapy and their plan is to work with him and start getting him ready for getting up and around after he finishes the radiation on his hips. Dr. R had started out the door, but then he stopped, turned around, looked at Billy with a rather concerned look on his face, and said that he wants to do a metabolic bone scan (they are just special X-rays of the entire body) before they do too much as far as getting him out of the wheelchair. That is scheduled for next Tuesday. It will give us a pretty good idea of how Billy's bones are doing.

Oh, before I forget, while Billy is still eating, he is not eating very much at a time. He was weighed again today, and he has lost a few pounds again.

He is going to try to get them back on before he sees the nutritionist again. I told him I think it is because he has not been eating the protein shakes like he had been. He had been drinking one or two of them a day, along with what he was eating. The last few days he has been eating about the same, but he has not been drinking the shakes. He said that he is going to try to get those few pounds back on in the next few days before he gets weighed again, and he had a protein shake today. I will see if I can get him to have a couple of them a day, like he had been doing.

Our prayers are

- that his counts stay good;
- that he doesn't get too fatigued with the radiation and chemo; and
- that he begins to eat more, his bones heal, for strength, and that the use of his hand will improve.

Thank you all for your prayers and support!

God is good, all the time!

—Dione

Tuesday, May 12, 2009, 9:35 p.m.

> For we are His workmanship, created in Christ Jesus for good works, which God prepared beforehand that we should walk in them.
>
> —Ephesians 2:10

> Walk in Grace—Living a life in Christ is to be where He is; it is to know heavenly realities on earth. Nothing is too hard for Christ. Grace means that when Christ lives within us, all that we have and all that we are is His gift.

> We cannot boast in what He has given, we simply live in gratitude, walking according to His grace.[9]

It was a fairly busy day today with no time for a nap, but all went well and Billy was feeling pretty good. He ate pretty well today and had a shake as well. Physical therapy did an evaluation with him today, and he will be seeing them three times a week. They will work on strength and endurance, keeping in mind the limitations that Dr. R has given.

The pain management appointment went well. It was decided to leave him on the doses he is currently on. They are not unreasonably high doses, and Billy is showing no signs of being over medicated, so we are leaving things as they are. He won't see pain management again until next month, unless something comes up and we feel he needs to see them before then.

I told you last night that the first round of chemo knocked the cancer down pretty good, but there is a ways to go. I think I can give you a pretty good idea of where things are without getting into stuff that will get confusing. I am going to give it a try, and hopefully this will make sense. There are two heavy chains in the blood and two light chains. Billy's cancer is in one of the light chains, so the ratios I am going to give are just in the light chains of blood, not all of the blood. I know that's as clear as mud. Anyway, before the first round of chemo, the cancer cells to good cells ratio was 2100 to 1. After the first round of chemo, it was 314 to 3. That is quite a difference, but as I said before, he still has a ways to go. They will check this again at the end of the month.

I did see Dotty today, and Marty is still throwing up blood. They will be doing some tests to check things out and see what is going on for sure and what they can do about it. I told her that we are praying for them and that we have asked others to pray as well. She was very grateful and said that is the best thing anyone could do for them.

The kids will be here Thursday evening!

Thank you, Stan and Marlene!

---

9 Ibid., pg. 1407

God is good, all the time!

—Dione

—∞—

Wednesday, May 13, 2009, 9:03 p.m.

> Have you not known? Have you not heard? The everlasting God, the Lord, the Creator of the ends of the earth, neither faints nor is weary. His understanding is unsearchable. He gives power to the weak, and to those who have no might He increases strength.
>
> —Isaiah 40:28-29

We had sunshine and warm weather today, and it looks like storms tonight. There is a pretty big thunderstorm headed our way, but it looks like many other areas are dealing with the same thing. I hope everyone stays safe with the storms tonight.

We sat outside a couple of times today and enjoyed the warm air and sunshine. It was a fairly quiet day, with occupational therapy this morning and radiation this afternoon. Billy then took a good nap before supper. He will have a blood draw and get his Decadron tomorrow. The last thing he has tomorrow is his radiation at 1:15, so he will be able to get a nap in the afternoon before the kids get here tomorrow!

Things seem to be going well with this round of chemo. There is no rash like last time.

Our prayers are that he will continue to eat well and feel pretty well, that counts will stay good, and that the treatments will continue to do their job.

God is good, all the time!

—Dione

Thursday, May 14, 2009, 10:37 p.m.

> And let the peace of God rule in your hearts, to which also you were called in one body; and be thankful.
>
> —Colossians 3:15

The kids made it! They arrived at around 9:10 this evening. Billy had taken a nap late this afternoon, so we had them come over for a little while. There were lots of smiles and hugs. They also brought me a beautiful necklace for Mother's Day. They are really sweet! They headed for the hotel about 10:00 and will be over in the morning to spend the day with us. Billy just has a couple of appointments tomorrow, so we will be able to spend pretty much all day with the kids.

Billy did pretty well today, and occupational therapy is going well. He only has Friday and Monday left for his radiation on his hips, and then he will have a metastatic bone scan on Tuesday to see how his bones are doing.

Thank you for all of your prayers and support.

God is good, all the time!

—Dione

Information I feel I need to add here: Before getting sick, Billy was very active in our church, our church association, with his Road Riders for Jesus group (a motorcycle group), was doing some fill in pastoring, and was the state coordinator for Church Renewal. Kaylyn and Max had gone to North Carolina with Billy and helped with a Church Renewal weekend, and Kaylyn, Max, Levi, and I had also helped Billy with one in Missouri.

Friday, May 15, 2009, 9:07 p.m.

> And He said to me, "My grace is sufficient for you for My strength is made perfect in weakness." Therefore most gladly I will rather boast in my infirmities, that the power of Christ may rest upon me.
>
> —2 Corinthians 12:9

> In Weakness He Is Strong—Beware of your strength, for it can lead to self-reliance. Glory in your weakness, for it can lead to humility and dependence upon God. He can show Himself strong through a willing servant. God gives strengths and weaknesses; let Him work through both. [10]

Wonderful! That is a good way to describe our day. We have had a wonderful day with the kids! Billy had occupational therapy at 10:30, and Stan and Marlene brought the kids over at about 9:30. Billy and I were already sitting outside enjoying the sunshine and beautiful morning. Stan and Marlene brought some things for lunch and other goodies. They wanted to see the room, so we brought the things to the room, and then Stan and Marlene headed out to spend their day with some friends and checking out Tulsa. The kids went to the library to hang out while Billy had OT. He was supposed to have PT at 11:30, but we talked to them while at OT and canceled his PT for today since the kids are here. They thought it was a much better idea for Billy to spend the time with the kids.

Billy has eaten really well today. Marlene brought some chips and salsa, some other dip, barbecued beef and pork for sandwiches, and a few other things. Billy ate a really good lunch, and everyone else enjoyed it as well.

After lunch the kids hung out in the room while Billy had radiation, and then we had them meet us on the main floor, and we all went outside. Kaylyn, Max, and Cassy visited with Billy while Justin, Levi, Faith, and

---

[10] Ibid., pg. 1393

I went for a walk on the walking path. We all enjoyed the fresh air and sunshine. After getting something to drink, we went back to the room and let Faith open her birthday presents from Billy and me. She was surprised that she had presents, but she was very happy and I think she liked them.

It was about 3:00 by the time Faith opened her presents, and Billy was getting tired, so the kids and I decided to watch a movie on the big-screen TV in the family room on the second floor while Billy took a nap. It was agreed that I would get Billy up around 4:30 after the movie got over. (It was just an hour and a half.)

Benny and Pam arrived a little after 4:00 to visit. At 4:30 Faith informed me it was time to get Dad. I told her to just wait a couple more minutes because I was in the middle of a conversation with Benny and Pam. A few minutes later, Levi told me it was after 4:30 and I needed to get Dad. I went to get Billy, but he was sound asleep, so I decided to give him a few more minutes.

Stan and Marlene were bringing pizza at around 5:30 or so for supper. Billy thought pizza sounded good and the kids all agreed, so being very kind, Stan and Marlene were willing to pick it up and deliver it while they were out and about with their friends. Faith and I went to get Billy at 5:00. We had to wake him up, but he felt like he had a pretty good nap, so he was feeling pretty well.

Benny and Pam joined us for supper, and we continued to visit. Stan and Marlene dropped the pizza off and then returned a little after 7:00 with hot Krispy Kreme donuts. We all visited until a little after 8:00, and then Stan, Marlene, the kids, Benny, and Pam headed over to the hotel so the kids could swim and Benny and Pam could visit with Stan and Marlene for a little while.

Billy ate a really good supper, and then he ate a doughnut as well, so he ate really well today. We have both really enjoyed visiting with the kids and meeting Benny and Pam. (They were the youth leaders at our church's lay renewal weekend. They live in Oklahoma, and the kids love them.)

Thank you, Stan and Marlene. (Stan is the song leader at church, and Marlene is his wife.) We had a great day! And thank you to Benny and Pam for coming to see us. We really enjoyed meeting and visiting with you.

God is good, all the time!

—Dione

Saturday, May 16, 2009, 8:33 p.m.

> Therefore humble yourselves under the mighty hand of God, that He may exalt you in due time, casting all your care upon Him, for He cares for you.
>
> —1 Peter 5:6-7

Stan, Marlene, and the kids headed home between 1:30 and 2:00. We had a nice visit with the kids this morning, and Stan and Marlene got an ice cream cake for Faith's birthday. Everyone enjoyed it for desert.

We really enjoyed our visit with the kids this weekend, and we are very proud of them. They are doing a great job taking care of each other, and they are all growing up way too fast! Keep up the good work, guys. *We love you!*

God is good, all the time!

—Dione

Sunday, May 17, 2009, 10:20 p.m.

> Make a joyful shout to the Lord all you lands! Serve the Lord with gladness; come before His presence with

> singing. Know that the Lord, He is God; it is He who has made us, and not we ourselves; We are His people and the sheep of His pasture. Enter into His gates with thanksgiving, and into His courts with praise. Be thankful to Him, and bless His name. For the Lord is good; His mercy is everlasting, and His truth endures to all generations.
>
> —Psalm 100

Brenda and Tom (Church Renewal folks from North Carolina) stopped by for a little while today. We had a very nice visit with them, and they prayed with us. It was good to have visitors today, as the day after the kids leave is a bit of a bummer day. Thank you, Brenda and Tom. We enjoyed your visit!

Billy is still eating and feeling pretty good. He has a busy day tomorrow. He has OT, and PT, a blood draw, radiation and an appointment with the radiation oncologist or his nurse practitioner, an appointment with Dr. R (oncologist) and then his IV chemo and Decadron, as long as the blood work is okay. He has rested most of today, since he won't have time tomorrow.

Praises:

- Billy is eating pretty well.
- He is feeling pretty well.
- He has had no rash or fever during this round of chemo.
- We are seeing some improvement in his hand (I forgot to mention that on Friday, the occupational therapist had Billy see if he could pick up chess pieces with his right hand. She really didn't think he would be able to, but he did! She is pleased with how well Billy's hand is improving.)
- He has not had to use his breakthrough pain medication in over a week.

Prayers:

- Billy will continue to eat well.

- He will feel pretty good and continue to gain strength and endurance.
- The bones will recover.
- The cancer will continue to be knocked down.

Thank you all for your prayers and support. We are truly blessed!

We are also very blessed to have six very special children who are handling things really well. Kaylyn is doing a great job of taking on some very adult responsibilities, and Max and Cassy are being very good to help where they can. Justin, Levi, and Faith are helping out by not causing trouble (or at least not too much), and they are all looking out for each other and helping out. We are very proud of you guys and know that you are each a very special gift given to us by God. We love you guys!

God is good, all the time!

—Dione

Tuesday, May 19, 2009, 8:50 p.m.

> For I consider that sufferings of this present time are not worthy to be compared with the glory which shall be revealed in us.
>
> —Romans 8:18

Yesterday was very busy and ended up being very long too. Billy's blood counts were good, so he got his IV chemo and Decadron. His potassium was low, so he was given IV potassium after the Decadron and Velcade (IV chemo). It takes four hours to give potassium through the IV, so it was about 10:45 before we got out of the infusion center last night.

After talking to Dr. R yesterday, we know that the stem cell rescue is no longer a consideration. The doctors who do the stem cell rescues are very picky about the chemo protocol, and Dr. R has had to change the protocol for Billy. He had no choice. If he had pushed forward with the protocol the stem cell doctors require, it would have killed Billy. Dr. R is not concerned about it, and neither are we. The chemo drugs Billy is getting are Revlimid (an oral pill taken fourteen days, then seven days off) and Velcade (IV chemo that is currently being given twice during the fourteen days). Billy is also taking Decadron, which is a steroid that he receives four times during the fourteen days. The Revlimid and Decadron alone are 90 percent effective in putting multiple myeloma into remission. Dr. R is adding in as much of the Velcade as Billy can handle because it will help the Revlimid and Decadron to be that much more effective. Hopefully I have not caused too much confusion. The current plan (as we understand it) is to push forward with the eight rounds of chemo (the second round is just being finished up), which is the Revlimid, Velcade, and Decadron, and get the MM in remission. Then once it is in remission, Billy will receive maintenance treatments from time to time to keep the MM in remission. As I said, that is the way we understood it, but things can change as new treatments are discovered.

Billy finished the radiation on his hips yesterday, and we had an appointment with the nurse practitioner. Billy's hips no longer hurt him, so the radiation seems to have done the job. We asked about the knot that is still in the middle of his back and the one on his right shoulder. Just in case you do not know what I am talking about, I will explain. Before we ever came to CTCA, a big knot had developed on Billy's right shoulder blade and in the middle of Billy's back on his spine. Those knots were caused by the cancer, and while the radiation to those areas did help with the pain and the knots went down some, they are still there. We asked if the knots in either place could be what were causing the problem with the nerves and the issues in his right hand. We also wanted to know if anymore could be done about it. The first answer is yes; most likely the knot in the middle of the back is compressing some nerves and causing or contributing to the problem in the right hand. The second answer is that there is nothing more they can do for it. OT is about all we can do at this point to get it working better, and it is helping, so we will continue with it.

Billy had the metastatic bone scan (basically just special x-rays) done today. They did not have the results yet this afternoon, so we will check back tomorrow. This test will give the doctor an idea of how the bones are doing and what kind of shape they are in. How it turns out will determine the restrictions the doctor will give Billy. Currently he is restricted to the wheelchair. We are hoping things are improving enough that he will be able to start doing some walking. The condition of Billy's bones when we arrived here is why he has not been allowed to travel. We are hoping things have improved enough that even if he has to continue using the wheelchair, he will be able to travel home before long.

Praises:

- His counts remain good.
- Radiation is complete.
- Billy is no longer in pain.
- He is still eating pretty well.
- He has stayed healthy.
- The kids remain healthy.
- Billy is feeling pretty well.

Prayers:

- That the chemo continues to stay on track
- That Billy's right hand continues to improve
- That the results from the bone scan are good
- That Billy continues to stay healthy

Thank you all for your prayers and support.

God is good, all the time!

—Dione

> Oh, give thanks to the Lord, for He is good! For His mercy endures forever.
>
> —Psalm 107:1

Chapter 9

Wednesday, May 20, 2009, 8:57 p.m.

> For we were saved in this hope, but hope that is seen is not hope; for why does one still hope for what he sees? But if we hope for what we do not see, we eagerly wait for it with perseverance.
>
> —Romans 8:24-25

We got the results of the metastatic bone survey from yesterday. We were a bit disappointed with the results, and Billy was pretty down for a little while. When it was compared to the bone survey done the first week we were here, there is no change. This means the bones are no better, but they are no worse. Billy is restricted to the wheelchair with minimal weight bearing for another two months, when they will do another bone survey. When they say minimal weight bearing, they mean he can pull the wheelchair up to the bathroom door and then walk to the toilet while holding on to something or using a cane. This was not at all what Billy was hoping for.

The bone survey also showed that there are a couple of vertebra that are either partially or completely collapsed. One is right where the neck and shoulders meet, and the other is in the middle of his back where there is a knot. They are going to do an MRI of the spine on Friday to get a better look at them, as well as the rest of the spine. If they are partially collapsed, there is plastic cement type stuff that they can inject into the area to give it support. The way we understand it is if the vertebra is completely collapsed, there isn't anything they can do for it. They believe that one of these areas is where the nerves to his hand are being pinched. I don't think we will have the results of the MRI until Tuesday since Dr. R is not here on Friday.

Billy doesn't have too much going on tomorrow, just some OT, a blood draw, and his last dose of Decadron for this round of chemo.

Bob and Phyllis (national coordinator for Church Renewal) stopped by for a little while today. They were on their way to Oklahoma City and made a point to stop in and see us. It was really good to see them, and if you have never met these two, you really are missing a blessing. After the disappointing news about the bone survey earlier in the day, it really helped to have the visit. I know it did Billy a lot of good. Once again we see God at work with His perfect timing. Thank you, Bob and Phyllis, for taking the time to stop in!

Praises: Billy continues to be healthy and feeling pretty well, and the OT and PT are going well. He is also still eating pretty well.

Prayers:

- That counts are still good tomorrow
- That the bones will begin to heal
- That the MRI will show them what they need to see and they will be able to help with Billy's back

The kids are visiting again this weekend, so we are looking forward to that. We are still praying that we will be able to come home before long. We know it will just be for a few days here and there, but we would still like to be able to come home some. We know that Billy will be able to go home when it works out, even though he will need to continue using the wheelchair. However, we didn't think to ask if he will need to have a hospital bed when he is home. There are a few things we will have to find out and have lined up before we are able to start making trips home, but we will get there.

God is good, all the time!

—Dione

> Oh, give thanks to the Lord, for He is good! For His mercy endures forever.
>
> —Psalm 107:1

THURSDAY, MAY 21, 2009 9:06 P.M.

> Therefore humble yourselves under the mighty hand of God, that He may exalt you in due time, casting all your care upon Him, for He cares for you.
>
> —1 Peter 5:6-7

Billy is feeling better about things today. He was pretty disappointed to start with yesterday, but after thinking it through and praying, he felt a lot better. He realizes it is going to take time for the bones to heal, and the fact they were not any worse was a good thing.

The Lord is so good, and He always provides. We received an e-mail today, and a very sweet person has said that if Billy needs a hospital bed then he has one that Billy can use. We will check with the doctor on Tuesday to confirm this, but we are pretty sure the doctor will still want him to use one. Having a hospital bed that we can just put in the house and have there when we need it is great! Otherwise we would have to rent one each time we were going to be home, and that would be a hassle. My mom and dad are planning to move our bed to their house and then the hospital bed and a twin bed can be put in our bedroom and we won't have to have the hospital bed in the living room. Like I said, we will have to check to find out for sure if he will need a hospital bed, but at least we will have everything covered if he does.

Billy has an MRI of his spine scheduled for the morning. We most likely won't have the results until Tuesday because Billy's oncologist who ordered the MRI is off tomorrow.

God is good, all the time!

—Dione

> Oh, give thanks to the Lord, for He is good! For His mercy endures forever.
>
> —Psalm 107:1

Friday, May 22, 2009, 8:30 p.m.

> Therefore we do not lose heart. Even though our outward man is perishing, yet the inward man is being renewed day by day. For our light affliction, which is but for a moment, is working for us a far more exceeding and eternal weight of glory, while we do not look at the things which are seen, but at the things which are not seen. For the things which are seen are temporary, but the things which are not seen are eternal.
>
> —2 Corinthians 1:3-5

Billy had the MRIs of his spine done today. We should have results on Tuesday. Other than that, he just had OT and PT today.

Billy's parents came down Thursday and headed home after lunch today. We had a good visit with them and enjoyed ourselves.

We have to tell you all that we are so very *blessed!* We have an *incredible* support system thanks to all of you. You are all truly amazing, and we are so very thankful for all of your prayers, encouragement, support, and all that everyone is doing. We have been told by several people who work here that we have more visitors than anyone else. They have commented, "You must really be loved." We do feel loved and as I said, truly *blessed! Thank you!*

The kids will be here tomorrow, and we are looking forward to their visit!

We love you all and are very grateful for all you are doing for us.

God is good, all the time!

—Dione

> Oh, give thanks to the Lord, for He is good! For His mercy endures forever.
>
> —Psalm 107:1

Saturday, May 23, 2009, 9:14 p.m.

> Delight yourself also in the Lord, and He shall give you the desires of your heart. Commit your way to the Lord, trust also in Him, and He shall bring it to pass. He shall bring forth your righteousness as the light, and your justice as the noonday.
>
> —Psalm 37:4-6

> Delight Yourself—The greatest source of joy in life comes from a relationship with God. All other pleasures stem from that source.[11]

It has been a great day! Mike, Heidi, Amy, and Aaron brought the kids down to visit. *Thank you!* We knew Mike and Heidi were bringing the kids, but Amy and Aaron were a bonus. We enjoyed visiting this afternoon with everyone, and then at supper time, the adults left the kids with us for a few hours. we spent the evening visiting with the kids. It was a very pretty evening, so we sat outside and had a wonderful evening.

11 Ibid., pg. 639

We are really proud of how well the kids are doing and what great kids they are. The Lord has blessed us in such amazing ways. Kaylyn is such a capable young lady. She has taken on several adult responsibilities, and she is doing great with them. In doing so, she is setting a wonderful example and being a good witness. Max is just a stand-up young man and is doing his best to set a good example for others and be a witness. He recently led someone to Christ while playing an online computer game. Cassy is growing into quite the young lady, and although she is sassy and keeps everyone on their toes, she is always willing to help. She is also always witnessing and setting a good example. On Wednesday evening her cousin was having trouble with using bad words, so she sat down with him and her Bible and showed him Scripture. Then she talked to him about how we should conduct ourselves. Justin, Levi, and Faith are also doing a great job just being good and watching out for each other, as well as helping out where needed. We love you guys and are very proud to be your parents!

While sitting outside this evening, we saw Dotty and Marty. Thank you for your prayers for them because Marty is doing really well now. He looked good and is unhooked from everything. He had been hooked up to fluids and was being fed by IV because he could not eat anything. He is now eating and drinking on his own and keeping things down. He was really happy about it too.

We will meet the gang for breakfast in the morning and then spend the day with them. It should be a great day!

God is good, all the time!

—Dione

> Oh, give thanks to the Lord, for He is good! For His mercy endures forever.
>
> —Psalm 107:1

Sunday, May 24, 2009, 4:48 p.m.

> But those who wait on the Lord shall renew their strength; They shall mount up with wings like eagles, they shall run and not be weary, they shall walk and not faint.
>
> —Isaiah 40:31

> Wait—Waiting on the Lord is an expression of faith. When circumstances bear down on us, it is tempting to orchestrate our own relief effort. Yet if we will tenaciously trust the Lord, He will renew our spirit and strengthen us for any challenges.[12]

We had another great day with the kids! We enjoyed visiting with Amy, Aaron, Mike, and Heidi as well. Thanks again for bringing the kids down!

They all came over a little after 8:00 this morning to have breakfast, and we just spent the day visiting after that. They headed out about 4:15, and then Billy laid down for a nap. We really enjoyed our weekend, and the kids will be back Thursday and Friday.

Tomorrow will be a very quiet day, with just a blood draw late in the morning.

God is good, all the time!

—Dione

> Oh, give thanks to the Lord, for He is good! For His mercy endures forever.
>
> —Psalm 107:1

12 Ibid., pg. 846

Monday, May 25, 2009, 9:19 p.m.

My favorite Psalm:

> Oh Lord, our Lord, how excellent is Your name in all the earth, Who have set Your glory above the heavens! Out of the mouths of babes and nursing infants You have ordained strength, because of Your enemies, that You may silence the enemy and the avenger. When I consider Your heavens, the work of Your fingers, the moon and the stars, which You have ordained, What is man that You are mindful of him, and the son of man that You visit him? For You have made him a little lower than the angels, and You have crowned him with glory and honor. You have made him to have dominion over the works of Your hands; You have put all things under his feet, All sheep and oxen—Even the beasts of the field, The birds of the air, And the fish of the sea that pass through the paths of the seas. O Lord, our Lord, How excellent is Your name in all the earth!
>
> —Psalm 8

Billy just has a blood draw today, so it was pretty quiet. The technician decided to draw the blood the old-fashioned way and not access the port today since Billy shouldn't need the port the rest of the week. When the lab tech was looking for a vein, Billy said he couldn't really make a fist with his right hand because of the nerve issues. She said that she had a nerve issue at one time due to a car accident and it took a long time to get it back to normal. Billy asked her how long a "long time" was. She thought and said it took about a year and a half to get things back to normal and get all of the strength back, but it is all good now.

It won't be too busy this week because this is the week off of chemo. The kids will be back on Thursday and Friday. Thank you, Dad!

Billy has rested quite a bit today. We really enjoyed our weekend! We have such great friends and an incredible support system. Thank you! We love all of you!

God is good, all the time!

—Dione

> Oh, give thanks to the Lord, for He is good! For His mercy endures forever.
>
> —Psalm 107:1

Tuesday, May 26, 2009, 9:12 p.m.

> For we were saved in this hope, but hope that is seen is not hope; for why does one still hope for what he sees? But if we hope for what we do not see, we eagerly wait for it with perseverance.
>
> —Romans 8:24-25

Max and Jim built a wheelchair ramp at the house today. They are getting things set up so whenever it works out for us to go home, it will all be ready. Kaylyn said that it looks really good, and she is going to try to get a picture of it for us.

I talked to Libby, our care manager, today, and Billy will have to have a hospital bed when he is at home. We have been offered the use of a hospital bed (thank you, Ron!), so that will get set up at the house as well so it will be ready when we get home.

I also asked Libby about the MRI results. She gave me the results, but we are not completely clear on what all they mean. We have a couple of questions about whether they can do anything to help. We will talk with Dr. R in more detail on Monday. According to Libby, the disease is throughout the entire spine, and there are compression fractions throughout the spine. It also shows multi-level stenosis. Stenosis is a narrowing, so this means a narrowing of the spinal column, and multi-level means it is narrowing in more than one place (at least that is my understanding). There is some pressure on the cord at T-4 and T-5, and this is what is causing the nerve issue in his right hand. I am not sure how much sense any of this makes, and as I said, we are still a little unsure of what it all means. Hopefully we will have a better understanding and know more after we see Dr. R on Monday.

I also talked to Libby about Billy's bones healing. I told her that it was our understanding that the bones would not really begin to heal until the cancer is in remission. She said, "Yes, that is correct, unless God chooses to heal them. God still does miracles, and that is always a possibility." I like Libby.

Our prayers are that Billy will continue to feel pretty well and eat well; that the cancer will continue to be beat down and put in remission; and that his bones will not get any worse and will be able to heal.

Thank you for your prayers and support!

God is good, all the time!

—Dione

> Oh, give thanks to the Lord, for He is good! For His mercy endures forever.
>
> —Psalm 107:1

Wednesday, May 27, 2009, 4:08 p.m.

> Oh, love the Lord, all you His saints! For the Lord preserves the faithful, and fully repays the proud person.

> Be of good courage, and He shall strengthen your heart,
> all you who hope in the Lord.
>
> —Psalm 31:23-24

It is a cloudy, cool, dreary day. There hasn't been any rain, but it is very overcast. We have just been lazy this afternoon and watched a movie.

Billy has been eating pretty well—not great but not bad. He is feeling pretty well and has not had any hints of fevers. We are very grateful for that.

We talked to Renee (the OT) this morning about the MRI results, and she said that things do not look any worse than they did two months ago. Billy asked her if compression fractures mean what it sounds like—that there are breaks. She said that basically yes, it means the vertebra are compressed or collapsed and they have done that because there are cracks or breaks in them. Not all of the vertebra are broken, but there are multiple compression fractures. She also told us that there are actually some pieces (we assume of vertebra) floating in there, but they are not touching anything that will cause a problem. She seemed to think there might be something they could do to help support or stabilize things, but she didn't go into detail because she said the doctor would know better what could be done, if anything. We will talk to Dr. R about it on Monday. We all agreed that the fact that it isn't any worse is a good thing.

Dad is bringing the kids down tomorrow! I talked to Kaylyn earlier today, and she said all of the kids are looking forward to visiting again. In OT, they have had Billy play catch. I picked up a ball like they use so the younger kids could play catch with Billy for a few minutes. I thought they would get a kick out of Dad playing ball with them.

From what Kaylyn said, they are getting things organized to get our bed moved out of the house and move the hospital bed and a twin bed in. Jim and Max have the wheelchair ramp built, and things are pretty much in order for whenever we can make it home. We will be praying that will be sooner than later.

Once again I must say *thank you* to everyone who is praying for us, taking care of kids, and giving in so many ways. We are *blessed*! I told Leigh (who works in the cafeteria here) that Dad was bringing the kids down again. She was very excited and said that she just loves how our family and friends visit and bring the kids down. She said that is how it should be; families and friends should be there for each other, and she is just thrilled with how you all are taking care of us. She said that it is an excellent example and testimony. Billy and I feel extremely blessed to have such an incredible support system!

We were down by the clinic a little early to check in for OT this morning, so we just sat out in the hall for a few minutes. (For those of you who haven't been here, there are chairs all along both sides of the very wide hall.) As we were sitting there a sixty-four-year-old lady (she told us her age) came up to us and asked how we were doing. She was talking to us like we knew her. We must have had confused looks on our faces because she said that we didn't know her. However, she and her husband had seen us several weeks ago, and she told her husband, "That young man is very sick." Billy was sweating really badly at the time, and I was wiping the sweat away.

She looked at Billy and said, "It is wonderful to see you looking so much better. You are looking very good."

Billy thanked her and told her that is what everyone keeps telling him. She then told us that she and her husband pray for as many of the people here as they can. They remember the faces. She was really pleased to see that Billy had improved so much. It was pretty neat!

While we were in rehab this morning, we discovered that they do reflexology here. Bill and Kay, did you know there is a place on the wrist just above where you would wear your watch that you can rub to relieve nausea? I don't know how well it works, but one of the guys was trying it out today. They showed him how to find the sore spot, and he was rubbing away.

God is good, all the time!

—Dione

> Oh, give thanks to the Lord, for He is good! For His mercy endures forever.
>
> —Psalm 107:1

Thursday, May 28, 2009, 9:29 p.m.

> That which we have seen and heard we declare to you, that you also may have fellowship with us; and truly our fellowship is with the Father and with His Son Jesus Christ.
>
> —1 John 1:3

> That you also—As you walk with the Lord, learn from Him, and see His activity, be sure to share the blessing. Others need to hear and know the goodness of God as well.[13]

Dad and the kids arrived in time for lunch. It was a beautiful day today, so we enjoyed visiting outside after lunch and again after supper.

This afternoon Dad went to check into the hotel, and we took the kids to our room so we could give Kaylyn her birthday present. She seemed very pleased. Billy changed his cell phone plan and put her and me on a family plan. We got Kaylyn a really nice phone with a camera as her sixteenth birthday present. She seemed very happy with it.

Levi was past ready to go to the hotel and go swimming by the time they left at 8:40 or so. I think they are going to go swimming at the hotel after breakfast before they come over tomorrow. Billy has an appointment at 11:00 and then another one at 11:30, so he will be able to sleep in, and then we will have all afternoon with Dad and the kids.

---

13 Ibid., pg. 1494

Today and tomorrow is CTCA's Celebration of Life. Apparently they do it every year, and it is in honor of all of the center's five-year survivors. Tonight they had a special deal going on around supper time, and then they took anyone who wanted to the new part of the building they are working on. People were given permanent markers, which they used to write Scriptures on the floors of the new part of the building. Carpet will be laid over the floors, but the Scriptures will still be there. Tomorrow they have several things going on. The only one I really know anything about is that they will have several five-year survivors telling their stories. They have a giant tree on one of the walls in the lobby area. The tree leaves are brass plates with the names of five-year survivors on them. There were over seven hundred on the tree, and this week they have added two hundred more! Pretty cool!

God is good, all the time!

—Dione

> Oh, give thanks to the Lord, for He is good! For His mercy endures forever.
>
> —Psalm 107:1

Thank you all, for prayers, support, and all that you are doing. We love you!

Friday, May 29, 2009, 8:50 p.m.

> Praise the Lord! I will praise the Lord with my whole heart. In the assembly of the upright and in the congregation. The works of the Lord are great, studied by all who have pleasure in them. His work is honorable and glorious, and His righteousness endures forever. He has made His wonderful works to be remembered; The Lord is gracious and full of compassion.
>
> —Psalm 111:1-4

We enjoyed the day with the kids! They left a little after 6:00. Billy and I enjoyed the visit, and I think the kids did as well.

The Celebration of Life continued today. The five-year survivors were talking to patients this morning and handing out HOPE pins. A gentleman from North Carolina spoke to Billy. He was very encouraging.

Thank you to everyone who is helping with moving the beds around tomorrow. We just hope to get to come home and put all of your work to use before too much longer.

Have a good weekend, and thank you for the prayers and everything you are doing.

God is good, all the time!

—Dione

> Oh, give thanks to the Lord, for He is good! For His mercy endures forever.
>
> —Psalm 107:1

Chapter 10

Sunday, May 31, 2009, 3:45 p.m.

> And we have such trust through Christ toward God. Not that we are sufficient of ourselves to think of anything as being from ourselves, but our sufficiency is from God.
>
> —2 Corinthians 3:4-5

On Friday Billy saw the nutritionist, and she was very pleased. He weighed the same as he did when she saw him about three weeks ago. She encouraged him to try a few more vegetables and other healthy things, but for the most part, she was just pleased to see that he was no longer losing weight.

Billy spent more of yesterday just resting and relaxing. Then in the evening, our good friends Russ and Trish stopped by with their little one, Christian. Christian looks just like his Dad and is a very sweet, happy little guy! We really enjoyed our visit with the three of them. Thank you for coming to visit, Russ, Trish, and Christian!

Billy is once again just resting and taking it easy today. Russ and Trish gave him a Bugs Bunny DVD, and Billy has been really enjoying it today. Thank you, guys!

Thank you to everyone who helped with moving the beds on Saturday! We are very grateful for everything everyone is doing. We have wonderful family and friends, and we love every one of you!

Billy will see the OT and have blood drawn in the morning, and then we will see Dr. R. If all is well, chemo will begin again tomorrow evening. The big prayer for tomorrow is that everything will be okay to start chemo again. We will also be talking to Dr. R about the MRI and the condition of Billy's back.

Thank you all for your prayers and support!

God is good, all the time!

—Dione

> Oh, give thanks to the Lord, for He is good! For His mercy endures forever.
>
> —Psalm 107:1

MONDAY, JUNE 1, 2009, 9:24 P.M.

> Blessed be the God and Father of our Lord Jesus Christ, the Father of mercies and God of all comfort, who comforts us in all our tribulation that we may be able to comfort those who are in any trouble, with the comfort with which we ourselves are comforted by God. For as the sufferings of Christ abound in us, so our consolation also abounds through Christ.
>
> —2 Corinthians 1:3-5

Billy was able to start his chemo today, and we had an appointment with Dr. R this afternoon. We discussed the MRI results. There are multiple compression fractures all along Billy's spine. What concerns Dr. R most is that right below where the neck and shoulders connect, there are pieces of vertebra that are pointed back toward the spinal cord. They are not touching it but are headed that direction. A fall or being shoved into something just right could cause Billy to be paralyzed if those pieces of bone are shoved into the spinal cord. Dr. R said Billy needs to be very careful.

Dr. R also said that Billy's shoulder (Billy understood it to be the ball joint part of the shoulder) is basically gone. The bone is not broken but has basically just dissolved. Dr. R said he didn't know if there was such a thing as a shoulder replacement, or if there is, he didn't know if Billy had enough bone in that area to do it.

After going over the results, Dr. R said that Billy will never be the man he was a year ago, but Dr. R wants to do everything he can to give Billy the best quality of life he can for however long that may be. That said, he went to talk to one of the radiologist oncologists to see if he knew if there was anything that could be done to help with the situation in Billy's back.

Dr. R found out that there is a surgeon in Tulsa (not at CTCA) who has been able to do amazing things with backs. This surgeon uses the plastic cement type stuff that I have mentioned before to build up in between the vertebra that have compression fractions and help give the spine more support. He also does more invasive things, but he does it all with laser (if we understood correctly). He doesn't cut the back open. Dr. R told us to think about it and if we wanted, then he would have the radiation oncologist give all of Billy's X-rays, bone surveys, and MRIs to this surgeon to look at and see if he feels he could do anything to help. Dr. R said that he cannot really tell us that we should or shouldn't talk to this doctor; that is up to us. However, he did say that if it were him at Billy's age, he would want to know if there was anything that might help give his spine more support. We are just to let him know if we want this other doctor to look at all of Billy's scans and MRIs.

Dr. R also said that Billy's hips and femurs look pretty good, so there is no reason Billy can't walk. He just needs to start out slowly and only walk maybe one hundred yards the first day or two and then work up from there. If he gets tired or hurts, then he is to use the wheelchair. Billy was very pleased to hear that he will not have to be in a wheelchair all the time and will be able to walk. Dr. R did caution that he is to be extremely careful and not to take a chance on falling. He is not to hurry or get distracted, and he is to use the wheelchair as much as he feels he needs to. Dr. R also said that Billy needs to keep using a hospital bed to help prevent twisting and strain on his back and right shoulder.

Billy did ask if he would be able to get back on his motorcycle at some point, and Dr. R said not right away, but in a year or so he should be able to get on it again. He said Billy would need to start out just in the parking lot and work up to out on the road. The big thing is that Dr. R does feel the bones will thicken and rebuild, although the shoulder and back can't really repair themselves—at least not completely.

Billy was very glad to hear that he should be able to get back on his motorcycle at some point, and being able to walk pleased him as well. Dr. R also noticed that Billy's right hand is doing better. It has a long way to go, but it is getting better.

Our prayers are that Billy will do well with this round of chemo, with no fevers, and he will continue to eat well. Continue to pray for the bones, including protection for his spine and right shoulder because those are the areas in the most danger. Also pray that the right hand will continue to improve and he will continue to gain strength.

Thank you all for your prayers and sticking with us!

God is good, all the time!

—Dione

> Oh, give thanks to the Lord, for He is good! For His mercy endures forever.
>
> —Psalm 107:1

Tuesday, June 2, 2009, 8:55 a.m.

Good morning, everyone! I wrote a long update last night. If you haven't seen it, you will want to read it, but I felt something needed to be added this morning. We know that we have a large number of people praying, and we have seen those prayers answered in big ways, so I am asking for more prayer today. Debbie (Dr. R's nurse) called before 8:00 this morning. They had drawn another CBC late yesterday afternoon, and Dr. R didn't see those results till this morning. The one from Thursday had looked good—not over the top but good. However, the one yesterday showed that Billy's white count is down to 2.3, so I am not to give Billy the Revlimid. He will have a blood draw again on Friday. Please pray that the white count will come up to where it needs to be by Friday.

He did get the Decadron and Velcade last night. Billy is somewhat discouraged today because we are not sure how this will play out or what it means for us getting on a schedule where we can come home. The Revlimid is also very important in fighting the cancer. We do know that the cancer is now under control. It is not gone, but it is not running rampant.

Edited to add: My sweet husband is doing much better now. He was pretty down just after the call that the white count was down, but he has bounced back and is in a good mood and doing good again. Thank you for the prayers.

I also wanted to point out something I was pretty sure of, but we had it confirmed today. When they say the white count is 2.3, it means that it is 2,300; normal is 4.2 to 7 (4,200 to 7,000). Billy's white count is about half of what it should be, but it is not real bad. They are not going to give him any shots or anything. They just want to re-check the white count on Friday and see how it has done.

Thank you for your prayers!

God is good, all the time!

—Dione

Tuesday, June 2, 2009, 9:09 p.m.

> I have been crucified with Christ; it is no longer I who live, but Christ lives in me; and the life which I now live in the flesh I live by faith in the Son of God, who loved me and gave Himself for me.
>
> —Galatians 2:20

It was a pretty, day and we spent some time this morning and this evening sitting outside. Billy did some walking today, and he thought that felt great! He walked from our room to the elevator about three times, and then physical therapy had him walk as well. It really pleased Billy, and several people we see every day were very happy to see him up and walking.

Thank you for all of your prayers, notes, and support!

Not much is going on tomorrow, just OT, so it will be a quiet day.

God is good, all the time!

—Dione

> Oh, give thanks to the Lord, for He is good! For His mercy endures forever.
>
> —Psalm 107:1

Thursday, June 4, 2009, 3:57 p.m.

> A friend loves at all times, and a brother is born for adversity.
>
> —Proverbs 17:17

> A Friend and a Brother—God does not ask anything of us He has not already demonstrated Himself. As He is our Father, and His people are our brothers and sisters, we are to act toward others with the same love, grace, compassion, and sacrifice God showed us in Christ.[14]

When I read the above, I thought of all of our friends and family and everything they are doing for us. *Thank you all* for your prayers, and everything you are all doing for us. We are truly blessed with the best friends and family anyone could ask for. We love you all!

It is a beautiful day! We have spent some time outside today, and Billy has done some walking. He just had OT earlier today and will get his Decadron a little later. We talked to a nurse in the infusion center yesterday, and she made a really good suggestion. Billy has had his port accessed since last Thursday, so they will need to take the needle out today. She said that they could go ahead and draw his blood for the CBC this evening when he goes in for his Decadron and that way they can de-access Billy's port and they won't have to re-access it again tomorrow just for a blood draw. We will hear from Dr. R's nurse tomorrow about the CBC results and whether we can start back on the Revlimid or not. Pray that the white count will be back to normal.

Take care, and God bless you all. We are very thankful for every one of you!

God is good, all the time!

—Dione

> Oh, give thanks to the Lord, for He is good! For His mercy endures forever.
>
> —Psalm 107:1

---

14 Ibpg. 758

Friday, June 5, 2009, 3:58 p.m.

> The Lord shall judge the peoples; Judge me, O Lord, according to my righteousness, and according to my integrity within me.
>
> —Psalm 7:8

> My Righteousness—It is not always easy to live a righteous life, but God sees our integrity and He rewards us accordingly.[15]

Good news! Billy's white cell count is up, and we continue the Revlimid tonight! Thank you for all your prayers! Other than that, Billy had PT and OT today. PT had him walk quite a bit.

Since we didn't have a lot to report today and I have gotten several questions about CTCA, I thought I would just give you some history about Cancer Treatment Centers of America. The following is from a CTCA brochure:

> Cancer Treatment Centers of America was created in 1988. However, the origin of our treatment philosophy goes back to the early 1980s following the tragic death from cancer of our founder's mother, Mary Brown Stephenson.
>
> After his mother's diagnosis, Richard J. Stephenson embarked on a mission to find the most advanced and effective cancer treatments available. He hoped his efforts would enable his mother to recover and remain an integral, irreplaceable part of his life and the lives of his children.
>
> The Stephensons were disappointed by what they found. What were regarded as world-renowned cancer treatment facilities were focused more on the clinical and technical aspects of cancer treatment, ignoring the

15 Ibid., pg. 638

human side of it and the multidisciplinary nature of the disease. Mrs. Stephenson did not live to watch her grandchildren grow and mature.

To keep his mother's memory and spirit alive, Richard vowed to change the face of cancer treatment. He selected a group of outstanding oncologists and challenged them to find a way to deliver whole-person cancer treatment in a compassionate, nurturing environment.

Richard founded a *hospital in northern Illinois* where the CTCA model of care was first implemented. He ensured its success by keeping his staff members focused on one thing—making a difference in the lives of people who have cancer.

Since then, the experts at CTCA have been committed to revolutionizing cancer care. As a result, Cancer Treatment Centers of America is the only institution of its kind in the nation.

By implementing the Mother Standard of care, *CTCA cancer doctors* provide patients with the same warmth, unconditional support, and respect we would extend to our own mothers, fathers, sisters, brothers, or other loved ones.

Our clinicians take an aggressive and individualized approach to cancer treatment. They combine the latest medical, surgical, and radiation therapies with supportive therapies like nutrition, naturopathic medicine, mind-body medicine, oncology rehabilitation, and spiritual support. This whole-person approach gives those fighting cancer new options and hope.

The CTCA network of treatment facilities presently includes cancer hospitals in Zion, Illinois, Philadelphia, Pennsylvania, and Tulsa, Oklahoma, and a comprehensive care program in Seattle, Washington. In early 2009, CTCA opened its newest cancer hospital in Goodyear, Arizona.

If you want more information about the history of CTCA the website is: www.cancercenter.com/about-us/history.cfm.

God is good, all the time!

—Dione

Sunday, June 7, 2009, 5:03 p.m.

> Through the Lord's mercies we are not consumed, because His compassions fail not. They are new every morning; Great is Your faithfulness. "The Lord is my portion," says my soul, "Therefore I hope in Him!"
>
> —Lamentations 3:22-24

> Every Morning—Every day God expresses His love for us in fresh personal ways. We ought to watch daily to see how God uniquely demonstrates His love and compassion for us.[16]

Billy's parents came down for the weekend, and we had a very nice visit. Billy has a blood draw today, and we have an appointment with Dr. R first thing in the morning. One of the nurses in the infusion center is one who was working the Sunday morning when Billy was admitted with pneumonia. She told him that he looks 100 percent better.

With Billy getting up and doing some walking, we have been able to evaluate just how much shorter he is due to the compression fractures. I knew he was not as tall as he used to be, but I had not realized how much shorter he has become. Due to the compression fractures, his back is much shorter; it is like it has been squished down. We were talking about it today, and I said I thought he was probably four inches shorter. Billy says he is at least four, maybe closer to five inches shorter than he was. It is really quite a difference and takes a little getting used to.

16 Ibid., pg. 961

God is good, all the time!

—Dione

> Oh, give thanks to the Lord, for He is good! For His mercy endures forever.
>
> —Psalm 107:1

Monday, June 8, 2009, 8:32 p.m.

> But may God of all grace, who called us to His eternal glory by Christ Jesus, after you have suffered a while, perfect, established, strengthen, and settle you. To Him be the glory and the dominion forever and ever.
>
> —1 Peter 5:10-11

We had an appointment with Dr. R first thing this morning. Dr. R is pleased with how Billy is doing and the progress being made. He is going to quit giving Billy the Velcade. The Velcade tends to drop Billy's counts, and then he has to stop all treatment. The Revlimid and Decadron have been proven to be very effective in putting multiple myeloma into remission, so we will continue those. Billy asked Dr. R if he still felt that eight rounds of chemo would put him in remission. Dr. R said that he is quite confident it will and then we will discuss the options for continued treatment to keep him in remission.

Dr. R is also going to see about getting the MRIs and X-rays to the orthopedic surgeon to take a look at. From what he said, they had already sent them over, but through some odd events today, we discovered that there was some wires crossed somewhere and it was unclear whether they had made it to the surgeon yet or not. Libby, our care manager, was making some phone calls and getting things straightened out so it will get done. It sounds like it will just be delayed for this week because the radiologist here who knows the surgeon is on vacation this week. At any rate, they are working on getting things taken care of so everything can be looked at and a recommendation can be made.

Thank you all for sticking with us and most important for all the prayers. I am sure you have all noticed that God has really been working, and prayers are being answered, so *thank you*!

God is good, all the time!

—Dione

> Oh, give thanks to the Lord, for He is good! For His mercy endures forever.
>
> —Psalm 107: 1

(Say, did you know that there is another Psalm that's first verse is exactly as the above verse? Are you curious? Check out Psalm 118:1. I thought that was pretty cool.)

Tuesday, June 9, 2009, 7:53 p.m.

> Show me Your ways, O Lord; teach me Your paths. Lead me in Your truth and teach me, for You are the God of my salvation; on You I wait all the day.
>
> —Psalm 25:4-5

Billy had an appointment with Dr. A today. Billy is doing really well and in little to no pain all the time, so they left things as they are, and we will see him again in a month. He also had OT and PT, and everything went well. He is doing a decent amount of walking and getting along with it very well. He is also using his right hand a little more and doing a few more things for himself.

They will do a blood draw again tomorrow to make sure his counts are still staying up and all is going well with this round of chemo. Thursday he has a follow up with Dr. K, the radiation oncologist. That will be an easy appointment because Billy has had no problems or side effects related to the radiation. He will also get his Decadron again on Thursday.

Our prayers are that things continue to go well and that his counts stay good.

God is good, all the time!

—Dione

> Oh, give thanks to the Lord, for He is good! For His mercy endures forever.
>
> —Psalm 107:1 or 118:1

Wednesday, June 10, 2009, 8:43 p.m.

God is good, all the time! The blood draw looked good today. Billy's hemoglobin has actually gone up since the draw on Sunday. Dr. R said that taking out the Velcade would reduce the need for blood transfusions, and this seems to be the case. Billy did need to get potassium today, but all of his other counts were good. He will be able to complete this round of chemo.

Tomorrow is busy because Billy will get his Decadron, he has OT and PT, and he has a follow-up appointment with the radiation oncologist.

Billy is feeling pretty well, although he is a little more tired today. He is approaching the end of this round of chemo, and he tends to be a little more tired toward the end of a round. His fatigue is not very bad, but needs a bit more rest. He is still eating really well, and he did get his walking in today. He will get his walking in tomorrow with PT because

Glen tends to put him through his paces, and they cover quite a bit of ground.

Things seem to be progressing nicely. We haven't heard anything else about whether the MRIs and X-rays have made it to the orthopedic surgeon. I think they will have to wait until the radiologist gets back from vacation since he is the one who knows this orthopedic surgeon. We know we will hear something when they know something.

Have a good night, and thank you for all the prayers.

God is good, all the time!

—Dione

Chapter 11

Friday, June 12, 2009, 8:32 a.m.

We are home! We are surprising the kids. They did not know we were coming home, and I didn't want to put anything on here and have them see it. My dad will be bringing the kids to the house later on this morning. He is going to tell them they are going to go for a hike and then take them a roundabout way of getting here. Today is Kaylyn's sixteenth birthday. Our plan was to show up at her surprise birthday party, but we were able to come home yesterday instead of today and I just can't wait all day to see the kids. This way we will have a little time with just the kids. It is *so* nice to be home!

Billy got his Decadron yesterday morning and then had a couple of other appointments. We were able to leave by 2:00 and were home around 7:00. Billy is feeling good and is very happy to be home. We will be home for ten days. We have to go back on Sunday, June 21. After that, the plan is to be at CTCA for twelve to thirteen days at a time and then be home for eight to ten days at a time. That is a much better schedule than being there for almost three months.

We will be in town a couple of times this week for blood draws. At least one of those days we will be stopping by to visit Farm Bureau. If you would like us to let you know what day we are coming, we can do that. Justin, you have our phone numbers and e-mail if this is a busy week and one day would be better than another. We have to be in town Monday and Thursday if one of those works better.

Have a great day. We will!

God is good, all the time!

—Dione

Friday, June 12, 2009, 11:27 a.m.

Attention, attention: if you have not read the most recent post, you might want to go back and read it. We are home.

We will be home until Sunday, June 21. Visitors are welcome because we would love to see everyone. We will be at church on Sunday. If you would like to visit, we just ask that you call first since Billy may need a nap from time to time and we will need to go into Jefferson City twice this week for blood draws. If you are driving by and just want to stop for a few minutes, just knock and we will let you know if it is a good time. Billy is feeling well, and he is actually the one who told me to post this. As the week goes on, if he is getting tired and visiting needs to be limited, I will post and let you all know.

My dad brought the kids out, and even though the Suburban was sitting in the driveway, they did not believe we were home until I opened the door. They are as happy as we are.

God is good, all the time!

—Dione

Sunday, June 14, 2009, 8:15 p.m.

> Bless the Lord, O my soul; and all that is within me, bless His holy name! Bless the Lord, O my soul, and forget not all His benefits: Who forgives all your iniquities, who heals all your diseases, who redeems your life from destruction, who crowns you with lovingkindness and

> tender mercies, who satisfies your mouth with good things, so that your youth is renewed like eagles.
>
> —Psalm 103:1-5

It is great to be home! We are loving it! Billy is doing really well. He is feeling pretty well and even grilled the brats last night for supper. We went to Sunday school and church this morning, and my youngest nephew was baptized. Devin went forward back in April but did not want to be baptized until Billy and I could be there. It was great to be at church and see everyone!

After church Mom, Dad, John (my brother), and Dru and the boys (my sister and two nephews) came out for grilled hamburgers. They spent the afternoon visiting, and we had a good time.

Tomorrow Billy has a blood draw in Jefferson City, and then we will go to Farm Bureau to see everyone. Billy is looking forward to the day. We will be home by later in the afternoon and all evening. We will be home the rest of the week except for a blood draw on Thursday. Billy is really enjoying visiting, so if you would like to visit, just let us know, or stop in if we are at home.

Prayers are that everything will look good with the blood work and he will not need blood or potassium and that his white count will be good. He is finishing up this round of chemo this evening as he takes the last pill for this round. Our prayers that there will be little to no side effects over the next few days. (There weren't any issues last round). Also pray that he continues to feel good so he can enjoy this week at home.

God is good, all the time!

—Dione

> Oh, give thanks to the Lord, for He is good! For His mercy endures forever.
>
> —Psalm 107:1

Monday, June 15, 2009, 9:45 p.m.

> I will love You, Oh Lord, my strength. The Lord is my rock and my fortress and my deliverer: My God my strength, in whom I will trust; my shield and the horn of my salvation, my stronghold. I will call upon the Lord, who is worthy to be praised; so shall I be saved from my enemies.
>
> —Psalm 18:1-3

We had another great day at home! Well, partly at home. We went into town. We ate at Chili's (thank you, Farm Bureau family!) and then stopped at Sears to get Max a couple pair of jeans (he's skinny and tall, so it is hard to find something that fits him). We then went over to Farm Bureau for a visit. Everyone really enjoyed visiting there. I know Billy was very happy about seeing everyone. It was very nice to meet all of you! Thank you all for stopping in to see Billy and for all of your support through all of this. For those who weren't there, they put us in a big meeting room where Billy could just sit down in a very comfortable chair, and then everyone came to him. That was wonderful because he intended to walk through the different departments, and he really didn't need to do that much walking.

Billy is still feeling well, and is really enjoying seeing everyone he can. We have really missed everyone. He had been hurting for months before we left, so it has been quite some time since he has been able to enjoy visitors. We will be home all day tomorrow, so if you are thinking about stopping in, you are welcome to do just that. Being home and seeing family and friends is really good for both Billy and me, and the kids are enjoying it too.

God is good, all the time!

—Dione

> Oh, give thanks to the Lord, for He is good! For His mercy endures forever.
>
> —Psalm 107:1 and 118:1

Tuesday, June 16, 2009, 10:51 a.m.

I did update last night in case you missed it . . .

God is good, all the time! We are very pleased this morning! I just talked to Libby, our care manager, and she had just received Billy's blood test results from yesterday. Everything looks great! She said, "You couldn't ask for better." His white cell count is normal, and everything else is either normal or very close. This is wonderful since he just finished this round of chemo on Sunday. It also shows that Dr. R was right—the Velcade was what was knocking Billy's counts down so bad, and the right decision was made to take him off of it. It also shows that his bone marrow is beginning to recover.

Thank you, thank you for all of your prayers! We continue to be amazed at how God is working. God is on his throne, and He answers prayers!

God is good, all the time!

—Dione

> Oh, give thanks to the Lord, for He is good! For His mercy endures forever.
>
> —Psalm 107:1

Wednesday, June 17, 2009 8:34 p.m.

> You will show me the path of life; In Your presence is fullness of joy; at Your right hand are pleasures forevermore.
>
> —Psalm 16:11

> In Your Presence—True joy comes not from receiving God's blessings but from knowing and spending time with God.[17]

Another great day at home! Kaylyn and Max had a puppet show this morning in Jefferson City. Cassy road along and we made a stop at Wal-Mart for some odds and ends before going on to drop Kaylyn and Max off for their puppet show. Then this afternoon I dropped the kids off at the pool to swim for a couple of hours. Stacey (youth leader from church) and some other youth from church were there as well. The kids had a good time swimming and are tired and a little pink this evening.

I fixed one of the kids' favorite meals this evening and the boys didn't even complain that it was there turn to clean up.

Billy has had a good day and is just enjoying being home. He has another blood draw tomorrow, but after the good results from Monday, we are not concerned about it. However, prayers never hurt anything =) We will also stop by Farm Bureau again, as there is a person or two he didn't see on Monday. Other than that there isn't much planned, so if you were thinking of stopping in tomorrow afternoon or evening would be good. If you want, call first to make sure we are back from Jeff City.

We will leave for Tulsa Sunday afternoon and are hoping all will go well. We really think it will, in which case we will be back home on the 29th or 30th. We know we will have to see how everything goes, but are thinking positive. There is a possibility that we will be at home for most or all of

---

17 Ibid., pg. 643

July. I will keep you all posted on that, we will have a better idea after we meet with Dr. R on Monday (22nd).

Thank you all for your continued prayers, they are working.

God is good, all the time!

—Dione

> Oh, give thanks to the Lord, for He is good! For His mercy endures forever.
>
> —Psalm 118:1

Friday, June 19, 2009, 8:46 p.m.

> Righteousness and justice are the foundations of Your throne; Mercy and truth go before Your face.
>
> —Psalm 89:14

This week is going to fast! Kaylyn and I did a lot of running today. I took her to California, Missouri, to take her driving test. We arrived before 10:00, but she didn't even get to start her car. She walked out with the examiner, and he said, "We already have a problem." The tags on her car expired in April. We had no idea. If we got the notice, it was around the time when Billy was diagnosed and we were getting ready to go to Tulsa, but we don't remember getting it. Anyway, the tags had to be current before she could take the test. Of course, the car needed an inspection, so we tried a couple of places in California. The first one couldn't do it until tomorrow, and the other one did inspect it but wouldn't pass it. We came back to Russellville where we had it inspected at our usual place, and it passed no problem.

We then went back to California to the DMV and waited our turn. They were busy so that was a thirty-minute wait or so. Once the car was legal, we went back to take the driving test. Kaylyn was pretty disappointed because she failed. What bugged her most is the examiner told her that she is an excellent driver. She has good control of the vehicle. She knows where she is and what is going on around her. The things she flunked for are things that a lot of drivers don't do. She didn't use her turn signal when she pulled away from the curb and when she pulled out of the parking place—things like that. The examiner told her that she won't have any trouble passing the test now that she knows what they are watching for. She is planning to try again on the first Friday in July. We should be back from Tulsa then, and she will be on vacation with a friend this next week while we are in Tulsa.

Billy is still feeling pretty well. We stopped in at Farm Bureau again after his blood draw yesterday. He enjoyed the visit.

I called Libby yesterday to check on Billy's Revlimid. We had not heard anything from Biologics (the pharmacy where we get the Revlimid). Billy called them and took their survey a week and a half ago or more (the survey basically questions you on rather you will share the drug, if you understand the seriousness of the drug and why it cannot be shared and why it must be disposed of properly if it is not all used). In the past, after he took that survey, they have called us within a few days and made arrangements to get it delivered by overnighting it to us. I was getting a little concerned that we hadn't heard from them. We also needed to make sure they could either get it to us before we left or just get it to us in Tulsa.

I left a message with Libby that we had not heard anything about the Revlimid. Then I called Biologics and asked them about it. They said our insurance would no longer pay for it through them and we would have to use a specialty pharmacy. They gave me the name and phone number for the other pharmacy and said they were sending the information to Libby as well. Libby called later in the day, and she had not heard anything about it. I gave her the name and number of the specialty pharmacy, and she called them yesterday. She called us this morning and told us that the authorization from the insurance company was only good through today, so she got the ball rolling and made them promise they could get it processed today. She said if they didn't call us by early afternoon to call her back and she would get after them. The pharmacy did call and made arrangements to have it delivered at CTCA on Monday. Billy only takes the Revlimid once a day, and we still have three pills since he couldn't take it for three days on the last round. That gives us a couple of days in case something happens. Libby told them it was an emergency and we had to have it no later than Monday. They assured us that it will be there Monday, so I do not anticipate any problems.

Thank you all for your prayers and any and everything else you have done for our family. We have an incredible network of family and friends. We are so very thankful for each of you, and we love you all.

Thank you to our church for the special gift. We love all of you and are so very blessed to have such a wonderful church family! Your support has been amazing and beyond anything we could imagine!

God is good, all the time!

—Dione

> Oh, give thanks to the Lord, for He is good! For His mercy endures forever.
>
> —Psalm 107:1

Saturday, June 20, 2009, 9:44 p.m.

> Even to your old age, I am He, and even to gray hairs I will carry you! I have made, and I will bear; even I will carry, and will deliver you.
>
> —Isaiah 46:4

Our days at home for this round have come to an end. We leave for Tulsa tomorrow. It sure went by fast! I didn't get half the things done I planned to. Oh well, I guess they will be there for next time.

We had a few visitors today, and I took some of the kids into town. We needed to pick up Levi's insulin and other supplies, and some of the kids needed a few things. Everyone should be set for a while now.

Kaylyn is packed for her trip to the Wisconsin Dells with her good friend Kayla. Billy and I are packed as well, and we will head out after lunch tomorrow. If all goes as we hope, we should be home June 29 or 30. Hopefully this time it will be for about four weeks, but we will see how it goes.

The kids gave Billy his Father's Day cards and presents this evening. They didn't think they would really have time tomorrow. They did a very nice job picking out the cards, and they got him a movie and cap. They came across a "Built Ford Tough" cap and couldn't pass it up. They have all decided their dad is about the toughest or strongest person they know. Billy had told them not to worry about getting him anything, so he was surprised and quite pleased. The kids were really sweet.

I will continue to keep you all up on what is going on. We have an appointment with Dr. R on Monday afternoon and will go from there. Blood will be drawn tomorrow evening after we get down there, so they will have the results to look at on Monday. We expect all to be well since it has been all week.

God is good, all the time!

—Dione

> Oh, give thanks to the Lord, for He is good! For His mercy endures forever.
>
> —Psalm 107:1

Chapter 12

SUNDAY, JUNE 21, 2009, 11:20 P.M.

> I have set the Lord always before me; because He is at my right hand I shall not be moved.
>
> —Psalm 16:8

We are back in Tulsa at the Cancer Treatment Centers of America, our home away from home. We are even back in the exact same room on the fourth floor that we spent almost three months in, which I thought was interesting. The trip went fine, and of course, Billy drove the entire way. His back was a little sore and tired when we got here, and he did take some breakthrough pain medication on the way down, but he did pretty well. He is sound asleep and has been for a while now. Unless something changes there are no early appointments tomorrow, so he can sleep in or at least spend a good part of the morning just resting.

Kaylyn headed off on her vacation today. They are staying in St. Louis tonight and will get up early in the morning to go on to the Wisconsin Dells. She is feeling much better about not getting her driver's license on her first try. I think it helped that several people at church today told her they didn't pass the first time either. Max was saying he would probably pass his first try since he knows from Kaylyn trying what they will be watching for. Kaylyn didn't find that amusing at all.

Thank you all for your continued prayers and support. Billy did great while he was at home, and I am so thankful for that.

God is good, all the time!

—Dione

> Oh, give thanks to the Lord, for He is good! For His mercy endures forever.
>
> —Psalm 107:1

Monday, June 22, 2009, 4:48 p.m.

> But I rejoiced in the Lord greatly that now at last your care for me has flourished again; though you surely did care, but you lacked opportunity. Not that I speak in regard to need, for I have learned in whatever state I am, to be content: I know how to be abased, and I know how to abound. Everywhere and in all things I have learned both to be full and to be hungry, both to abound and to suffer need. I can do all things through Christ who strengthens me.
>
> —Philippians 4:10-13

Today started out a bit strange but has turned out to be a good day. When we got what was supposed to be our schedule under the door this morning, it said that there were no appointments for this week. We knew better than that because I had taken the last schedule we had gotten before going home, and it showed an appointment with Dr. R this afternoon as well as appointments OT all week. I made a couple of calls. I found out that OT and PT needed to get new orders and then they would get Billy on the schedule, and we ended up with an appointment with Dr. R at 10:30 this morning, so it all worked out.

Dr. R says things are continuing in the right direction with the cancer (less disease is showing up), and he is pleased. He also had some new information that came out of the big oncologist meeting the end of

May, when the top oncologists from all over the world met. The report backed up what Dr. R had already been doing for Billy's treatment. We are treating Billy with the correct drugs for multiple myeloma, and the correct protocol is being used. Dr. R ordered another metastatic bone scan for tomorrow. He wants to take another look at the bones and make sure there are no new lesions. He said that what had already been damaged will pretty much look the same, or at least he expects it to, but he wants to make sure there are no new areas developing.

We discussed Billy taking the Decadron orally and how often we would have to be back here if Billy can tolerate it. If all goes well this week, then Billy will get his Zometa (bone builder) on Monday (June 29), and then we can be home for . . . are you ready? Are you wondering? Can you guess? Okay, I'll tell you . . . . We can be home for six weeks! We will come back every six weeks for a checkup with Dr. R and to get Zometa, as well as to do any other tests or anything Dr. R feels is needed at the time. Once the cancer is in remission, which we expect to achieve by the eighth round of chemo in September, then we will discuss where to go from there.

Billy's blood counts were good today, except that he needed potassium. Apparently the Revlimid is not hurting most of his counts but does tend to knock out the potassium. Debbie (Dr. R's nurse) said that Billy can take potassium pills at home, so he won't have to get it by IV. There are even some that are smaller than the usual potassium horse pills. We will discuss that more at our next appointment and get the prescription for the potassium. We will go to the infusion center in a little while to get the potassium by IV for this time.

Billy asked about the orthopedic surgeon, and Dr. R and Debbie said that the orthopedic surgeon is supposed to call us. They don't have his name or anything because the radiologist who knows the orthopedic surgeon was supposed to get the MRIs and x-rays to him. The radiologist said that he did send everything to the orthopedic surgeon, so Dr. R was going to check with the radiologist and make sure everything went where it was supposed to. He also got our cell phone number again to give to them and make sure they have the correct number to contact us. I guess the ball is in their court now. I know Debbie and Dr. R were surprised that we hadn't heard anything, and they weren't too happy that we haven't. Maybe the guy is just really busy. We will just have to wait and see what happens.

Our prayers are that Billy will do well with the oral Decadron and that all will continue to go well with his chemo. Also, please pray that his right hand will continue to improve and his bones will be able to heal. I guess it wouldn't hurt to pray that the orthopedic surgeon will get a chance to look at things and give us a call as well.

God is good, all the time!

—Dione

> Oh, give thanks to the Lord, for He is good! For His mercy endures forever.
>
> —Psalm 107:1

Tuesday, June 23, 2009, 7:00 p.m.

> Be merciful to me, O God, be merciful to me! For my soul trusts in You; and in the shadow of Your wings I will make my refuge, until these calamities have passed by. I will cry out to God Most High, to God who performs all things for me.
>
> —Psalm 57:1-2

We stayed inside again today because it was really hot out. Billy had OT and PT today, and he did a lot of walking. He walked quarter mile in PT as well as walking down to his appointments today. He took his Decadron yesterday and had no trouble with it at all. It looks like there will be nothing to keep us from going home on Monday afternoon or Tuesday at the latest. We are currently planning to go home Monday afternoon. There are just a few appointments this week, so it is going to be a long week, but knowing we can go home so soon will help.

Pray that nothing comes up to prevent us from being able to go home on Monday, as well as that Billy just continues to improve.

God is good, all the time!

—Dione

> Oh, give thanks to the Lord, for He is good! For His mercy endures forever.
>
> —Psalm 107:1

Wednesday, June 24, 2009, 8:50 p.m.

> The Lord is my strength and my shield; My heart trusted in Him, and I am helped; Therefore my heart greatly rejoices, and with my song I will praise Him.
>
> —Psalm 28:7

It was very hot again today, as it apparently was many places. Billy just had OT today, so it was a pretty quiet day. He walked down for OT and supper; he didn't even take the wheelchair. Everyone has noticed that he is walking instead of riding, and they think it is great.

Tomorrow we have a blood draw and OT. We will check on the results from the blood draw before he gets his chemo pill tomorrow evening, but I don't expect there to be any issues since his counts have been doing really well. He also takes his Decadron again tomorrow, but again, we don't expect a problem since he didn't have any trouble on Monday.

We talked to Kaylyn, and she is having a really good time. They have discovered their favorite water slide. The only problem is all the stairs they have to go up to go down the slide, but they are getting their exercise. They went on a carriage ride and rode the Ducks today. Kaylyn said she took a bunch of pictures.

Max is enjoying haying with Grandpa Jim and has even been able to drive the tractor and do a little mowing. Cassy is doing a really good job with Levi's diabetic stuff. Everything is going well, and everyone is pleased that we will be home soon and able to stay home for weeks.

God is good, all the time!

—Dione

> Oh, give thanks to the Lord, for He is good! For His mercy endures forever.
>
> —Psalm 107:1

Thursday, June 25, 2009, 8:02 p.m.

> Now may the God of hope fill you with all joy and peace in believing, that you may abound in hope by the power of the Holy Spirit.
>
> —Romans 15:13

Another day down and a little closer to getting home! We just had OT and a blood draw today. Counts are still good, so we continue chemo this evening. He also took his Decadron again today, and that went well too.

OT has been working with Billy this week on different things he can do while at home to keep his hand improving as it has been. There are certain ways he needs to use it to help keep that going. Most of the exercises are just simple things that make the hand work in normal ways. Since there really isn't anything she is doing with him that he can't do at home, we don't plan to try to get him into OT or PT while we are at home. The PT has just been having him walk, and there are a few exercises he has Billy do. They are also all things Billy can do at home. The kids and I may just have to make a point to remind him to do the different things he needs to do, but I think he will do fine. He has some papers with instructions on how to do the different things. He also has the resistance band the PT made for him and the putty stuff the OT made for him to use, so he should do fine.

Continue to pray that Billy's counts will stay good, that his hand will continue to improve, and that he will continue to feel well and gain strength. He still has a long way to go as far as getting his strength back, but he feels much better than he has for quite some time. Also, Kaylyn will be traveling home with her good friend Kayla and Kayla's sister, grandma, and aunt tomorrow, so please pray that they will have a safe trip home.

God is good, all the time!

—Dione

> Oh, give thanks to the Lord, for He is good! For His mercy endures forever.
>
> —Psalm 107:1

FRIDAY, JUNE 26, 2009, 7:24 P.M.

> He shall cover you with His feathers, and under His wings you shall take refuge; His truth shall be your shield and buckler.
>
> —Psalm 91:4

> The safest place in the world is whenever someone is covered by God's truth.

Billy had OT today, and Renee (the OT) suggested that we might see if Dr. R would give us an order for hand therapy Billy could do while at home. We would just have to find an OT in Jefferson City who can do the hand therapy. Billy has a bunch of things Renee has taught him that he can do at home, so he will be able to keep working on his hand on his own. We will see what Dr. R says Monday. We really don't think he will have a problem with giving us the order.

Tomorrow is Saturday, so we don't have anything we need to do. We were thinking we might go out to eat. We just won't go during one of the actual meal times because we have been told there are pretty long waits at restaurants in this area at meal time. We were thinking we might just have a late breakfast and then go to lunch at about 3:00 or so. We will see what Billy wants to do tomorrow. It was actually his idea.

Our prayers are that Billy's blood counts will continue to be good. He will have a blood draw again on Sunday since the appointment with Dr. R is at 8:30 on Monday morning. His counts were okay yesterday but not as high as they had been. They were still fine for doing chemo, but since they had come down a little since the last draw on Monday, I am praying that they do not continue to go down. Billy also says he feels fine, but he seems a bit more tired today. It is nothing drastic, and it is reasonable considering he has been on his chemo since Monday. However, he has tired easier today and just not had quite as much energy. He has not had much appetite today, but he did eat okay. He said he wasn't hungry but then decided to at least eat something. Once he started eating, he ate better than either of us thought he would, which was good. You might remember his appetite and energy in your prayers, as well as his counts.

Kaylyn made it home today. Thank you for the prayers for a safe trip. She had a good time, and we look forward to hearing all about it and seeing all of her pictures when we get home. She will also be taking her driving test again next Friday.

God is good, all the time!

—Dione

> Oh, give thanks to the Lord, for He is good! For His mercy endures forever.
>
> —Psalm 107:1

Saturday, June 27, 2009

> Oh Lord, You are my God, I will exalt You, I will praise Your name, for You have done wonderful things; Your counsels of old are faithfulness and truth.
>
> —Isaiah 25:1

It is very quiet today, as it usually is on the weekends, although I think more people went home this weekend than usual. Maybe they are just hanging out in their rooms and are not out when we are. We did go out to eat today. We waited until about 3:00 and then one of the center's drivers took us in one of the Lincolns. They are really good to you around here! Billy has eaten really well today, and we are both still full.

Billy has a blood draw tomorrow, so as always, pray that results are good. We have an early appointment with Dr. R on Monday, and then Billy will get his bone builder and get his port de-accessed. He had it accessed Monday, and it has been accessed all week.

Since we have not heard anything from the orthopedic surgeon here in Tulsa, I decided to try something. We know that the University of Missouri Hospitals and Clinics have some very good orthopedic surgeons. Dr. Dan, who operated on Cassy's femur back in 2006 and my nephew's this past year, is one of them, and his e-mail address is on the website. I got on the hospital's website and found that they have a spine center, and Dr. Dan is part of that team. Dr. Dan specializes in pediatric orthopedic surgery, and he does scoliosis surgeries. I don't think he would be the one to operate on Billy, but one of the other surgeons in the spinal group does all kinds of spine surgeries.

I e-mailed Dr. Dan and gave him some background on what is going on with Billy and what the MRI showed. I then asked him if he thought there was a doctor there who could help Billy's back, and if so, would they be willing to look at the MRIs and X-rays of Billy's back. I don't expect to hear anything from him until sometime next week, but since he put his e-mail out there for people, I do think he will read it and at least give me some kind of answer. The other doctors did not have e-mail addresses, so I thought I would try this first. We are also going to check with Libby either Monday or later on next week and see if she will contact the surgeon here in Tulsa for us. If she could give us his number, we could also call him. We know she has his name but are not sure if she has his number. However, we can locate the number if we have the name, so we will see what we can find out.

Thank you all for your prayers and everything else that has been done and is being done for us. We have an amazing support system with our family and friends. Our church family has done so much for us. We can never repay or thank you all enough. Just know that we are very thankful for every one of you, and we love you all very much.

God is good, all the time!

—Dione

> Oh, give thanks to the Lord, for He is good! For His mercy endures forever.
>
> —Psalm 107:1

Sunday, June 28, 2009, 4:45 p.m.

> Rejoice always, pray without ceasing, in everything give thanks; for this is the will of God in Christ Jesus for you.
>
> —1 Thessalonians 5:16-18

It was a little cooler today, and we sat outside for a little while this morning. Our laundry is almost dry, and then I will get everything ready to go tomorrow!

Our prayers are that blood counts will be good and the Suburban will start without any trouble. The Suburban doesn't like to start after it has sat for a few days, and I wasn't sure it was going to start when we headed home the last time. Billy knows a couple of tricks, and it finally took off.

Thank you all for your prayers. I know some of you who read this we have never met, and there is a good chance we never will. However, your prayers are greatly appreciated, and we are very thankful for you.

We hope to visit with many of you over the next few weeks while we are at home!

God is good, all the time!

—Dione

> Oh, give thanks to the Lord, for He is good! For His mercy endures forever.
>
> —Psalm 107:1

Chapter 13

Monday, June 29, 2009, 10:00 p.m.

We are home! I think we are going to have to do something as far as a vehicle because the Suburban is having more problems all the time. There were a couple of times today when Billy talked really nice to it because we weren't sure it was going to keep running, but we made it. God is good! We were able to head home at about 10:40 this morning and arrived at Billy's parents' house at about 4:30. The kids were helping fix supper, and we were invited to eat there. Max has been helping Jim hay this week, and they came in for supper.

We went over the results of the metastatic bone survey with Dr. R this morning. There are no new areas of concern, which is good. We also went over the test results that tell Dr. River how things are going as far as the cancer, and so far so good. Dr. R gave us the numbers that show how much cancer there is. They don't make much sense other than that they are going down. The first of these tests done the end of March showed the cancer number was 609, then in April it was 166, and the last one done in the first part of June was 77, so we are making good progress.

Billy's white count was a little too low (not low enough to worry about him getting sick), so he cannot take his Revlimid until we get the results of his blood tests on Thursday. We will have to get into Jefferson City first thing Thursday morning to get the results early enough to find out if he can take his Revlimid Thursday evening and over the weekend. His last day for this round is Sunday.

We will be home until August 2, and this time we should only be in Tulsa for a couple of days. We have an appointment with Dr. R and a follow-up appointment with pain management on August 3. Whether we have to be there more than just that Monday will depend on what Dr. R orders on that Monday. If he just orders blood tests and the Zometa, then we will be done Monday but may wait until Tuesday to come home depending on how late it gets by the time we are done.

We did see Libby for just a few minutes before we left this morning, and she does not have the name of the orthopedic surgeon. We told her Dr. R had checked with Dr. MK about it last Monday, and she said that was good, so we will see what happens. I did not hear anything from the doctor at the university today, but I really didn't expect to this soon.

Visitors are very welcome. We will be home long enough this time to see everyone who wants to see us. Billy loves visitors. Since he is limited in what he can do and loves to visit anyway, it is really good for him, and he enjoys company. If he is to tired or getting worn out and needs a nap, he will let you know. Everyone at CTCA thought the ten days home did Billy a world of good, so he should be doing wonderful after five weeks at home.

Our prayers are for Billy's white count to come up. Dr. R also started Billy on potassium pills since he has been needing potassium about every other week. They are not the usual horse pills but are still pretty good size. I think it would be good to also pray that we will hear something from an orthopedic surgeon, although I am wondering if there is a reason we have not heard from anyone yet, since all things are in God's time. However, prayer is always good.

Thank you all for your prayers and support. It is very nice to be home, and we hope to visit with as many of you as we can.

God is good, all the time!

—Dione

TUESDAY, JUNE 30, 2009, 9:11 P.M.

> Now to Him who is able to do exceedingly abundantly above all that we ask or think, according to the power that works in us, to Him be glory in the church by Christ Jesus to all generations, forever and ever. Amen.
>
> —Ephesians 3:20-21

> God's Best—God does not need our grandiose plans and creative imagination. He is prepared to do far more in or lives than we could ever imagine, if we are willing to wait on His will and to trust Him to accomplish it through us.[18]

It is good to be home. We are already starting to get back to normal stuff. Today Cassy and I went grocery shopping. We now have plenty of food and snacks in the house. Next we will have to decide what we are going to have for supper tomorrow evening. Oh how nice it is to have such a normal dilemma. I have already been given several suggestions, so I don't think we will have too much trouble figuring it out. We are enjoying the pretty weather today, and the kids have really enjoyed playing outside since it wasn't too hot.

Billy is feeling pretty well and is enjoying being home. He slept in this morning and then took a nap today. We let the older three stay up for a while last night and visit with us, so it was around 11:30 before we all went to bed. That is fairly late for Billy but really not that unusual on a day when he has taken his Decadron, which he had yesterday morning.

We are planning to go to the fireworks in Eldon on Friday. We have started going every year because Eldon has a really good fireworks show. The kids love it and look forward to it every year. We will then go to my Mom and Dad's for the Fourth. My sister and nephews will be there, and this has become a tradition. It will be especially nice this year since there for a while we weren't even sure if we would be home for the Fourth. We are very blessed!

---

18 Ibid., pg. 1408

God is good, all the time!

—Dione

> Oh, give thanks to the Lord, for He is good! For His mercy endures forever.
>
> —Psalm 107:1

Wednesday, July 1, 2009, 9:51 p.m.

> But as for me, I trust in You, Oh Lord; I say, "You are my God." My times are in Your hand; Deliver me from the hand of my enemies, and from those who persecute me. Make Your face shine upon Your servant; save me for Your mercies' sake.
>
> —Psalm 31:14-16

It was a pretty quiet day. I took the older four kids to church tonight for youth group. It is hard to believe we have four kids in the youth group!

Billy is feeling well and getting along pretty well. He is pretty limited in what he can do, so he really enjoys visits because they help pass time.

Our prayers are that blood counts will be good again tomorrow so he can finish up this round of chemo. He has missed doses for Monday, Tuesday, and today, so it would be best if he didn't miss anymore. This is his fourth round, and he will finish it on Sunday. He will then have a week off before starting his fifth round. The plan is to have him in remission by the end of the eighth round; so far things are headed that way. (Each round is two weeks on and one week off.)

Kaylyn is going to try taking her driver's test in Eldon tomorrow. They won't be giving one in California on Friday since it is a holiday, so she decided to try it in Eldon.

God is good, all the time!

—Dione

> Oh, give thanks to the Lord, for He is good! For His mercy endures forever.
>
> —Psalm 107:1

Thursday, July 2, 2009, 10:15 p.m.

> For our heart shall rejoice in Him, because we have trusted in His holy name.
>
> —Psalm 33:21

Thank you for all the prayers! I checked with Libby this afternoon, and Billy's blood work was perfect. He will take his chemo each evening through Sunday to finish up this round.

Billy had his Decadron today, so he is not quite ready for bed, even though it is almost 11:00. He tends to stay up later on the days when he takes his Decadron. But again prayer has been answered because he is not having any trouble taking his Decadron.

Kaylyn didn't get her license again today. She was a bit bummed to start with, but the things she missed were all things she should know. She is either just nervous and not remembering to do it or just isn't trying hard enough. She will try again next Thursday and plans to pass. She is going to review the manual and work on it that way. I told her that we could go out and practice. I could give her a practice test, paying attention to the things she seems to be having trouble remembering to do.

Oh, I forgot to tell you all something kind of funny. At our last appointment with Dr. R, Billy told him that he thought he knew the answer but he was going to ask anyway. Billy then asked Dr. R about shooting his rifles with his left arm and hand. His left shoulder is in better shape than his right, but not by a lot, it has a lot of bone deterioration as well. Dr. R sat back in his chair, grinned, and said, "We have a medical term for that. It's called stupid." He then told Billy that he can shoot a smaller-caliber pistol that does not have much kick. I guess Billy forgot that he can't shoot with that shoulder right now anyway because his port is on that side.

I thought I had the laundry pretty well caught up today, and then I went by the kids' hamper. It was full! Oh well, I will keep working on it.

Thanks again for all the prayers and support! You all are amazing!

God is good, all the time!

—Dione

> Oh, give thanks to the Lord, for He is good! For His mercy endures forever.
>
> —Psalm 107:1 or 118:1

Saturday, July 4, 2009, 8:26 p.m.

> And the Lord, He is the One who goes before you. He will be with you, He will not leave you nor forsake you; do not fear nor be dismayed.
>
> —Deuteronomy 31:8

We ended up not going to the fireworks last night. Kaylyn and Max had a puppet show at a RV camp at the lake. They said there was a good turnout and they thought everything went well. Then they went to the fireworks with Robert and Stacey. They thought they were pretty good but not as good as years past. They still enjoyed their evening, and they always have fun with Robert and Stacey.

Last night, since we didn't go to the fireworks, Cassy, Faith, and I made cookie bars to take to my parents' house today, and then we played cards. The kids were able to watch some fireworks from the deck, so they were happy. Everyone is looking forward to getting together with my family today. Last year we were able to watch all kinds of fireworks from our front yard, so this evening we will be keeping an eye out for fireworks.

I have some good news about finding a surgeon for Billy's back. You may remember that I had e-mailed the doctor at the university who did the surgery on Cassy's femur when she broke it in 2006. I gave him some information about Billy's situation and the condition of his back. Then I asked if he felt there was a doctor there who might be able to do the kind of surgery Billy would need or at least look at the MRIs and X-rays and see what he thinks. Dr. Dan forwarded my e-mail to a Dr. C, who does all kinds of spinal surgeries at the Missouri Spine Center. Dr. C e-mailed me and said that he would be happy to look at Billy's MRIs and X-rays and discuss what can be done. He gave me the name and number of who to call to make an appointment and get the needed test results to them. Of course, CTCA and the Missouri Spine Center were closed yesterday for the holiday, so I will be making the needed phone calls during the first part of the week to get the needed connections made and get MRIs and other information to Dr. C. Billy and I feel it is unlikely they will be able to do the surgery until after he is in remission, but we don't know for sure. Regardless, it will be good to know what can be done.

Billy is still feeling pretty well and is doing well with his last few days of chemo. (This round ends on Sunday.) He even got out and about for a while yesterday with his dad and Kaylyn.

Happy Independence Day! We all need to pray for our military and their families, as well as our leaders and this country. Our freedom did not come free, and if we don't pay attention and fight for it, we could lose it.

God is good, all the time!

—Dione

> Oh, give thanks to the Lord, for He is good! For His mercy endures forever.
>
> —Psalm 107:1

Sunday, July 5, 2009, 7:43 p.m.

> As you do not know what is the way of the wind. Or how the bones grow in the womb of her who is with child, so you do not know the works of God who makes everything.
>
> —Ecclesiastes 11:5

We had a very nice day at Mom and Dad's yesterday. We just spent the day visiting and relaxing, and it was very nice. We also enjoyed going to church this morning.

I have had several things bouncing around in my head all week and have decided to try and put them down here, even though they may seem random. Hopefully they will make sense, but I can't guarantee it, so feel free to stop reading here.

Life is very interesting and quite an adventure. I have no idea why some people deal with terrible diseases or bad accidents and others don't. I have heard many times, "Why do bad things happen to good people?" I have no idea, but I have another question: "Why not?" Why shouldn't bad things happen to good people? We all live in the same sinful world, and we are all sinful people. In reality, people aren't good. We are sinners. We are born sinners. We may be innocent at birth, but we are still sinners. Since we are all sinners living in a sinful world where the devil is free to roam, why would any of us think bad things can't happen to us?

God didn't promise us easy lives or lives without struggles, illness, or trials, but He did promise to always be with us if we accept His Son as our Savior. Jesus was the only truly good person to walk the earth, and bad things happened to Him.

Billy and I know that the Lord brought us together. I knew from the time I was four years old that I wanted to marry a farm boy and have eight to twelve children. As I grew older, I began praying for my husband. I wanted a Christian, farm-grown boy, and I wanted to have a bunch of kids and homeschool them. I met Billy in Sunday school, and as I got to know him, I knew he was very special. Since I was born in Denver, Colorado, grew up in Nebraska (until I was fourteen anyway), and ended up in Missouri via a nine-month stay in Wichita, Kansas, and Billy grew up in Missouri, he has always said that only the Lord could have put us together.

Billy has always been a very special man of integrity with a close relationship to God. Those are things that drew me to him. My parents, brother, and sister have always thought a lot of Billy as well. I have told him many times that he is a very special man, and I am very thankful and blessed to have him as my husband. He has always amazed me and the kids with his ability to talk to people in the hospital or those dealing with tough situations. The kids and I have talked about how those are his God-given abilities. The Lord gives him the words, and that is why he always seems to know what to say. When Kaylyn, Max, and I helped Billy with a lay renewal weekend in Neosho, Missouri, we were amazed at how he led the weekend and how the Lord gave him the wisdom and words he needed. Max even commented that he just hoped he could someday talk to people the way his dad does. He was referring to how Billy had spoken in front of everyone and led the weekend, as well as the fact people were seeking Billy out and asking for his guidance. Max said that his dad seemed to be so wise, and people wanted his help and advice. He just hoped that he could be at least a little like that someday.

When I tell Billy how special he is, he always says he isn't much. I know that most people who know Billy are aware that he is a godly man of integrity, but I have been thinking about all he has been through lately and how well he has handled it. He truly is amazing, and I am incredibly blessed.

Billy has always been very strong and able to do anything he chose. He was one of the first ones called when someone needed help moving or just about anything else. He worked on the vehicles and other things around here. He helped at church work days and many other things. He went on multiple mission trips. He loves riding his motorcycle and has always enjoyed shooting his various guns. Billy went from doing all those things, as well as many others, to being confined to a wheelchair to where he is now. He is six inches shorter due to the compression fractures in his back. He has limited use of his right hand. He has some limited mobility in his neck and back. His bones, particularly in his back and ribs, are very fragile. He must use a hospital bed to help avoid twisting and putting weight and pressure on his bones. He is much weaker than he used to be. I think he has the right to feel sorry for himself, be angry, ask "Why me?" or be down or depressed, at least part of the time, but he isn't. He does occasionally get grumpy or a little down, but it is very seldom and doesn't last long. He is accepting of what he is dealing with and simply doing the best he can.

He has always been concerned with whether he is genuine. By that I mean he wonders if what he believes and talks shows in the way he lives his life. I have told him that it does, but I believe through all of this that it has shown even more. He has worried if he has set an example of living the advice he gives others when they are facing something tough in their lives. I think he is setting a good example and living his life the way he says he believes.

I told you all this would be a post of random thoughts! I could go on and on about the kids as well, but for now I will leave it with the fact Billy and I are very proud of them. They are very special, and we are very blessed!

I cannot thank you all enough for your prayers, gifts, and help. Again, the Lord has blessed us beyond what we deserve and we are extremely grateful!

God is good, all the time!

—Dione

> Oh, give thanks to the Lord, for He is good! For His mercy endures forever.
>
> —Psalm 107:1

Monday, July 6, 2009, 9:03 p.m.

> Be anxious for nothing, but in everything by prayer and supplication, with thanksgiving, let your requests be made known to God; and the peace of God, which surpasses all understanding, will guard your hearts and minds through Christ Jesus.
>
> —Philippians 4:6-7

Billy and I went into Jefferson City today for a blood draw. We also went by Farm Bureau. We are so very thankful for the Farm Bureau family and all they have done and are doing for us. Thank you all for the gifts, prayers, support, and encouragement. Billy is really looking forward to the day when he returns to work. He misses all of you.

We did take the red Tempo into town today. It is a stick shift and not the smoothest ride, but Billy wanted to give it a try. He thought we might try taking it to Oklahoma next time if he got along with it okay. I was not so sure about that idea because I am not sure I would trust it to go that far. After taking it to Jefferson City today, he decided it might be okay to drive for blood draws to save a little gas, but any farther than that would not be such a good idea. His back was pretty tired and a bit sore after driving the Tempo today. Billy had also forgotten that the car has a couple of issues, so taking it to Oklahoma is not an option. However, I was pleased that he could drive it since he had to shift with his right hand. I think his shoulder would get tired or even sore if he drove it too much, but it might not.

The kids cleaned house today, so if you would like to visit, feel free to stop in. We have a few things to do this week, so you might want to call and make sure we are here, but we all enjoy company. Billy really enjoys visiting.

Thank you to everyone for your prayers and support. We feel that we are very blessed in so many ways, and we love you all.

God is good, all the time!

—Dione

> Oh, give thanks to the Lord, for He is good! For His mercy endures forever.
>
> —Psalm 107:1

Tuesday, July 7, 2009, 10:24 p.m.

> Being confident of this very thing, that He who has begun a good work in you will complete it until the day of Jesus Christ.
>
> —Philippians 1:6

I talked to Arlene at the Missouri Spine Center today. Billy has an appointment with Dr. C on Monday, July 13. I called CTCA, and they are faxing the needed medical records and are overnighting the MRI and metastatic bone scan discs. It was late enough today that they will go out tomorrow. I will check on Thursday afternoon and make sure Dr. C received everything. I really love CTCA. They are so easy to work with. I just called them and told them what I needed and where it needed to go, and it was taken care of—no jumping through hoops or twenty questions or anything. I have tried getting medical stuff from doctors' offices before, and it was like pulling teeth. Hopefully it will be a good visit and we will get some good information and maybe even a plan of how they can help Billy's back. Dr. C had openings in the first part of August, but he really wanted to see Billy as soon as he could. I am taking that as a good thing.

The kids spent quite a bit of time outside this afternoon and evening. This evening was quite nice out until the bugs started trying to eat us. I think the kids were outside most of the afternoon trying to avoid me and the laundry, but that's okay. It was good for them, and I am picky about folding the laundry and usually do it myself anyway. Besides, they spent most of yesterday cleaning house, and I have had plenty of help with meals and things. When I go to the kitchen to start working on lunch or supper, I have at least a couple of volunteers right there ready to help. It is so nice.

I will take at least some of the kids to church tomorrow night, but otherwise we have a day at home with no running. Billy has a blood draw again Thursday morning and nothing scheduled for Friday or Saturday—at least not yet. Billy is feeling pretty well, so if you are thinking about visiting, he would love to see you. We should be home at least most of what is left of the week.

Kaylyn will be taking her driver's test again on Thursday. She is determined to pass this time and has been reading the manual. We have also been quizzing her some, and she has been going over the various situations in her mind to help it all stick in her. She has a job lined up that she is to start on July 15, so it would be a big help for her to have her license. She has a vehicle because as her great-grandma gave her a Tempo a couple of years ago, so she is all set other than the license. I think she will make it this time.

I'd like to give you a little update on Levi. Levi is our nine-year-old type 1 diabetic. His sugar readings were very crazy for a while with everything that has been going on with Billy. When we first went to Tulsa, Levi's numbers were really bad. He would run very high during the day, and then when he went to bed, his sugar would drop like a rock. I think it was because during the day he was stressed and worried, and after he went to sleep, he quit worrying and relaxed. There were quite a few nights when Max stayed up, checked on him, and fed him snacks off and on until 1:00, 2:00, or even 3:00 in the morning. We made some very odd adjustments to his insulin, and I e-mailed his doctor and told him what was going on. The doctor said we were doing fine and it would just be a matter of doing the best we could. Levi is doing great now! His sugar readings are pretty close to as good as we can get. He has only been having a few highs here and there, and they are just a little high. He has not been having lows. He had a few readings that were pushing low, but they were still okay. He is doing well at night too.

As always, thank you for your prayers and all of your support. We love you all! Our prayers for this week are mainly that Billy will continue to feel well and that he will continue to improve. One ongoing prayer is that the chemo will continue to work and he will be in remission by the end of the eighth round of chemo. He just finished his fifth round and will begin his sixth round on Monday, as long as his blood counts are okay.

God is good, all the time!

—Dione

> Oh, give thanks to the Lord, for He is good! For His mercy endures forever.
>
> —Psalm 107:1

Chapter 14

THURSDAY, JULY 9, 2009, 1:50 P.M.

> Now may the God of hope fill you with all joy and peace in believing, that you may abound in hope by the power of the Holy Spirit.
>
> —Romans 15:13

Kaylyn got her driver's license today! She is thrilled, and I have already sent her to town to pick up Billy and Levi's prescriptions. She couldn't wait to go somewhere and not have to have one of us with her. She took Cassy with her, and they were both excited about going somewhere on their own. I can already see how Kaylyn having a license is going to be very helpful for us. Kaylyn and Max have a puppet show on Sunday evening, and Kaylyn will be able to drive to it. We won't have to take them, and no one will have to pick them up. Pretty cool! But it is also a bit scary for Billy and me. It is hard to believe Kaylyn is old enough to drive.

Billy is feeling pretty well. He is taking a much-needed nap right now because he didn't take one yesterday. We all went to church last night and enjoyed the evening. It is really nice to be doing regular things. This reminds me—I need to see about the laundry again.

If counts are all good, then Billy will start chemo again on Monday evening. We also have our appointment at the Missouri Spine Center on Monday.

God is good, all the time!

—Dione

> Oh, give thanks to the Lord, for He is good! For His mercy endures forever.
>
> —Psalm 107:1

—∞—

Friday, July 10, 2009, 10:15 p.m.

> Be still, and know that I am God; I will be exalted among the nations, I will be exalted in the earth!
>
> —Psalm 46:10

> Be Still—We busy ourselves with inconsequential activities. We fill our lives with incessant noise, commotion, and busyness that distract us from God's presence. It is in the stillness that we find God.[19]

Billy is feeling well and has been enjoying having company. Robert and Stacey were out last night, and Steve and Linda came out this evening. We all enjoyed the visits. Thanks for coming out, guys.

So far we are pleased with our dealings with the Missouri Spine Center and Dr. Choma. Arlene, who works in his office, has called a couple of times to make sure we know how to get there and let us know that they did receive the medical records by fax as well as a disc with the MRIs and metastatic bone survey. When Arlene called this morning to tell us that they did get the MRIs and other information, she said that Dr. Choma was already looking at them. We will see what he has to say on Monday.

Faith went to a Girls in Action (her Wednesday night group at church)get together today. They cooked and ate and I am not sure what else. Faith enjoyed herself. Thank you, Betty and Susan!

---

19 Ibid., pg. 666

When Steve and Linda were here this evening, we were talking about having an archery tournament for the Royal Ambassadors (Levi's Wednesday night group at church)s. Levi wrote down instructions for a game and the object. This is what he wrote: "Put a heart on the target. The object is to picture the arrow like God's hand coming down and touching your heart." We all thought that was pretty good.

God is good, all the time!

—Dione

> Oh, give thanks to the Lord, for He is good! For His mercy endures forever.
>
> —Psalm 107:1

Saturday, July 11, 2009, 11:23 p.m.

> Peace I leave with you, My peace I give you; not as the world gives do I give to you. Let not your heart be troubled, neither let it be afraid.
>
> —John 14:27

Today has been a pretty quiet day. Billy slept in this morning after not taking a nap yesterday. He continues to feel well, and we are very thankful for that. Charlie and Cathy came by for a visit late this afternoon, and we enjoyed their company. Then Billy's mom and dad brought their computer up this evening for Billy to work on. I think he is looking forward to having something to do.

Kaylyn and her friend Kayla went to a movie and did a little shopping today. They seemed to have a good time and thought it was pretty cool to not have any parents along.

Max, Faith, and I went to the beauty shop in Russellville. I needed a haircut. Max got a trim, which was badly needed but not so much wanted. It looks good, and Billy was even happy with it. Faith is letting her hair grow out so she can have it cut for Locks of Love. She wants to give her hair to have a wig made for a little girl with cancer. When it gets long enough and she has it cut, we can take it to CTCA because there is a lady there who will see that it gets where it needs to go. Faith's hair is really thick, so she had it thinned a little and the ends trimmed and evened up. She is pleased with it since it is easier to brush.

I actually had the laundry caught up for a few minutes! Cassy helped me fold five baskets of laundry this evening. However, everyone took showers, so it is no longer caught up. *Sigh*. Oh well, such is life.

Thank you all for your continued prayers, calls, visits, messages, encouragement, and support. We are so very blessed, and we love you all!

God is good, all the time!

—Dione

> Oh, give thanks to the Lord, for He is good! For His mercy endures forever.
>
> —Psalm 107:1

Sunday, July 12, 2009, 8:45 p.m.

> From the end of the earth I will cry to You, when my heart is overwhelmed; lead me to the rock that is higher than I. For You have been a shelter for me, a strong tower from the enemy. I will trust in the shelter of Your wings.
>
> —Psalm 61:2-4

> My Rock—We are frail and weak. Life's hectic pressures can easily overwhelm us. Yet God is above all our problems. He is an immovable rock, undaunted by our worst trials. When God reaches down and lifts us up, we see life from an entirely new vista—God's perspective.[20]

We all enjoyed going to Sunday school and church this morning. It is so nice to be back in church. It is one of our very favorite places to be. I taught my first—and second-grade Sunday school class and really enjoyed being back. Hopefully the kids enjoyed it too.

Kaylyn and Max had a puppet show this evening with the puppet group. They seemed to think it went well. Kaylyn was able to drive, so no one had to pick her and Max up, and we didn't have to run them anywhere. Kaylyn starts work tomorrow, and she is ready and excited.

Billy has been a little tired today. He said that it isn't that he feels bad. He is just a bit off and tired. He did get a nap today but is thinking he might go to bed a little earlier tonight. He has a blood draw in the morning, and we will go from there to Columbia for his appointment with the orthopedic surgeon or spine surgeon or whatever he is officially called. As long as everything looks okay with the blood work, he will begin his fifth round of chemo tomorrow evening.

We continue to feel your prayers and thank you for them, as well as for everything else everyone is doing. We love you all.

God is good, all the time!

—Dione

> Oh, give thanks to the Lord, for He is good! For His mercy endures forever.
>
> —Psalm 107:1

20 Ibid., pg. 675

Monday, July 13, 2009, 9:15 p.m.

> For I, the Lord your God, will hold your right hand, saying to you, fear not, I will help you.
>
> —Isaiah 41:13

Today was pretty good day and informative. First thing today Billy had a blood draw. His counts all look good, so round five of chemo begins this evening.

After the blood draw we went to the Missouri Spine Center in Columbia to meet with Dr. C. We really liked Dr. C, and he spent quite a bit of time with us. He had looked at the MRIs CTCA had sent. We told him about the concerns Dr. R has with Billy's back and the possibility of a bad fall or minor car accident causing paralysis. Dr. C said that he was also very concerned. In the middle of Billy's back where they have already done radiation there is one vertebra that is completely collapsed and a couple of others that are not in the best shape. Where the neck and shoulders connect there is also a collapsed vertebra that is broken, and although there isn't truly a piece floating around, it is closing in on the spinal cord. This is the area where there is the biggest concern of a fall causing paralysis.

Dr. C pointed out the narrowing of the spinal column on the MRI. He also pointed out several areas were the cancer is showing up in the spine. He said that what they normally do for collapsed vertebra is to go in and cut out the collapsed vertebra and put in a spacer thing along with a rod on each side of the spine and screw them to the bone. However, in Billy's case he cannot do that because there is not enough solid bone for him to screw anything to. The surgery would be way too risky for Billy and would not hold. He said that we should have the area where the neck and shoulders meet radiated to kill the cancer in that area to prevent further breakdown, which could pinch the spinal cord. We will be getting that arranged with CTCA. He also said that it is up to Billy, but if Billy would like, then he will write a prescription and make arrangements for Billy to get a back brace. The purpose of the brace would be to give the back some support from the outside and help prevent further breakdown in the spine. He said that it is up to Billy. Billy is going to do some research on this particular type of brace and see what he thinks.

Dr. C said that the bone is trying to repair itself, but until the cancer is truly in remission, it can't do too much. He feels that once the cancer is in remission, then the bone will repair. However, it cannot rebuild the collapsed and broken vertebra. He said what is there will harden so that it will be strong and prevent further breakdown or closing in on the spinal cord. I asked him if the surgery he was talking about should be done after the cancer is in remission, and he said, "Not necessarily." He did not seem to think that the surgery would be worth the risk unless the spinal cord was being compromised.

Dr. C told us several symptoms to watch for, and if Billy is having any of them, then we are to call him and he will take another look at things. We were very pleased with him and how he explained things. He told us that he was very concerned about Billy when we contacted him. He asked that in September when the cancer is in remission that we let him know, because he will be worrying about Billy. We feel that we found a good doctor and learned a lot. For now we need to continue working on getting the cancer in remission and get the area at the neck and shoulders radiated, and we will go from there. Billy will look into the back brace, but as Dr. Choma told him, if he doesn't think he will wear it, then there isn't any point in getting one.

Thank you all for your continued prayers, messages, encouragement, and support. Our prayers for this week are that Billy continues to feel well, that his counts stay up, and wisdom for deciding on the back brace.

God is good, all the time!

—Dione

> Oh, give thanks to the Lord, for He is good! For His mercy endures forever.
>
> —Psalm 107:1

Tuesday, July 14, 2009, 9:00 p.m.

> You enlarged my path under me, so my feet did not slip.
>
> —Psalm 18:36

> Enlarging My Path—God may not change the path you are on, but He will help you keep sure footing as you navigate it.[21]

I really like the above message, and I completely agree with it. I know for a fact in my life and that of my family that the Lord is walking every step of the way with us. I believe He is right there giving us the strength we need each day. This new path isn't easy. Sometimes it is just plain hard or disappointing, but God is there, and he gets us through. I can't imagine how anyone would get through anything like this without God. We will continue to take it one day at a time and look to the Lord to guide us and get us through, which is the only way I think we will make it.

Billy has felt pretty good today. He even did some vacuuming. He had the kids doing some cleaning, and he decided to vacuum for a little while. When his back got tired, he quit, but he did pretty well. He has been doing the exercises with his hand, and today he was testing it a bit to see if he could see any improvement. I think he was pleased because he has found there are several things he is able to do now that he was not able to do two weeks ago. Slow progress is fine; we are just glad to see progress.

Max and I did some running in town today. He has a research report to do, so we went to the library and then picked up some odds and ends since we were in town. He is going to do his report on Adolf Hitler. I am not sure what made him think of Hitler except that we have watched several things on the History Channel about World War II. He was looking at his choice of topics, and one of them was to do a biography about someone. He seemed to think Hitler would be interesting, and he wanted to do

21 Ibid., pg. 645

something different since most people usually pick a nice or hero-type person. It will be interesting to see how this turns out.

The girls went over to Bill and Kay's today. For those of you who do not know, Bill and Kay go to our church and are our neighbors. Bill is battling pancreatic cancer, and he fell and broke his little finger. If his platelets are okay tomorrow, then he will have surgery to set that little finger. The girls went over to help Kay with her house cleaning. I think they ended up doing as much playing as helping, but they enjoyed it.

I have been working on getting all of the kids' school work from this past year finished up. I am getting all the grading done and the tests and other things ready to mail. I have made pretty good progress. I just need to proof read some book reports and a couple of things, and then it will be ready to mail. I have also been going through this next year's books and getting their assignments all set up. I have made it through Kaylyn and Max's, so again, I am making progress.

Tomorrow I will try to catch the laundry up again. I did have it caught up for about an hour or two over the weekend.

Visitors are always welcome. Billy is continuing to do well, and he enjoys visitors. The kids (with encouragement from Billy) are keeping the house picked up and clean, so you won't have to be afraid.

God is good, all the time!

—Dione

> Oh, give thanks to the Lord, for He is good! for His mercy endures forever.
>
> —Psalm 107:1

Thursday, July 16, 2009, 9:16 p.m.

> Therefore He is also able to save to the uttermost those who come to God through Him, since He always lives to make intercession for them.
>
> —Hebrews 7:25

> Constant Intercession—We will face temptations and difficult circumstances. At times our strength may fail and our faith may waiver, but we have this hope: Christ our high priest forever intercedes for us with the Father. He is victorious and intends to bring us victory as well.[22]

Thank you all for your prayers! Billy's blood work was all good today, so this round of chemo continues without an interruption (at least so far).

I also talked to Libby about having Dr. C fax her his recommendation for Billy to have radiation where his neck and shoulders meet. She said that would work great and she will get his appointment set up with radiation oncology so we can get his radiation when we are there next time. I then called Dr. C's office and left a message about getting his recommendation faxed to Libby. I will check on it Monday if I don't hear anything before then, just to make sure everything was taken care of.

We had to get a new hot water heater today. We knew it was coming and have been babying the old water heater for a while, but it finally gave up. There was nothing more that we could do to revive it. The last time Billy worked on it back in November or early December we knew the next time it acted up, it would be time to replace it. We weren't sure how long it would hold up at that time, so it did pretty good to make it this long. Thankfully, we found a plumber who does a lot of work in mobile homes, and he was very good and quick.

---

22 Ibid., pg. 1465

Thank you for your continued prayers and support. We have a pretty amazing group of friends and family, and we are thankful for every one of you, as well as for those who are praying for us who we have never met. Thank you all! We love you!

God is good, all the time!

—Dione

> Oh, give thanks to the Lord, for He is good! For His mercy endures forever.
>
> —Psalm 107:1

PS: My mom's friend Nelda is putting together a benefit for our family. (Thank you, Nelda!) It is on Saturday, July 25, at the Elks Lodge. It is a dinner, auction, and dance. The dinner begins at 1:00 and goes till 7:00, with the auction starting at 7:00. There is a 50/50 raffle drawing as well. The dinner is BBQ pork steaks or brats with sides, dine in or carry out. The cost is an $8 per plate donation for adults and $5 for kids twelve and under.

Friday, July 17, 2009, 9:32 p.m.

> Cast your burden on the Lord, and He shall sustain you; He shall never permit the righteous to be moved.
>
> —Psalm 55:22

> Cast Your Burden—Why should we shoulder our burdens alone when almighty God wants to carry them for us? Genuine trust in God places every care into His hands.[23]

[23] Ibid., pg. 672

What a beautiful day! We have had a very enjoyable day. We decided to take the kids to a movie this afternoon. We had planned to go to *Night at the Museum 2*, but the website said it was playing at 1:45, and when we got there, it wasn't playing until 5:10. Since I did not bring Levi's insulin with us, that wouldn't work. We ended up going to *Ice Age 3*. Everyone enjoyed it. I got a kick out of listening to Faith giggle and laugh. She loved it! Billy chuckled several times too, and judging from the way the kids were repeating particular lines on the way home, they all liked it. The kids spent pretty much all evening outside, and I sat outside while visiting on the phone with my sister.

We had a message when we got home that Dr. C's assistant was faxing Billy's records to Libby. I will need to call Libby Monday about Billy's blood work, so I will make sure she received the fax.

Billy is feeling fairly well and enjoying the pretty weather. He is going to have Max help him take the cover off the motorcycle in the morning and start it so he can listen to it for a few minutes.

Thank you all for your continued prayers and support. We are very thankful and truly blessed! We hope you all have a wonderful weekend!

God is good, all the time!

—Dione

> Oh, give thanks to the Lord, for He is good! For His mercy endures forever.
>
> —Psalm 107:1

Saturday, July 18, 2009, 6:30 p.m.

> Whenever I am afraid, I will trust in You. In God (I will praise His word), in God I have put my trust; I will not fear. What can flesh do to me?
>
> —Psalm 56:3-4

Today was another beautiful day! Today is Max's fifteenth birthday. It is hard to believe he is fifteen! He is quite the young man, and we are very proud of him. Billy and I took him shopping for a birthday present and then out to eat. We enjoyed our afternoon out, and I think Max had a good day as well. We are going to all watch a movie in a little while, and we will have grandparents, aunts, uncles, and cousins over one evening next week. I asked Max what kind of cake he would like, and he decided on homemade cinnamon rolls. I expected that since my homemade cinnamon rolls are one of his favorite things.

Billy is feeling pretty well, but I think he is a little tired this evening. He didn't get a nap yesterday or today, and he is looking tired to me, although he says he's not too tired. Since he knows how he feels, I will try not to pester him about it.

It is just two weeks from tomorrow till we go back to Tulsa. We are really enjoying our time at home. Thank you for your continued prayers and encouragement.

God is good, all the time!

—Dione

> Oh, give thanks to the Lord, for He is good! For His mercy endures forever.
>
> —Psalm 107:1

Sunday, July 19, 2009, 11:39 p.m.

> He has made everything beautiful in its time. Also He has put eternity in their hearts, except that no one can find out the work that God does from beginning to end.
>
> —Ecclesiastes 3:11

Today was a very nice day. We all enjoyed Sunday school and church this morning. We had a really nice visit with Denzil and David this afternoon. Thank you for the tomatoes and blackberries. We have already been enjoying them.

Billy has a blood draw in the morning, and our prayers are that counts will be good. Monday is the beginning of his second week of this round of chemo, and typically it is the day his counts are low and he can't take his chemo for three days until his counts are checked again on Thursday. We are hoping that counts will be good and he won't miss any chemo this week.

Thank you all for your prayers, and be sure to pray for each other as well. I know of several who need prayers, and I just want you to know that we are praying for you. God knows everyone and their needs, so even if you don't know specific needs, if people are brought to your mind, it is good to pray for them. Please know that we feel very blessed and are extremely grateful for all of your prayers and all you do for us. Your prayers are felt; thank you.

God is good, all the time!

—Dione

> Oh, give thanks to the Lord, for He is good! For His mercy endures forever.
>
> —Psalm 107:1

Chapter 15

Monday, July 20, 2009, 8:00 p.m.

> And in that day you will say: Praise the Lord, call upon His name; declare His deeds among the people, make mention that His name is exalted.
>
> —Isaiah 12:4

Thank you for the prayers! Billy's counts are good, so the second week of chemo continues. This is his fifth round of chemo, and during the last two rounds, this was the blood draw where counts were low and he couldn't take chemo for three days. We are very pleased that counts were good today.

Just as a reminder, chemo rounds are two weeks on chemo and then one week off. He will finish this round on Sunday and will begin round six when we are back in Tulsa on August 3.

Billy is feeling pretty well, although he took his Decadron today, and being a steroid, it can do odd things too him, like make him sweat and at times just feel a bit odd or off. Thankfully it doesn't last too long, and he will be feeling more like himself tomorrow.

The kids washed windows and made sure the house was clean today, so as always, visitors are welcome. Billy enjoys visiting.

God is good, all the time!

—Dione

> Oh, give thanks to the Lord, for He is good! For His mercy endures forever.
>
> —Psalm 107:1

WEDNESDAY, JULY 22, 2009, 10:00 P.M.

> Fight the good fight of faith, lay hold on eternal life, to which you were also called and have confessed the good confession in the presence of many witnesses.
>
> —1 Timothy 6:12

It was a nice day today. I worked on some more school stuff to get it ready for the upcoming school year. Max spent the day helping Grandpa Jim work on the lawnmower. They should have it back together and running in the morning, and then Max will mow. Billy had a nice afternoon nap and is feeling pretty well. The kids and I all went to church this evening and there was a nice turnout. It is really nice to be back at church!

Billy is on the downhill side of this round of chemo and has done very well. He has a blood draw tomorrow, so hopefully his counts will still be good and he will get all of his chemo in this round. Other than being a bit tired and needing a nap from time to time, he is really feeling pretty good. He was outside this morning while his dad and Max were taking the deck off the lawn mower. When he came in, he said that is the closest he has come to doing anything for quite a while. He then said he really didn't do much, but at least he got his hands dirty. It isn't that he hasn't been doing anything, because he has worked on his mom's computer and I think he is done with it. He has done a few things around the house, as well as playing foreman and giving the kids guidance on some things.

God is good, all the time!

—Dione

> Oh, give thanks to the Lord, for He is good! For His mercy endures forever.
>
> —Psalm 107:1

Saturday, July 25, 2009, 10:04 p.m.

> You are the light of the world. A city that is set on a hill cannot be hidden. Nor do they light a lamp and put it under a basket, but on a lamp stand, and it gives light to all who are in the house. Let your light so shine before men, that they may see your good works and glorify your Father in heaven.
>
> —Matthew 5:14-16

Thank you! Thank you! Thank you to everyone who helped with the meal, bought meals, gave a donation, participated in the auction, and anything else at the benefit for us today. We appreciate it more than we can tell you all! We were there this evening from 5:00 till after 8:30 and really enjoyed visiting with several of you. We are very blessed. It is amazing how the Lord is taking care of things and using many people to do it.

Billy had taken a good nap this afternoon and really enjoyed visiting this evening. His last day of chemo for this round is tomorrow. Again, thank you all for everything, including your prayers, support, and encouragement. We are very blessed!

God is good, all the time!

—Dione

> Oh, give thanks to the Lord, for He is good! For His mercy endures forever.
>
> —Psalm 107:1

Sunday, July 26, 2009, 10:55 p.m.

> It is God who arms me with strength, and makes my way perfect.
>
> —Psalm 18:32

We all enjoyed Sunday school and church this morning. Kaylyn and Max had a puppet show this afternoon, so they stayed in town. Kaylyn had to work for about an hour this evening, and then they came home. She is working at Southwest Animal Hospital. She is currently kennel help but learned today that they are pleased with her work, and before long, she will be trained as a technician. She is pretty happy about that. She is currently working seven days a week but also found out that she only has to do that while another person is on vacation. She was happy about that as well. She doesn't mind the number of hours but likes the idea of not working every single day all the time.

Billy is tired today, and his back is fairly tired. He did more standing then he should have last night, but he enjoyed himself. He said he really isn't in pain; his back is just tired. He did get a good nap this afternoon, so that helped some. Tonight he took his last chemo pill for this round. He has a blood draw tomorrow, and when I call to check on it, I am going to see if Libby was able to get the radiation set up for when we are down there this time.

Thank you all for your prayers and all that you do.

God is good, all the time!

—Dione

> Oh, give thanks to the Lord, for He is good! For His mercy endures forever.
>
> —Psalm 107:1

Monday, July 27, 2009, 10:08 p.m.

> But I will sing of Your power; Yes, I will sing aloud of Your mercy in the morning; for You have been my defense and refuge in the day of my trouble. To You, O my strength, I will sing praises; for God is my defense, my God of mercy.
>
> —Psalm 59:16-17

> My Refuge—We would never know God as our strength if we never needed a refuge. It is through life's trials and triumphs that we come to experience the rich array of God's ways.[24]

I really like this verse and the message from the *Blackaby Study Bible*. As my Grandpa used to say, "Think about that!" I think these warrant some thinking about.

Prayers continue to be answered because Billy's blood counts were all good again today. That makes three weeks straight with good counts! Thank you all for your prayers! As always, they mean more then you could know, and we are very thankful for all of you.

Billy has not felt as well the last couple of days. I knew he was pretty tired and his back was tired yesterday. He really didn't look or act like he felt very good. This morning he admitted that he really didn't feel very well and his back was hurting. I gave him breakthrough pain medication, and a few hours later he said that he should have taken some yesterday because he was feeling better since his back wasn't hurting. That means he was hurting yesterday but didn't admit to it. Hmmm, tough guy I guess. He took a pretty long nap again this afternoon and was feeling quite a bit better this evening. He doesn't look as tired this evening either, so that is good.

---

24 Ibid., pg. 674

He had a meeting he had planned to go to this evening, but he has a busy day tomorrow with a lunch meeting. Then we have friends coming out for supper tomorrow evening, so he decided to just rest this evening. I think it did him some good because he seemed to be feeling better all evening. He plans to go to his lunch meeting tomorrow and then take a nap in the afternoon so he should be rested for both events, and he is looking forward to his day.

God is good, all the time!

—Dione

> Oh, give thanks to the Lord, for He is good! For His mercy endures forever.
>
> —Psalm 107:1

Wednesday, July 29, 2009, 12:03 a.m.

I really liked the verse from last time. It just really jumped out at me, so I am going to use it again.

> But I will sing of Your power; Yes, I will sing aloud of Your mercy in the morning; for You have been my defense and refuge in the day of my trouble. To You, O my strength, I will sing praises; for God is my defense, my God of mercy.
>
> —Psalm 59:16-17

> My Refuge—We would never know God as our strength if we never needed a refuge. It is through life's trials and triumphs that we come to experience the rich array of God's ways.[25]

25 Ibid. pg. 674

It was a good day. Billy went to lunch with C. B. and enjoyed himself. That is the first time he has gone anywhere by himself in many months, and he did just fine.

Our very good friends Russ, Trish, and their little boy Christian came out for supper this evening, and we all had a good time. Thank you for the fish and shrimp, guys! It was yummy! It was a very nice visit, and the guys did the cooking outside, so that was nice too.

I talked to Libby today to make sure she had received the information from the surgeon in Columbia and to see if Billy would be able to do the radiation when we go to CTCA this time. She said she had just received the fax yesterday and she would have one of the schedulers call me and get things set up. It wasn't long before I got a call from the scheduler. Billy has an appointment with one of the radiation oncologists on Monday, August 3. When we meet with them, they will set up the CT simulation to get Billy marked for the radiation, and then the radiation will begin a day or two later. We are figuring if they do the same type of radiation and schedule they did on the other spots then he will begin radiation either Tuesday or Wednesday and will have ten days. That means we will be in Tulsa at least fourteen to sixteen days this time. It will all depend on the radiation schedule and how his counts do since he will also be getting chemo at the same time. We are glad they are getting the radiation scheduled since that is the main recommendation the surgeon had for him.

Thank you for the continued prayers. We love you guys!

God is good, all the time!

—Dione

> Oh, give thanks to the Lord, for He is good! For His mercy endures forever.
>
> —Psalm 107:1

Wednesday, July 29, 2009, 10:51 p.m.

> Brethren, I do not count myself to have apprehended; but one thing I do, forgetting those things which are behind and reaching forward to those things which are ahead. I press toward the goal for the prize of the upward call of God in Christ Jesus. Therefore let us, as many as are mature, have this mind; and if in anything you think otherwise, God will reveal even this to you.
>
> —Philippians 3:13-15

Billy was fairly tired today and had some pain in his back, so he just rested most of the day and took some breakthrough pain medication, which did help. The older four kids had a youth get together at the Russellville pool this evening. The parents were supposed to come too, but Billy decided just to stay home and take it easy. Faith went to the Cole County Fair with the neighbors, so I took the rest of the kids to the pool. Robert grilled and the kids swam while the parents visited. It was nice, and everyone seemed to have a good time.

Faith had a ball at the fair. She was so cute when she came home between 10:30 and 11:00. She came in the door bright eyed and asked if the other kids were in bed. I told her that they were all in bed and she said, "Yes!" It was the first time that she had stayed up after everyone else was in bed. She told us all about her evening, and she had a great time. She petted goats and rode rides and saw all kinds of things. She thought it was great!

Billy has a blood draw in the morning. We expect everything to be good since he hasn't had any chemo this week and everything was good Monday.

Thank you all for your continued prayers and support in so many ways.

God is good, all the time!

—Dione

> Oh, give thanks to the Lord, for He is good! For His mercy endures forever.
>
> —Psalm 107:1

Thursday, July 30, 2009, 10:17 p.m.

> Like the appearance of a rainbow in a cloud on a rainy day, so was the appearance of the brightness all around it. This was the appearance of the likeness of the glory of the Lord.
>
> —Ezekiel 1:28

> God's Majesty—Christians in the midst of adversity do not need a better understanding of their plight; they need a fresh vision of God's majesty. No matter what the crisis is, God is sovereign.[26]

Billy slept in a little this morning. He has a spot in his back that has been hurting him off and on. He has taken breakthrough pain medication a couple of times in the last couple of days. The area that is hurting seems to be in the ribs that wrap around the back. We know from the first CT that was done that his ribs are affected by the cancer. Since we have an appointment with the oncologist and the radiation oncologist on Monday, we will tell them both about it. Billy thinks it may just be due to the fact he has been doing more while at home. We will see what they think.

His blood work was good today, as we expected. We also received Billy's Revlimid (oral chemo) today. He will start it again on Monday. We did get calls from CTCA today reminding us of all of his appointments on Monday as well as the check in Sunday evening, so all is a go. It is hard to believe it is almost time to head back down already. It is amazing how fast the time goes! It is time for me to start thinking about packing.

---

26 Ibid.,967

I have been able to get several things done this time at home. I have pretty much everything done with the kids' school work that I can do right now, and things are ready for them to start back to school in September.

Thank you for your prayers and for checking in. We are very blessed and love you all.

God is good, all the time!

—Dione

> Oh, give thanks to the Lord, for He is good! For His mercy endures forever.
>
> —Psalm 107:1

Friday, July 31, 2009, 10:56 p.m.

> Thus God, determining to show more abundantly to the heirs of promise the immutability of His counsel, confirmed it by an oath, that by two immutable things, in which it is impossible for God to lie, we might have strong consolation, who have fled for refuge to lay hold of the hope set before us.
>
> —Hebrews 6:17-18

> Our Hope—Our hope lies not in ourselves but in the relationship of Christ. He is absolutely faithful. His promises to us always come to pass. Our confidence in the future lies within Him, not within ourselves.[27]

We all had a little outing today. Kaylyn didn't have to work this morning, so we all went to Sam's. We picked up stuff for the kids to fix for lunches

[27] Ibid., pg. 1464

while we are in Tulsa, as well as some snack stuff for the kids and for us to take with us.

Then this evening we enjoyed visiting with Dee and her girls. We had a nice visit with Dee, and the kids seemed to have a good evening playing outside. It was a very nice evening, although according to the kids the mosquitoes were bad.

Billy has felt pretty good today, other than having some pain in his ribs on the right side, kind of under his arm and around the back. He did need breakthrough pain medication twice today, but it helped.

I called the medical supply company that delivers the hospital bed to our room when we are in Tulsa. They need a prescription to send a bed, so I called and left our care manager a message about it. I didn't hear back from her, even though she is usually very good about letting me know when things are taken care of, so I called the company back to see if they had gotten the fax. It was after 5:30, so they put me in touch with the person on call for the weekend. He was not in the office, so he will check on it first thing in the morning to get it all set up and then give me a call to let me know they have it taken care of. He talked like they would be able to have the bed in the room sometime on Sunday so it will be there when we get there. We will see if it all works out. I called guest services before calling the medical supply company, and they gave me the room number, which I gave to the medical supply company, so they should be able to get it all taken care of.

With this trip home, I have learned a little more about how some things work and who to call first to get things taken care of. The other day I called the pharmacy we get the chemo from to see about getting a new prescription. I found out that they need the doctor to fax them the prescription before they can do anything, so next time I will just remind Libby to get the ball rolling on that. Then I called the medical supply company about the bed. Since I was the one who called them to pick the bed up when we were ready to leave, I thought I would just get it all set up for when we go back. However, again they need a prescription from the doctor, so again I will just call Libby and remind her to get the ball rolling on the bed next time.

Thank you for the continuous prayers. Billy will have several doctor appointments on Monday, and we will talk to the oncologist and radiation oncologist about the pain in his ribs. He also has a follow-up appointment with the pain doctor. When we get there on Sunday evening they will take several tubes of blood to run tests to see where we stand with the cancer. We will have most if not all of those results when we see Dr. R on Monday morning. Prayerfully, all will be still headed in the right direction.

Have a good weekend!

God is good, all the time!

—Dione

> Oh, give thanks to the Lord, for He is good! For His mercy endures forever.
>
> —Psalm 107:1

Saturday, August 1, 2009 11:08, p.m.

> While He was still speaking, some came from the ruler of the synagogues' house who said, "Your daughter is dead. Why trouble the Teacher any further?" As soon as Jesus heard the word that was spoken, He said to the ruler of the synagogue, "Do not be afraid; only believe."
>
> —Mark 5:35-36

> Do Not Fear—God may test our faith by allowing obstacles to come between our prayers and the answer. The test is overcome when we believe God's word is true regardless of the circumstances and the conditions. Then He will make the answer known.[28]

28 Ibid., pg. 1191

There was a lot packed into the day today. I worked on some laundry and packing to start with this morning and then realized I needed to go to the bank and post office. I went to Russellville on the way back (thankfully very close to home), the brakes seemed to go out on the red Tempo. I am glad it is a stick because I could down shift to slow it down. Since I was close to home, I just went slower than usual. Billy figured a line broke or something as I was slowing down to turn on to Mt. Olive off of AA. When I stepped on the brakes, they started to take hold and then the pedal just went onto the floor without doing much of anything. I think Jim (Billy's dad) and Max are going to take a look at it later this week. There isn't a hurry since we won't need it for a while.

I think Max and Jim are going to crawl under the house and see what they can find before they worry about the car. Levi discovered water in the vents this morning. Our heating/AC vents are in the floor. Max checked it out and discovered there was water actually running (a small stream) through the vents, starting with the vent next to the air conditioner. He got the shop vac out and sucked the water out of the vents. He found that the vent in the boys' room must be a low spot because it had the most water in it. We have no idea how long this has been going on, other than it wasn't doing it before we left for Tulsa last time. Max is pretty sure it has just been a few days, but we really don't know. Billy and Jim and the rest of us agree that there must be something broken or stopped up under the house, which is allowing the condensation from the AC unit to run into the vents somewhere. It looks like Max and Jim will be crawling under the house on Monday. Thank you, Jim!

When I came back from Russellville this morning, my mom, dad, and brother, John, were here. They came out to visit for a little while, and we enjoyed it.

Right after lunch, Faith and I went into Jefferson City to pick up a refill prescription for Billy, and I planned to pick up Levi's test strips as well. However, our insurance won't pay for the refill until tomorrow. The pharmacy was going to fill the prescription, and then Kaylyn will pick them up on Monday since she has to go to work and will be in town anyway. We also had some other errands to run and odds and ends to pick up. We got everything done and made it home around 3:00. My laundry was done by then, so I went back to packing.

I was working on packing and double checking some things when Doris (Billy's mom) called to see if we had plans for supper. I had something I could fix but hadn't really gotten started on it yet. Doris and Jim had pizzas they thought they would bring up and we could cook them. We didn't need much encouragement for that, everyone thought pizza sounded good. Thank you, Doris and Jim. We enjoyed it! We also had a nice visit.

Doris and Jim only stayed until around 7:00, so we all watched a movie after they left. Then I trimmed Billy's hair. Unfortunately, I tried something a little different (he told me to). It didn't work as well as we would have liked, but after a bit more trimming, it turned out all right. I think it will look better in a few days when it doesn't have the fresh-cut look, but for the most part it looks pretty good. Then Billy got his shower and tucked in. It was almost 11:00 by then, so it was a pretty full day.

Billy did pretty well today. For the most part he felt good. He did have some pain this afternoon and took some breakthrough pain medication, and then he took his really strong breakthrough pain medication before getting in the shower.

Oh, the medical supply company in Tulsa called me about 11 this morning to let me know that everything was set and they would have the hospital bed in the room for us tomorrow. He said that everything had been taken care of yesterday, so they would have it ready for us.

We will go to Sunday school and church in the morning, then come home and have a bite of lunch, and then I will get the Suburban loaded. We need to be in Tulsa around 7:00 for registration and then a blood draw. We will try to leave no later than 1:30.

Thank you all for your continued prayers and support! We love you all!

God is good, all the time!

—Dione

Oh, give thanks to the Lord, for He is good! For His mercy endures forever.

—Psalm 107:1

Chapter 16

MONDAY, AUGUST 3, 2009, 9:53 P.M.

> And my God shall supply all your needs according to His riches in glory by Christ Jesus. Now to our God and Father be glory forever and ever. Amen
>
> —Philippians 4:19-20

We made the trip to Tulsa in exactly five hours yesterday. It was a good trip, and Billy did well. He felt better when we got here than last time. They did have the hospital bed in the room, and we are on the fourth floor again, just down a different hall. Our room is a little bigger than the last one because they put us in a handicap room. The extra space is nice.

We met with Dr. R this morning, and he is pleased with how Billy is looking and doing. Dr. R is not sure whether the stem cell rescue is worth pursuing. He has a couple of reasons for this. One is that the Revlimid is fairly new in treating multiple myeloma, and it is more effective than anything else they have used, so medical professionals are not sure if a stem cell rescue or transplant is even needed anymore when using Revlimid. Second, he is not sure Billy is even a candidate for it anymore because of the way treatment had to be done to save his life when we first got here.

Dr. R recommended that we do some online research about transplants for multiple myeloma and then call the CTCA at Zion, Illinois, and the Mayo Clinic in Rochester to gather information and get their opinion on whether to try a transplant or rescue. Dr. R simply doesn't know if the benefits are worth the risks or if it is even necessary with the Revlimid being so effective. He told us the best thing to do is to become as informed as we can and then make our decision on what to do. He will support and help us either way. Billy asked him what he would say if, when Billy finishes his eight rounds of chemo and is declared to be in remission, he just says, "Thanks, Doc," calls it good, and just does checkups after that. Dr. R said that would be fine with him, and he isn't even sure that wouldn't be the best thing to do. We will be doing a lot of praying about this while we gather our information. I can tell you that Billy and I have never been too sure we liked the idea of a stem cell rescue, so we will definitely be carefully looking into it and praying for guidance.

This afternoon we met with Dr. F, the radiation oncologist. We feel that appointment went well, although it looks like we will be here for close to three weeks or so instead of the two we were hoping for, but we will know more on Thursday. Dr. F wanted to gather some more information before scheduling radiation. He wants to make sure that where he radiates will be the most benefit for Billy. Billy had an X-ray of his ribs done today and will have an MRI of his entire back on Wednesday. Dr. F is also consulting with two other doctors, a neurosurgeon and a neurologist, because he wants to be sure that when he does the radiation, if at all possible he can help the nerve issue with the right hand. We will meet with him again on Thursday afternoon and hopefully will get a plan of action at that time.

Our prayer requests are that we will be given wisdom and understanding as we do our research and make our decision about whether to pursue a stem cell rescue or transplant of any kind. Please also pray that blood counts will stay good through this round of chemo. Billy's potassium and white count were a little low today. They were not low enough to be a problem at this point, but since chemo started today, we want the counts to continue to stay good.

We continue to be thankful for and cherish your prayers. We love you all and are very blessed by you.

God is good, all the time!

—Dione

> Oh, give thanks to the Lord, for He is good! For His mercy endures forever.
>
> —Psalm 107:1

Wednesday, August 5, 2009, 4:45 p.m.

> Be strong and of good courage, do not fear nor be afraid of them; for the Lord your God, He is the One who goes with you. He will not leave you nor forsake you.
>
> —Deuteronomy 31:6

Billy spent two hours in the MRI machine today. They did MRIs of almost all of his back. We will see the radiation oncologist again tomorrow afternoon to see what the plan for radiation is. We will then have a better idea of how long we will need to be here.

I have been doing some research online, as Dr. R suggested. I can't say that we are very pleased with what we are finding. Of course, like everything else on the Internet, some sites make things sound pretty positive and others are not very positive at all. I contacted CTCA at Zion today through an online chat. They are going to get some information together for me and then give me a call so we can discuss things. I told them that Billy is being treated here, and they took Billy's name. I will wait for them to call and see what we can find out.

We understand that many MM patients have done the stem cell rescue and have done very well with it. One of the big issues with Billy is that the oncologist isn't even sure it is possible for him to have the stem cell rescue, in which case the mini transplant might be an option. However, what I have been able to find says that they do the stem cell rescue first and then the mini transplant. One site I found says that the mini transplant is still in clinical trials, but I could not find anything to indicate how old that information is, so that may not be the case. We will continue to see what information we can gather. With what I have found so far, we are just not sure the risks are worth it since the oncologist has said that with this newer chemo, he is not even sure it would be necessary. Billy has said, "What we are finding just doesn't give me the warm fuzzies." We will have to see what I find out from Zion.

Billy has a blood draw tomorrow, so our prayers are that counts will continue to be good. We would also ask for prayer for wisdom and guidance as we continue to try to gather information to make a decision on future treatment.

Thank you all for your continued prayers and encouragement.

God is good, all the time!

—Dione

> Oh, give thanks to the Lord, for He is good! For His mercy endures forever.
>
> —Psalm 107:1

Thursday, August 6, 2009, 4:15 p.m.

> God is our refuge and strength, a very present help in trouble. Therefore we will not fear, even though the earth be removed, and though the mountains be carried into the midst of the seas; Though its waters roar and be troubled. Though the mountains shake with its swelling. There is a river whose streams shall make glad the city of God, the holy place of the tabernacle of the Most High.
>
> —Psalm 46:1-4

Blood work was drawn today, and it is okay. Billy's counts are a little low but still okay, so chemo can continue. His counts will be checked again on Monday.

We did meet with Dr. F again today. All of the doctors here and other medical staff had a lunch meeting where they discussed Billy's case. They were all (about forty people) in agreement to have the MRIs looked at by an orthopedic oncologist in Philadelphia to see if he feels anything can be done to stabilize the area where the cervical and thoracic spine meet. They are connected to him by computer, so he will be able to look at the MRIs from May and yesterday over the computer. We were told we would hear something before the end of the day tomorrow on what the plan is.

The focus was on deciding how to proceed with the neck area. The doctor didn't say anything about the rib area. We didn't think to ask about it at the time. When they call us with the plan for the neck area, we will ask about the ribs, or I will just either call or go down and catch someone from that office and remind them to have Dr. F look at the X-rays and let us know about that area as well.

Our prayers are that we will get a plan of action concerning the neck area and radiation. Billy is not very happy with all the waiting we have had to do this week. He had hoped to have several days of radiation done already, and nothing had been started yet. We also pray that the blood counts will remain good as this round of chemo continues.

Thank you so much for your continued prayers. We love you all.

God is good, all the time!

—Dione

> Oh, give thanks to the Lord, for He is good! For his mercy endures forever.
>
> —Psalm 107:1

Friday, August 7, 2009, 6:35 p.m.

> "If I say, "My foot slips," Your mercy, O Lord, will hold me up. In the multitude of my anxieties within me, Your comforts delight my soul.
>
> —Psalm 94:18-19

Well, we continue to wait. We didn't hear anything from Dr. F today. Since he was waiting to hear from another doctor, he only has so much control over how soon he gets his information. We hope to hear from him on Monday. Billy is not good at waiting, so it will be a long weekend.

I called Dr. F's office today to remind them that we didn't hear anything about the X-rays on the ribs. We didn't hear anything back about that today either, but I figure they will go over that when they call about the other. Again, we will wait until Monday.

I talked to Libby today, and they do not have all of the results back from the tests they ran to determine where things are with the cancer. She was going to let Dr. R know that we are waiting to hear about those tests, so as soon as he gets the results, he will let us know how things look. It could be later on next week; some of those tests take a little time.

I also learned while talking to Libby that they have sent all of Billy's records, along with the discs of his scans, to the CTCA in Zion, Illinois. Libby talked to one of the doctors there who does the various kinds of transplants (stem cell rescue, mini transplants, and others). He is going to take a look at all of Billy's records and see if Billy is eligible for any of the transplants, and if so, then he will contact us with all of the information so we can make a decision. All of this was discussed in the meeting the doctors had yesterday. From what one of the nurses said, Billy was their only topic yesterday, and they discussed every aspect of his care and how best to proceed. Everyone was in agreement with the decisions made. Now we just have to wait for them to get all of their information together and give us the plan so we can make our decision on it. Hopefully we will hear something fairly early on Monday.

Billy talked to the guy who looked at our air conditioner today. Billy's dad took a look at the unit, but it wasn't something he could fix, so he called someone. The air conditioner and coils need to be replaced, and it is recommended that we go ahead and replace the furnace as well. We understand why and agree that it would be a good idea, but we are still thinking it over. The excitement never ends! Oh well, such is life.

We continue to feel your prayers and be blessed by all of you! Thank you for sticking with us! We love you all!

God is good, all the time!

—Dione

> Oh, give thanks to the Lord, for He is good! For His mercy endures forever.
>
> —Psalm 107:1

Saturday, August 8, 2009, 7:12 p.m.

> "For the mountains shall depart and the hills be removed, but My kindness shall not depart from you, nor shall My covenant of peace be removed." Says the Lord, who has mercy on you.
>
> —Isaiah 54:10

Well, as expected, it is going to be a long weekend. Today is dragging out, and I expect tomorrow to be about the same. I am praying we hear something before noon on Monday. Billy is not good at waiting, and not being home makes it worse. I think he understands why Dr. F wants to be completely sure of things before starting radiation, but he would be a much happier camper if we had heard something yesterday.

We did not hear anything about the X-rays on the ribs either. However, his ribs have not been hurting him this week, so maybe there is nothing serious going on there. One of the nurses wondered if maybe twisted wrong and pulled something. Billy doesn't remember doing anything like that but thinks it could be possible. We shall see.

We did get out for a little while today. We went out for BBQ. It was pretty good, and then we walked around a little in the strip mall area were the BBQ place was. We went into a store that sells new and used movies, games, and all kinds of things. We enjoyed looking around for a little while.

Thank you all for your prayers and encouragement. They mean a lot to us! You are all very special to us, and we love you all!

Our prayers are that we find something out Monday as far as the plan for radiation. Also, please pray that his counts will continue to be good so he can continue his chemo through next week and not miss any. This is his sixth round of chemo, and so far there have only been two rounds (I think) that he made it all the way through without missing any.

Thank you again for your prayers and support!

God is good, all the time!

—Dione

> Oh, give thanks to the Lord, for He is good! For His mercy endures forever.
>
> —Psalm 107:1

Monday, August 9, 2009, 6:41 p.m.

> As for God, His way is perfect; The word of the Lord is power; He is shield to all who trust in Him.
>
> —Psalm 18:30

> Create in me a clean heart, O God, and renew a steadfast spirit within me.
>
> —Psalm 51:10

Well, Billy has waited all he can wait. We talked to Renee in Dr. F's office today. She had not had a chance to talk to Dr. F about the rib X-rays yet, and she didn't know if he had heard from the other doctor. Billy's ribs have not hurt him for a week and he has appointments here on August 31, so we have decided to go home tomorrow. We will wait to hear from them while we are at home with the kids. That gives them time to hear from the doctor they are waiting on and they can get a plan put together. Then if radiation is in the plan, we will do it when we come back on August 31.

Unless we hear something first thing in the morning to change our plans, we are headed home in the morning and will be home for about three weeks.

Billy's blood counts were okay again today, so chemo continues. This is his second week of this round. He has just one more blood draw for this week, and that is on Thursday.

Thank you all for your continued prayers and support. We love you all!

God is good, all the time!

—Dione

> Oh, give thanks to the Lord, for He is good! For His mercy endures forever.
>
> —Psalm 107:1

Tuesday, August 11, 2009 10:03 p.m.

> O Lord, our Lord, how excellent if Your name in all the earth, who have set Your glory above the heavens! Out of the mouth of babes and nursing infants You have ordained strength, because of Your enemies that You may silence the enemy and the avenger. When I consider Your heavens, the work of Your fingers, the moon and the stars, which You have ordained, what is man that You are mindful of him, and the son of man that You visit him? For You have made him a little lower than the angels and You have crowned him with glory and honor. You have made him to have dominion over the works of Your hands; You have put all things under his feet, all sheep and oxen—even the beasts of the field, the birds of the air, and the fish of the sea that pass through the paths of the seas. O Lord, our Lord, How excellent is Your name in all the earth!
>
> —Psalm 8

Thank you all for your continued prayers and support! We are home, and Billy is feeling well. Traveling went well today, and it is nice to be home with the kids.

We will just enjoy being at home and let the doctors figure out the plan from here. Levi has a clinic appointment for his diabetes on Friday, so I will be able to take him to that. Max is ready to take his test for his learner's permit, so we will get that done before long.

Billy is continuing his sixth round of chemo and will have a blood draw on Thursday. Things seem to be progressing well. We will make further decisions when we are given the information needed to do so. Until then we will just enjoy being at home with the kids.

Thank you again for the prayers. Many of you are also in our prayers. We feel the prayers daily and know they have played a big role in how well Billy is doing. Love you all!

God is good, all the time!

—Dione

> Oh, give thanks to the Lord, for He is good! For His mercy endures forever.

—∞—

Wednesday, August 12, 2009, 10:27 p.m.

> Your eyes saw my substance, being yet unformed, and in Your book they all were written, the days fashioned for me, when as yet there were none of them. How precious also are Your thoughts to me, O God! How great is the sum of them!
>
> —Psalm 139:16-17

> Precious Thoughts—God's thoughts toward you are infinite, wonderful, and tender. Let Him share them with you and they will become precious to you.[29]

It's very nice to be home. Billy is feeling pretty well. He was just a bit tired today after traveling yesterday. He slept in a bit this morning and then took a three-and-a-half-hour nap today. Although the traveling does make him rather tired, he isn't hurting with the new Suburban (well new to us). In the black Suburban we wouldn't even make it halfway through the trip before he needed breakthrough pain medication. He didn't have to take any breakthrough pain medication this time. There are more seat adjustments, so he is able to get more comfortable. Even though he gets tired, at least he isn't hurting.

Kaylyn and Max had a puppet show this morning, so Max just rode in to work with Kaylyn, and then they met the puppet team afterward. I wasn't

---

29 Ibid., pg. 732

sure how I would like Kaylyn being old enough to drive, but I like it, at least for the most part.

Tomorrow is blood draw day, and other than that, it has been a pretty quiet day. Billy and Cassy have wanted me to do pulled pork for quite some time, so that is what we are having for supper tomorrow. Hopefully they will be pleased with it.

We don't expect too much excitement the rest of the week—just laundry, house cleaning, fixing meals, and the usual stuff.

We hope you are all doing well and want you all to know that we are very blessed by all of you and very thankful for your prayers and everything! Love you all!

God is good, all the time!

—Dione

> Oh, give thanks to the Lord, for His mercy endures forever.
>
> —Psalm 107:1

Thursday, August 13, 2009, 7:57 p.m.

> He guards the paths of justice, and preserves the way of His saints. Then you will understand righteousness and justice, equity and every good path. When wisdom enters your heart, and knowledge is pleasant to your soul.
>
> —Proverbs 2:8-10

It has been a pretty quiet day. Billy took Kaylyn with him for his blood draw this morning. He is feeling okay but still a bit tired. He finishes this round of chemo on Sunday, and he tends to be a little more tired around the end of the second week.

Billy's blood counts were okay, so chemo continues, and that is good news, since he has gone several weeks with good counts. This morning we got a call from one of the care managers at CTCA. (Our care manager is out this week.) They heard back from the Cancer Treatment Centers of America at Zion, Illinois, and Billy is not eligible for any of the transplants. Dr. R will discuss our options with us at our next appointment with him on August 31. This is one less decision we have to make since it is not an option. We will just have to see what the next step might be when we go back at the end of the month.

Thank you all for your continued prayers. Billy's counts staying up for so long is definitely an answer to prayer, and we are very grateful. We love you all!

God is good, all the time!

—Dione

> Oh, give thanks to the Lord, for He is good! For His mercy endures forever.
>
> —Psalm 107:1

Friday, August 14, 2009, 7:22 p.m.

> And Moses said to the people, "Do not be afraid. Standstill, and see the salvation of the Lord, which He will accomplish for you today. For the Egyptians whom you see today, you shall see again no more forever. The Lord will fight for you, and you shall hold your peace."
>
> —Exodus 14:13-14

> Stand Still—Following God's will can sometimes be difficult. Don't panic; stay where God has led you. Quitting or fleeing is evidence of a doubting heart. Remain where God placed you and you will witness the miraculous.[30]

Billy is feeling pretty well and was not as tired today. He just has three more days of this round of chemo and then just two rounds left. As I said yesterday, when we meet with Dr. R at the end of the month, we will discuss what, if anything, we will do when he finishes his eighth round of chemo. As for the possibility of more radiation, we have not heard any more on that. The radiation oncologist at CTCA was waiting to hear from on orthopedic oncologist in Philadelphia. Our care manager will be back in the office this next week (as far as we know), so we will check with her on whether they have made any progress with that decision. We are going to see if she will check into it and let us know whether to plan on any radiation when we go back to Tulsa.

Faith rode along with Levi and me to Columbia this morning for Levi's clinic appointment for his diabetes. Dr. B was really pleased with how Levi is doing, as was the dietitian. I really like Dr. B. He not only checked Levi out and went over his numbers, insulin doses, and other information, but he also asked about Billy as well as the rest of us. He wanted to know how all of us were doing with everything going on. He is concerned that we each have someone we can talk to and that we are all handling the stress and everything okay. He felt that Levi and Faith both seemed to be doing well. He asked each of them several questions. He had Levi grinning from ear to ear and blushing when he asked him if he is good to his sister. Levi said that sometimes he is. Dr. B then told him that he needed to be really good to her because when they get older, he might like some of her friends and he would want Faith to be saying good things about him. Levi seemed to get quite a kick out of that, and Faith found it pretty funny too.

While Dr. B asked about all of us, he was most concerned about Max. My dad took Levi to his last clinic appointment in April, and Max and Kaylyn went along. Dr. B remembered that Max was very quiet, and he just felt

---

30 Ibid., pg. 83

that Max was keeping things bottled up and not talking to anyone. He thought Max seemed the most worried and was trying to deal with things on his own. I told him that at that time, several of us were a little worried about Max, but Max is doing quite well. We have learned a few things about talking to Max and the things that are important for us to talk to him about one on one. It is really neat to have a doctor who is concerned about every aspect of the patient, not just how his numbers are. I don't think we can get a better report than what Dr. B said before leaving the room. He looked at me and said, "Your family is amazing, Levi is doing great, and I wouldn't change a thing. Just keep it up. Let us know if we can be of help to you." Dr. B and the dietitian also told me to update them from time to time on things by e-mail. That is another thing neat about dealing with Dr. B and the dietitians; I can e-mail them with questions and they always get back to me within twenty-four hours.

Thank you all for continuing to remember us in your prayers. We love you all!

God is good, all the time!

—Dione

> Oh, give thanks to the Lord, for He is good! For His mercy endures forever.
>
> —Psalm 107:1

Saturday, August 15, 2009, 8:23 p.m.

> The Lord your God in you, the mighty One, will save; He will rejoice over you with gladness, He will quiet you with His love, He will rejoice over you with singing.
>
> —Zephaniah 3:17

Today is Billy and my seventeenth anniversary. In some ways it doesn't seem like it has been seventeen years, and in others it seems like we have always been together. We met around the time Billy turned fifteen and I turned sixteen. We have been together pretty much ever since then. Billy has always said that God put us together since he was born and raised in Missouri and I was born in Denver, lived in Nebraska until I was fourteen, and then lived in Wichita, Kansas, for nine months before moving to Missouri.

We have enjoyed and been blessed in our seventeen-year marriage. There have been ups and downs, as in everyone's marriage, but we have never had a real fight or major argument and have grown closer and love each other more with each passing year. We think so much alike that when one of us says, "I have been thinking about such and such or that we should do this or that," the other one will say, "I was just thinking the same thing." It can be a little strange at times.

Thanks to Linda for spending the evening with us and bringing some yummy Mexican food! Levi was very happy to get his nachos.

Billy is feeling pretty well, and he enjoys visiting, so if you would like to stop in, just let us know. We would love to see you!

As always, we are very thankful for and blessed by your continued prayers and encouragement. We love you all!

God is good, all the time!

—Dione

Monday, August 17, 2009, 8:17 p.m.

> Now to Him who is able to keep you from stumbling, and to present you faultless before the presence of His glory with exceeding joy, to God our Savior, who alone

is wise, be glory and majesty, dominion and power, both now and forever. Amen.

Jude 24-25

Faultless—Don't let your circumstances or failures discourage you. Your spiritual victory is not based on your wisdom or strength or ingenuity. It depends entirely upon Christ and His ability to hold you in His hand. He can cleanse you from every impurity; His forgiveness will allow you to one day stand before Him faultless.[31]

Things continue to go well. Billy is feeling pretty well, and his blood counts were good today. This is his week off of chemo, and he has only two more rounds to go. At least that is the current plan. We have an appointment with Dr. R on August 31, and we will discuss options at that time.

When I was talking to Libby today, I found out that Dr. F has been out sick for a week. When I call her later in the week to check on Billy's next blood draw, I will see if Dr. F is back. I told her that we just want to know whether to plan on radiation when we come back down. Hopefully Dr. F will be back to work before long and we can find something out so we know what to plan for when we go back.

Thank you all for the continued prayers, encouragement, and support. It is such a blessing and encouragement to have all of you out there praying for us. We have really seen prayers answered, and I know that Billy doing so well has a lot to do with all the prayers. Thank you! We love all of you!

God is good, all the time!

—Dione

[31] Ibid., pg. 1507

> Oh, give thanks to the Lord, for He is good! For His mercy endures forever.
>
> —Psalm 107:1

Tuesday, August 18, 2009 8:30 p.m.

> Therefore we also, since we are surrounded by so great a cloud of witnesses, let us lay aside every weight, and the sin which so easily ensnares us, and let us run with endurance the race that is set before us, looking unto Jesus, the author and finisher of our faith, who for the joy that was set before Him endured the cross, despising the shame, and has sat down at the right hand of the throne of God.
>
> —Hebrews 12:1-2

> Faith—Faith is demonstrated through action. Sometimes faith results in incredible victory, healing, and miraculous deliverance. Other times it is expressed by confidence and peace in the presence of continued pain, suffering and rejection. Genuine faith perseveres in both trial and triumph.[32]

Billy has felt pretty well today. The air conditioner was replaced today, and the new one works much better. Billy and I stayed at the house since the guys were replacing the AC, but the kids took advantage of the nice day and went down to the creek. They met up with Bill, Kay, and two of their grandkids for a weenie roast and playing in the creek. They had a really good time.

32 Ibid., pg.1470

We had a nice visit with my sister and her boys this afternoon. The boys start school tomorrow and my sister had today off, so they came out to visit for a little while. I think everyone enjoyed the visit.

Thank you all for your continued prayers, encouragement, and kindness! We love you all!

God is good, all the time!

—Dione

> Oh, give thanks to the Lord, for He is good! For His mercy endures forever.
>
> —Psalm 107:1

Thursday, August 20, 2009, 8:52 a.m.

> This is my comfort in my affliction, for Your word has given me life.
>
> —Psalm 119:50

> Life—God's word does not simply provide devotional thoughts. It brings us to Him and He gives us life.[33]

Yesterday was a pretty full day. Kaylyn had a pretty challenging day, but she handled it like the together young lady she is. We are so very proud of the responsible young lady Kaylyn has grown into. I think anyone who knows her understands just how special she is.

Max passed his tests for his learner's permit! We have another driver in the house, although one of us has to be in the vehicle with him. He was pleased that he passed the first time. He was nervous when he was doing

33 Ibid., pg. 720

the part of the test where he had to look into the little machine and tell the guy which side the light was flashing on and then what road signs he saw. The young police officer (he was wearing a uniform like an officer, so I assume he was) who was doing that part of the test had a fun personality, and he saw that Max was nervous, so he played with him a bit. He had Max look into the machine deal and had him read the letters off. Then he told Max to tell him which side he saw the flashing light on, right or left. I was watching Max, and he looked and looked and finally very tentatively said, "Both?" The young man grinned big and said that was correct. I think he knew what he was doing and was playing with Max a bit. Max's picture even turned out well on his permit.

We received a call from the radiation oncology department at CTCA yesterday, and we will be returning to Tulsa this Sunday (August 23). Dr. F is still out sick, but Dr. K (he did Billy's other radiation treatments) came back part time for a few days to get some patients started on their radiation. Dr. K had left CTCA. His last day was August 3. He apparently left on very good terms, and Dr. F was hoping he would eventually decide to come back. Anyway, what all of this means is that we have an appointment with Dr. K on Monday morning, and they will then do the CT simulation and radiation will begin. They will be doing radiation where the neck and shoulders meet. Since we will be meeting with Dr. K on Monday, we will make sure he has seen the X-rays of the ribs as well. We will go down after church on Sunday, and we expect to be there a little over two weeks as they get the radiation done.

We weren't very sure we liked the idea of going back a week early, but after thinking about it, it does work out for the best. This way we should be back by the time I planned to have the kids; start school. Levi has been practicing his handwriting, and Faith has been doing some simple math to start getting back in the swing of things and refresh her memory a little. I think Justin and Cassy were planning to do some math review next week to get them started.

We know that God is in control and everything will work out the way it is supposed too, so we will continue to trust Him to walk us through each day. Thank you all for your prayers, encouragement, and being there for us. We love you all!

God is good, all the time!

—Dione

> Oh, give thanks to the Lord, for He is good! For His mercy endures forever.
>
> —Psalm 107:1

Thursday, August 20, 2009, 9:43 p.m.

> What is man that You are mindful of him, and the son of man that You visit him? For You have made him a little lower than the angles, and You have crowned him with glory and honor. You have made him to have dominion over the works of Your hands; You have put all things under his feet.
>
> —Psalm 8:4-6

While I did laundry and finished up some school things, the kids went with Grandpa Ron and the boat. The kids had a great time and really enjoyed the boat! Thanks, Grandpa Ron!

Billy's blood counts were good again today. They have been doing really well. Thank you all for the continued prayers. I talked to Libby, and she was glad they had things ready for the radiation. She was going to get the prescription for the hospital bed faxed over to the medical supply company, and I will call tomorrow to make sure everything is set for Sunday.

Thank you all for the continued prayers and support. You are all great, and we love you!

God is good, all the time!

—Dione

> Oh, give thanks to the Lord, for He is good! For His mercy endures forever.
>
> —Psalm 107:1

Friday, August 21, 2009, 9:24 p.m.

> By faith Abel offered to God a more excellent sacrifice than Cain, through which he obtained witness that he was righteous, God testifying of his gifts; and through it he being dead still speaks. By faith Enoch was taken away so that he did not see death, "and was not found, because God had taken him" for before he was taken he had this testimony, that he pleased God. But without faith it is impossible to please Him, for he who comes to God must believe that He is, and that He is a rewarder of those who diligently seek Him.
>
> —Hebrews 11:4-6

> Impossible—Regardless of what else you do for God, your life is not pleasing to Him if it is not characterized by faith. You will face situations where you must practice faith in order to live a life that glorifies Him.[34]

Some of the kids and I went into town to pick up prescriptions and some odds and ends today. It was a pretty day to be out and about. I planned to grill hamburgers for supper since it was so nice. Kaylyn volunteered to do it, so she took care of supper for us. She did a good job.

Tomorrow I will do laundry and pack, and then we will head for Tulsa after church on Sunday.

34 Ibid., pg. 1469

Thank you all for your continued prayers and support. We are very blessed by all of you!

God is good, all the time!

—Dione

> Oh, give thanks to the Lord, for He is good! For His mercy endures forever.
>
> —Psalm 107:1

Chapter 17

SUNDAY, AUGUST 23, 2009, 9:18 P.M.

> For this reason I also suffer these things; nevertheless I am not ashamed, for I know whom I have believed and am persuaded that He is able to keep what I have committed to Him until that Day.
>
> —2 Timothy 1:12

We are now back in Tulsa at the Cancer Treatment Centers of America. We arrived around 6:00, and the drive went well. Just after we headed out, I called the medical supply company to make sure the hospital bed would be here when we got here. The guy on call for the weekend was not aware that Billy's bed needed to be delivered, but he asked what time we would arrive. He said it would be in the room when we arrived, and it was.

We are on the third floor instead of the fourth this time, and we are on the other side of the hall from where we have always been, so we have an entirely different view out of our window.

Billy did well with the trip even though he wasn't feeling that great when he got up this morning. He seems to have felt better as the day has gone on, although his ribs are hurting him again from time to time. He has not had to take any extra pain medication and did not have any trouble with the drive, but it did get his attention for a little while this morning and again this evening. We will be asking Dr. K about the rib X-rays tomorrow.

Tomorrow morning is the appointment with Dr. K, and we should get the plan for the radiation schedule. There will also be a blood draw tomorrow because the seventh round of chemo starts tomorrow.

Thank you all so very much for your continued prayers and support. When you think about it, we have come a long way since March, and Billy has made many improvements. We know that prayer has played a major part in that, which means all of you have had a part in it as well, and we are very blessed! Love you all!

God is good, all the time!

—Dione

> Oh, give thanks to the Lord, for He is good! For His mercy endures forever.
>
> —Psalm 107:1

Monday, August 24, 2009, 5:31 p.m.

> But by the grace of God I am what I am, and His grace toward me was not in vain; but I labored more abundantly than they all, yet not I, but the grace of God which was with me.
>
> —1 Corinthians 15:10

We had a good appointment with Dr. K this morning. He took a look at the rib X-rays, and it appears that there are healing fractures. He prefers to have CTs done to get a better look, so when they did the CT simulation this afternoon, they took a CT of the ribs so Dr. K can make the final decision on whether to radiate the ribs as well. He seemed to think they most likely would do the ribs, and they can do them at the same time as the neck area. Billy asked him about the shoulders, so he took a look at some X-rays and an MRI that showed the shoulders. Billy asked how bad the shoulders were and if Dr. K thought they would heal. Dr. K said that the bones still have their shape. They do have a lot of holes in them, and the bone is soft or thin, but he believes they will harden and repair over time. Billy was very glad to hear that.

Dr. K looked at the most recent MRI of the entire spine to determine if any other areas need to be radiated. He was showing us how there is at least a little cancer in every vertebra in Billy's back. We got a bit of a kick out of him. As he was looking at it and pointing out the cancer, he said, "Hmm, it's a mess." You have to love an honest doctor who speaks a language we can understand. He said that the spine is very fragile right now, and as far as Billy's exercise and activities, walking is about the most physical thing he should do. However, he did not see any other areas that should be radiated at this time. He said we will keep an eye on it and if Billy has any new areas of pain or nerve issues, then they will take another look.

All of that is to tell you that the CT simulation was done today, and it will take them a little while to get everything set up and ready. They had to make a special mask thing they will put over Billy's face and head to hold his head perfectly still. If they do the ribs, they will do them at the same time, and radiation will begin on Wednesday. There will be ten days of radiation, and they cannot do it on the weekends or Labor Day, so if all goes well, with no delays due to low counts, the last day will be September 9, so we will see how it all goes.

Billy's blood counts were good today, so we will begin the seventh round of chemo this evening.

We are very thankful for your thoughts and prayers. We love you all!

God is good, all the time!

—Dione

> Oh, give thanks to the Lord, for He is good! For His mercy endures forever.
>
> —Psalm 107:1

Tuesday, August 25, 2009, 9:34 p.m.

> When you are in distress, and all these things come upon you in the latter days, when you turn to the Lord your God and obey His voice "(for the Lord your God is a merciful God), He will not forsake you nor destroy you, nor forget the covenant of your fathers which He swore to them."
>
> —Deuteronomy 4:30-31

We had just a quiet day hanging out in the room today. Billy took his Decadron yesterday after lunch. It is a good thing he only takes it twice a week during the chemo weeks because we never know what it might do. Sometimes he gets the munchies and just eats and eats, other times he has trouble going to sleep that night, and sometimes he goes to sleep okay but keeps waking up. Last night it kept him awake. I think this is the worst it has been as far as that goes because as he was awake until almost 3:00 a.m. This morning when he took his pain medication at 7:00 he decided he was ready to get up, but by 8:30 he was getting a bit sleepy and by 9:00 he was dozing. He slept off and on most of the day, but it doesn't look like that is going to affect his sleeping tonight because he is getting sleepy again.

He is scheduled to begin radiation tomorrow afternoon. It will be good to get that started. He will then have radiation once a day, Monday through Friday for ten days, unless his counts drop. If his counts drop too much, they won't be able to do the radiation until they come back up, so we will have to see how it goes. He is taking his chemo every evening right now.

Our prayers are that radiation will go well and his counts won't drop too much. Just to give you an idea of how many prayers have been answered, I will just mention a few things:

- On Sunday, March 29, Billy was admitted to the ICU with pneumonia, and his mental status was altered. He was in pretty bad shape, and we have learned since then that they really didn't know at that time if he would survive. He was in the ICU for four days and then moved to a regular floor. During the time he was in ICU is when his right hand really deteriorated, and he basically lost the use of it. Thanks to your prayers and God's goodness, he was released as an outpatient in just under a week.

- After beginning his radiation and chemo, he basically quit eating and was losing more weight and not regaining his strength. Prayers went up, and again God was good. Billy has been eating well for the most part ever since and has been getting stronger as time goes on.

- When we arrived back in March, they confined Billy to a wheelchair, which was very hard for him to deal with. Prayers continued to be offered up, and just two weeks after being very upset about being told he would have to continue using the wheelchair, a metastatic bone survey was done and it was decided he could get out of the wheelchair. Again, that was an answer to prayer.

- After basically losing the use of his right hand altogether, you all continued to be faithful in your prayers, and as always, God was good. That right hand began to improve and continues to improve. Believe me, it has come a long way since he was in patient back in March. He can't really sign his name yet, but he can print numbers and letters quite well, and his typing is improving with it as well. He is also regaining some strength in it and is now able to pick things up.

- His blood counts have now held for seven weeks! Amazing!

- One of the things I find quite amazing and believe it is all because of God's goodness and your prayers is that Billy has continued to remain healthy (has not even caught a cold since he had pneumonia) through all of this, and the kids and I have remained healthy as well. When you think about it, that is truly God's grace and definitely answered prayers.

I thought it was a good time to count some blessings and take a look at some answered prayers. Thank you all for your continued faithfulness in keeping Billy and our family in your prayers. We love you all!

God is good, all the time!

—Dione

> Oh, give thanks to the Lord, for He is good! For His mercy endures forever.
>
> —Psalm 107:1

Wednesday, August 25, 2009, 9:56 p.m.

> He who dwells in the secret place of the Most High shall abide under the shadow of the Almighty. I will say of the Lord, "He is my refuge and my fortress; My God, in Him I will trust."
>
> —Psalm 91:1-2

It was pretty warm here today, but it is supposed to be cooler, with a very good chance of rain tomorrow. They could use the rain around here, so it would be good. They served supper outside tonight in their picnic area. They had a Luau theme, and the food was very good. We did eat inside because it was still pretty warm outside at supper time.

Radiation began today, and they are doing Billy's ribs as well as the neck area. They are hitting the ribs from six different directions and the neck from five directions.

Chemo continues, and Billy will have a blood draw tomorrow. We want those counts to continue to stay up so he can continue not only the chemo but the radiation as well.

Thank you for the continued prayers. We love you all!

God is good, all the time!

—Dione

> Oh, give thanks to the Lord, for He is good! For His mercy endures forever.
>
> —Psalm 107:1

Thursday, August 27, 2009, 7:23 p.m.

> I wait for the Lord, my soul waits, and in His word I do hope.
>
> —Psalm 129:5

> My Soul Waits—There is no point in rushing ahead with our lives if God does not go with us. It is always better to wait on the Lord than to proceed without Him.[35]

Billy's blood counts were good today, so radiation and chemo continue. Billy took his Decadron today. We will see what it does this time and how late it keeps him up.

Billy will have radiation again tomorrow, and then Saturday and Sunday will be pretty quiet. We are going to go out to eat on Saturday, and Billy thought we would go get ice cream on Sunday. Other than that, I will do the laundry, and that will be about it for the weekend.

Thank you so much for your continued prayers and for checking in to see how things are going. We love you all!

---

35 Ibid., pg. 727

God is good, all the time!

—Dione

> Oh, give thanks to the Lord, for He is good! For His mercy endures forever.
>
> —Psalm 107:1

Friday, August 28, 2009, 8:35 p.m.

> Let us hold fast the confession of our hope without wavering, for He who promised is faithful.
>
> —Hebrews 10:23

Billy went down for his radiation this morning, and I stayed in the room to wait for his chemo to be delivered (this will get him through his last round). His radiation was at 9:45, and yesterday he was done by 10:10. At 10:30 this morning he wasn't back, and I was beginning to wonder about him. He didn't take his phone because he can't have it on him during the radiation. I was debating whether to go down and see what was going on when the phone in the room rang. It was around 10:45, and it was Billy. He was in the lobby and told me to just come down.

I went down, and we got coffee and went to sit outside. He was delayed this morning because the girls who do the radiation were concerned about what appeared to be a reaction of some kind on his chest and shoulders. They figured it was from the mask they put on him because there is mesh that goes across his chest and shoulders. They wanted him to see the radiation oncologist's nurse practitioner, Veria, but she was backed up, so they said to come back at around 1:00. The area does not hurt or itch. It is just red.

We saw the nurse practitioner this afternoon, and she was not too concerned. She gave us some cream to keep on it, and the two-day break from radiation over the weekend should help. Billy didn't think it was a big deal, but the radiation nurses are very protective of their patients (as are all the nurses), and they insisted he had to see Veria about it. Veria really wasn't any more concerned than Billy but said that we do need to keep the cream on it and watch it.

Monday will be a busy day that begins early. We will have to be down in the clinic by 7:45 for the appointment with Dr. R. This should be an interesting appointment because we will discuss options for when the eighth round of chemo is finished, and we will also go over the test results that tell us where things are at with the cancer. We are a little nervous about this appointment because we are not sure what the next step might be after the eighth round of chemo. Will there be some kind of maintenance dose of chemo from time to time (just a thought we have had)? Will we just come back every three months or so for tests and go from there? Or is there something else? We just don't know, and sometimes the unknown is the hardest part. I know Billy has been thinking pretty hard about what the future might hold while I have been trying not to think about it too much. Hopefully some of the unknowns will be answered on Monday.

After the appointment with Dr. R on Monday, Billy will have radiation. Then we will go to the infusion center for his Zometa. He will have his port accessed and a blood draw done on Sunday evening. After his Zometa, he has an appointment with pain management. It will be a busy morning. We have seen Dr. R's nurse in the clinic area a couple of times this week, and when we saw her yesterday, she wanted to know when our appointment with Dr. R is. She had seen us earlier in the week and was watching for our appointment but hadn't seen us on the schedule. Billy told her his appointment is at 7:45 Monday morning, and she said that is very early, since she gets here about 7:40 and we see her first. She told us that if she is a little late, to cut her some slack. Of course Billy gave her a hard time, but she gives it right back. She is a sweet little thing and always very happy (like pretty much everyone here). She has been really pleased with how well Billy has done. As with everyone else, she was worried about him for about the first month we were here.

Thank you all for checking in and for your prayers. In some ways it seems like it has been a very long year, and then other times it is hard to believe August is basically over. We will continue to take it one day at a time and walk through each day with the Lord right beside us. Love you all!

God is good, all the time!

—Dione

> Oh, give thanks to the Lord, for He is good! For His mercy endures forever.
>
> —Psalm 107:1

Saturday, August 29, 2009, 9:59 p.m.

> God is my strength and power, and He makes my way perfect.
>
> —2 Samuel 22:33

> Therefore do not worry about tomorrow, for tomorrow will worry about its own things. Sufficient for the day is its own trouble.
>
> —Matthew 6:34

It has been a very pretty and quiet day. I got the laundry done, and we went out to eat. We also went to Target and picked a few things up. Billy has felt pretty good today, and not much is going on. The red area on his chest and shoulders has gone away. It had faded a lot by bedtime last night, and tonight it is gone.

It will be quiet again tomorrow. I think we may watch a couple of movies we brought along, and Billy said we would probably go get ice cream. Then tomorrow evening he will get his port accessed and blood drawn in the infusion center. We may sleep in a bit tomorrow since we have to be up early Monday.

Round seven of chemo continues, and so far so good. Thank you all for your support and prayers. Also, thanks to Brenda, Robert and Stacey, and Bill and Kay for keeping the kids this week. They had a good time and really enjoyed their week. We love you all! Thanks for checking in.

God is good, all the time!

—Dione

> Oh, give thanks to the Lord, for He is good! For His mercy endures forever.
>
> —Psalm 107:1

MONDAY, AUGUST 31, 2009, 6:43 P.M.

> I cry not to the Lord with my voice; with my voice to the Lord I make my supplication. I pour out my complaint before Him; I declare before Him my trouble. When my spirit was overwhelmed within me, then You knew my path. In the way in which I walk they have secretly set a snare for me.
>
> —Psalm 142:1-3

> You Knew My Path—We are sometimes overwhelmed by our circumstances. But though life bewilders us, God sees clearly what lies ahead for us. He knows where He intends to lead us.[36]

[36] Ibid., pg. 733

This evening we are trying not to think too far ahead and take it one day at a time. We are just walking with the Lord and trusting in Him because He knows what He has in store for us.

We did not go out for ice cream yesterday because Billy was not feeling very well. At about 4:00 I took his temperature, and he was running a fever, so we went to the infusion center early (he was to have a blood draw there yesterday evening). They did a chest X-ray (it was clear), took blood for cultures, gave him fluids, and ended up giving him antibiotic as a precaution. We were able to come back to the room because his fever came down.

We had an appointment with Dr. R first thing this morning, and while the news was not what we were hoping for it, could be worse. The Revlimid is not going to achieve remission. While the cancer cell count has continued to come down, it seems to have leveled off. It is now at thirty-one cancer cells to every three good cells. Dr. R is doing some more blood tests. We will do a twenty-four-hour urine capture tomorrow, and they did a metastatic bone survey today. We will meet with Dr. R again on Friday to discuss where to go from here. He said that we need to hit the cancer hard now before it starts getting a hold and climbing again. He said that there are other drugs that work for this cancer, so we need to find one that will put it in remission. He is planning to have something figured out when we meet with him Friday.

After the appointment with Dr. R, we went to the infusion center for Billy's Zometa. The nurse told us that the blood cultures grew out gram negative rods, and we needed to talk to the infusion doctor. The infusion doctor told us that the antibiotic the doctor started Billy on last night is the one needed for this infection, which explains why his fever broke in the night and has not been back. The doctor said if his fever comes back, if he is chilling, if he just isn't feeling well, or if something new comes up, we are to go back to the infusion center. He thinks the antibiotic will take care of it and Billy will do fine.

Thank you all for your continued prayers. We are very blessed by your prayers, encouragement, and support. Thanks for hanging with us and checking in. We love you all!

Specific prayers for the next several days are

- that the antibiotic works to clear up the infection;
- that his blood counts stay high enough for radiation and chemo to continue. They are lower than normal but so far still high enough to continue the radiation and chemo;
- wisdom for Dr. R in determining the best treatment from here; and
- protection for Billy's bones because they are very fragile and of great concern.

God is good, all the time!

—Dione

> Oh, give thanks to the Lord, for He is good! For His mercy endures forever.
>
> —Psalm 107:1

Tuesday, September 1, 2009, 8:00 p.m.

> Great is our Lord, and mighty in power; His understanding is infinite. The Lord takes pleasure in those who fear Him, in those who hope in His mercy.
>
> —Psalm 147:5, 11

> The Lord Takes Pleasure—God is pleased when people reverently submit to Him. Our humble surrender to His will brings Him pleasure, because in yielding we are inviting Him to pour out His loving mercy on us.[37]

Billy is feeling quite a bit better today compared to the last couple of days. It was a beautiful day, and we sat outside for a while this morning.

---

37 Ibid.,pg. 736

Then we went out for ice cream this afternoon. Radiation was done this morning, and it was a pretty quiet day.

Thank you all for your support, encouragement, and prayers. This seventh round of chemo ends on Sunday, and there are five more doses of radiation.

Prayers continue to be

- that the antibiotic clears up the infection and Billy stays healthy;
- that the blood counts continue to be up enough to continue chemo and radiation;
- wisdom for Dr. R and other doctors to find the best plan for Billy; and
- continued protection for Billy's bones.

We continue to be thankful and blessed by all of you. We love you all! We will be praying for all of you to stay healthy and ask that you would all pray for each other as well.

God is good, all the time!

—Dione

> Oh, give thanks to the Lord, for he is good! For His mercy endures forever.
>
> —Psalm 107:1

Wednesday, September 2, 2009, 8:26 p.m.

> Seek the Lord and His strength; Seek His face evermore! Remember His marvelous works which He has done, His wonders, and the judgment of His mouth.
>
> —1 Chronicles 16:11-12

> The Lord will guide you continually, and satisfy your soul in drought, and strengthen your bones; You shall be like a watered garden, and like a spring of water, whose waters do not fail.
>
> —Isaiah 58:11

There wasn't too much going on today. Billy had radiation this morning and then rested for the rest of the day. He napped a couple of times today. With the radiation and chemo, along with not feeling very well for a couple of days, he is a bit fatigued. He was feeling okay today, other than needing some extra rest.

Tomorrow he will have a blood draw and radiation, and then we will meet with Dr. R again on Friday.

Prayers:

- For protection for the bones
- That the blood counts stay good
- For a new plan to achieve remission

Thank you to everyone who has left notes of encouragement, and as always, we are very grateful for the prayers. We love you all and thank you for checking in.

God is good, all the time!

—Dione

> Oh, give thanks to the Lord, for He is good! For His mercy endures forever.
>
> —Psalm 118:1

Thursday, September 3, 2009, 9:12 p.m.

> These things I have spoken to you, that in Me you may have peace. In the world you will have tribulation; but be of good cheer, I have overcome the world.
>
> —John 16:33

> But Jesus looked at them and said to them, "With men this is impossible, but with God all things are possible."
>
> —Matthew 19:26

Well, Billy's blood counts are pushing the low side. I called Libby to check on them, and she said they were getting low but should be okay. She was going to check with Dr. R to make sure and let us know if it was a problem. As I said, it is pushing the low side, but he is able to take his chemo this evening. We will see about the rest of this cycle when we talk to Dr. R in the morning.

Billy has done quite a bit of napping today. As he gets close to the end of a cycle of chemo, he is usually more tired, and when you add in radiation, it wears him out. Because of this, he just rested most of the day. We had talked about going to Target this afternoon, but he wasn't up to it today. We may go tomorrow.

Thank you for your continued prayers, support, and messages. They all mean a lot to us, and we are blessed to have you all out there pulling for us. We love you all!

Prayers:

- That Dr. R will have a plan for us tomorrow
- That his counts continue to hold without dropping too much
- For Billy's overall health
- For health for each other and your families

We will be keeping all of you in our prayers as well.

God is good, all the time!

—Dione

> Oh, give thanks to the Lord, for He is good! For His mercy endures forever.
>
> —Psalm 107:1

Friday, September 4, 2009, 4:00 p.m.

> But my eyes are upon You, O God the Lord; In You I take refuge; do not leave my soul destitute.
>
> —Psalm 141:8

> Keeping our eyes on God is our only sure protection in difficult circumstances. A crisis is not the time to focus on people; our safest refuge is always in God.[38]

The appointment with Dr. R went pretty well this morning. The metastatic bone survey revealed that things are pretty much the same with the bones, which is actually good, since that means they are no worse. Billy's blood counts are just a bit too low to continue chemo, so Billy will not be taking any more Revlimid. He had three days left in this cycle, but he will not be taking them. All of the blood work and urine tests revealed that his kidneys are functioning normally. Dr. R says that is amazing. God is good! The cancer is basically staying steady. The cancer numbers have not gone up, and they have not gone down. Dr. R was relieved by this because it means the cancer is not rebounding, which he was a little concerned about. Dr. R needs more time to go through the huge amount of information he has on treating multiple myeloma. He is giving Billy two weeks off of chemo, and we will meet with him again on September

---

38 Ibid., pg. 733

18. We won't know how long we will need to stay until we find out what Dr. R's plan for treatment is.

While Dr. R was reviewing the blood work, he found the blood culture report from Sunday when Billy had a fever. Both cultures (from the arm and the port) came back positive for salmonella in the blood. Dr. R said this means Billy has blood poisoning, and while he has been doing well on the antibiotic he is on, Dr. R wanted the infectious disease department to be consulted to make sure the antibiotic is the correct one, and he didn't feel seven days was enough. We got a call about lunch time that Billy is on the correct antibiotic, but he needs to be on it longer to make sure the infection clears up. They called it into the pharmacy, and I picked it up, so we are set.

The radiation is staying on track, so it looks like we will still be going home Wednesday, September 9 and will then return on September 17 for our appointment with Dr. R on September 18. Because of the H1N1 virus as well as it just being the time of year for flu and other illnesses, we are to pretty much stay home unless we have to get out. This means we are not to go to church, and I will be doing the grocery shopping and running other errands shortly after we get home. I will try to pick up everything I can so we can avoid going to the store. This will be hard for the kids as well as for Billy and me because they will not be able to go to church either. Homeschooling has an advantage because the kids will be staying home (other than Kaylyn working) with us, so they won't be bringing stuff home with them. While we don't want any of us to get sick, it can be very dangerous for not only Billy but also Levi. We will be able to have visitors (as long as they are healthy) and go to other people's homes (as long as no one in the house is sick), but we are to avoid groups of people.

The kids and I are supposed to start helping cook the Wednesday-evening meals at church in a couple of weeks, and Billy and I are trying to figure out a way that we can still help. We are thinking that I will take kids in and help cook and then we will leave before everyone gets there and the serving starts. Some of this may sound like we are being overprotective or taking drastic measures, but this is something we really need to do to protect Billy and Levi. Besides, the doctor told us this is what we need to do.

Thank you all for your continued prayers, messages, and support. You continue to bless us with all that you do, and prayers are being answered.

Prayers:

- That radiation is completed without a delay so we can go home for a few days
- That Dr. R is able to come up with a good plan for Billy
- That we all stay healthy, but especially Billy and Levi
- That Billy's infection clears up without any complications

Continue to pray for each other to stay healthy, and we will be praying for all of you as well.

God is good, all the time!

—Dione

> Oh, give thanks to the Lord, for He is good! For His mercy endures forever.
>
> —Psalm 107:1

Sunday, September 6, 2009, 11:46 a.m.

> When He had called the people to Himself, with His disciples also, He said to them, "Whosoever desires to come after Me, let him deny himself, and take up his cross, and follow Me, For whoever desires to save his life will lose it, but whoever loses his life for My sake and the gospel's will save it."
>
> —Mark 8:34-35

> Deny Self—You cannot follow Jesus if you have not first taken up your cross and given up your right to your life. You will never be able to take up your cross if you remain self-centered rather than God-centered.[39]

Billy is feeling pretty well. It is very quiet around here because many of the patients went home for the long weekend. Billy did get his pneumonia shot yesterday, and they checked his vital signs. All was good. There was no sign of fever, so the antibiotic is taking care of the infection in the blood.

We had planned to let the kids go to church today, but after much discussion and thinking, we felt since the kids are healthy, it would be best to start keeping them home now. It was a very hard decision to make because the kids love their church family and love going to church. I have to say we are amazed and very proud of how they are handling all of this. They did not complain or pout or anything. They seem to understand that while this all seems drastic, it is what the doctor has recommended and what we need to do for now. I know everyone thinks their kids are great (and they should), but we sure have great kids! We love them so much!

Speaking of the kids, today is Justin's twelfth birthday. He chose to wait until we get home for us to give him his birthday present (as did Cassy). Justin was born just before 5:30 a.m. Justin was the only one of the kids we had not settled on a name for when he was born. We had thought of names, but the ones I came up with Billy didn't care for, and I didn't care for the ones he came up with. As soon as Justin was born, the first thing I said was, "Oh no, we don't have a name!" The nurses found that funny and assured me it was okay and really not that unusual. I knew Mom was waiting for us to call with the news of his birth, but I wouldn't let Billy call anyone until we named him. It took almost an hour, but we got it done. We love you, Justin!

Thank you all for your continued prayers, support, and encouragement. We are very blessed and grateful for all of you. We love you!

---

[39] Ibid., pg. 1196

Our prayers continue to be as before, including praying for each other's health. We will continue to keep all of you in our prayers.

God is good, all the time!

—Dione

> Oh, give thanks to the Lord, for He is good! For His mercy endures forever.
>
> —Psalm 107:1

Tuesday, September 8, 2009, 8:50 p.m.

> But I will hope continually, and will praise You yet more and more.
>
> —Psalm 71:14

> Continual Hope—The righteous never lose hope, no matter how long God's answer takes, no matter how difficult the problem. Because they know God intimately, they continue to hope, praising Him continually as they wait on Him.[40]

We are going home tomorrow! We will only be home for a week before we have to be back to meet with Dr. R, but it will be so nice to be back home! We will head out after Billy's radiation in the morning. We also have to meet with the radiation oncologist, but we should still get headed home by 11:00 or so.

Before I go any further, *happy birthday, Cassy!* Cassy is thirteen today, and that gives us three teenagers. We *love* you, Cassy! Wow, where does the time go! Cassy was our little drama queen. (Max would argue that

40 Ibid., pg. 682

she still is, but that's just an older brother for you.) She has always been full of it and just a lot of fun. She has a very quick wit that will keep you on your toes.

While Billy is feeling okay, the radiation is taking its toll. He has been more fatigued in the last couple of days, and his throat has become quite sore. The sore throat is from the radiation. Dr. K told us that along with the fatigue, the only other side effect would be a sore throat. Unlike most sore throats, it is very low in the throat, and it is bothering Billy quite a bit today. It is odd that as much pain medication as he is on that his throat would hurt that much. I guess it is because of the difference in the kind of pain. While he is still eating, he isn't eating that much. Hopefully getting home and having food he is used to will help. I think we are both a bit homesick, and we are *so* ready to get home and see the kids. I think just being home will help how he feels, and I know being with the kids will help too.

Thank you all for checking and for your continued prayers. We love you all!

God is good, all the time!

—Dione

> Oh, give thanks to the Lord, for He is good! For His mercy endures forever.
>
> —Psalm 107:1

Chapter 18

Thursday, September 10, 2009, 9:17 p.m.

> For I know the thoughts that I think toward you, says the Lord, thoughts of peace and not of evil, to give you a future and a hope.
>
> —Jeremiah 29:11

It is nice to be home! We drove through rain most of the day yesterday but had no problems. I did the grocery shopping today and tried to pick up anything we might need for the next couple of weeks. Billy and I will have to head back to Tulsa on September 17, but we don't know how long we will have to be there this time.

Billy had an appointment with the radiation oncology nurse practitioner after his final radiation treatment yesterday. His white count is still low, but it did come up some over the weekend. They felt okay with finishing up his treatment but cautioned that the count is still low. He told her that his throat was sore from the radiation. She said that will last a couple of weeks but also looked at his throat to make sure there wasn't anything else going on. It was good that she checked because he has thrush and needed medication for it. She called the prescription into the pharmacy there at CTCA, and I was able to pick it up and not delay our trip home. Billy's throat is still pretty sore, but hopefully it won't take long for the medication to help, although the soreness from the radiation will last a while.

The kids and I (except Max) went to church this morning and helped the ladies get the kitchen ready to start cooking Wednesday-night meals next week. Since there were just a few of us meeting at church and we knew everyone was healthy, we were comfortable going to help. Kaylyn worked this morning, so she met us at church when she was done. Then she brought all of the kids home except Justin, because he went grocery shopping with me. We all had a good day, and it was good to see some of the ladies. The ladies also had presents for Cassy and Justin and cake for a snack at around 10:30. It was very nice! Thank you, ladies, we enjoyed the morning!

We are settled in and ready to hang out for a while. I took orders on what everyone wants to eat over the next week or so and picked up groceries accordingly, so they should all be happy with meals.

Thank you all for your continued prayers, support, encouragement, and messages! We are so grateful and blessed by all of you. Thank you for checking in. We love you all!

God is good, all the time!

—Dione

> Oh, give thanks to the Lord, for He is good! For His mercy endures forever!
>
> —Psalm 107:1

SATURDAY, SEPTEMBER 12, 2009, 9:10 P.M.

> Now, therefore, you are no longer strangers and foreigners, but fellow citizens with the saints and members of the household of God, having been built on the foundation of the apostles and prophets, Jesus Christ Himself being the chief cornerstone, in whom the whole building, being fitted together, grows into a holy temple in the Lord, in whom you also are being built together for a dwelling place of God in the Spirit.
>
> —Ephesians 2:19-22

> Together with Christ—In His characteristic orderly way, God fashions His dwelling place. Jesus is the cornerstone and each believer is a building block. The unified, divine temple—the body of Christ—displays God's glory.[41]

Thank you all for checking in, for sticking with us through this adventure, and most of all for your prayers and encouragement! You are all very special to us, and we are blessed by you!

It is so nice to be at home! We have been enjoying the kids, and we have laughed a lot. Those of you who know the kids know that they all have good senses of humor and can be pretty quick witted. It has gotten pretty silly around here several times, and we have loved it! We are just laughing, watching movies and TV (tonight has been bull riding all evening), and enjoying our time together. Since we start school on Monday, we have been letting the kids stay up later than we would otherwise (except Faith since she tends to doze off by 10:00), and we have let them sleep in (except Kaylyn because she has had to work). Tomorrow will begin earlier bedtime.

Billy is still pretty fatigued from the radiation. He doesn't feel too bad; he just feels tired. He has been sleeping in and getting about an hour nap during the day. His throat continues to be pretty sore. He thinks it might be a tad better, but he isn't sure. Since his throat is going to hurt for about two weeks from the radiation, it is hard to tell whether it is hurting from the thrush or the radiation. We continue to doctor it, and the one medication turns the inside of his mouth and tongue a really cool shade of purple. Kaylyn would love to get a picture of his purple tongue, but so far Billy will not let her. She is hoping to talk him into it before he is done with his medication.

I put off folding laundry yesterday and ended up doing two more loads today. I finally got all six loads folded this evening. However, there are still two loads of towels that will need folded tomorrow. Oh well.

---

41 Ibid., pg. 1407

Phone calls and visits are welcome (as long as you're healthy). Billy enjoyed visiting with Joe on the phone this morning. He really enjoys visiting and always has, so if you were thinking of checking in and talking to him for a few minutes or stopping by, it would be welcome. He had hoped to go by Farm Bureau to see everyone this time, but that just isn't a good idea, so hopefully next time.

Prayers:

- That his throat will get to feeling better
- That his counts will be up when we get back to Tulsa
- That Dr. R will have a plan that will work
- That everyone continues to be healthy

Also continue to pray for each other. There are so many dealing with health issues or other complications in life. We all need to remember each other in our daily prayers. We need to support and hold each other up.

We love you all, and we will keep you all in our prayers.

God is good, all the time!

—Dione

> Oh, give thanks to the Lord, for He is good! His mercy endures forever.
>
> —Psalm 107:1

Monday, September 14, 2009, 8:52 p.m.

> For He shall give His angels charge over you, to keep you in all your ways. In their hands they shall bear you up, lest you dash your foot against a stone.
>
> —Psalm 91:11-12

We started school today, and the first day went very well. Yesterday when I asked the kids if they were ready to start school, they said no. If you ask them if they like school, they will tell you no. However, they all jumped right in this morning, and I heard more than one kid say, "I like this." "Mom, did you know . . . ?" "Mom, look at this." There were plenty of smiles, and everyone had something to say about something they learned today. It was a very good school day. Levi came in early this afternoon from playing outside and said he was looking for something to do. I suggested that he could do some school, and then he wouldn't have as much to do later in the week. He said, "Okay," which surprised me a little. He did enough extra today that he will have very little to do on Friday. Guess who likes most of his school but won't admit it when asked?

Billy's throat is feeling much better today. This has worked out really well because he took his Decadron today and has been munching a lot of the day. He hasn't been quite as tired today either. Faith and Levi were very pleased this afternoon. They have a movie they have wanted Billy to watch with them, and he watched it this afternoon. Since they have seen it a few times, they knew what parts were funny and were very pleased that Dad found them funny too.

Thank you for your prayers and encouragement. We love you all!

God is good, all the time!

—Dione

> Oh, give thanks to the Lord, for He is good! For His mercy endures forever.
>
> —Psalm 107:1

Tuesday, September 15, 2009, 8:15 p.m.

> The Lord is my strength and song, and He has become my salvation; He is my God, and I will praise Him; My father's God, and I will exalt Him.
>
> —Exodus 15:2

> I will sing of the mercies of the Lord forever; With my mouth will I make known Your faithfulness to all generations. For I have said, "Mercy shall be built up forever; your faithfulness You shall establish in the very heavens."
>
> —Psalm 89:1-2

We watched *The Passion of the Christ* this evening. Cassy and Justin had not seen it yet but have asked several times if we would watch it with them. I am so very grateful for what Jesus did for us! The Lord has so much for us! I am also very thankful that I know my husband, my children (as well as many family members and friends), and I will meet again in heaven, no matter what this earth holds for us. During the years when we were having our children, some people thought we were crazy (a few knew we were). Some commented on the fact it is very expensive to raise children and because we had so many, we would never have anything. Billy's and my response to them was this: "What does it matter what we have? We are only on this earth for a short time. Eternity is what matters, and while we cannot take our things with us to heaven, we can take our children. We understand that they must make the decision, but we can teach them and guide them and pray that they will accept Jesus as their Lord and Savior." Our children have done that, and while I am their mother and a bit partial, I believe their faith shows in their young lives.

Kaylyn was three years old when she asked Jesus into her heart. She has always been wise and mature for her age. It was one evening when Billy was out of town with work. I had already put Max to bed, and Kaylyn and I were on the floor coloring. She looked up at me and said, "Mom, how do I get Jesus to come into my heart?" I explained it to her, and she said she wanted to pray "right now," so she did. I was not sure a three-year-old really understood what she was doing, but she sure seemed too. A little while later when I put her to bed, I was about to turn the light out in her room when she sat up and said, "Mom, wait, I need to pray again." My thought was, *Oh, I was right. She really didn't understand, and she is going to pray the prayer again.*

Any question about whether she knew what she had done was erased by the prayer that followed. She bowed her head and very sincerely prayed, "Jesus, thank You for coming into my heart. I love You." We talked to her about being baptized, but she was afraid of being dunked under the water. She asked us why you are supposed to be baptized, and we told her that it was because Jesus was baptized and it was a way to tell everyone that you had asked Jesus into your heart. She said that until she was ready to be baptized, she would just tell everyone, and that is about what she did. She was baptized after Max. When she saw that Max could do it, so could she.

Max was not quite five when he asked Jesus into his heart, and he knew he wanted to be baptized right away. All during the service he would ask me every few minutes, "When is it time to go up?" Billy had told him he would go with him, but Max didn't need anyone to go with him. The piano player had barely gotten started on the hymn of invitation when Max actually ran to the front. He was so cute and so very pleased with what he was doing!

Cassy was six when she asked Jesus into her heart. She knew exactly what she was doing and how to do it, but she did need me to go up with her when it was time to go forward to let everyone know and ask to be baptized. On the Sunday morning Cassy was to be baptized, it was discovered that the heater had not been turned on in the baptistery, and she was given the option of waiting until the following Sunday because the water was very cold. Cassy was ready and would not wait. She was quite the trooper and was freezing when she came out, but she was grinning from ear to ear (with blue lips).

From the time Justin was two until he asked Jesus into his heart when he was six, Max kept after him. Max knew that to go to heaven you had to have Jesus in your heart, and he worried about Justin. Justin was two years old, and the kids were playing in the backyard when Max came running in panic stricken because Justin had crawled under the fence and was in the pasture. Justin was fine, but Max was freaking out. After getting Justin back into the yard and calming Max down, I got him to tell me what had him so upset. Take into account Max was five when Justin was two. Max was all upset because out in the pasture is our lagoon. It isn't right behind the house—Justin would have to walk a little ways through the pasture to get to it—but still, it is a body of water in the pasture. Max was terrified that Justin would fall in and drown, and because he hadn't asked Jesus into his heart, he wouldn't go to heaven. I tried to explain how little guys weren't accountable yet because they didn't understand. Max, however, took it upon himself to make sure Justin understood that he needed to ask Jesus in his heart.

Cassy led Levi to Christ. She explained things to him over a period of time, and when he really started asking questions, Cassy answered most of them. It was Cassy who led him in the prayer to ask Jesus into his heart. When Levi was ready to go forward and ask to be baptized, he could hardly wait. On the Sunday he decided he was going forward, he started to follow Bro. Brian to the front of the church after the greeting time. I grabbed him and asked him what he was doing. He told me he was going to go tell Bro. Brian that he wanted to be baptized. I took him back to the pew and made him wait, which he did, on pins and needles. I have often wondered what might have happened if I had let him go forward when he wanted to. I didn't let him go because I wasn't sure if it was proper, but as I thought about it later, it would have been pretty cool to start a service out with a decision.

When Faith asked Jesus into her heart, she wanted to be baptized on the same day she went forward to tell Bro. Brian. We told her she could not be baptized that same day because they weren't ready but she could be baptized the next Sunday, which she chose to do even though Kaylyn and Max were with the puppet team and couldn't be there to see it. Kaylyn tried talking her into waiting until they could be there, but she would have none of that. It was time to be baptized, and she already had to wait a week longer then she planned.

I know I have gone on and on, but I am so blessed and thankful for all that the Lord has done.

Billy has felt pretty good today, and his throat is a lot better. We enjoyed my dad visiting this afternoon. At least some of the kids and I are going to go help cook the meal for church tomorrow. We will spend a few hours in the afternoon helping get the meal ready and will then pick up a few things before coming home.

Thank you, Susan, for the offer of books from the library. While we are at church tomorrow, I may borrow a couple to take to Tulsa with me. If I do, I will be sure to fill out a card or leave you a note.

Thank you all for checking in and for your prayers! We love you all!

God is good, all the time!

—Dione

> Oh, give thanks to the Lord, for He is good! For His mercy endures forever.
>
> —Psalm 107:1

Wednesday, September 16, 2009 10:11 p.m.

> The refining pot is for silver and the furnace for gold, but the Lord tests the hearts.
>
> —Proverbs 17:3

> Heart Tests—God will regularly test your heart, but not for His benefit—He already knows its condition. His tests show you what He already sees. He will allow pressure, criticism, temptation, and pain to bear upon

> you so you see what lies within you. Such tests reveal what you are really like.[42]

Justin stayed home with Billy this afternoon while I took the rest of the kids to help get the meal ready at church. Bro. Brian came out to visit with Billy this afternoon, and Billy really enjoyed the visit. Justin acted as host. When we left, he seemed very pleased to be staying home with Dad.

Faith and Levi really wanted to go with the older kids and me to help at church. Billy told them that they could go, but only if they helped. They were not to go just to horse around and goof off. They both made sure that they helped, and they did a pretty good job. We had a good time in the church kitchen with the ladies. It was so nice to be at church and helping in the kitchen.

Billy and I will head for Tulsa after lunch tomorrow. I called today to make sure Billy's hospital bed will be there tomorrow when we get there, and I was assured that it will be there.

Thank you all for your continued support and prayers. We don't know what the plan will be or how long we will need to be there this time. We should have at least some idea of what will be going on when we meet with Dr. River on Friday.

God is good, all the time!

—Dione

> Oh, give thanks to the Lord, for He is good! For His mercy endures forever.
>
> —Psalm 107:1

42 Ibid., pg. 758

Chapter 19

Thursday, September 17, 2009, 10:22 p.m.

> My flesh and my heart fail; but God is the strength of my heart and my portion forever.
>
> —Psalm 73:26

Everything went well on the drive down, and we made good time, although, it was kind of hard to leave this time. The hospital bed is here, and we are on the fourth floor, which will make the housekeepers happy (at least the fourth-floor housekeepers). We have been on the fourth floor for every stay except this last time, and the fourth-floor housekeepers gave us a hard time for not being on their floor. (They told us before to request the fourth floor.) We have been in this room before.

Billy took his Decadron after lunch today, and that gave him a little more energy for the trip, so he was not as tired when we got here.

After we got registered, they drew blood from Billy's right arm. However, he also had to have cultures drawn from his port, so we had to go to the infusion center and have his port accessed for that. They are checking to make sure the infection he had in his blood is gone. The preliminary report will be in by the time we have the appointment with Dr. R in the morning, but it can take up to three days to get the final report on the cultures.

We will find out in the morning what Dr. R has come up with, and that should give us an idea of how long we will need to stay this time.

Thank you all for checking in and your continued prayers, support, and messages. We love you all!

God is good, all the time!

—Dione

> Oh, give thanks to the Lord, for He is good! For His mercy endures forever.
>
> —Psalm 107:1

Friday, September 18, 2009, 8:12 p.m.

> Cast your burden on the Lord, and He shall sustain you; He shall never permit the righteous to be moved.
>
> —Psalm 55:22

Billy is back on Velcade (an IV chemo drug). Dr. R said that he had several to choose from, but the Velcade has been the most effective with multiple myeloma. There are a few things still up in the air and yet to be decided for sure. The Velcade will be given twice a week for five weeks and then one week off. We do not know how many cycles will be needed—if five weeks will be it or if there will be more. Dr. R did not say, and I am not sure he knows just yet. We think he is waiting to see how things go before determining how many cycles. Dr. R agrees that we need to stay here for the first week to see how Billy's counts do. If all goes well, there is a possibility we will be able to do treatments in Columbia at home.

I e-mailed Kay this morning to get the name of the facility and doctor where Bill is going. I also talked to Linda this afternoon, and she recommended the same facility and gave me the name of another doctor there. I will be giving Dr. R the information on Monday so he can contact them and see if they will be willing to work with him and let Billy do treatments there. If we are able to do treatments at home, it will mean a lot of running because Billy will have to have blood draws on Mondays and Thursdays in Jefferson City and then chemo on Tuesdays and Fridays in Columbia. We figure we can handle the running if we can be home. Like I said, there are several things up in the air, so we will take it one day at a time and see how it all works out. Billy got his first dose of Velcade today.

The cultures taken last night have not grown anything yet. We asked the nurse in the infusion center about it this afternoon when Billy got his Velcade, and she said that it usually takes forty-eight hours. She said if anything grows over the weekend, it throws a red flag and they will call us to get Billy started on treatment right away. When the infection showed up last time, the culture from the right arm was positive in twenty-four hours, so I take it as a good sign that we have not heard anything.

Billy has been a little tired today from the drive yesterday but has felt pretty good. Taking the Decadron yesterday before we left helped some, and they gave him a little more Decadron with his Velcade today. It usually takes him a day or two to completely recover from the drive, but he seems to be doing better than usual today. He is eating well too.

Prayers:

- That Billy's counts hold so he can take the Velcade without any problems
- That Missouri Cancer Associates will be willing to work with Dr. R so we can do treatments and be at home

Thank you for your prayers, support, and messages and for checking in. We love you all! We will be praying for all of you and ask that you would keep each other in your prayers and look out for each other. Thanks!

God is good, all the time!

—Dione

> Oh, give thanks to the Lord, for He is good! For His mercy endures forever.
>
> —Psalm 107:1

Saturday, September 19, 2009, 7:10 p.m.

> Wait on the Lord; Be of good courage, and He shall strengthen your heart; Wait, I say, on the Lord!
>
> —Psalm 27:14

> Wait!—Acting is easy. Waiting is not. Yet strength comes from waiting on God.[43]

We all have times in our lives when we have to wait on something. We may just be waiting for time to pass, as children do when they are waiting for their birthdays or Christmas, or we may be waiting for a decision to be made, or the results of a medical test. No matter what it is, waiting can be hard.

This week finds us waiting to see how well Billy will tolerate the Velcade and if his counts will hold. We will also be waiting to find out if we can do treatments in Columbia. (I will give Dr. R the contact information on Monday.)

We have waited on medical issues before. When Max was two, we waited to see if he had meningitis. He didn't. More than once we waited on test results when Cassy was little and had urinary tract and kidney infections but her symptoms indicated something else going on. One time they were even sure her appendix needed to come out. However, all tests were negative for anything else, and her appendix was fine. We waited all night in the PICU in Columbia with Levi to see if the IV insulin would bring his sugar levels down and keep him from going into a coma,

---

43 Ibid., PAGE NUMBER.

and it did. When Cassy broke her femur, it was at 2:30 on a Tuesday. We waited until 9:00 on Wednesday evening before they were able to do the surgery. The pain Cassy was in was terrible, at times more than she could take, but she made it to surgery. This is not the first time we have been waiting on something since this all started with Billy, but as with all the other things we have waited on, we continue to pray and ask that the Lord to take control and for His will to be done.

Billy and I have talked about it, and we know how we would like all of this to turn out. We are not shy in sharing our desires with the Lord, but we also know that we must allow the Lord to make the decision, and His will that must be done. He will never let us down regardless of how He answers our prayers. He is in control, and we are His.

I am reading *The Hiding Place* by Corrie Ten Boom. I know her story, but I had never read her book. In the book Corrie's older sister talks about how there I isn't one place safer then another place in this world. For some reason, that really struck me. We are safe, no matter where we are or what is going on. As long as we are in the Lord's will, everything will be fine. It may not be fun or happy or even what we really want, but if we just hang on to the Lord, it will be fine, and we will be able to get through anything. Only He knows what the future holds, and only He knows what is best.

Billy is feeling fairly well today and is eating well. He seems to have the munchies today. That is most likely because he had a dose of IV Decadron with his Velcade yesterday, and that was after taking his Decadron on Thursday, so he had an extra dose. Dr. R knows about it and has discontinued the IV Decadron since Billy is taking the oral. Having an extra dose doesn't hurt him a bit; it has just made him hungry.

Prayers continue to be

- that Billy will tolerate the Velcade well and his counts will hold;
- that we will be able to do treatment in Columbia; and
- that everyone stays healthy.

We will be praying for you all as well, and thank you for checking in. Thank you for the support, messages, and prayers! We love you all!

God is good, all the time!

—Dione

> Oh, give thanks to the Lord, for He is good! For His mercy endures forever.
>
> —Psalm 107:1

Sunday, September 20, 2009, 9:53 p.m.

> You are my hiding place; You shall preserve me from trouble; You shall surround me with songs of deliverance.
>
> —Psalm 32:7

> Let Your mercy, O Lord, be upon us, just as we hope in You.
>
> —Psalm 33:22

There is not much to report today. It was a beautiful day outside. Billy didn't get much sleep last night. We both stayed up pretty late. The last time I looked at the clock was at 1:30 this morning. Billy said that he dozed a little but really didn't get to sleep until around 4:00 this morning. He was not hurting, feeling bad, or anything like that. He was just awake. We figure it had something to do with the two days of Decadron.

Since Billy didn't sleep much last night, he slept a good part of today. He has been trying to stay awake since late this afternoon so he can go to sleep tonight and not get his days and nights turned around. He will get Decadron twice a week while he is getting the Velcade, so we will see how it goes.

Tomorrow morning he will have a blood draw and then chemo in the afternoon.

Thank you all for continuing to check in and most of all for your prayers. We have seen many prayers answered and are very thankful. We love you all!

God is good, all the time!

—Dione

> Oh, give thanks to the Lord, for He is good! His mercy endures forever.
>
> —Psalm 107:1

MONDAY, SEPTEMBER 21, 2009, 6:23 P.M.

> Ah, Lord God! Behold, You have made the heavens and the earth by Your great power and outstretched arm. There is nothing too hard for You.
>
> —Jeremiah 32:17

Thank you all for your continued prayers. God is working. (He always is!) This morning we gave Libby the information about the Missouri Cancer Associates in Columbia. This afternoon Libby called to let us know that Billy has an appointment with Dr. V at MCA on Wednesday, September 30. She already faxed Dr. V Billy's medical records, and I will go to radiology in the morning and have them get all of Billy's scans put on discs so we can take them with us. The plan is for us to go home after Billy gets his chemo on Monday. We will then meet with Dr. V on Wednesday and go from there. If all goes well, Billy will be able to get his treatments at MCA with Dr. V overseeing, per Dr. R's direction. That is what we are hoping for anyway.

Billy got his chemo this afternoon. His counts were still good but had dropped some since the first dose of chemo on Friday. His blood pressure was a little high, so the nurse checked with the infusion doctor, who then talked to Dr. R. It is believed that the Decadron could be what is causing his blood pressure to be up a little. Neither doctor was very concerned because it is just a little high. The doctors decided to just watch it and see how it does.

Prayers:

- First, we are very thankful for Libby being able to get us an appointment with Dr. V so quickly and that we are going home.
- That counts will be able to hold so chemo can continue
- That there will be no blood pressure issues

God is good, all the time!

—Dione

> Oh, give thanks to the Lord, for He is good! For His mercy endures forever.
>
> —Psalm 107:1

Tuesday, September 22, 2009, 8:56 p.m.

> One generation shall praise Your works to another, and shall declare Your mighty acts. I will meditate on the glorious splendor of Your majesty, and on Your wondrous works. Men shall speak of the might of Your awesome acts, and I will declare Your greatness. They shall utter the memory of Your great goodness, and shall sing of Your righteousness. The Lord is gracious and full of compassion, slow to anger and great in mercy. The Lord is good to all, and His tender mercies are over all His works.
>
> —Psalm 145:4-9

> I Will Meditate—Understanding God and His awesome works does not come easily. Truly, we will never plumb the depths of God's majesty, but through careful meditation we will grasp something of His greatness.[44]

Billy slept well last night and felt good today. He took his Decadron yesterday, and it made him sweat quite a bit over night. This meant he had moisture under his dressing for his port, and it needed to be changed. Since the port dressing already needed to be changed, we covered it with an aqua guard, and he took a shower before we went to the infusion center for the dressing change. It worked out for the best because as the aqua guard had come loose by the time the shower was over, so the dressing was very wet.

Every time you go to the infusion center for any reason, they take vital signs. Billy's blood pressure is still running a bit high, but he had Decadron again yesterday. Since it was the same as yesterday and the doctors were not overly concerned, the nurse wasn't too concerned either. It will be checked again on Thursday, so we will see how it does.

Prayers:

- That Billy's blood pressure does not go higher, making it a new concern (they will treat it if need be)
- That his counts will hold up through treatment
- That Dr. V at Missouri Cancer Association will agree to work with Dr. R and treatment can be done there

I forgot to mention yesterday that we asked Libby about the treatment cycles. Dr. R had told us that if Billy's counts would hold, he would get Velcade twice a week for five weeks and then one week off. However, he didn't say if there would just be one cycle of five weeks or if there were more planned. Libby checked for us, and at this time Dr. R has not planned any farther ahead than the five weeks. He is going to just see how Billy does with first five-week cycle, and we will go from there.

---

44 Blackaby, *Blackaby Study Bible*, pg. 735

Thank you all for checking in and your continued prayers. We love you all!

God is good, all the time!

—Dione

> Oh, give thanks to the Lord, for He is good! For His mercy endures forever!
>
> —Psalm 107:1

Wednesday, September 23, 2009 9:18 p.m.

> And not only that, but we also glory in tribulations, knowing that tribulation produces perseverance; and perseverance, character; and character, hope. Now hope does not disappoint, because the love of God has been poured out in our hearts by the Holy Spirit who was given to us.
>
> —Romans 5:3-5

It was a beautiful day! Billy and I got out this morning and went to Target. He is very picky about his bottled water and was almost out of his favorite. We also promised the kids some Jelly Belly jelly beans, and Target has a big selection of flavors. We picked those up as well.

Billy slept well last night and is feeling pretty good. He will have a blood draw in the morning and chemo in the afternoon tomorrow. We will also be able to pick up the discs with all of his scans on them. We will take them to the doctor's appointment in Columbia next Wednesday. I need to check with Libby tomorrow and see if we need to make an appointment with Dr. R before we go home. Billy is currently scheduled to see him on Thursday, October 1, but since we have an appointment in Columbia on September 30, we will be cancelling the appointment with Dr. R. When we saw Dr. R on Friday and talked about working it out to see a doctor at home, he told us we could cancel it if need be or see him sooner if needed. I will check with Libby tomorrow and see what we need to do. It may depend on Billy's counts tomorrow.

Prayers:

- That his counts are good for chemo tomorrow
- That things work out for treatment at home
- Remember to lift each other up

Thank you all for checking in and for your prayers. We will keep you all in our prayers. We love you!

God is good, all the time!

—Dione

> Oh, give thanks to the Lord, for He is good! For His mercy endures forever.
>
> —Psalm 107:1

Friday, September 25, 2009, 2:58 p.m.

> Confess your trespasses to one another, and pray for one another, that you may be healed. The effective, fervent prayer of a righteous man avails much.
>
> —James 5:16

> (Blackaby Study Bible) Fervent Prayer—You do not have to be a spiritual giant before God answers your prayer. Yet God expects you to enter His presence with a keen sense

> of need for His involvement in your life. The prayers of a desperate sinner gain God's immediate attention.[45]

We have seen another prayer answered in a *big* way. Yesterday Billy had his blood draw in the morning and was supposed to have his chemo in the afternoon. We were in the infusion center. The nurse was getting everything ready to start his chemo when she checked his counts, and they were just a little low. She called Dr. R to see if he wanted to go ahead with the chemo. Dr. R decided not to give chemo yesterday but instead recheck the counts this morning and see what they did. The nurse really did not expect them to come up in such a short time. We were both pretty discouraged because his counts becoming such an issue so soon in the course of a five-week treatment cycle worried us a bit.

We knew you all were praying about his counts, and we did some heavy praying ourselves. Blood was drawn this morning, and the nurses in the infusion center agreed with us that we would all expect his counts to be okay today. We talked to Libby at about 2:00 this afternoon, and Billy's counts look great today! Not only did they come up enough, but the white count and the ANC (infection fighters) almost doubled! That is amazing! God is good, all the time! They had to reorder the chemo, and Billy will be getting it in about thirty minutes.

Our plan is for Billy to get his chemo on Monday, and then we will head home. The appointment with the doctor in Columbia is on Wednesday. If all goes well, then Billy will begin treatment in Columbia on Friday. If for some reason the doctor there will not work with Dr. River and us, then we will be headed back down here for chemo on Thursday. No one is expecting a problem with the doctor in Columbia working with us. Then we will need to come back to Tulsa October 21 for an appointment with Dr. River and Dr. Axness (the pain doctor). We should only have to stay a couple of days.

Prayers:

- First, thank You, Lord, for bringing the counts back up so chemo can continue!

---

45 Ibid., pg, 1479

- That they will work with us in Columbia
- That Billy's counts continue to stay up

I know there are many who will be traveling and others who are battling illnesses, so let's remember to pray for each other. There are so many who need prayers, and it isn't right for us to keep so many prayer warriors to ourselves. We will keep all of you in our prayers.

Thank you all for checking in and for your prayers! We love you all!

God is good, all the time!

—Dione

> Oh, give thanks to the Lord, for He is good! For His mercy endures forever.
>
> —Psalm 107:1

Saturday, September 26, 2009, 8:41 p.m.

> Blessed is that man who makes the Lord his trust, and does not respect the proud, nor such as turn aside to lies. Many, O Lord my God, are Your wonderful works which You have done; and Your thoughts toward us cannot be recounted to You in order; if I would declare and speak of them, they are more than can be numbered.
>
> —Psalm 40:4-5

Nothing much is going on today. Billy will have his blood draw tomorrow evening and then get his chemo mid-morning on Monday. After chemo Monday morning, we are heading home!

The appointment with the doctor in Columbia is on Wednesday afternoon. We continue to pray that will work out. If it doesn't, we have to be back in

Tulsa by 8:00 a.m. on Thursday. That is not really something we want to do, but we will if we have to. If all works out with the doctor in Columbia, then I have several phone calls to make to get appointments in Tulsa cancelled and rescheduled.

We are so thankful for all of your prayers! We are still amazed with the difference in the blood counts from Thursday to Friday. The fact the nurses really didn't expect to see much of a difference makes it even more amazing. It was truly an answered prayer! Such a drastic change in twenty-four hours impressed everyone. The white count went from 2.5 to 4.7 (normal is 4.0 to 10.0). The count for what Dr. R calls the infection fighters was also a bit too low for chemo on Thursday. It was 1.38 and went up to 3.52. When we talked to Libby yesterday, she was thrilled and very encouraging. She really expects the doctor in Columbia to work with us but also advised us as a precaution not to cancel any blood draws, chemo, or anything here until we know for sure.

We are so very thankful for all of you! Thank you for your prayers and for checking in. We love you and keep you in our prayers.

God is good, all the time!

—Dione

> Oh, give thanks to the Lord, for He is good! For His mercy endures forever.
>
> —Psalm 107:1

SUNDAY, SEPTEMBER 27, 2009, 7:48 P.M.

> Two are better than one, because they have a good reward for their labor. For if they fall, one will lift up his companion. But woe to him who is alone when he falls, for he has no one to help him up. Again, if two lie down together, they will keep warm; but how can one be warm

> alone? Though one may be overpowered by another, two can withstand him. And a threefold cord is not quickly broken.
>
> —Ecclesiastes 4:9-12

> Friendships—The Christian life is not to be lived in isolation. As you link your life with other believers, you will experience God's love and grace through these relationships.[46]

We are very blessed to have so many friends walking with us down this road. Thank you all for sticking with us and for your prayers and support!

I have most things packed, and we just got back from getting the blood draw done. Chemo is scheduled for mid-morning, and then we will head home!

I hope you all have a great start to your week, and we will keep you in our prayers.

God is good, all the time!

—Dione

> Oh, give thanks to the Lord, for He is good! For His mercy endures forever.
>
> —Psalm 107:1

46 Ibid.,pg. 781

Tuesday, September 29, 2009, 8:42 p.m.

> A man's heart plans his way, but the Lord directs his steps.
>
> —Proverbs 16:9

We were able to get Billy's chemo at around 10:00 yesterday morning and headed for home at about 11:45. We arrived home just after 5:00. It is so nice to be home! I think the kids are as glad to have us home as we are to be home.

Billy had a double dose of his Decadron yesterday, which worked out for the best. Traveling on the days Billy takes his Decadron works out well because he doesn't get as tired. He ended up with a double dose because he took it orally before we went to the infusion center and then they had it ordered IV to go with his chemo.

Since we knew Billy wouldn't be ready for bed until fairly late because of the Decadron, we let the kids stay up late with us. Levi and Faith were both in bed by 10:30, but the rest of us stayed up until just after midnight. It was nice.

Faith and Levi were the only ones who had school to do today. The rest of the kids did today's school work yesterday. They were all talking about how long it had taken them and the fact it made for a long day of school, but it helped them pass time. They were really glad they had done it when we let them stay up late, since that meant they were able to sleep in this morning, as did Billy.

We are hoping our plans will come together to stay home for the rest of treatment. However, since we aren't sure, I did not unpack yet. If we are not able to stay home, we will need to be back in Tulsa at 8:00 on Thursday morning. With that said, the more we learn about Dr. V (who we meet with tomorrow afternoon), the better we will feel about this working out.

Prayers:

- Dr. V agrees to work with us!
- That Billy's counts stay up so treatment goes smoothly
- That everyone continues to stay healthy

Thank you all for your prayers and for checking in! We love you all and will keep you in our prayers.

God is good, all the time!

—Dione

> Oh, give thanks to the Lord, for He is good! For His mercy endures forever.
>
> —Psalm 107:1

Chapter 20

Wednesday, September 30, 2009, 10:22 p.m.

> I know that You can do everything, and that no purpose of Yours can be withheld from You.
>
> —Job 42:2

The appointment with Dr. V went well today—at least after a little while it turned out to be a good thing. At first Billy wasn't sure he was going to like Dr. V at all, and my mind was spinning trying to figure out what to think. Thankfully, once he slowed down a little (he was talking super-fast to start with) and we answered his questions about why Dr. R had done things this way or that way, we were able to ask him some questions and became more comfortable with him.

There was a lot of discussion, and Dr. V gave us his opinion on what should have been done with Billy's treatment as well as what he thinks should be done next. The long and the short of it is that he did agree to do the treatment as Dr. R has directed! God is good! However, he also wants to talk to Dr. R about his ideas on what Billy's treatment should be from here on out. Billy and I told him that we had no problem with him talking to Dr. R, and who knows, maybe two heads are better than one. But we specifically asked him if he would do the treatment as Dr. R has directed, and he said that if that is what we want, he will do that. What this comes down to is we will be able to stay home until October 21, and Billy begins his treatments in Columbia on Friday. They will be able to do the blood draw for the CBC just before giving the treatment. If the counts are good, he will get treatment. This means we do not have to go into Jefferson City twice a week for blood draws. We will just go to Columbia twice a week for blood draws and chemo! We will only have a couple of appointments in Tulsa when we go back and should only be there two to three days. If Dr. R and Dr. V talk and come up with something better for treatment, then we will go from there.

We are all thrilled that we will be staying home for a while. I was telling the kids that we will be in Columbia most or all morning Friday, and Faith said, "But you will be home the same day! You won't be gone for a week or two."

We spent the rest of the afternoon and evening (after the doctor's appointment) at church. It was great to be there! Our revival starts on Sunday and runs through Wednesday. This year our revival will be preached by all in-house preachers. We have two retired pastors who will preach, and then Billy and one of our other men who have been licensed but have not been pastors of a church (yet) will also preach. Billy is preaching next Wednesday (October 7) night and has been working on his sermon. We didn't know for sure until today if we would be here for Billy to be able to preach. I will actually unpack tomorrow!

Thank you all for your prayers and checking in. We love you all and keep you in our prayers.

Thank you again for your prayers! God is good, all the time!

—Dione

> Oh, give thanks to the Lord, for He is good! For His mercy endures forever.
>
> —Psalm 107:1

Friday, October 2, 2009, 3:19 p.m.

> And now, Lord, what do I wait for? My hope is in You.
>
> —Psalm 39:7

Today we need prayers for wisdom and guidance. Dr. V called yesterday, and he has talked to Dr. R. Treatment for today was cancelled, and things were rescheduled for Wednesday, October 7. Dr. V thought Billy should have a week's break after the chemo he has had recently, and he has a different idea for treatment. Dr. V told me yesterday that Dr. R agreed to Dr. V's treatment plan. We are to be in Columbia at 8:45 in the morning on Wednesday for a blood draw, and then we will meet with Dr. V to find out what the plan is.

We plan to talk to Dr. R before Wednesday to get it directly from him that he is in agreement with Dr. V. We would also like to hear for ourselves his opinion of Dr. V's treatment plan. Since our plan was just to have Dr. V oversee the current treatment plan, it was surprising to have him basically decide he was going to take over the treatment. We are not opposed to him taking over the treatment if that is what is best for Billy, but there is a lot to think about since everything is changing so quickly, and in some ways it feels like we are starting over.

Billy is feeling good, and we are all enjoying being home together. School is going well, and the kids are great.

Billy enjoys visits and phone calls, so anyone is welcome to stop in.

Thank you to the Farm Bureau family for all the cards and Debbie for the green beans. Fresh green beans are one of our favorites. Justin brought them by this morning. Thank you, Justin. We also want to say thank you to our church family for all of their support in so many ways. You all are the best, and we love you!

Thank you all for checking in and most of all for the prayers. We love you all.

Our heads are spinning a little with all of the recent information from Dr. V and the quick change in things.

God is good, all the time!

—Dione

> Oh, give thanks to the Lord, for He is good! For His mercy endures forever.
>
> —Psalm 107:1

Sunday, October 4, 2009, 10:07 p.m.

> Your words were found, and I ate them, and Your word was to me the joy and rejoicing of my heart; for I am called by Your name, O Lord God of hosts.
>
> —Jeremiah 15:16

> Joy—God's word can bring joy even in the midst of heartache and suffering. Our circumstances can become dismal in an instant, but God's word to us is a source of strength and unquenchable joy.[47]

We have really enjoyed our weekend! We just hung out and enjoyed spending Saturday with the kids. Today was busy but very nice. We went to Sunday school and church this morning. Our revival started this morning. Kaylyn and Max left with the puppet team before church was over because they had a puppet show in Tuscumbia. We came home for about three hours because we had a carry-in meal this evening before our service. We went back into church and helped get ready for the carry-in meal. It was a great day!

Billy is feeling well and is not as tired as he had been. I will call Dr. R tomorrow and talk to him or his nurse to get some questions answered. However, we did some research of our own last night, and from everything we have read, we are finding Dr. R was correct in how he was doing things. We may just have to ask Dr. V to administer the chemo as directed by Dr. R, which is all we wanted him to do in the first place. Everything we have been finding in our research is saying that there is

47 Ibid., pg. 902

no standard of care for multiple myeloma, and the treatment needs to be tailored to the individual based on things like the level of disease, the damage done by the disease, and so on. This is what Dr. R has been doing. Dr. R also gives us all the information, including the positives and negatives of the various treatments, and he will tell us what he thinks would be best. He also recommends that we do our own research and then we are able to make an informed decision about treatment. He does not push or bully because he believes the final decision is up to the patient.

We don't meet with Dr. V again until Wednesday, so we will have a chance to talk to Dr. River and make a decision on how we want to handle the appointment with Dr. V. In the meantime, we will continue to enjoy our time at home and attend the revival at church, with Billy preaching the final night on Wednesday.

God is good, all the time!

—Dione

> Oh, give thanks to the Lord, for He is Good! For His mercy endures forever.
>
> —Psalm 107:1

Monday, October 5, 2009, 11:04 p.m.

> For He Himself is our peace, who has made both one, and has broken down the middle wall of separation.
>
> —Ephesians 2:14

We talked to Dr. R this afternoon. We feel much better about seeing Dr. V and discussing whatever plan he might have. Dr. R said that he had a good talk with Dr. V, and he found him to be very intelligent and knowledgeable. Dr. R said that while the final decision on treatment is ours, he feels that what Dr. V has to offer is something we need to go with. We will meet with Dr. V Wednesday morning and find out exactly what the plan is and where we go from here.

Dr. R said that while there is no standard of treatment for multiple myeloma, each facility or hospital has put together their own standard. Dr. V has a particular way to treat MM, and Dr. R agrees it is something we should do. It appears that the Lord has opened a new door so we will step through and see what we find.

We went to revival again this evening and heard Mark preach. It was a good message, and we enjoyed being there.

Thank you all for checking in and for your prayers and support. We love you all and continue to keep you in our prayers.

God is good, all the time!

—Dione

> Oh, give thanks to the Lord, for He is good! For His mercy endures forever.
>
> —Psalm 107:1

WEDNESDAY, OCTOBER 7, 2009, 12:07 P.M.

> Blessed is the man You choose, and cause to approach You, that he may dwell in Your courts. We shall be satisfied with the goodness of Your house, of Your holy temple. By awesome deeds in righteousness You will answer us, O God of our salvation, You who are the confidence of all the ends of the earth, and of the far-off seas; who established the mountains by His strength, being clothed with power; You who still the noise of

> the seas, the noise of their waves, and the tumult of the people.
>
> —Psalm 65:4-7

> Awesome Deeds—Do not pray to God unless you are prepared to accept His response. His answers are awesome and perfectly righteous, as He is.[48]

We did see Dr. V this morning, but there is currently not too much to report. He decided to let Billy have one more week off of chemo, and Billy is to take his Decadron. We will then begin chemo next week (we see him again Wednesday), and from what we understand, he is planning to do the Velcade once a week (we were doing it twice) and then add the Revlimid back in at a lower dose than Billy was getting before. Any changes that might be made will depend on Billy's counts and response to the treatment. At any rate, it was a good visit with Dr. V, and we are much more comfortable with him and his decisions. We will continue to see Dr. R at the end of chemo cycles or as needed. We are currently scheduled to see him on October 22.

We are getting ready to head for church to help fix the meal for this evening. This is the last night of our revival, and Billy is preaching at 7:00 this evening. We have attended every service, and the Lord has really spoken through all of the preachers, as well as the wonderful music. We were all talking on the way home last night about how even though none of the preachers got together and discussed the verses they were going to preach from or their messages, they all went together. The Lord has really used these men and has given them messages from Him. It is very exciting!

Thank you all for your continued prayers, support, encouragement, and messages. We love you all!

God is good, all the time!

—Dione

48 Ibid., pg. 677

> Oh, give thanks to the Lord, for He is good! For His mercy endures forever.
>
> —Psalm 107:1

Thursday, October 8, 2009, 9:58 p.m.

> And we know that all things work together for good to those who love God, to those who are called according to His purpose.
>
> —Romans 8:28

This is what Billy says concerning this verse in relation to his multiple myeloma: "God is in control, and His will is right. He has promised to use everything for good, but there is nothing that says everything we encounter will be good. God does not cause everything we encounter. Some things are not even allowed by Him but are merely a result of the corrupt, sinful world in which we live. God has a plan, and His will is good and perfect. The best we can strive for is to seek His will so He will receive the honor and the glory."

We had a good day yesterday. We went to church at around 1:00 to help fix the meal. Billy went in with us and did some visiting with us in the kitchen and going over his notes for his sermon. He did well preaching and seemed to handle the long day pretty well.

For tonight's update, I am going to give you some information we have not said anything about because we were waiting to see what actually happened. When we met with Dr. V last week (our first appointment), one of the things he was talking about that threw us for a loop was that he believes Billy can have a stem cell rescue at Barnes, and he feels it is the best treatment. That is one reason we really wanted to talk to Dr. R, since the Cancer Treatment Center at Zion, Illinois, said Billy was not eligible. Dr. R told us that since there is no standard of treatment for MM, each facility has its own standard. Dr. R told us that Barnes is an excellent facility, and if Dr. V can get us there to talk to the transplant doctors, it is well worth our time. As always, he told us that the final decision is up to us, but he felt we did need to see what they have to say. If they feel they can do the transplant, we will need to listen to what they have to say and make the decision that is best for us.

When we saw Dr. V yesterday, he asked if we had talked with Dr. R. Dr. V told us that he had talked things over with Dr. R and they were both in agreement that getting Billy to see the transplant doctors at Barnes is well worth it. Dr. V sent all of Billy's records to one of the transplant doctors yesterday and said that we would hear from them by sometime next week. Well, they called today, and we have an appointment with one of the transplant doctors on Tuesday at 11:15. They will draw blood, and then we will see the doctor. We will then go from there. It is one step at a time, and only the Lord knows what the next step is.

Billy's counts were a little low yesterday. That was the biggest reason he didn't get chemo, so our prayers are for counts and wisdom as we talk to more doctors.

Thank you to Maryann for the fresh green beans and new potatoes and also to Ruth for all of the goodies!

Thank you all for checking in, your prayers, and all that you are doing and have done for our family. We are so blessed, and we love you all! We are keeping you in our prayers.

Next week will be interesting. We have an appointment at Barnes on Tuesday, and then we see Dr. V again on Wednesday. We continue to pray for wisdom and guidance. God is in control!

God is good, all the time!

—Dione

> Oh, give thanks to the Lord, for He is good! His mercy endures forever.
>
> —Psalm 107:1

FRIDAY, OCTOBER 9, 2009, 8:54 P.M.

> Trust in the Salvation of the Lord. How long, O Lord? Will You forget me forever? How long will You hide Your face from me? How long shall I take counsel in my soul, having sorrow in my heart daily? How long will my enemy be exalted over me? Consider and hear me, O Lord my God; enlighten my eyes, lest I sleep the sleep of death; lest my enemy say, I have prevailed against him; Lest those who trouble me rejoice when I am moved. But I have trusted in Your mercy; my heart shall rejoice in Your salvation. I will sing to the Lord, because He has dealt bountifully with me.
>
> —Psalm 13

> Where Is God? When God is distant, that is not the time to trust your feelings. Review all God has graciously done for you and said to you, and let that be the standard by which you understand His love for you.[49]

I hope everyone has had a good day. It has been a pretty good day here. Billy has felt good, and he had some of the kids help him organize a couple of the bookcases this afternoon.

Cassy helped me bring in the two big plastic tubs of fall/winter clothes out of the shed, and I went through those. I also went through all of the coats and jackets the kids have, and we now have a couple of boxes of clothes and coats for the Samaritan Center.

---

49 Ibid., pg. 642.

Max, Cassy, and Justin are going to help at the church work day tomorrow, and Kaylyn has to work. I have laundry to get done and school to check, so I will stay busy. Levi and Faith are hoping it won't be raining so they can spend some time playing outside.

Thank you all for your continued prayers and support. We are very thankful and love you all!

God is good, all the time!

—Dione

> Oh, give thanks to the Lord, for He is good! For His mercy endures forever.
>
> —Psalm 107:1

Sunday, October 11, 2009, 7:30 p.m.

> So teach us to number our days, that we may gain a heart of wisdom.
>
> —Psalm 90:12

It has been a nice weekend but quiet. Kaylyn worked Saturday and then went to a wedding, so she was gone all day. When Kaylyn went into work on Saturday morning, she dropped Max, Cassy, and Justin off at church to help with work day, and they spent all morning and afternoon helping.

I checked quite a bit of school work and got a few odds and ends done. Levi and Faith made brownies with peanut butter chips. They were very pleased with themselves.

We all enjoyed church this morning, and then my sister and her two boys came out for the afternoon. Several of the kids spent quite a bit of the afternoon outside while the rest of us spent the afternoon visiting. It was a very nice day!

Even though tomorrow is a holiday, we are going to do school. We will then take Tuesday off since Billy and I have to go to St. Louis for his appointment at Barnes on Tuesday.

Thank you all for your prayers and support. We love you all and keep you in our prayers.

God is good, all the time!

—Dione

> Oh, give thanks to the Lord, for He is good! For His mercy endures forever.
>
> —Psalm 107:1

Tuesday, October 13, 2009, 9:09 p.m.

> But may God of all grace, who called us to His eternal glory by Christ Jesus, after you have suffered a while, perfect, established, strengthen, and settle you. To Him be the glory and the dominion forever and ever. Amen.
>
> —1 Peter 10:11

Okay, let's see if I can explain everything from today and make sense. First, we like the two doctors we met with from the transplant team. I will call them Dr. W and Dr. G. Both Dr. W and Dr. G explained things very well and answered our questions. Now I need to figure out where to start so this all makes sense.

Just so everyone knows, we have talked to the kids and explained all of this to them. One of the hardest things about today was something Dr. R told us, but there are some things you really hope are not true. It is true, the kids know about it, but as we have talked with each other and the kids, God is in control, and *He* has the final say! There is no cure for multiple myeloma (at this time). With just chemo alone, it has been known to be kept in check for around three years or so. A stem cell transplant gives another three years. Without a transplant, Billy's life expectancy is three years, give or take a little. With a stem cell transplant, his life expectancy is six years, give or take a little. Again, God is in control, and we know He can simply heal Billy if He so chooses. Dr. G also told us today that there are a couple of new drugs that are almost approved that can make a difference in treatment, and there could be a major breakthrough in the next few years. God is in control!

Now for the actual treatment information. First Dr. G had the technician draw about fourteen tubes of blood today for all kinds of tests. He also needs a bone marrow sample so he can see exactly what is going on and how much myeloma is in the bone marrow. Dr. G is concerned that Billy's counts have not rebounded or recovered as they should throughout his treatment, and he wants a good look at the marrow to see what is going on. Once he gets all of the test results back, he will put the treatment plan together as to whether to do the transplant sooner or do some more treatments and do the transplant later. When he has the treatment plan in place, we will meet with him again, go over the plan, and make the final decision on whether to proceed.

We have an appointment with Dr. V in the morning, so Dr. G was going to call him and have him do the bone marrow collection tomorrow. There will not be any chemo treatments until Dr. G gets all the test results and decides whether to do more chemo first or move forward with the transplant. Billy is supposed to get his bone builder tomorrow. Dr. G's nurse was going to check with our insurance to see if they will allow Dr. V to do the other tests needed for the transplant (an EKG, an X-ray of the lungs, and a bone scan) or if they have to be done in St. Louis.

Once it is determined that the transplant can be done and we agree to it, the actual transplant is done by first harvesting the needed stem cells for transplant. That will mean a seven—to eight-day stay in St. Louis, but it is outpatient. Billy will have to have shots once a day for four days to increase the number of white cells he is making. On the fourth day, he will get a shot in the morning, and then later in the day, they will place another catheter (like his port) to use just for the stem cell stuff. On day five, he will get a shot, and then they will start harvesting the stem cells. The harvesting will go on for two to three days until they get five million cells, which are then frozen. Whether the transplant is done right away or later on has not yet been decided.

The transplant will proceed by Billy being admitted to Siteman Cancer Center and given very high doses of chemo for two to three days to completely wipe out his bone marrow. Then a day or so later, they will infuse his cells back into him. He will remain in the hospital for two to three weeks while his immune system rebuilds. We will have to stay in St. Louis for another week for them to monitor how he is doing. The time frame is a guide because any complications will make the stay longer. If he responds quickly and his immune system rebuilds quicker than expected, he will be able to come home sooner.

We will continue to take this one step at a time. The current step is to get all of the testing done.

Prayers tonight are that Dr. V can take care of all the needed testing to prepare for the stem cell transplant and that the bone marrow extraction will go well and not cause Billy too much pain or discomfort.

Thank you all for your prayers and for checking in. We love you all!

God is good, all the time!

—Dione

> Oh, give thanks to the Lord, for He is good! For His mercy endures forever.
>
> —Psalm 107:1

Wednesday, October 14, 2009, 10:40 p.m.

We saw Dr. V this morning, and he did the bone marrow biopsy. He promised Billy that he would not feel it, and he would not remember it. He kept his promise. They put Billy under right in the office, and Dr. V extracted the bone marrow in about five minutes or less. The nurse and I then took Billy down the hall in a wheelchair to get his bone builder. It is an IV infusion that takes two hours. Billy was out of it for a while and slept most of the time he was getting the infusion. He has done very well, and the spot where they took the bone marrow is not hurting him. It may be a bit sore tomorrow, but then again, it might not since it still isn't bothering him.

Since we have to do a twenty-four-hour urine capture tomorrow and take it back to Columbia on Friday, Dr. V scheduled an appointment for us to see him again on Friday morning. He said they will have the preliminary bone marrow results back by then and we can go over them. He expects the transplant team to want Billy back in St. Louis next week, but we will see how it all works out.

We will not be going to Tulsa next week. We were scheduled to be back in Tulsa on October 21 for a blood draw and then appointments with Dr. R, Dr. A, and the radiation oncologist on October 22. Dr. V can write the prescriptions for the pain medications and any of Billy's other meds, and that is the reason we were seeing Dr. A. Dr. R just wanted to talk to us after we talked to the transplant doctors, and we can do that over the phone. The appointment with the radiation oncologist was just a follow up from Billy's last round of radiation, and because he isn't having any problems, we can answer all their questions over the phone if need be. It was going to be a quick trip, but Billy, the kids, and I are glad that we don't have to go. We may end up back in St. Louis next week, and if that is what we need to do, that is what we will do.

Thank you for the encouraging messages in the guestbook. After talking to the transplant doctors yesterday, we feel much better about proceeding with this. We really feel the Lord had a reason for closing the door on the transplant through Cancer Treatment Centers of America at Zion but has now reopened it. We will just take it one step at a time and see where we go from here. God is in control, and we trust Him!

Thank you to Bro. John for coming to the Siteman Cancer Center and praying with us yesterday. It was good to see you. Billy has already decided that when we are there for the stem cell harvest, we will take you up on going out to dinner. Thank you for your message, Pat.

When I updated last night, I left something out about our day that was interesting. Bro. John was the pastor of Mt. Olive ten years ago. Billy and I met at Mt. Olive, we were married at Mt. Olive, and all of our kids were born while we were attending Mt. Olive. Anyway, Bro. John is now pastoring a church in the St. Louis area, and when he found out we would be there, he called and then came and prayed with us before the appointment. We had a nice visit, and while we were visiting, another man sitting just a few chairs away asked if we were from Jefferson City. We told him where we were from and found out he is very good friends with Don and Shirley, who attend Mt. Olive, and he goes to church with Bro. John's daughter's in-laws and sees Bro. John's grandson quite often. Jim is a very nice man, and we had a good visit with him again after the appointment with the doctors while we were waiting for more blood to be drawn. It was an interesting day all around.

I have a feeling Billy will sleep in tomorrow. After the bone marrow extraction and his two-hour bone builder infusion, we to church. I helped (a little) with getting the meal ready for tonight, and we stayed through business meeting. Billy went to bed at around 10:30, and he was pretty wiped out. He said his back was done for the day. I wasn't sure he would want to go to the church this afternoon or if he would be up to staying through the evening, but he seemed to do pretty well. We don't have to go anywhere tomorrow, so he can just spend the day resting.

Thank you all for your prayers, support, encouragement, and messages. We love you all and keep you in our prayers. We will keep walking this road one step at a time.

God is good, all the time!

—Dione

> Oh, give thanks to the Lord, for He is good! For His mercy endures forever.
>
> —Psalm 107:1

Thursday, October 15, 2009, 10:17 p.m.

> Therefore I turned my heart and despaired of all the labor in which I had toiled under the sun. For there is a man whose labor is with wisdom, knowledge, and skill; yet he must leave his heritage to a man who has not labored for it. This also is vanity and a great evil.
>
> —Ecclesiastes 2:20-21

> Created for Eternity—Food drink, laughter, and earthly treasures are all temporary pleasures. But God created us for so much more. His kingdom is eternal. Abundant life begins when we submit to Him.[50]

We didn't have to go anywhere today. Kaylyn went to work, but the rest of us just hung out at home. I got five loads of laundry folded and got caught up on checking a lot of the school work.

Thank you to Ken and Joyce for bringing supper and Bro. Brian for showing them the way to our house. It was very good, and not needing to cook supper is one reason I got several things done. Thank you!

We have an appointment with Dr. V at 11:15 tomorrow. He was sure he would have the preliminary back on the bone marrow, so he can go over it with us. We are going to leave early and take all of the kids tomorrow. Kaylyn needs a new pair of cowboy boots, so we are going to Larry's Boots for sure, and then we will see what else we do. Billy thought the drive would be pretty with the leaves changing.

---

50 Ibid., pg. 779

Thank you all for your prayers and encouragement. We love you all!

God is good, all the time!

—Dione

> Oh, give thanks to the Lord, for He is good! For His mercy endures forever.
>
> —Psalm 107:1

Friday, October 16, 2009, 6:14 p.m.

> Now faith is the substance of things hoped for, the evidence of things not seen.
>
> —Hebrews 11:1

The appointment with Dr. V was short and sweet today. He was very pleased with the preliminary bone marrow report. He said that if he didn't already know Billy's diagnosis. He would not have guessed it because the bone marrow looked almost normal. (God is good!) He said that means now is the time to harvest the stem cells and proceed. He expects the transplant doctors to want us in St. Louis by the end of next week to start the process. The transplant doctors will have the bone marrow results and the urine test results on Monday or Tuesday. Dr. V said that if we do not hear from them by Wednesday, we need to call him. He was very excited and is sure they will be moving forward with the next step right away. Dr. V used to work at Siteman as a transplant doctor, so he has a very good understanding of how they do things. We feel God used Dr. R to get things where they are now, and we are very thankful.

We decided since the appointment with Dr. V wasn't supposed to be a very big deal, we would make it a family day out. We had a great time! We didn't do anything very exciting, but we all went and we all enjoyed it. We love spending time with the kids, and they are so much fun! We went to Larry's Boots, and Kaylyn was able to find a new pair of boots and a shirt that looks great on her! She was very pleased. This is the first time she has done any shopping since she started working, at least that I can think of, and she enjoyed it. We than went to the doctor's appointment which only took fifteen to twenty minutes. We went out for lunch and then to Sam's. Like I said, we didn't do anything very exciting, but we all enjoyed it just the same.

Kaylyn, Max, Cassy, and Justin will be gone Saturday and most of Sunday because they are going with our church youth group on a mini mission trip. They will be preparing, serving, and cleaning up a meal at a homeless shelter in Springfield on Saturday. They will be doing the noon meal. They then have a surprise outing in the evening. The kids don't know what it is, but the parents do. I don't know about the rest of the youth, but not knowing what they will be doing is about to drive our kids nuts. They will spend the night at a church and then attend church in Springfield before coming home on Sunday.

Since Levi's birthday is on Sunday and it will just be Faith and Levi home with us on Saturday, we are going to fix Levi's cake. He has requested a turtle cake; he will get his presents from Billy and me. We got him a movie he has really been wanting and a board game. We will spend the day playing games with Levi and Faith and watching movies. It will just be a quiet day with the youngest two. It will be a bit odd to only have two kids at home, but I know Levi and Faith are looking forward to it. We plan to enjoy the day.

Thank you for your prayers and checking in. We love you all and keep you in our prayers.

God is good, all the time!

—Dione

> Oh, give thanks to the Lord, for He is good! For His mercy endures forever.
>
> —Psalm 107:1

Sunday, October 18, 2009, 8:07 p.m.

> Do not withhold Your tender mercies from me, O Lord; let Your loving-kindness and Your truth continually preserve me.
>
> —Psalm 40:11

It has been a very nice weekend. Kaylyn, Max, Cassy, and Justin went to Springfield with our youth group and helped at a homeless shelter part of Saturday. Then they played paintball and went barn swinging. They spent the night in a church in Springfield and went to Sunday school and church down there today. It sounds like the youth group did a great job, and they had a good time.

Apparently Justin should try his hand at bull riding because he set a new record on the mechanical bull at the barn swing place. The old record was something like forty-seven seconds. Justin rode it for fifty-five seconds and then again for seventy-seven seconds. Max managed seventy seconds but couldn't top Justin.

Levi, Faith, Billy, and I had a good time at home yesterday. Faith and Levi helped me make Levi's birthday cake, and we gave him his presents. We gave him the movie *Monsters vs. Aliens* and the original Clue game. He has wanted to see the movie since it was in the theaters, and he loves the Clue game. Levi and Faith have already played it nine times. Billy played and won a game, then Mom and Dad were out yesterday afternoon and Mom played twice, winning both games. I played three games with them yesterday evening. I won one, Levi won one, and Faith won one. I also played one game with them today and Faith won that one, and Levi and Faith played each other some today. Levi tends to accuse too early and misses by one. He has the game figured out, but he is afraid someone will accuse before he does, so he tries to soon. Anyway, the movie and game were a big hit, and everyone had a good weekend!

Billy is feeling well and even worked on his truck some yesterday, although that ended up frustrating him and wearing him out. He drove the truck last Saturday, and it ran fine. However, he tried to start it yesterday and it wouldn't start. It did try to start a couple of times, but then it wouldn't even try. Billy has an idea of what the problem might be. He wore himself out and was pretty frustrated by the time he gave up messing with it. He slept really good last night. He is going to have Max and his dad help him work on it another day.

I will call Cancer Treatment Center tomorrow and cancel all of this week's appointments there. We are also planning to talk to Dr. R later in the week because he is supposed to get copies of all of the tests.

Thank you all for your prayers, encouragement, messages, and checking in. We love you all and keep you in our prayers.

God is good, all the time!

—Dione

> Oh, give thanks to the Lord, for He is good! For His mercy endures forever.
>
> —Psalm 107:1

Tuesday, October 20, 2009 8:47 p.m.

> Blessed is the man who endures temptation; for when he has been approved, he will receive the crown of life which the Lord has promised to those who love Him. Let no one say when he is tempted, "I am tempted by God," for God cannot be tempted by evil, nor does He Himself tempt anyone.
>
> —James 1:12-13

> Withstanding Temptation—God knows what is within our heart, we do not. He will allow us to undergo trials and temptations as a way of bringing to the surface those things in our lives that are impure or ungodly. When we repent of our sin and learn from our failures, we grow into Christian maturity.[51]

It has been a beautiful couple of days! The kids have loved the weather, as have Billy and I. Billy is feeling good and even getting out and doing a few things. Yesterday Billy, Max, and Billy's dad worked on the truck. The problem appears to be the starter, so they took the starter somewhere to be worked on.

Today Billy and I went into town to run an errand, and then we did the grocery shopping for the meal at church tomorrow. Sheri usually does the shopping, but she is sick, so we will be praying that she is feeling better quickly.

Billy has enjoyed getting out and doing something the last couple of days, although it does wear him out much quicker than it used to. Tonight his legs are even a bit tired from all of the walking and standing he's done over the last couple of days.

The kids are doing great, and school is going well. I have school work to catch up on checking again. It is just one of those things that always needs done, like laundry, dishes, and fixing a meal.

We have not heard anything from any doctors, but I did get the appointments in Tulsa cancelled. We are enjoying being at home and doing our everyday stuff. Until we hear from the doctors and things change, we will continue to enjoy our everyday stuff.

Tomorrow we will be at church by 12:30 or so to get the meal started for tomorrow evening. Dr. V told us to call him on Wednesday if we didn't hear from the transplant doctors by then. However, he then said that they may not have all of the test results until Wednesday. We won't be home

---

51 Ibid., pg. 1475

after noon, but they have both cell phone numbers, so if the doctors really need to get a hold of us, they will be able to.

Thank you all for your continued prayers and checking in. We love you all and keep you in our prayers. The flu stuff seems to be going around again, so let's all pray for each other because it can be some pretty nasty stuff.

God is good, all the time!

—Dione

> Oh, give thanks to the Lord, for He is Good! For His mercy endures forever.
>
> —Psalm 107:1

Wednesday, October 21, 2009, 9:40 p.m.

> Blessed be the God and Father of our Lord Jesus Christ, who according to His abundant mercy has begotten us again to a living hope through the resurrection of Jesus Christ from the dead, to an inheritance incorruptible and undefiled and that does not fade away, reserved in heaven for you, who are kept by the power of God through faith for salvation ready to be revealed in the last time. In this you greatly rejoice, though now for a little while, if need be, you have been grieved by various trials, that the genuineness of your faith, being much more precious than gold that perishes, though it is tested by fire, may be found to praise, honor, and glory at the revelation of Jesus Christ, whom having not seen you love. Though now you do not see Him, yet believe, you rejoice with joy inexpressible and full of glory, receiving the end of your faith—the salvation of your souls.
>
> —1 Peter 1:3-9

Billy, Jim (Billy's Dad) and Max worked on the red cars break lines today. They spent a good part of the day working on them and Billy was to worn out to go to church this evening. His back was just too tired and he needed to rest. He is feeling pretty good, he just gets tired out rather easy.

The rest of the kids and I went into church a little after noon to help cook the meal for this evening. Sheri is still sick, so we continue to keep her in our prayers. We had lots of help in the kitchen today. Thank you, Ruth, Garnet, and Candy! Kaylyn and Cassy's desserts turned out really well too. We always have a good time in the kitchen.

We haven't heard anything from the transplant doctors. We really didn't expect to hear from them just yet since they weren't going to have all of the test results until today.

I think Billy, Jim, and Max will finish up the work on the car's brake lines tomorrow. Max doesn't seem to think it will take very long. Not much else is planned for tomorrow, just the usual stuff at home.

Thank you all for your continued prayers and support. We love you all and keep you in our prayers.

God is good, all the time!

—Dione

> Oh, give thanks to the Lord, for He is good! For His mercy endures forever.
>
> —Psalm 107:1

Friday, October 23, 2009, 11:56 p.m.

> And those who know Your name will put their trust in You; for You, Lord, have not forsaken those who seek You.
>
> —Psalm 9:10

Billy is feeling good, and it has been nice to have a week without a doctor's appointment. We still have not heard from the transplant doctors. I need to call Dr. V on Monday to see about getting new prescriptions for Billy's pain meds, so I will let him know that we have not heard anything.

It has been a pretty quiet week, which is fine with us. Kaylyn has to work tomorrow morning, so she is going to drop Max and Justin off at church to help some of the guys work on some new Sunday school rooms. Then tomorrow afternoon, Kaylyn, Cassy, and I are going to do a little shopping with my sister.

Thank you, Sandy and Georgia, for bringing supper last night! We all enjoyed it! We also enjoyed the visit. Come back anytime. Billy loves visiting, and the kids and I enjoy company, so anyone thinking about stopping in is welcome.

Thank you all for your continued prayers, support, encouragement, and messages. We love you all and are very blessed to have such a wonderful support system!

Hold your loved ones close, and be sure to tell them how much you love them. We have no idea how much time any of us have, so we need to be kind to each other and make sure our loved ones know how much they mean to us.

God is good, all the time!

—Dione

> Oh, give thanks to the Lord, for He is good! For His mercy endures forever.
>
> —Psalm 107:1

Saturday, October 24, 2009, 10:13 p.m.

> Then you will call upon Me and go and pray to Me, and I will listen to you. And you will seek Me and find Me, when you search for Me with all your heart.
>
> —Jeremiah 29:12-13

It was a beautiful day! We really enjoyed the sunshine and great temperatures. Kaylyn dropped Max and Justin off to help at church as she went to work this morning, and then picked them up on her way home. This afternoon Kaylyn, Cassy, and I had a good time shopping with my sister. We found a few things and just had a good time being pretty silly at times. If you get Cassy a large caramel coffee, she gets pretty silly and keeps everyone laughing. It seemed to rub off on Dru, which kept us all in stitches for a while. We saw Steve, Linda, Rick, and Joany in the middle of all the silliness. Hopefully we didn't scare them too much.

After getting back from helping at church, Max then helped Billy and Grandpa Jim work on the truck. It sounds like it took a good part of the afternoon, but it is running again!

Thank you for your prayers and for checking in. We love you all and keep you in our prayers.

God is good, all the time!

—Dione

> Oh, give thanks to the Lord, for He is good! For His mercy endures forever.
>
> —Psalm 107:1

SUNDAY, OCTOBER 25, 2009, 8:59 P.M.

> Teach me Your way, O Lord; I will walk in Your truth; unite my heart to fear Your name. I will praise You, O Lord my God, with all my heart, and I will glorify Your name forevermore. For great is Your mercy toward me, and You have delivered my soul from the depths of Sheol.
>
> —Psalm 86:11-13

> God's Ways—God's ways are not our ways. We do not think like He does. God must teach us His ways if we are to live by them.[52]

We enjoyed going to Sunday school and church today, and other than that it has been a pretty quiet day. We have just taken it easy this afternoon.

I am not sure what this week might bring. We expect to hear from the transplant doctors in the first part of the week. I will be calling Dr. V tomorrow about some prescriptions, so I will let him know that we have not heard anything yet. We have really enjoyed the week of just being home with no doctor appointments. However, we also know that Billy's counts need to be checked, and we need a decision on the next step for treatment so we can get started.

Thank you all for your prayers and all you do for us. We are very thankful for all of you!

---

52 Ibid., pg. 695

God is good, all the time!

—Dione

> Oh, give thanks to the Lord, for He is good! For His mercy endures forever.
>
> —Psalm 107:1

Chapter 21

Tuesday, October 27, 2009, 2:05 p.m.

> In You, O Lord, I put my trust; Let me never be ashamed; Deliver me in Your righteousness. Bow down Your ear to me, deliver me speedily; be my rock of refuge, a fortress of defence to save me. For You are my rock and my fortress; therefore, for Your name's sake, lead me and guide me.
>
> —Psalm 31:1-3

I called Dr. V's office yesterday and talked to his nurse. I told her that we had not heard from the transplant team and that Billy did not have any blood counts or other blood work done last week since we didn't have an appointment with Dr. V and we didn't go to St. Louis. She said she would call the transplant team and check with Dr. V about whether we needed to make an appointment with him and have counts done. We didn't hear anything back from her on that. She did put the prescriptions we needed in the mail, and we received them today.

Today we received a schedule with almost a full day of appointments for Friday at the Siteman Cancer Center. There is not a doctor's appointment scheduled but several tests. There is a RVG (heart test) on the second floor at 11:00; a skeletal survey (X-rays of the entire body) at 12:15 on the sixth floor; a chest X-ray and EKG at 1:30 on the third floor; and a PFT (pulmonary function test/ breathing test) on the eighth floor at 3:30. It looks like we will be there most of the day, and we will be all over the building. I guess that is one way to learn our way around.

Since there is not an appointment with the doctors, we are thinking that means they will have to see the results of all of these tests first and will then schedule an appointment to meet with us, but we don't really know. This is all new to us, so we will just take it one step at a time and see where we go from here.

Apparently we will not have to see Dr. V this week since we did not hear back from the nurse. Since Billy is not on any chemo or other treatment, it may not be as important to get the blood counts every week. We will go help prepare the meal at church for tomorrow night and enjoy another week at home, or most of a week.

Billy is still feeling pretty well. He gets tired pretty easy—much easier than he would like—and of course there are many things that he simply can't do, and that gets rather frustrating for him. However, he is very thankful (as are we) that he is not in pain and feeling good. That means a lot even if he can't do everything he would like to.

We are all staying healthy and pray that all of you are healthy as well. We are very thankful for all of your prayers, and we know that they play a very big part in how well things are going. Thank you, and we love you all! Thanks for checking in, and we will continue to keep you all in our prayers.

God is good, all the time!

—Dione

> Oh, give thanks to the Lord, for He is good! For His mercy endures forever.
>
> —Psalm 107:1

THURSDAY, OCTOBER 29, 2009, 9:16 P.M.

> Lift up your heads, O you gates! And be lifted up, you everlasting doors! And the King of glory shall come in.

> Who is this King of glory? The Lord strong and mighty, the Lord mighty in battle. Lift up your heads, O you gates! Lift up, your everlasting doors! And the King of glory shall come in. Who is this King of glory? The Lord of hosts. He is the King of glory.
>
> —Psalm 24:7-10

It was so nice to see sunshine yesterday! We went to church at about 12:30 yesterday so we could help fix the meal for the evening. We all had a good day and enjoyed being in the kitchen and at church. The day was a little long for Billy, but he did pretty well.

We are headed for St. Louis in the morning and will be there all day. We still haven't heard from any doctors, so we are assuming that means we will not see the doctors tomorrow but will just do the tests and will then hear from the doctors after they have seen the results of all the tests.

Other than the tests tomorrow, there really isn't too much going on. Kaylyn worked today, and she and Cassy both have plans tomorrow afternoon. Kaylyn is going to drop Cassy off so she can spend the night with a friend, and then Kaylyn and a friend of hers are going shopping and out to eat.

Oh, we did have a little excitement yesterday when Cassy's rabbit, Thumper, got out of her pen. She is a big gray rabbit and weighs around ten pounds. The kids have a pen fixed for her in the backyard. She has done really well for a very long time and not dug out, but she has started digging out recently. Cassy happened to look out the window into the backyard while she was doing school yesterday morning, and there sat Thumper under the picnic table in the backyard. Several of the kids went out and tried for a while to catch her but didn't have any luck because she went under the house.

When we pulled into the yard last night after church, a cotton tail rabbit went hopping across the yard, and there sat Thumper by the car port. She was just looking around like she wasn't sure what to do. Kaylyn, Cassy, and Max jumped out of the Suburban and commenced to trying to catch her. Billy kept her in the headlights so they could see her, and it didn't take long for Max to catch her. He dove for her, and although he missed to start with, he confused her enough that she didn't know which way to go and he was able to grab her. We were rather entertained by the show, and Thumper is back in custody.

Thank you all for your prayers, support, and encouragement. You all mean a lot to us, and we are very blessed by you.

God is good, all the time!

—Dione

> Oh, give thanks to the Lord, for He is good! For His mercy endures forever.
>
> —Psalm 107: 1

Friday, October 30, 2009, 9:09 p.m.

> But You, O Lord, are a shield for me, My glory and the One who lifts up my head. I cried to the Lord with my voice, and He heard me from His holy hill. I lay down and slept; I awoke, for the Lord sustained me.
>
> —Psalm 3:3-5

> Peace—True peace comes not from the absence of adversaries but from trust in God. Nothing can disrupt your sense of peace when God exercises His presence in your life.[53]

[53] Ibid., pg. 636

It was a long day, and Billy is pretty worn out. We will hear something about the tests the first part of the week and will then have an idea of what the next step will be.

It is a good thing we have already met with two of the transplant doctors and are comfortable with them, or Billy would have called everything off today and we would not be going back. The heart test was fine. They injected radioactive isotopes as well as something else into him and then a few minutes later began taking some kind of pictures of his heart. The machine they used was repositioned three times and was left in place for ten minutes at a time to take pictures. It just required Billy to lay on a gurney. However, the guy doing the test raised and lowered the gurney a couple of times, and he did not do it gently.

The skeletal survey was almost more than Billy could take, and like I said, if we were not already comfortable with the transplant doctors, I think Billy would have said forget it and we would have gone home right then. The skeletal survey was just X-rays of Billy's entire body. However, it took thirty minutes, and he came out hurting more than he has hurt since back before they had his pain under control. Thankfully I had some Fentora with us, which is his high-powered breakthrough pain medication. He took it, and it did the trick. He has not had to take any of it since he was doing radiation. He would take it before a treatment because he had to lie on a hard table, and they knew he would be hurting by the time they were done if he didn't have it.

For the X-rays he had to lay on a metal table. The X-ray technician then moved the table around some and moved the machine some to get it in position, which was fine for the most part. The metal table itself was a bit of a problem for Billy, but the technician pushing him around on the table to get him in the position she wanted was very painful for Billy. She then had him in a chair (like a metal folding chair), and without any warning, she shoved the chair, which hit him right in the middle of the back. That was also very painful for him. We know that we are a little spoiled by the great care that they took with Billy in Tulsa, but this was just uncalled for and unnecessary. There were a couple of other things that did not impress us, but the experience with the X-rays was by far the worst. For the most part the chest X-ray, EKG, and pulmonary test were not a problem. Billy is thankful that today's tests are all over.

The kids got along fine today. Kaylyn and Cassy left a little before 2:00. Cassy is spending the night with a friend, and Kaylyn will be home in a little while after going out with a friend. I got a kick out of Kaylyn and Cassy on Wednesday when they realized they would be gone for part of the day while Billy and I were in St. Louis. They both asked if I was sure it was okay for them to go since that would mean Max would be home with the younger three. The kids are all old enough that they are fine home with Max. I thought it was funny that Kaylyn and Cassy are such mother hens that they would think one of them has to be home for things to be okay when Billy and I are not home.

Kaylyn doesn't have to work tomorrow and is looking forward to sleeping in. Max is going to be working with some of the guys at church, and then Kaylyn and Max have a puppet show (along with the puppet team) at the Russellville Park tomorrow in the late afternoon. Depending on weather and how Billy is feeling, we may all go watch their puppet show.

We continue to pray for wisdom and God's guidance. We plan to just relax and enjoy the weekend, and we will see what the first part of the week brings as we hear from the doctors about the test results.

Thank you all for your prayers and kindness. We are so very blessed by all of you. We love you all!

God is good, all the time!

—Dione

> Oh, give thanks to the Lord, for He is good! For His mercy endures forever.
>
> —Psalm 107:1

Saturday, October 31, 2009, 9:06 p.m.

> Yes, we had the sentence of death in ourselves, that we should not trust in ourselves but in God who raises the dead, who delivered us from so great a death, and does deliver us; in whom we trust that He will still deliver us, you also helping together in prayer for us, that thanks may be given by many persons on our behalf for the gift granted to us through many.
>
> —2 Corinthians 1:9-11

We are very grateful for all of your prayers and support. We are very blessed to have so many people praying for our family, and we feel your prayers daily. Thank you. We love you all and keep you in our prayers.

It has been a pretty quiet day. I took Max in to help work on the new Sunday school rooms at church. Since he has his learner's permit, he drove in. The brakes are holding pretty well in the red Tempo and it is a stick, which Max loves to drive, so we took it. It sounds like they put up quite a bit of drywall at church today, so a good day.

Billy really slept in today because he was completely exhausted from his day yesterday. The fact that we stayed up until almost midnight visiting with Kaylyn and Max contributed to his exhaustion. However, at the time we were visiting, none of us felt tired. Max was still up with Billy and me when Kaylyn got home between 10:30 and 11:00. Billy had talked to Max on the phone when we were in St. Louis yesterday and told him that when we got home, he would tell him all about the day. He had not done that yet, so with Kaylyn being home too, he decided to tell them about the day. Kaylyn also told us about her day, so we were just enjoying our visit and didn't realize it was getting so late. Billy was thinking about trying to go to his Road Riders for Jesus (RRJ) motorcycle groupmeeting this morning, but after his day, he wasn't sure he would be able to get up and get there. Then when he looked at the clock when we were going to bed, he decided he wasn't even going to try. Oh well, we always enjoy visiting with the kids (any and all of them), so it was well worth the time and getting to bed a bit later. We love our kids! They are great kids. We are very blessed!

Unfortunately, the puppet show at the park in Russellville this evening ended up being a no go due to equipment failure. We all went up to the park and they got everything unloaded and set up. However, they could not get the CD to play. They tried and tried, but it just wouldn't work. No one was sure what the problem might be. They didn't have time to go back to the church and get different equipment, so they just had to pack everything back up. It was a bit of a bummer, but it happens—thankfully not often. As far as I know, this is the first time since Kaylyn and Max have been in the puppets that equipment failure has been this bad. Apparently it all worked the last time they used it, so they had no reason to think there would be a problem. It was just one of those things. In a way it was good for the puppet team because where they were set up, the wind was blowing through and it was pretty cool; the puppet group all looked cold.

It was so nice to see the sunshine today! Justin, Levi, and Faith spent most of the day outside. They have really missed being outside with all the rain lately. We will get Cassy back after church tomorrow. (She is staying with her buddy from church.) I am sure she has had a great time, but we will be glad to have her home. I have told the kids and Billy before—and I know that it is odd—but things just don't feel right when not all the kids are home at bedtime. It isn't so bad when they are gone during the day. I have gotten used to Kaylyn working, and Max has been gone helping at church fairly often. Justin has helped at church some as well, and that isn't a big deal, but when they are not all in their beds at bedtime, things just aren't right, or at least they don't feel right to me.

Enjoy your day of rest tomorrow. I know we will. We all look forward to Sunday school and church and then a quiet afternoon. Kaylyn and Max have another puppet show tomorrow evening.

God is good, all the time!

—Dione

> Oh, give thanks to the Lord, for He is good! For His mercy endures forever.
>
> —Psalm 107:1

Sunday, November 1, 2009, 8:23 p.m.

> Therefore, my beloved brethren, be steadfast, immovable, always abounding in the work of the Lord, knowing that your labor is not in vain in the Lord.
>
> —1 Corinthians 15:58

Today was a beautiful, sunshiny day! The kids spent a lot of time outside again today, and we all enjoyed Sunday school and church this morning. Cassy and Justin spent quite some time getting the rabbit's pen fixed so she could be back out in the yard. She has spent the last several days in the playhouse since they haven't been able to get the pen fixed.

Billy is getting recovered from Friday. He has not been as tired or sore today. I made cinnamon rolls this afternoon, which made everyone happy. Cinnamon rolls are one of Max's favorite things, and he commented a couple of weeks ago that I needed to make them again. He was very pleased when he discovered I was making them. Everyone really likes them, but they make Max especially happy. This evening everyone is full of cinnamon rolls and taking it easy.

I hope everyone had a good day and was able to enjoy the sunshine. Thank you for your prayer and support. We love you all!

God is good, all the time!

—Dione

> Oh, give thanks to the Lord, for God is good! For His mercy endures forever.
>
> —Psalm 107:1

Monday, November 2, 2009, 8:47 p.m.

> My brethren, count it all joy when you fall into various trials, knowing that the testing of your faith produces patience. But let patience have its perfect work, that you may be perfect and complete, lacking nothing.
>
> —James 1:2-4

There were no phone calls from any doctors or nurses today, so we will wait and see if they call tomorrow. Because Dr. G's nurse said that she would call today, I did expect a call, but I did not hold my breath. Good thing!

It was another beautiful day! We love the sunshine, and the kids really enjoyed being outside. Kaylyn did have to work, but she was thankful for the sunshine as well. Max got the four-wheeler out, and I think Faith enjoyed that as much as Max did. Faith loves to ride with her big brother. Thumper the rabbit was out again today. She looked quite happy being free, and I have suggested that they just let her run free during the day and then catch her just before dark. However, the kids are not comfortable with that idea, especially Cassy. Cassy worked most of the afternoon trying to fix the pen, but she didn't have any luck, so Thumper is staying in the playhouse until we can figure something out or get some new pen-making materials.

Billy went in to Farm Bureau for a while today and really enjoyed visiting. He went by himself, and the kids and I thought it was good for him to get out on his own. It seemed to do him good, and he enjoyed himself.

I spent most of the day after we finished school washing up all the bedding. I think I did six loads of bedding today, but everyone has clean sheets, pillow cases, and blankets. I don't know if the kids have finished making their beds yet or not, but they will shortly, since it will be bedtime before long. Faith has already fallen asleep on the couch. She had a busy day playing outside.

Thank you all for checking in! We are so very blessed by all of you, and we love you all!

God is good, all the time!

—Dione

> Oh, give thanks to the Lord, for He is good! For His mercy endures forever.
>
> —Psalm 107:1

Chapter 22

Tuesday, November 3, 2009, 10:43 p.m.

> But also for this very reason, giving all diligence, add to your faith virtue, to virtue knowledge, to knowledge self-control, to self-control perseverance, to perseverance godliness, to godliness brotherly kindness, and to brotherly kindness love. For if these things are yours and abound, you will be neither barren nor unfruitful in the knowledge of our Lord Jesus Christ.
>
> —2 Peter 1:5-8

> A Living Nature—God does not love us because we are lovable, but because it is His nature to do so. Allow His divine nature to work in your life so you love others the way God does and so the world can see Him through you.[54]

Well, we got no phone calls today, but we did get another schedule via FedEx. We don't get the warm fuzzys from the lack of personal communication, but this is apparently how things work. We are supposed to be in St. Louis at 3:00 on Saturday afternoon to begin the harvesting process. Billy will get a shot on Saturday, Sunday, Monday, and Tuesday morning. He will have a catheter placed on Tuesday morning and will then get a different kind of shot on Tuesday evening. Wednesday will begin the actual harvest, which will continue for three to five days depending on how long it takes to get the needed cells. We will then

[54] Ibid., pg. 1490

come home for a couple of weeks and go back to St. Louis to begin the transplant process on Monday, November 30. Billy will be admitted on that day. He will then be an inpatient for two to four weeks depending on how he does, and we will need to stay close to the hospital for one week following the transplant. If all goes really well, we could be home the week of Christmas. However, most likely it will be the week or so after Christmas. We will just have to see how it goes.

I took Levi and Faith to town this afternoon to do some shopping. The older kids have all been out and about doing various things, but Levi and Faith have just been at home other than the usual church activities. They have not complained but occasionally ask if we are going anywhere. Faith needed some new shoes and clothes, Levi still had birthday money burning a hole in his pocket, and I needed to get some groceries and odds and ends, so away we went. We had a very nice day, and they were really good. Faith has a couple of very nice outfits and cute shoes. The only problem is she looks more grown up all dressed up.

Billy and the older kids seemed to enjoy their afternoon hanging out. We will head to church a little after noon tomorrow to help fix the meal for tomorrow night. I will be doing some packing a little later in the week, and we will head for St. Louis around noon on Saturday.

Thank you all for sticking with us! We are very blessed by your prayers and everything you do for us. We love you all! Hopefully we will be able to get Internet access when we are in St. Louis so I can continue to update.

God is good, all the time!

—Dione

> Oh, give thanks to the Lord, for He is good! For His mercy endures forever.
>
> —Psalm 107:1

Thursday, November 5, 2009, 2:26 p.m.

> This is the message which we have heard from Him and declare to you, that God is light and in Him is no darkness at all. If we say that we have fellowship with Him, and walk in darkness, we lie and do not practice the truth. But if we walk in the light as He is in the light, we have fellowship with one another, and the blood of Jesus Christ His Son cleanses us from all sin.
>
> —1 John 1:5-7

> Word Study Fellowship—The Greek word koinonia, translated "fellowship," needs many English words to present its full meaning. When used for a person's relationship with God, it means people can have fellowship with Him, an intimate relationship that impacts every area of life. It also implies partnership with Him in His work. It expresses sharing between two parties, each one giving freely to the other. Furthermore, it relates to the stewardship people have over that which God entrusts to them. Koinonia is the outflow of God's love in practical expression (1 Cor. 1:9; Eph. 3:9). The same word is used to describe the relationship between God's people. The manner in which God has shared His life with us is the same measure we are to love other people in the kingdom of God.[55]

We had a good day yesterday, spending most of the day at church. We did get a phone call this afternoon from the transplant doctor's nurse. Talking to her and being able to ask a few questions helps our outlook on things. We really didn't have any questions about this coming week and planned to ask our questions about the transplant while we are there this time. However, since she called, we asked.

When Billy is admitted for the transplant (on November 30), I will be able to stay in the room with him, and they have wireless Internet, so we will

[55] Ibid., pg. 1495

be able to use the computer. Billy will be able to have visitors. They just ask that those who come to visit are healthy, and any children under thirteen will undergo a health screening on the floor before going into the room. That is not a problem. I will have to ask Dr. B (Levi's diabetic doctor) about Levi's flu shot, since Billy cannot be around someone who has had a vaccination with a live virus, at least not during and just before the transplant. I had planned to get Levi's flu shot at his clinic appointment this month, but we may have to put it off until after Billy recovers from the transplant. How long we have to stay in St. Louis after Billy is released from the hospital will depend on how Billy is doing and how soon Dr. V is willing to take over his care.

Billy told the nurse about his experience with the X-ray technician last Friday. She was sorry to hear about the experience and said she would let Dr. G know and they would also talk to that department. Billy could not remember the name of the gal who took the X-rays, but the nurse said that they can track down exactly who it was. She also said the technician should know they are to be careful with Dr. G's patients because of the bone issues with multiple myeloma. Billy told her that if he has to go for X-rays there again, he will not let that same gal do them. The nurse understood and agreed that he shouldn't.

All is well at our house, and we pray you are all doing well too. Thank you for your prayers and support. They mean a lot. We love you all!

God is good, all the time!

—Dione

> Oh, give thanks to the Lord, for He is good! For His mercy endures forever.
>
> —Psalm 107:1

Saturday, November 7, 2009, 7:21 p.m.

> My soul, wait silently for God alone, for my expectation is from Him, He only is my rock and my salvation; He is my defense; I shall not be moved. In God is my salvation and my glory; the rock of my strength, and my refuge, is in God. Trust in Him at all times, you people; pour out your heart before Him; God is a refuge for us.
>
> —Psalm 62:5-8

I thought I would do this early today since I need to get my packing done yet. We enjoyed going to Steve and Linda's for a movie night last night. Thank you, Steve and Linda! As always, there was good company, good friends, good food, and lots of fun.

We will head out around noon. We have our reservations made for the week (Thanks, Mom!), and Billy has an idea of where the hotel is and how to get there, as well as having it programmed into the GPS.

Billy will have a blood draw and his first cell-boosting shot today. Then he will just have a shot tomorrow. Monday he will have a shot and an appointment with the pheresis (cell removal) people, and we will drop signed paperwork off at Dr. G's office. Tuesday will be an earlier morning because Billy will get his shot at 8:00 a.m. Then his catheter will be placed at 9:00, and at 5:15 he will get a different kind of shot that will make the cells in his bone marrow "slippery" so they will "slip" into the blood stream. On Wednesday morning, the cell collection will begin. Billy will lay back in a recliner for three to six hours each day as they harvest his cells. He will get the "slippery" shot each evening. This will go on for three to five days depending on how long it takes them to get all the needed cells. From the schedule we have and from what the doctor told us, they expect to have enough cells by the third day if not before, so we should be able to be home next weekend, but we will see how it goes.

Thank you all for sticking with us and for all your prayers. As we begin the next step, we are blessed to have all of you with us, and we feel your prayers daily. We are also sending up prayers for Bill and Kay today. Bill has pancreatic cancer, and his treatment has gone pretty well. However, he had to have his spleen removed yesterday, and there were some complications. From our understanding, he is expected to do okay, but it means a longer stay in the hospital, which is not Bill's thing. You are in our prayers, Bill and Kay. We love you!

Thanks again for checking in. We love you all!

God is good, all the time!

—Dione

> Oh, give thanks to the Lord, for He is good! For His mercy endures forever.
>
> —Psalm 107:1

Sunday, November 8, 2009, 7:29 p.m.

> Cause me to hear Your loving-kindness in the morning, for in You do I trust; cause me to know the way in which I should walk, for I lift up my soul to You. Teach me to do Your will, for You are my God; Your Spirit is good. Lead me in the land of uprightness.
>
> —Psalm 143:8-10

> Cause Me to Know—We can acquire knowledge, but only God can give wisdom. Only He knows the best paths for us. Only He can guide us unerringly.[56]

Well, so far so good. Billy got his shot of cell growth stuff yesterday and today. They actually give two shots each time. If I understood the nurse correctly yesterday, one shot is the stuff to make the bone marrow produce

56 Ibid.,pg. 734

more stem cells and the other is something to help the body absorb the first shot because the stuff is very thick. There are several possible side effects from these shots, but so far Billy has not had any of them, so hopefully it will stay that way.

Tomorrow Billy will get another of these shots, and we will meet with the pheresis department for the pheresis evaluation. Pheresis is the process of removing the stem cells from the blood, and the plan is to start that on Wednesday.

On Tuesday Billy will get his shot, and then they will place a catheter to be used for the pheresis process. Then in the early evening, he will get a Mozobil shot. The Mozobil is what makes the stem cells slip out of the bone marrow and into the blood so they can collect them. Wednesday morning will begin the pheresis process, where he is in a recliner and they collect the cells. I will explain this better once I see how it actually works. I have an idea from what they have told us, but I am not sure what I have pictured is actually how it works, so we shall see. We had been told that he would lay in the recliner for three to six hours. However, one of the nurses yesterday said that it would most likely be closer to the six hours (possibly seven) than three. Again, we shall see.

So far things are going well. Thanks for checking in, and most of all, thank you for your continued prayers and support! We cannot tell you all how much it means to us that you all continue to pray for us and are so very kind. We truly are blessed! We love you all!

God is good, all the time!

—Dione

> Oh, give thanks to the Lord, for He is good! For His mercy endures forever.
>
> —Psalm 107:1

Monday, November 9, 2009, 10:18 p.m.

> Then you shall call, and the Lord will answer; You shall cry, and He will say, "Here I am."
>
> —Isaiah 58:9

> "Peace I leave with you, My peace I give you; not as the world gives do I give to you. Let not your heart be troubled, neither let it be afraid."
>
> —John 14:27

Billy got his third cell-boosting shot today, and so far so good. We also met with the pheresis people and now have a little better understanding of that process. Billy will get a catheter placed tomorrow that will be used for the pheresis and transplant process. The port he has does not handle a large enough volume for the process. There will be an in and out on the catheter, and the blood will come out one tube through tubing and into a machine that separates the white cells from the red. The stem cells are actually the immature white cells, and that is what they are after. We were told today that how long it takes is based on his blood volume because they will take his entire blood volume out and put it back four times each day during pheresis. Due to his size and weight, they said it would take right around five hours. He will be in a comfortable recliner (according to the nurse and doctor) and have his own TV with DVD player. They have a large selection of DVDs to choose from, we brought some DVDs from home as well, and there are snacks. He can watch TV or movies or just nap. The pheresis will start at 8:00 a.m. on Wednesday

The catheter will be placed tomorrow morning at around 9:00. This one is not completely under the skin like the port is. The catheter will require a dressing change once a week when we are home. I will be taught how to do the dressing change.

We have heard that Bill is doing better. He will still be in the hospital for a few more days, but he is improving each day.

Our prayers are

- that the placement of the catheter will go well;
- that there will be lots of stem cells so the collection can be completed by Friday; and
- we are also very thankful that everyone has stayed healthy.
- Levi's blood sugars have been running very high in the last few days, so if you think about that, I ask that you would pray we get them in check. If they are not better by noon tomorrow, he will be getting some extra insulin.

Thank you all for your prayers, support, and encouragement! We love you all and keep you in our prayers.

God is good, all the time!

—Dione

> Oh, give thanks to the Lord, for He is good! For His mercy endures forever.
>
> —Psalm 107:1

Praise the Lord! Oh, give thanks to the Lord, for He is good! For His mercy endures forever.

—Psalm 106:1

> Oh, give thanks to the Lord, for He is good! For His mercy endures forever.
>
> —Psalm 118:1

Tuesday, November 10, 2009, 8:45 p.m.

> May the Lord answer you in the day of trouble; may the name of the God of Jacob defend you; may He send you help from the sanctuary, and strengthen you out of Zion; may He remember all your offerings, and accept your burnt sacrifice. May He grant you according to your heart's desire, and fulfill all your purpose. We will rejoice in your salvation, and in the name of our God we will set up our banners! May the Lord fulfill all your petitions. Now I know that the Lord saves His anointed; He will answer him from His holy heaven with the saving strength of His right hand. Some trust in chariots, and some in horses; but we will remember the name of the Lord our God. They have bowed down and fallen; but we have risen and stand upright. Save, Lord! May the King answer us when we call.
>
> —Psalm 20

The catheter placement went well today, although they were supposed to do it at 9:00 and it was 10:45 before they got started. Billy was awake the entire time, and it went very well. It is an interesting little piece of equipment with three lines coming off of it. Each line can have an IV hooked up to it.

We were missing our sweet, loving, kind, careful nurses from Cancer Treatment Centers of America at one point today. When we went in for Billy's Mozobil shot this evening, we asked the nurse if Billy's dressing on his catheter needed to be changed. The gauze on the catheter was soaked with blood, and it had oozed out from under the dressing. There was even a little blood on Billy's shirt. When we told the nurse that we thought it might need to be changed, she said they don't change them until the next morning. We said that if that was the case that's fine, but we would like her to look at it and see what she thought. She seemed very bothered that we wanted her to look at it. When she did look at it, she continued to be irritated, but she said she would change it since that is what we wanted. Billy tried to tell her that if it didn't need to be changed then she didn't have to change it. We didn't know and just wanted her to look at it. She went ahead and changed the dressing, but she was not happy about doing it. She made that clear because she was quite rough about it. Billy felt that she did it for spite since she really didn't want to change the dressing. She made it very clear that she was annoyed with the entire thing.

We keep being told that the nurses on the transplant floor are the sweetest, kindest nurses we will meet. We are praying that what they are telling us is so because we have not been comforted by the lack of kindness and compassion in the nurses and some of the other staff so far. I know many people think they are wonderful, but Billy figures that is because they have not experienced the level of care he had in Tulsa.

I do have to say that the nurse and the doctor we met from the pheresis department yesterday were very nice and actually showed more concern and compassion than most here have so far. In fact, the doctor we met with checked with another doctor to make sure the pheresis process wouldn't pull off Billy's pain medications because it can remove some medications. She called this afternoon to let us know that the doctor does not think it will affect the pain medications, but he is concerned that five hours in the recliner could get uncomfortable for Billy, so they asked him to bring his breakthrough pain medication along just in case. As long as it is truly a comfortable recliner, as we have been told, it shouldn't be a problem, since Billy sits in a recliner all the time and does fine.

Tomorrow begins the next part of this process as they start removing the stem cells. It will be a long five hours or so because I am not able to stay with Billy during the process. I will be able to go back and see him for a few minutes a few different times during the process, but otherwise I will have to stay in the waiting room or wander the hospital. I will take my book, and I can take the computer, but we will see.

Thank you all for your prayers and support. We love you all, and you are all very special to us!

Our prayers are

- that they will be able to get plenty of cells by Friday;
- that Billy will not have any problems with the process; and
- that Levi's numbers will straighten out.

I talked to Kay today, and Bill is improving, just slower than they would like. They are hoping he will go home tomorrow. We are keeping you in our prayers, Bill and Kay.

God is good, all the time!

—Dione

> Praise the Lord! Oh, give thanks to the Lord, for He is good! For His mercy endures forever.
>
> —Psalm 106:1

Wednesday, November 11, 2009, 7:57 p.m.

> Oh, sing to the Lord a new song! Sing to the Lord, all the earth. Sing to the Lord, bless His name; proclaim the good news of His salvation from day to day. Declare His glory among the nations, His wonders among all people. For the Lord is great and greatly to be praised; He is to be feared above all gods. For all the gods of the peoples are idols, but the Lord made the heavens. Honor and majesty are before Him; strength and beauty are in His sanctuary. Give to the Lord, O families of the peoples, give to the Lord the glory due His name; bring an offering, and come into His courts. Oh, worship the Lord in the beauty of holiness! Tremble before Him, all the earth. Say among the nations, "The Lord reigns; the world also is firmly established, it shall not be moved; He shall judge the peoples righteously." Let the heavens

> rejoice, and let the earth be glad; let the sea roar, and all its fullness; let the field be joyful, and all that is in it. Then all the trees of the woods will rejoice before the Lord. For He is coming, for He is coming to judge the world with righteousness, and the peoples with His truth.
>
> —Psalm 96

God is good! Thank you, thank you for all of your prayers! Not only did everything go very well today, but they collected 5.5 million cells, which means they collected all they needed in one day! (The goal was 5 million.) We have to call Pam (Dr. G's nurse) in the morning. As far as we know, all we have to do is get things figured out so I can do the dressing changes on Billy's catheter. The pheresis nurse who called to let us know that all the cells had been collected said that we needed to check with Pam in the morning and find out the next step. As I said, to our knowledge, the only thing we need to know has to do with the care of the catheter, and then we should be able to head home. Our plan is to be home sometime tomorrow. Pam isn't in the office until 9:00, so we will call her as soon as she gets in and go from there.

The pheresis nurse was wonderful! We keep being told the transplant nurses are the best, and while she isn't a transplant nurse, the pheresis is part of the transplant process, so we expect to have wonderful nurses for the transplant. The pheresis process was quite interesting and went very well. Billy was comfortable in the recliner and had no side effects or issues of any kind. All in all, it was a very good day!

We were very glad to hear that Bill was able to go home today. Get well soon, Bill!

Thank you all for your prayers! We have felt those prayers all week and are very grateful for them. We love you all!

God is good, all the time!

—Dione

> Praise the Lord! Oh, give thanks to the Lord, for He is good! For His mercy endures forever.
>
> —Psalm 106:1

Friday, November 13, 2009, 9:02 p.m.

> Yet if anyone suffers as a Christian, let him not be ashamed, but let him glorify god in this matter.
>
> —1 Peter 4:16

> Suffering for Righteousness—Suffering is common to all people. We have the choice of suffering as a result of our sin and rebellion, or suffering as a result of righteousness. The former is at the hand of God and the latter is in the hand of God.[57]

We made it home around 4:30 yesterday afternoon. It would have been a few hours earlier, but an issue came up with Billy's new catheter and that had to be taken care of. Billy got up about 6:30 and had blood running down his side from the catheter. Blood had oozed out under the dressing and started running down his side. He wiped it away, but it kept oozing and was bright red blood. Since the catheter is in a major artery, we thought it would be best to get it checked out and not mess around. We got the dressing changed (after waiting well over an hour), and it looked pretty good. However, within two hours, just after getting checked out of the hotel and getting gas, Billy noticed that he had fresh blood on his shirt. I looked at the catheter, and sure enough, blood was oozing out from under the dressing once again. We called Pam (our nurse coordinator), and she sent us over to interventional radiology at the main Barnes hospital to have the catheter fixed. It took just over an hour to get taken care of, but everything is good now. We have had no more problems with the catheter.

---

57 Ibid., pg. 1486

We have talked to Pam, and she wondered when we thought we were supposed to be back for the transplant. We told her that our schedule said we are to be back on November 30. Well, apparently the schedule was wrong. We have to go back on November 20, one week from today. Billy will be checked into the hospital in the late afternoon or early evening next Friday. According to Pam, this means we will be home and Billy will be feeling better by Christmas. We return to St. Louis on November 20, Billy will be admitted, the high-dose chemo will be given on Saturday and Sunday (at least that is what we understand), he will have a break on Monday, and then the stem cell infusion will be done on Tuesday. Billy will remain hospitalized for two to three weeks depending on how he does and how fast his counts recover. So far things have gone very well, so we anticipate good results.

Billy's counts are great after all of the shots he had for building his cells. If you would like to stop in for a visit this week, we would love to see you.

Thank you all for your continued prayers. We are very grateful for them! We love you all and keep you in our prayers.

God is good, all the time!

—Dione

> Praise the Lord! Oh, give thanks to the Lord, for He is good! For His mercy endures forever.
>
> —Psalm 106:1

Saturday, November 14, 2009, 7:24 p.m.

> For this is the love of God, that we keep His commandments. And His commandments are not burdensome. For whatever is born of God overcomes

> the world. And this is the victory that has overcome the world—our faith.
>
> —1 John 5:3-4

Kaylyn didn't have to work today, so she slept in. I took Max in and dropped him off at church so he could help with workday. Cassy went shopping with Linda and finally got some boots. She is very pleased with them. Thank you, Linda.

Billy is doing pretty well. He is just a bit fatigued. I thought I would try to explain something because there seems to be some confusion concerning the stem cell transplant. The confusion seems to be as to whether the stem cells that were harvested are "cleaned" to get rid of any possible cancer cells. Billy and I asked Dr. G this same question, and he answered it. Since the answer came directly from the transplant doctor, I feel confident that it is accurate.

They do have the ability to clean the stem cells; however, it has not proven to be effective or helpful. In the studies they have done, cleansing the cells versus not cleansing them made no difference in how soon people relapsed, and there is concern that it might even damage the good cells. This brings us to the answer for the question, do they or do they not clean the cells? The answer is, no, they do *not* cleanse the cells.

Chemo is given in the beginning (as Billy has had) to kill as much of the myeloma as they can and basically achieve a degree of remission. That is the best time to harvest the cells—when there is as little myeloma present as possible. The idea is that when you put the cells back into the patient, there will be very few myeloma cells, and the healthy stem cells will kill the cancer cells off as they rebuild the immune system. A stem cell transplant is not a cure (that is unless God chooses to use it as one). The stem cell transplant simply achieves a longer period of remission, or at least that is the hope. The doctors have made it very clear that they expect Billy to relapse; they just don't know how long it will be before it happens. They also hope to have found a new and better treatment before the relapse happens. How well the stem cell transplant works and how long Billy is cancer free is entirely up to the Lord. We believe that if the Lord so chooses, the stem cell transplant can be a cure, but we also understand that it may not be. Everything the doctors have told us, from Dr. R in Tulsa to Dr. V and Dr. G, is that Billy's best chance is the stem cell transplant. Really, regardless of the transplant it is all in the Lord's hands.

It is time to help Faith get some ice cream and watch a movie with the kids. Thanks for checking in, and as always, thank you for all of your prayers!

God is good, all the time!

—Dione

> Praise the Lord! Oh, give thanks to the Lord, for He is good! For His mercy endures forever.
>
> —Psalm 106:1

Monday, November 16, 2009, 8:45 p.m.

> Then he spoke to the children of Israel, saying; "When your children ask their fathers in time to come, saying, 'What are these stones?' then you shall let your children know, saying, 'Israel crossed over this Jordan on dry land;' for the Lord your God dried up the waters of the Jordan before you until you had crossed over, as the Lord your God did to the Red Sea, which He dried up before us until we had crossed over, that all the peoples of the earth may know the hand of the Lord, that it is mighty, that you may fear the Lord your God forever."
>
> —Joshua 4:21-24

> God's Glory—God gives us victory for His sake, not ours. When God works powerfully through us, people

> see His activity, not our ability. If we resist God's will, we lose the opportunity to glorify Him.[58]

It has been a very nice couple of days—well, if you don't count the rain that everyone is getting rather tired of. Oh well.

We all enjoyed Sunday school and church yesterday, as we always do. It is so good to see our church family and spend the day where we belong. This week is going to go by way too fast.

Kaylyn worked today, and Billy and I went into town to take care of some odds and ends. There are several things that have to be done this week, which will contribute to the week going by too fast.

Billy is feeling pretty well. He is getting over the fatigue from the stem cell harvest and commented yesterday and today that he just feels better.

I know I have said it before, but I don't think we can say enough how much you all mean to us! We are incredibly blessed by all of you! Our family, church family, friends, and the Farm Bureau family are truly wonderful and have blessed us in so many ways! There are also those of you who we have never met and don't really know, yet you all pray for us and encourage us—amazing! Thank you!

God is good, all the time!

—Dione

> Praise the Lord! Oh, give thanks to the Lord, for He is good! For His mercy endures forever.
>
> —Psalm 106:1

---

58 Ibid., pg. 257

TUESDAY, NOVEMBER 17, 2009 9:56 P.M.

Billy had a pretty good day, and he took a couple of naps in his recliner. I got my hair cut today, and Cassy had hers trimmed. I decided I had better get my hair cut since I will be staying with Billy in his hospital room. My hair was long enough that it would get pretty wild at night and required some taming each morning. I don't want a nurse to come in to check on Billy in the night and have my wild hair scare her. It should be much easier to deal with and less scary now.

Kaylyn didn't have to work today and she doesn't work tomorrow, but she and Max have a puppet show in the morning. There are times when it is really nice that she can drive. However, it can still be hard to believe that she is so grown up, and believe me, she is a very grown-up, special young lady! She is also excited that she will be able to drive the Suburban while Billy and I are in St. Louis for his transplant. Since I am able to stay in the hospital room with Billy, we are going to have my dad take us and leave us. That means the Suburban will be here for Kaylyn to drive when all of the kids are going somewhere, and that will prevent the carpooling that has had to be done in the past to get everyone to church and other places. Kaylyn was quite tickled at the idea of being able to drive the Suburban. She is so cute.

I have been watching the kids very closely this week, and it is amazing how good they are to each other! Yes, they argue and fuss with each other some but not very much. They really look out for each other and help each other, and the older ones have an amazing amount of patience with the younger ones. I really thought about it today when Max was playing a military game on his computer and Faith was watching him. She was asking him all kinds of questions about the game and why he was doing this and that. She was also telling Max how when Levi was playing that, he did it this way or that way. Max was very patient with her, answering all of her questions without ever sounding short, annoyed, or even just telling her to leave him alone. Max made Justin, Levi, and Faith's evening by playing a game with them after supper. When Billy and I are gone, Max is very good to check Levi's blood sugar at night and make sure he is doing okay. Levi does not follow any of the rules, and his blood sugar does very odd things when we are gone, so Max doesn't go to sleep until he is sure Levi is okay for the night.

Kaylyn and Cassy are very good at making the needed adjustments in Levi's insulin doses, and they make sure he gets the correct amount of food and the right balance with his meals and snacks. Kaylyn keeps track of things and refills Levi's prescriptions if needed when we are gone, and Cassy sees that the laundry stays washed up. They are both very good to help Levi and Faith with school work and other things as needed. They are pretty amazing young ladies.

Justin, Levi, and Faith are pretty good buddies and spend a lot of time playing together and just helping each other pass time. They play really well together. The kids are all very close and do such a good job looking out for each other and just caring for one another. They are all so special, and we love them *so* very much!

We will go to church at about 2:00 tomorrow afternoon and help prepare the meal for tomorrow evening. We all look forward to the time spent in the church kitchen each Wednesday, although Justin, Levi, and Faith do not spend a lot of time in the kitchen. They play around the church, and they do help some by setting up chairs and tables or anything else we come up with for them to do. They stop in the kitchen several times during the afternoon to see if there is anything they can do to help.

Thank you all for your prayers and checking in. We love you all!

God is good, all the time!

—Dione

> Praise the Lord! Oh, give thanks to the Lord, for He is good! For His mercy endures forever.
>
> —Psalm 106:1

Tuesday, November 19, 2009, 9:00 p.m.

> Your word is a lamp to my feet and a light to my path. I have sworn and confirmed that I will keep Your righteous judgments. I am afflicted very much; revive me, O Lord, according to Your word. Accept, I pray, the free will offerings of my mouth, O Lord, and teach me Your judgments. My life is continually in my hand, Yet I do not forget Your law. The wicked have laid a snare for me, yet I have not strayed from Your precepts. Your testimonies I have taken as a heritage forever, for they are the rejoicing of my heart. I have inclined my heart, to perform Your statutes forever, to the very end.
>
> —Psalm 119:105-112

Levi had a checkup at the clinic today, and that went very well. He has grown two and a half inches since August! They said that his diabetes is obviously being controlled since he is growing so well. They were very pleased with how he is doing and how well he understands everything. We will use regular insulin if needed, and otherwise things look good.

Billy was finally able to get a hold of our nurse coordinator at Siteman today. She had said that she would call us this week, but since we had not heard from her and we had some questions, we decided to call her. I called this morning, but she was coming in late today, so I left her a voicemail. I took Levi to Columbia for clinic this afternoon, and when Billy had still not heard from her by 4:00, he called her again. I will be able to stay in the room with Billy, as we were told, and I will be able to do laundry there. Billy will also be able to wear his own clothes.

We don't know yet what time we need to be there. I am supposed to call admitting in the morning to find out. After they get him admitted and we get settled, they will start the chemo tomorrow evening. He will have chemo tomorrow and Saturday. He will have Sunday as a day of rest, and then the stem cells will be infused on Monday. We will then be waiting for Billy's counts to come up. Billy was told today that it is expected to be two and a half to three weeks before he can be released from the hospital.

Whether we can come home right after he is released or have to stay in St. Louis will be up to the doctor, so we shall see.

Billy will be able to have visitors as long as they are healthy. The kids will be allowed to visit. They will just do a health screening on the floor for those under thirteen. Since St. Louis is much closer than Tulsa, the kids will be able to come visit for a day. We will play it by ear and go by how Billy is feeling as far as how soon we have the kids visit.

Thank you for all of your prayers and support. We love you all and keep you in our prayers.

God is good, all the time!

—Dione

> Praise the Lord! Oh, give thanks to the Lord, for He is good! For His mercy endures forever.
>
> —Psalm 106:1

Chapter 23

Saturday, November 21, 2009, 9:59 a.m.

The following post was written very early this morning, but due to some Internet connection issues, I was not able to get it posted, so I just saved it. We did get to bed at about 2:00 a.m., but Billy didn't really get any sleep until from 7:00 to 9:00 this morning. They gave him Decadron with his chemo and that tends to keep him awake. Since he got the Decadron a little after midnight, that pretty much took care of any sleeping for a few hours. He does not have any mouth sores this morning and is doing really well (other than lack of sleep) so far. As I mention below, the nurses are great!

> Blessed is the man who walks in the counsel of the ungodly, nor stands in the path of sinners, nor sits in the seat of the scornful; But his delight is in the law of the Lord, and in His law he meditates day and night. He shall be like a tree planted by the rivers of water, that bring forth its fruit in its season, whose leaf also shall not wither; and whatever he does shall prosper.
>
> —Psalm 1:1-3

Yes, for those of you who look at the time I post, it is 1:20 a.m. on Saturday, November 21. I called a little after 10:00 this morning (I guess technically yesterday morning) to see what time we were supposed to be here, and they did not know. They would not have a room ready until another gentleman was checked out, and they didn't know when that would be. They said they would call. We had not heard from anyone by 1:00, so I called a little after 1:00 and they still did not have a room ready and did not know when it would be. They said that they would call, but I was welcome to call as often as I liked. Billy called around 4:00, and they said it would probably be 7:00, and they would call if there was one ready earlier. At about 4:30, we decided to head out. At a little before 6:00, we were talking and started wondering what we would do if they didn't have a room tonight and we got here and they told us to come back tomorrow or Sunday. Billy called them again, and they assured us they would have a room; they just weren't sure what time. We stopped for supper and took our time, arriving a little after 8:00. When we got here, they were cleaning the room, and we were put in it about thirty minutes later.

The nurses are great so far! We are very pleased and thankful. They had to run IV fluids for at least two hours before they could give the chemo, and it was a little after 9:00 before they got those going. Chemo was finally given about 12:15 a.m. However, there was an emergency on the floor and things beyond the nurse's control that took time to take care of and that made things rather late. We are still waiting for Billy's evening pain medications (he takes one between 8:00 and 9:00 and the other at 10:30 normally). I was not allowed to give them to him because they have to do it, and due to the emergency, the doctor didn't get the prescriptions into the pharmacy. They have to get the methadone from across the street. I'm not sure what that means. They are supposed to be bringing them shortly. I suggested not giving them tonight since they are so far past due, but apparently that is not an option either. Oh well, we will get things lined out and on track.

The chemo was given at 12:15, and Billy will get it again at 10:00 a.m. He will continue to get IV fluids at least until after he gets the chemo in the morning, and then he will have the rest of tomorrow and Sunday off. He will then get his stem cells back on Monday, and that is about a thirty-minute infusion. The chemo's side effects are mouth sores, a sore throat, possible nausea and vomiting, diarrhea (apparently that is definite), hair loss, and fatigue. They consider this day—2 since he gets his cells back on Monday. Monday is day 0, and then we start counting up from there. Around day 3 (Thursday) is when the counts should bottom out and he will begin feeling his worst. This will last till day 7 or 8, and then he will gradually start feeling better as his counts start coming up. The nurse said that sometime between day 3 and 7, he will get a fever, and they will have to do all of the cultures, a chest X-ray, and such. She said it isn't if it is when because it is just what happens.

Hopefully I have made sense. If not, just leave any questions in the guest book and I will answer them and hopefully make more sense after a few hours of sleep, which I am going to see about getting now since Billy just got his meds.

Thank you all for your prayers and sticking with us on this new leg of our journey. We love you all!

God is good, all the time!

—Dione

> Praise the Lord! Oh, give thanks to the Lord, for He is good! For His mercy endures forever.
>
> —Psalm 106:1

Sunday, November 22, 2009, 12:04 a.m.

> Have I not commanded you? Be strong and of good courage; do not be afraid, nor be dismayed, for the Lord your God is with you wherever you go.
>
> —Joshua 1:9

> Be of Good Courage: God's presence makes a radical difference in a believer's life. A confident peace replaces fear and anxiety when you know God is with you.[59]

[59] Ibid., pg. 253

Day—2: Billy has continued to be on IV fluids and will be until about 11:00 tomorrow morning. He did have to have some Lasix today because he was retaining some fluid, but it seems to have done the job.

To help prevent mouth sores, which is one of the side effects of this chemo, they had Billy eat ice chips, popsicles, or ice cream to keep his mouth cold. He started with the ice or other cold stuff thirty minutes before the chemo began and continued for an hour after chemo was given. The chemo itself took around thirty minutes to run in. He has not had any mouth sores, and his mouth looks good. The most likely side effects will hit him about day 3 after chemo, so that would be Tuesday. They expect him to get diarrhea, have a very sore throat, have a lack of appetite, lose his hair, and experience fatigue.

Other than being pretty tired from basically no sleep last night, he has done really well today. He is starting to doze off, and the nurses and I expect him to sleep well tonight and then sleep a good part of tomorrow or at least most of the morning. We shall see. The nurse did say that he will get a fever and require blood cultures, a chest X-ray, and so forth. That is a given. It is just a matter of when he will get it. It will most likely happen between day +3 and day +7. She told us this evening that the earlier he gets the fever, the better, partly because if he doesn't get the fever while he is an inpatient, then most likely he will get it when we get home, and then he will have to be readmitted.

We were sorry to learn today that the patient who had the emergency last night passed away. Billy asked the nurse about it this evening when she came on, and she said that they did lose him. I do not know the family's name, but the Lord does, so if you would be led to do so, please say a prayer for this family. There is also someone who is struggling with making a salvation decision who really needs prayer. I do not know if she reads this site and do not want to embarrass or upset anyone, so I will not put a name, but again, the Lord knows who she is. She is a friend of my sister, Dru. When it comes down to it, the salvation decision is the most important decision we can make in our lives because it not only affects our lives here but also where we spend eternity. Prayers for healing are wonderful and very important, but a person's salvation is even more important than there earthly healing.

We were not sure if our cell phones would work in our room, but both phones do work. If you do not have our numbers and would like them, just e-mail me and I will give them to you. We have a nice room, and they have told us that visitors are welcome. They just ask that they be healthy, and when kids visit, they will not be able to wander around but will need to stay in our room. We are on the fifth floor. They do some transplants on the sixth floor as well.

I think I covered everything for today. If there is something I have not made clear or confused you on, feel free to ask and I will do my best to answer. Dr. G came in this morning, and he said that Billy's time as an inpatient is pretty much guaranteed to be a week and a half. That is very standard. He said that it is very rare for someone to get out in less than ten days, just as is it rather rare for them to have to stay longer. From what he said today, it sounds like once Billy is released, we will need to stay in St. Louis until after his first checkup, which will be two to three days after his release. That isn't too bad.

Prayers:

- That while the side effects are part of the process, they will not be to severe
- That the entire process will go well and most importantly that it will work
- That he will get his fever early but it will be short lived, with no complications

Thank you for your prayers and sticking with us. This sure has turned into quite the journey and a very interesting process. It has been pointed out to me by more than one nurse through all of this that I might consider being a nurse when the kids are older. In fact, the nurse practitioner at Levi's clinic mentioned it the other day. She said that after learning so much about diabetes with Levi and now that I am learning an entirely new area of medicine, it might be something to think about for the future. Hmm, as with so many other things these days, we shall see.

While I do not believe that the Lord did this to Billy or even that He gave Levi diabetes, I do believe that there is something to be learned from it.

There will be or is a purpose for us going through all of this. Billy and I do not know why Levi got diabetes, but we do know why he was diagnosed when he was. We were supposed to be at the university hospital when we were there with Levi. It was all about timing, and the Lord wanted us there at that time for a reason. Many of those reading this know what that reason was because we have told the story many times. Another day when I don't have much to post, maybe I will tell you about it then. Just know that the Lord does use everything for good, and His timing is perfect. We have seen if quite often in our lives.

Oh, before I close, thank you, Pam, for the suggestion of having some candy or something during the infusion of the stem cells. We actually have a big bag of Life Savers that my dad picked up for Billy yesterday. (Thank you, Dad!) Billy had asked for Life Savers, and I forgot to get them when I went to town the other day. I apologized to Billy for not getting them, and he said it wasn't a big deal and not to worry about it. Well, Miss Cassy would not accept that. She had Kaylyn call Grandpa Ron (my dad) yesterday to ask him to pick up Life Savers, and bring them out when he came. (Dad drove us down yesterday. Thank you, Dad!) When I told Cassy that Billy said it was okay and that I was sure I could get some later on, that was not acceptable as far as Cassy was concerned. She said, "He is going to be in the hospital for two to three weeks, and he needs Life Savers!" She wasn't too happy with me for forgetting them in the first place. One thing is for sure: you never have to wonder what Cassy might be thinking because she doesn't hesitate to tell you.

God is good, all the time!

—Dione

> Praise the Lord! Oh, give thanks to the Lord, for He is good! For His mercy endures forever.
>
> —Psalm 106:1

Sunday, November 22, 2009 9:00 p.m.

> Now this is the commandment, and which the Lord your God has commanded to teach you, that you may observe them in the land which you are crossing over to possess, that you may fear the Lord your God, to keep all his statues and His commandments which I command you, you and your son and your grandson, all the days of your life, and that your days may be prolonged. Therefore hear, O Israel, and be careful to observe it, that it may be well with you, and that you may multiply greatly as the Lord God of your fathers has promised you—a land flowing with milk and honey. Hear, O Israel: The Lord our God, the Lord is One! You shall love the Lord your God with all your heart, with all your soul, and with all your strength.
>
> —Deuteronomy 6:1-5

> But when the Pharisees heard that He had silenced the Sadducees, they gathered together. Then one of them, a lawyer, asked Him a question, testing Him, and saying, "Teacher, which is the great commandment in the law?" Jesus said to him, "You shall love the Lord your God with all your heart, with all your soul, and with all your mind."
>
> —Matthew 22:34-37

Day—1: So far so good. Billy has had no real side effects to speak of—at least not yet. They said to expect them on Monday or Tuesday. Billy still did not sleep very well last night, and he does not have as much of an appetite. However, he did eat okay once he decided to try something. He didn't feel hungry, but when he ate a little something, it woke his appetite up, and then he did better. He won't be getting anymore Decadron, so he should be able to sleep better. He did sleep a little more last night than the night before, and he has done a little napping today. Maybe that means the Decadron is wearing off. We have not seen the blood test results yet today. They don't draw blood until late in the day. Yesterday his counts had dropped from Friday. They said they would continue to drop pretty fast until they bottom out sometime in the next couple of days. Dr. G came in this morning. He said everything is looking good and is a go for the stem cells tomorrow. Billy will be getting them about mid-morning tomorrow.

The kids have had a good weekend (thanks, Steve and Linda) and are at the Thanksgiving meal at church, so they are eating really well this evening. If there is a day that I do not get an update done, do not worry. We are having Internet connection problems and at times just cannot keep a connection. Billy spent a good part of the day yesterday trying to figure out if it is our computer, maybe the wireless card, or if it is the network here. At one time he had almost decided it was our computer, but then after further investigation, he wasn't so sure. Either way, we have trouble maintaining a connection for any length of time.

Prayers:

- That the side effects will not be too severe when they do hit
- That the transplant goes well tomorrow. The only real possible issue with the transplant itself is if Billy has a reaction to the preservative they use. We do not expect any reactions, but you never know
- That things will go well after the transplant and Billy's counts will recover with no real issues

Thank you for your prayers and support. You all mean a lot to us, and we love you.

God is good, all the time!

—Dione

> Praise the Lord! Oh, give thanks to the Lord, for He is good! For His mercy endures forever.
>
> —Psalm 106:1

Monday, November 23, 2009, 4:57 p.m.

> Your eyes saw my substance, being yet unformed. And in Your book they all were written, the days fashioned for me, when as yet there were none of them. How precious also are Your thoughts to me, O God! How great is the sum of them!
>
> —Psalm 139:16-17

> Precious Thoughts—God's thoughts toward you are infinite, wonderful, and tender. Let Him share them with you and they will become precious to you.[60]

Day 0: Today is considered Billy's new birthday, or at least that is what the transplant nurse said. The actual transplant took place between 2:00 and 3:00. There are pre-meds and other things that have to be given to start with, and the cells also have to be thawed out. There really isn't much to it, and it all went very well. They did give Billy Benadryl, and since he was already sleepy today and working on catching up on his sleep, he has been sleeping since the transplant. He has had some trouble with nausea this afternoon. The nurses suggested he eat a light lunch before the transplant. We had been told transplant would be around noon, so he ate a little at about 11:00, but it didn't sit well. The nurse happened to be in here when he got sick, so they gave him something for it. Then they gave him some more anti-nausea stuff as part of the pre-meds for the transplant. He has not been awake long enough since then to try eating again, but the medicine did settle his stomach, so hopefully he won't have any trouble eating supper.

We talked to Dr. G again today, and he said Billy will be an inpatient for another ten to twelve days, depending on how he does. Once his counts come up, he still has to stay for another two to three days to make sure they are stable and stay up. We will then need to stay close until the first checkup, which will be two to five days after he is released from the hospital. We will just have to see how it goes, but so far so good.

---

60 Ibid., pg. 732

There is another couple here from Jefferson City. Jim is in his late sixties, and his wife, Judy, is staying with him as well. We followed each other around during the week of stem cell harvest, and Jim collected all of his cells in one day as well. He also had trouble with his catheter, just like Billy did, and had to have an extra stitch or two put in. Jim came back on Tuesday, November 17 to start his transplant. He had the transplant on Friday. They are on the sixth floor, so we had not seen them before today. I saw Judy today, and she said Jim is doing well. He is struggling with some nausea, but the medication the nurses give him takes care of it.

The kids are doing well, and they really enjoyed their weekend. Levi is doing well with his diabetes. We will have to see how things go and when Billy is comfortable having the kids visit. They don't really encourage kids to visit. They will allow your own kids to visit you, but they must stay in your room. Billy thought the kids could be in the family room part as well, but I read the little sign outside the family room, and that does not appear to be the case. However, there are many other sitting areas on other floors. When the kids visit, if it is too much to have all of them in the room at once, then I can stay with some of them in one of the other areas on another floor or we can wander the gift shop or something.

Thank you for sticking with us and for your prayers, support, and messages. We feel the prayers every day and are very grateful for them. We love you all and keep you in our prayers.

God is good, all the time!

—Dione

> Praise the Lord! Oh, give thanks to the Lord, for He is good! For His mercy endures forever.
>
> —Psalm 106:1

Tuesday, November 24, 2009, 8:02 p.m.

> Your hands have made me and fashioned me; give me understanding, that I may learn Your commandments. Those who fear You will be glad when they see me, because I have hoped in Your word. I know, O Lord, that Your judgments are right, and that in faithfulness You have afflicted me. Let, I pray, Your merciful kindness be for my comfort, according to Your word to Your servant. Let Your tender mercies come to me, that I may live; for Your law is my delight. Let the proud be ashamed, for they treated me wrongfully with falsehood; but I will meditate on Your precepts. Let those who fear You turn to me, those who know Your testimonies. Let my heart be blameless regarding Your statues, that I may not be ashamed.
>
> —Psalm 119:73-80

Day +1: So far so good. Billy slept well last night and has been more rested and awake today. He says he feels okay, but he seems a little fatigued. So far he has had none of the issues they are watching for. There seems to be some discrepancy as to when Billy will feel really bad, so we will just have to see how it goes. They are saying he will be an inpatient for ten to fourteen days after transplant, so that is ten to fourteen days from yesterday. We had been told his worst days would be from day three today seven after transplant, but today someone else told us it would be more like days eight to ten. We figure it all depends on the person, and we will just have to see how it goes and take it one day at a time.

Billy's potassium is low, so they will be giving him IV potassium around the time when he goes to bed. It is a four-hour infusion. He has been taking potassium in pill form, and we told the doctor we saw on Friday night when we came in about all of his meds. They took care of getting him his pain meds and have those on a good schedule, but they did not give him his potassium. The nurse doesn't know if it was an oversight or if because he has a blood draw every day, they decided to just see how it did. He has had potassium infusions before, so it isn't a big deal.

Thank you all for your prayers. We love you all!

God is good, all the time!

—Dione

> Praise the Lord! Oh, give thanks to the Lord, for He is good! For His mercy endures forever.
>
> —Psalm 106:1

Wednesday, November 25, 2009, 4:21 p.m.

> I will love You, O Lord, my strength. The Lord is my rock and my fortress and my deliverer; My God my strength, in whom I will trust; My shield and the horn of my salvation, my stronghold. I will call upon the Lord, who is worthy to be praised; so shall I be saved from my enemies.
>
> —Psalm 18:1-3

Day +2: This appears to be the beginning of the bad days. Billy woke up very early this morning (at around 3:00 a.m.) with some pretty bad nausea and some vomiting. About an hour later, the same thing happened, and the nurse gave him something for the nausea. However, it didn't seem to do much good, and after he vomited another time or two, they tried something else. He has no appetite today and has not drank very much. (They will hook him up to IV fluids if he doesn't drink enough so he won't get dehydrated.) The second medication for nausea did work for several hours until he had pills to take a little while ago, and then he vomited again. Overall he just feels really yucky today. We had been told days like this were coming, and hopefully the fact that he has started early means he will feel better that much sooner. He is getting a nap now, which is good. Earlier in the day he felt bad enough that he was having trouble resting. They have been keeping his pain meds on schedule, and he is not in pain. He just feels really yucky and is miserable. He has had no diarrhea, yet. However, with the vomiting and nausea issue today, we are grateful there is no diarrhea.

We don't have the counts for today yet. They just did the blood draw a little while ago. As of yesterday, the counts really had not dropped that much, so we will see how it goes. They ended up giving him his potassium in pill form. They gave him four pills that, although they were fairly big, were not too bad for him to take, other than the fact taking them brought on some nausea.

Prayer:

- That the worst days won't last too long and there won't be any complications
- That he will be able to regain at least some of his appetite before long (he has none today)
- That he will be able to rest even when feeling really crummy (he is napping really well right now)

Thank you for your prayers, support, encouragement, and notes in the guestbook and all that you are doing for us. We have an amazing support system, and it is a big help in getting through all of this. We love you all and keep you in our prayers.

God is good, all the time!

—Dione

> Praise the Lord! Oh, give thanks to the Lord, for He is good! For His mercy endures forever.
>
> —Psalm 106:1

Thursday, November 25, 2009, 5:00 p.m.

> Oh, give thanks to the Lord, for He is good! For His mercy endures forever. Oh give thanks to the God of gods! For His mercy endures forever. Oh, thanks to the Lord of lords! For His mercy endures forever: To Him who alone does great wonders, for His mercy endures forever; To Him who by wisdom made the heavens, for His mercy endures forever; To Him who made great lights, for His mercy endures forever—The sun to rule by day, for His mercy endures forever; The moon to rule by night, for His mercy endures forever.
>
> —Psalm 136:1-9

Happy Thanksgiving!

Day +3: Billy does feel a little better today. He doesn't feel good, but he does not feel as yucky as yesterday. They gave him nausea medicine just before his supper last night, and he was able to keep his supper down. They gave him a different nausea medicine this morning, and it has helped a lot. He has been able to keep his lunch and a couple of other things down. He has no appetite, so nothing sounds good, but he is eating a little anyway. They changed the nausea medicine today because they noticed the one they were using yesterday made him very sleepy, and he slept most of the day. He slept really good last night too. They generally do vitals every four hours around the clock, but the night nurse saw that he was sleeping well last night and decided to let him sleep.

We have not seen the blood test results yet today. They just drew them a little while ago. The results from yesterday showed that while his counts are coming down, they are still on the low side of normal. We have been told that once they started coming down, they would drop very fast, so we will see how that works out. We will just go one day at a time and see what happens.

We hope you are all enjoying your day. Thank you for your prayers, support, and messages and all that you do for us. We feel your prayers and are so very grateful for them. They keep telling us the worst days are yet to come, with diarrhea, continued nausea, hair loss, fever, extreme fatigue, and just feeling really bad. However, Billy has been known to not follow the normal pattern of things, so with prayer, who knows? He may not get as sick as they predict. Again, we will take one day at a time and deal with it as it comes.

Prayers:

- That there are no complications
- That he doesn't get as sick as expected

God is good, all the time!

—Dione

> Praise the Lord! Oh, give thanks to the Lord, for He is good! For His mercy endures forever.
>
> —Psalm 106:1

FRIDAY, NOVEMBER 27, 2009 10:18 P.M.

> He has delivered us from the power of darkness and conveyed us into the kingdom of the Son of His love, in whom we have redemption through His blood, the forgiveness of sins. He is the image of the invisible God, the firstborn over all Creation. For by Him all things were created that are in heaven and that are on earth, visible and invisible, whether thrones or dominions or principalities or powers. All things were created through Him and for Him. And He is before all things, and in Him all things consist.
>
> —Colossians 1:13-17

Day +4: We talked to all of the kids this morning and really enjoyed our visit with them. They all sounded really good and are doing well. We were talking to them at 11:00 this morning, which was partly by design because Billy's nurse today was holding the exercise class at 11:00. She had already told Billy a couple of times that she expected him to be there. However, she gave a little too much information, and it was not something Billy wanted to do. When she popped her head in about 10:55 and we were on the phone with the kids, she understood why he was not coming to the class. He had been dealing with nausea all morning as well and did not feel up to going to the class anyway. He was up walking around the room when she popped in a while later, and that made her happy.

As I mentioned, Billy is still dealing with a lot of nausea. He was trying to fight it on his own and not take anything, but he decided it wasn't worth it. Shortly after we got off the phone with the kids, he had them give him something for the nausea. It helped quite a bit, and he ate some lunch. It wasn't long after lunch when he began feeling pretty yucky again and the nausea was returning. They could not give him the same med because it had not been long enough, but they were able to give him a different one. However, that one is the one that makes him very sleepy, so he slept most of the day, from a little before 3:00 until almost 8:00 this evening. He did wake up long enough to eat a little around 6:00, so he ate twice today. It wasn't very much at a time, but it was twice instead of just once. He is very fatigued and gets worn out easily, which we were told would happen. I helped him with a shower a little while ago, and it wore him completely out.

The night nurse put the counts up a little while ago, and his white count is very close to 0 (0.4). His platelets and hemoglobin are dropping but are still holding well enough that he doesn't need any platelets or blood. They didn't have the ANC (infection fighters) figured yet, but with the white count at almost nothing, the nurse figured it was probably about there too. It had dropped more yesterday than the white count.

Thank you for checking and most of all for your prayers. We love you all!

God is good, all the time!

—Dione

> Praise the Lord! Oh give thanks to the Lord, for He is good! For His mercy endures forever.
>
> —Psalm 106:1

Saturday, November 28, 2009, 9:57 p.m.

Day +5: Nausea is still a big issue. However, Billy decided to take something for it first thing this morning, and that did help because he got on top of it. He has needed to continue taking meds for nausea through the day, but they have given him some relief. He hasn't been as miserable. He is rather fatigued and just doesn't have much go. The diarrhea began today. They will not give him anything for it until they have gotten two negative cultures. Each time he has diarrhea they take a sample and culture it to check for infections. The bad part is it can take most of a day to get results back on the culture. The nurse said this evening that means it will be two to three days before they can give Billy anything for the diarrhea. Thankfully, he is not going often and is not currently in danger of dehydration. He has been drinking enough that he has not needed any IV fluids. If the diarrhea picks up or he just can't drink enough, then they will hook him up to the IV fluids. He really doesn't have any appetite, but he did eat a little at three different times today. He has lost a few pounds since we have been here but not enough that they are concerned with it at this point.

Since today is day five after the transplant, they began the growth factor injections. The growth factor is Neupogen, which helps the body produce white cells. It is to help kick his new cells into gear and get them started engrafting (taking hold and growing). His ANC and white count pretty much hit bottom today. The white count is 200 (normal is 4,000 to 10,000), and the ANC is 0 (normal is 1,500). His hemoglobin (red cells) are 9,400 (normal is 12,000 to 15,000). They will give blood at 8,000. His platelets have also dropped. They are now 32,000 (normal is 150,000 to 200,000). They will give platelets at 10,000.

Billy officially has no immune system, and they are watching for fever, as well as any other signs of infection. He is supposed to let them know if anything changes, including if he just feels different or worse in any way. They are also watching his blood pressure because continued low blood pressures can be a sign of an infection somewhere. I didn't know that. I thought low blood pressure might be due to his lower blood counts. He did have one rather low pressure this afternoon—92/69—but the next two have been more normal. They figure the low one may have something to do with the fact he had just taken medicine for nausea. It is the one that makes him really sleepy, and he had been napping pretty well when the tech did his vitals. Regardless of the reason, his blood pressure has been looking good since then.

They continue to tell us to expect a fever and some kind of infection, which they will treat with IV antibiotics right away. They also have told him to expect to be very fatigued and feel weak and maybe even a bit dizzy over the next couple of days with his counts so low. While he is rather fatigued, as long as the nausea is under control, he doesn't feel very bad. He has been getting up a few times a day and walking around the room, and today he got out of the room and walked around in the halls. He does not want to leave the floor since he would have to wear a mask, and with his counts down so low right now, they would rather he not leave the floor. Today was the first time he had left the room since we arrived eight days ago.

Prayers:

- That his counts will come back up fairly quickly
- That there is nothing out of the ordinary
- That there are no serious complications
- That recovery goes well
- That there are not too many yucky days
- That this works!

Thank you all for your continued prayers and support. There is no way we could thank you enough. It means so very much to us. We are extremely blessed! We love you all!

God is good, all the time!

—Dione

> Praise the Lord! Oh, give thanks to the Lord, for He is good! For His mercy endures forever.
>
> —Psalm 106:1

Sunday, November 29, 2009, 7:36 p.m.

> "Therefore do not worry about tomorrow, for tomorrow will worry about its own things. Sufficient for the day is its own trouble."
>
> —Matthew 6:34

Day +6: Counts: ANC (infection fighters): 0; white count: 100; hemoglobin: 8,900; platelets: 22,000. Billy will need blood when his hemoglobin is down to 8,000 and platelets when they get down to 10,000. Most likely that will be in the next couple of days. Dr. G came in this morning, and everything is going as expected. They don't expect the counts to start coming back up for about five days. Dr. G said that it would be Thursday or Friday before he expected to see the counts coming back up.

Billy is feeling pretty yucky. He is pretty fatigued and weak. He said this morning that he just doesn't have any pep. He didn't have any more diarrhea until late this afternoon. Since his stool sample from yesterday was negative for infection, they gave him something for the diarrhea, but they also sent another sample to the lab. They will do that every twenty-four hours as needed. They want to make sure it is just the chemo causing the diarrhea and not that he has an infection in his gut. He has managed to drink enough that they have not had to give him IV fluids, but he is still eating very little. He ate about half a donut and three-quarters of a sandwich today, and that is all he has been able to eat. They are giving him nausea medicine as often as they can, but food just doesn't sound good and thinking about it doesn't sit very well with him. The nurse said this is normal and he is to just do the best he can. He did walk around the room a little today, even though he didn't feel like it. It is important for him to get up and walk a little each day to help keep his lungs clear and keep his strength up.

While he didn't have to be hooked up to the IV for fluids they, did have to give him potassium through the IV. We keep forgetting to ask Dr. G about Billy's potassium. He had been taking potassium at home, and I brought it with us and showed the doctor who was on the night we arrived, but they have not been giving him potassium. This is the second time this week he has needed potassium, so we made a note to ask Dr. G about it when he comes in tomorrow.

Thank you for your prayers, support, encouragement, and messages. We love you all!

God is good, all the time!

—Dione

> Praise the Lord! Oh, give thanks to the Lord, for He is good! For His mercy endures forever.
>
> —Psalm 106:1

Monday, November 30, 2009, 9:57 p.m.

> Those who trust in the Lord are like Mount Zion, which cannot be moved, but abides forever. As the mountains surround Jerusalem, so the Lord surrounds His people from this time forth and forever.
>
> —Psalm 125:1-2

Day +7: Things have apparently been rather crazy up here today with new patients who are being admitted. Our nurse said that some of them are new and others are patients who went home for the holiday and returned sick. Billy's counts are the same as yesterday except that his platelets have dropped to 11,000, so he will most likely need those tomorrow.

Billy is miserable today. He feels very yucky and has *no* energy at all. He has had trouble staying awake and has done a lot of napping. Dr. G was in this morning and said that is normal with counts this low, and Billy will most likely have another day or two like this. The good news is it is just part of it, nothing to be concerned about. However, it is not fun, and Billy just feels bad. He is still fighting diarrhea and nausea. His cultures continue to be negative, so they are able to give him something for both, but it only works for so long before symptoms arise again. Of course, then they give meds again. He did sleep really well last night, which had him wondering about things when he just couldn't stay awake this morning. It appears that things are all going as expected. The nurses continue to expect Billy to run a fever, but Dr. G said this morning that very rarely there will be someone who doesn't run a fever, so there is a chance, although very slim, that he might not run a fever.

Last night when the night nurse came in, she was surprised Billy still had his hair. We asked if everyone lost their hair, and she said that she has been here for twelve years and had only seen two people keep their hair. She said that when they lose their hair can vary, but it is pretty much a sure thing. Billy said that considering everything else losing his hair is not a big deal, but he could be the third one to not lose his hair. Again, we shall see.

We had a really nice visit with the kids over the phone around lunchtime. That was the highlight of the day. They sound really good and enjoyed their long holiday weekend. Faith has decided that Grandpa Ron and Uncle John watch way too much football, but it's okay because there is a TV downstairs so she doesn't have to watch football.

Prayers:

- That things continue to go as planned

- That there are no complications
- That Billy's counts start back up fairly quickly

Thank you for your support, encouragement, messages in the guestbook, e-mails, and most of all prayers. We definitely feel the prayers every day. We love you all!

God is good, all the time!

—Dione

> Praise the Lord! Oh, give thanks to the Lord, for He is good! For His mercy endures forever.
>
> —Psalm 106:1

Tuesday, December 1, 2009, 7:45 P.M.

Day +8: Things continue as we were told to expect. However, expected or not, it isn't pleasant. Nausea and diarrhea have not been as bad today. Billy is still feeling very fatigued and weak, although maybe a little better than yesterday. He has been able to drink enough to stay hydrated but has no appetite or desire to eat. The only thing he has eaten since Sunday afternoon is three cookies. The nurses are not very pushy about the eating. They encourage him to eat but have said they also understand how hard it is to eat right now. With him drinking enough, they are okay with things for now.

The nurses have continued to tell us to expect a fever, and sure enough, it showed up. His temperature had been creeping up a little through the afternoon yesterday, and when they did the late-evening vitals, his temperature was 101. That is the temperature they consider a fever and start treating. They gave him a broad-spectrum antibiotic for all gram-negative infections through his IV, drew blood cultures, and did a chest X-ray. They will change the antibiotic if the cultures show there is a need for something different. Billy will continue to get IV antibiotics every eight hours up to twenty-four hours before he is released from the hospital. They will stop the antibiotics twenty-four hours before he is released to make sure his fever does not return.

While Billy still has his hair, he has developed some sores in his throat, which was also expected. They are a bit of an irritation but not too bad, and he is doing his mouth rinses and a gargle that they started him on several days ago. The mouth rinse and gargle do help, but they cannot prevent the sores because they are from the chemo and they were just waiting for them to show up.

The nurses are very good, and the nurse this morning said that while all that is going on is pretty miserable and even concerning to us, they have not been surprised by any of it because it is all a normal part of this process. She also said that when the counts start back up, which will be any time from day +10 to day +14 (according to the norm), Billy will begin feeling much better, and it will be almost like a switch was flipped. The diarrhea will stop, the nausea will improve, his throat will start feeling better, and his energy will start to return. She also took a look at his counts from yesterday (we don't have the results of counts from today yet) and said that most likely he will need platelets this evening, but the red cell count (hemoglobin) had gone up just a little. When his hemoglobin drops too low, he will get packed red blood cells.

We decided not to worry about talking to Dr. G about the potassium since they are keeping an eye on it and giving potassium as needed. They had to give him potassium again last night. They have been giving it to him in his IV so he doesn't have any more pills to swallow since taking pills can set off the nausea. Considering the amount of potassium they have given him, what he had been taking at home would not be enough to keep up with things anyway. When we discuss his meds before he is released, we will talk to the doctor and make sure Billy's current prescription of potassium is going to be enough.

Oh, I can't remember if I mentioned that his kidney and liver functions are great. They are right where they want them. The chemo Billy had for the transplant can be very hard on the kidneys and liver, but there is no indication of any issues.

Thanks for hanging with us and continuing to pray. It makes a big difference. We love you all and keep you in our prayers.

God is good, all the time!

—Dione

Wednesday, December 2, 2009, 4:24 p.m.

> And He said to me, "My grace is sufficient for you, for My strength is made perfect in weakness." Therefore most gladly I will rather boast in my infirmities, that the power of Christ may rest upon me. Therefore I take pleasure in infirmities, in reproaches, in needs, in persecutions, in distresses, in needs, in persecutions, in distresses, for Christ's sake. For when I am weak, then I am strong.
>
> —2 Corinthians 12:9-10

Day +9: We don't have the counts from today, but yesterday's were still with ANC at 0, white at 0.2, hemoglobin at 8.4, and platelets at 3,000. Since they usually give platelets at 10,000, Billy did get platelets, but it wasn't until 4:00 this morning because they didn't have any until then. They expect him to need red blood cells tonight, but they won't know until the labs are back. His fever did return last night, but they had already begun a second antibiotic. The first antibiotic is a broad spectrum that covers all gram-negative infections, which are the really nasty ones, and then yesterday afternoon they started a broad-spectrum antibiotic that covers all gram-positive infections, which should cover everything else. The blood cultures they drew on Monday did start growing a gram-positive infection, but with the new antibiotic, it should be covered. They are continuing some testing on the positive culture to find out exactly what it is. They want to know exactly what it is so they know if there is a better antibiotic to treat it with or if they have it sufficiently covered. So far his fever has not returned, so we will see how it goes.

We do not know for sure if the diarrhea is gone because it seems to show up again as soon as we think it is over, but he hasn't had any since about 4:00 this morning. Hopefully he is done with it. All of the cultures from it have been negative, and they have done three, which is usually all they do. However, if it returns, they are going to do another culture just to be sure there isn't something more going on other than just the side effects of the chemo.

They have started a different mouthwash for the sores in his throat. They are not a big problem but seem to be a little worse. The new stuff he swishes and swallows instead of spitting out. The sores (thrush) in his throat are also a side effect of the chemo. We also shaved his head this morning. When he got up this morning, his hair was coming out by the handful, so he decided to go ahead and shave it instead of having all of the hair in his bed and all over everything. I think he looks fine, and the only comment he has made is, "It is what it is." He told the nurse there are much more important things to worry about and it isn't that big a deal. I think he was hoping he wouldn't lose his hair, but it isn't something he is going to let bother him either.

Billy is still not eating. He has eaten almost nothing since Sunday afternoon and has lost thirteen pounds since we arrived on the twentieth. The nurse told him that while they understand him not eating when he is feeling so rough, once his counts start coming up and he is feeling a little better, he needs to start eating because they won't release him from the hospital until he is eating and drinking okay. He didn't drink enough yesterday, so he is on IV fluids, and he has not drank much today. He feels about the same today as yesterday and is just resting and hoping his counts start coming up so he starts feeling a little better.

Jim and Judy, the couple from Jefferson City that we met when we were here for the stem cell harvest, came to see us today. Jim had his transplant on the twentieth, and he is going home tomorrow. His counts were at zero for four or five days, and then when they started back up, they jumped up fast. As of yesterday, Billy's counts had been at zero for four days, so we shall see how it goes. Jim had his head shaved yesterday. It had been falling out for several days, and he finally got tired of hair everywhere and decided to just let them shave it. He said he was very blessed because he really didn't even get very sick at all. He had just a little nausea, no diarrhea, and no infections or fevers. He said that he did have a few days when he was very fatigued, but he was very pleased with how he has done. It was nice to see them and encouraging. Billy figured it out after they left, and with Jim being released tomorrow, he will have been an inpatient for seventeen days. Billy figured if his counts will start coming back up, then it is still possible for him to be released after seventeen days, and that would be Sunday. We can hope.

I did the laundry today, and that turned out to be an adventure. They have a laundry room on the floor with a washer and dryer. I washed clothes last Thursday, and the washer didn't seem quite right. This morning when I went to do laundry, the washer was gone, and there was a pile of sand on the floor where it had been. Apparently the transmission went out on it. I asked if there was somewhere I could wash clothes, and they said I could use the washer on the sixth floor but that I then needed to use the dryer on the fifth floor. (We are on the fifth floor in room 5915.) I went up and down in the elevator several times to do my two loads of laundry. I talked to another lady who said the washer had quit working the other day, but she didn't know it was completely gone now. Billy thought it was silly that they have not replaced the washer. It isn't like there aren't any stores around where they could get one. Oh well, the laundry is clean, and we are good to go for several days. With any luck, we will be home before laundry needs to be done again.

Prayers:

- That he has no more fevers or diarrhea
- That the nausea goes away and there are no complications
- That Billy feels like eating
- That Billy's counts start coming back up soon and come up fast

Thank you all for your prayers. They are truly a blessing. We love you all!

God is good, all the time!

—Dione

> Praise the Lord! Oh, give thanks to the Lord, for He is good! For His mercy endures forever.
>
> —Psalm 106:1

Thursday, December 3, 2009, 10:52 p.m.

> Oh Lord, You have searched me and know me. You know my sitting down and my rising up; You understand my thought afar off. You comprehend my path and my lying down, and are acquainted with all my ways. For there is not a word on my tongue, but behold, O Lord, You know it altogether. You have hedged me behind and before, and laid Your hand upon me. Such knowledge is too wonderful for me; it is high, I cannot attain it.
>
> —Psalm 139

Day +10: Thank you, thank you for all the prayers! Billy is feeling quite a bit better today. He has been up walking in the halls a couple of times, which is a lot since for the last few days the most he did was go to the bathroom. He has had no nausea today and just a little diarrhea. He got blood last night, and that helped his color. He just looks better today. He has lost most of his whiskers, so by the time we get home, his head and face will both be smooth. Although he really doesn't have an appetite, he did eat some today. While it wasn't a large amount, he ate more today than he has in the last three days put together. He is also back on track with his drinking and has not needed IV fluids today. While we don't have the ANC yet, his white count was up to 0.5. It was 0.3 yesterday, and at its lowest was 0.1. We are hoping this works as Jim's did. Jim said that his came up a little one day and then jumped up big the next day and his counts were normal by day +12 or +13. He was released on day +14. If that would work for Billy, then he would be released on Sunday. We do know it will just depend on how he does, but it is good to know there is a chance.

One of his blood cultures from Monday did grow a bug. The doctor said that it is not one of the nasty bugs and one of the antibiotics he is on will cover it. He will be released on antibiotics because he needs to continue the one he is on for ten days, but that is no problem. While he is an inpatient he will get it through his IV, and then they will give it in pill form when he is released.

We had a bit of an adventure today. A little after 5:00 this evening our nurse came in and asked if we would mind moving up to the sixth floor. They had a patient on the sixth floor who was not doing well, and he needed to move them down to the fifth floor, but they did not have a room available. We agreed because it was not that big a deal. So I packed all of our stuff up, and at about 6:30 we were moved to the sixth floor.

I have to say I am very glad to see Billy feeling better. I also wanted to tell you that even sick, he is a pretty special guy. I think all of the nurses like him. He has not been demanding or grumpy, and he even apologizes when he has to call them for something. They just can't seem to get over that since their job is to do things for him. There were a couple of times when he had to page them twice before they came with his nausea medicine, and they apologized to him because they didn't get the first page. The first time he waited an hour before paging the second time. The nurse told him that she had not gotten the first page and told him not to wait more than ten minutes before paging a second time. He also apologized to her for seeming impatient because he knows there are other patients and she may have been in the middle of something important. She couldn't get over the fact he had waited that long because he didn't want to seem impatient or to bother her.

Last night Anna was his nurse. This is the first time he had Anna. When she came in, she told us that Sarah, who had been his nurse for the last couple of nights, was not happy when she didn't get Mr. Campbell. She told Anna that she was mad at her because she wanted Mr. Campbell. According to Anna, Sarah said that Mr. Campbell is really nice and very easy to take care of. Anna was in and out quite a bit until after midnight because of Billy's antibiotics and blood. Every time she came in she said that Sarah was still not happy about not getting Mr. Campbell. By then Anna had decided he was okay too and told Sarah it was just tough.

Thank you all so very much for your prayers! They mean a lot to us. We love you all!

God is good, all the time!

—Dione

> Praise the Lord! Oh, give thanks to the Lord, for He is good! For His mercy endures forever.
>
> —Psalm 106:1

Friday, December 4, 2009, 8:23 p.m.

> Oh, give thanks to the Lord, for He is good! For His mercy endures forever. Let the redeemed of the Lord say so, Whom He has redeemed from the hand of the enemy, and gathered out of the lands, from the east and from the west, from the north and from the south. They wandered in the wilderness in a desolate way; they found no city to dwell in. Hungry and thirsty,

> their soul fainted in them. Then they cried out to the Lord in their trouble, and He delivered them out of their distresses. And He led them forth by the right way that they might go to a city for a dwelling place. Oh, that men would give thanks to the Lord for His goodness, and for His wonderful works to the children of men!
>
> —Psalm 107:1-8

Day +11: God is good, all the time! Billy's white count and ANC took a big jump today! The white count up to 1.3 from 0.5 yesterday, and the ANC is up to 949 from 260 yesterday. The ANC has to be 1,000 for a couple of days before Billy can be released. The doctor came in late this afternoon. Dr. G is at a conference, so this was a different doctor. He said that we may just be able to go straight home when Billy is released and not have to stay in St. Louis until his first checkup. He talked like they will keep him over the weekend, and if all goes well, they will release him to go home and we will just come back to St. Louis for his checkup. It isn't definite, but he talked like it was a good possibility.

Billy had no diarrhea today but is still dealing with the nausea. The nausea was actually a little worse today than yesterday. He did eat a little today but not much. His platelets have dropped quite a bit again. They were twenty-one yesterday and are twelve today, so there is a good chance he will need those tomorrow. Things seem to be on track, and if all goes well, hopefully we will go home on Monday or Tuesday.

Prayers:

- That his counts finish coming up and hold
- That the nausea gets better and the diarrhea does not return
- That he has no setbacks
- That we get to go straight home from the hospital

Thank you so much for all the prayers! You all are wonderful, and we love you!

God is good, all the time!

—Dione

> Praise the Lord! Oh, give thanks to the Lord for He is good! For His mercy endures forever.
>
> —Psalm 106:1

SATURDAY, DECEMBER 5, 2009, 7:15 P.M.

> For You formed my inward parts; You covered me in my mother's womb. I will praise You, for I am fearfully and wonderfully made; Marvelous are Your works, and that my soul knows very well. My frame was not hidden from You, when I was made in secret, and skillfully wrought in the lowest parts of the earth.
>
> —Psalm 139:13-16

Day +12: Billy's counts continue to come up, and we are getting closer to going home. His white count is 4,000, up from 1,000 yesterday. The ANC count was 949 yesterday and is at 3,200 today! The hemoglobin came up some too, so it is starting to rebound on its own without Billy getting blood. His platelet count dropped to 9,000, so Billy will be getting platelets sometime tonight or early in the morning, as soon as they get them. The nurse said the platelets are the last thing to recover, but we should start seeing them holding their own and going up on their own before long. Until then Billy will get platelets as needed, and that can be done with him out of the hospital if needed.

Billy's diarrhea seems to be gone, but the nausea keeps hanging on. At times it hits all at once. Most likely he will be dealing with nausea for a while yet. Things don't taste right and he has no appetite, but he did eat a little today. The nurse put in an order so he can get Carnation instant breakfast three times a day. He tried that, and it went down okay. He seems to think he will have better luck eating when we get home, so hopefully that is the case. He is still very fatigued. He feels quite a bit better than he has for a few days, but he just doesn't have much energy. We went for a walk in the halls today, and it wore him out. It will take some time to build his strength back up.

We told the nurse what the doctor said about possibly staying an extra day and then going all the way home instead of staying in St. Louis. She said the doctors look at all the blood work at the end of the day and discuss their plan for the patient. She thinks we should be able to go home on Tuesday. We are so ready, and so are the kids!

Thank you all so very much for sticking with us, your messages and e-mails, and most of all, your prayers. We love you all!

God is good, all the time!

—Dione

> Praise the Lord! Oh, give thanks to the Lord, for He is good! For His mercy endures forever.
>
> —Psalm 106:1

Sunday, December 6, 2009, 8:06 p.m.

> Praise the Lord, all you Gentiles! Laud Him, all you peoples! For His merciful kindness is great toward us, and the truth of the Lord endures forever. Praise the Lord!
>
> —Psalm 117

Day +13: Billy has felt a bit better today. He started out taking nausea medication as a preventative, and it has helped a lot. He has not eaten much, but he ate more than he has been eating over the last few days. His counts are up even more. The white count was 5,700, the ANC was 4,620, and he doesn't need any blood or platelets. He had platelets last night, and that brought the platelet count up nicely. The ANC is the one that really counts. It had to be over 1,000 for two days before he could be released, and it was 3,200 yesterday. The doctor on the floor who came in this morning said he would talk to the transplant doctor about us going home. The nurse expects us to go home on Tuesday or maybe even tomorrow.

Late this afternoon Billy was hooked up to the IV pole to get his antibiotic, and I helped him into the bathroom. While we were in the bathroom, we heard the doctor stick his head in. I told him we would be out in just a minute, but he went on his way and didn't come back. We figure when the doctor on the floor comes in tomorrow morning, he will let us know what the plan is. The nurse agreed that would be the case. We definitely like Dr. G better than this other doctor. At any rate, it looks like we will be going home Monday or Tuesday! I can't wait!

Thank you all for your encouragement, messages, support, and most of all, prayers! We love you all!

God is good, all the time!

—Dione

> Praise the Lord! Oh, give thanks to the Lord, for He is good! For His mercy endures forever!
>
> —Psalm 106:1

Chapter 24

Monday, December 7, 2009, 10:23 p.m.

Day +14: *We are home! God is good, all the time!* The doctor signed Billy's discharge papers this afternoon. We filled all of his prescriptions—well, except for the antibiotic the pharmacy at the hospital was out of. We had to fill that one in Jefferson City on our way home. A couple of the nurses didn't seem very comfortable with the idea of us coming all the way home. However, the last time we saw the doctor, that is what he said he was going to let us do, and the gal who came in to go over discharge information knew we were going all the way home. We have to go back on Thursday for blood work to make sure no transfusions are needed, and then we go back on Tuesday, December 15 for Billy's checkup with Dr. G. It is so good to be home! Billy says he will eat and drink better at home, and I think he will.

I have to admit I am a little nervous about coming all the way home, especially since they did not do any blood work today. I would like to have known that his platelet count held or started going up and that the hemoglobin was holding okay. The nurses felt that after getting the platelets the night before last, Billy will start making them on his own. The platelets are just the last to recover. His hemoglobin had come up on its own Saturday but dropped a little yesterday. Billy says that it is only a couple of days before we go back for them to check his counts, and he is sure it will be fine. I have all of the information for what to watch for concerning low platelets and hemoglobin, as well as other reasons to call.

I know Billy will eat and drink much better at home. I was not sure what I would do to feed him if we stayed in St. Louis. He has eaten almost as much since we got home as he ate yesterday, not quite, but it's not too bad considering we didn't get home until around 8:30. Usually if you live more than two hours away from the hospital, they want you to stay in St. Louis. We are two hours and twenty minutes away, and my dad assured us he can make it in two hours or less. (Billy and I know he can.) If we need to go back for any reason, he will get us there. He will also be taking us back for the blood draw on Thursday and Billy's checkup next Tuesday. Thanks, Dad!

Prayers:

- That there is no fever
- That he has no bleeding or other issues that would send us back before Thursday
- That Billy is able to eat and drink as needed and regains his strength
- That this transplant took hold and remission will be achieved

Thank you so much for your prayers and all you do for us. We feel the prayers every day, and we know it is because of those prayers that we are home tonight. Thank you! We love you all!

God is good, all the time!

—Dione

> Praise the Lord! Oh, give thanks to the Lord, for He is good! For His mercy endures forever.
>
> —Psalm 106:1

PS: The closer to home we got, the better Billy said he felt. The kids are good medicine.

Tuesday, December 8, 2009, 10:14 p.m.

> The Lord is good, a stronghold in the day of trouble; and He knows those who trust in Him.
>
> —Nahum 1:7

> God Knows—God looks past our religious ritual and formulaic prayers and sees our hearts. He knows those who genuinely trust Him, and they will find God to be an unassailable fortress in times of distress.[61]

Day +15: We are enjoying being home. It is so nice! Billy is still struggling with nausea but has not done too bad today. He was able to eat two bowls of soup, and he drank a Boost, so he is making progress. He has also been able to drink the required amount of fluids. He is still rather fatigued, but hopefully as he becomes more able to eat, he will start regaining his strength. He is much happier at home, and he is enjoying the kids. Of course, I watch him very closely and at times I get on his nerves, but he only growls a little and then apologizes. He does seem to be doing okay; it is just going to take some time for him to regain his strength and get past the nausea and other issues. I will relax a little more after he has the blood work on Thursday and I know his platelets and hemoglobin are starting to rebuild on their own or he gets a transfusion if needed. It is still a concern to me that we left the hospital without them doing any blood work yesterday. Billy seems to think I worry too much, but I figure that is my job. I am pleased with how the day has gone and that his color is good. There is nothing going on to indicate an immediate concern. I am also happy to report the diarrhea is gone, and that is a real blessing.

Thank you all for checking in and for all you do. We are truly blessed with an amazing support system. Our families, friends, and church family have supported us in so many ways. It is quite amazing, and we are extremely blessed and humbled by all of you—both those we know and those we have never met. There are just no words to tell you all what an incredible blessing you are to our family and how much you all mean to us. Thank

---

61 Ibid., pg. 1098

you doesn't even come close, but that is the only thing I know to say. Thank you all, and may God bless every one of you because you are all such blessings to us. We love you all, and we keep you in our prayers.

Max asked a question last night, and it occurred to me that he might not be the only one wondering. He asked when we would find out if the transplant actually worked. Billy asked Dr. G that same question the day before transplant, and if I remember correctly, he said they would do a bone marrow biopsy in about three months to see how things look.

God is good, all the time!

—Dione

> Praise the Lord! Oh, give thanks to the Lord, for He is good! For His mercy endures forever.
>
> —Psalm 106:1

Wednesday, December 9, 2009, 8:51 p.m.

> Look upon me and Be merciful to me, as Your custom is toward those who love Your name. Direct my steps by your word, and let no iniquity have dominion over me.
>
> —Psalm 119:132-133

> Direct My Steps—God uses His word to guide us in our daily lives. We can find specific direction by turning to His word.[62]

Day +16: It was a long night. Billy went to bed around 11:00 but lay there and could not go to sleep, so he got up again and watched TV until about 1:00 a.m. He then had several episodes of nausea and vomiting until 5:00

62 Ibid., pg. 722

this morning. I suggested he take some of the nausea medicine and then take it as often as he can for a couple of days. Then he can back off of it a little and see how it goes. He has been trying not to take it too much and only took it once yesterday. We have two nausea medicines, and between the two, he can take something every three hours or so to stay on top of the nausea. I suggested the same thing yesterday and he just wanted to see how things went.

Today he decided to give my idea a try. I gave him the nausea medicine at 5:00, and he slept until 9:00 and then took the other one. I just kept up with when he could have a dose of each one through the day. This evening he said he thought we had finally gotten ahead of the nausea, and he was able to eat some this evening. He has done pretty well with his drinking today. I may not be the brightest bulb in the package, but I have a good idea from time to time. Hopefully we can stay on top of the nausea this way and it won't be too long before he gets past this.

We go to St. Louis in the morning for blood work and transfusions if needed. It is going to be cold out, but at least it sounds like we won't have any snow to deal with. Dad is going to take us, which is really nice. Thanks, Dad. How long our day is depends on whether Billy needs any transfusions.

The older four kids went to church, but Levi and Faith stayed home with Billy and me. Faith and Levi helped me fix supper, and we played several games. Levi won Clue and Blurt and Faith won Are You Smarter than a Fifth Grader? I have to admit I didn't try very hard, except for the Clue game, but just when I thought I had it, Levi accused, and he was right. I was really pleased with Faith and Levi playing Are You Smarter than a Fifth Grader? They are pretty smart! They each answered questions I didn't think they knew. Anyway, we had fun! Billy didn't play, but he laughed at us and with us.

Prayers:

- That Billy has no fevers or other complications
- That things will go well with blood draw tomorrow
- That the nausea goes away soon

- That Billy begins to regain his strength
- That the transplant did its job

Thank you all for your messages, support, encouragement, and most of all, prayers! We love you all!

God is good, all the time!

—Dione

> Praise the Lord! Oh, give thanks to the Lord, for God is good! For His mercy endures forever.
>
> —Psalm 106:1

THURSDAY, DECEMBER 10, 2009, 9:23 P.M.

> Look among the nations and watch—be utterly astounded! For I will work a work in your days which you would not believe, though it were told you.
>
> —Habakkuk 1:5

> Look!—God is at work in our midst. We do not have to coax Him to become involved in our world. We must open our eyes so we recognize and understand what He is already doing.[63]

Day +17: My dad took us to St. Louis this morning for Billy's blood draw. (Thanks again, Dad!) I am more relaxed this evening because Billy did not need blood or platelets! God is good, all the time! His hemoglobin has come up and is not far from normal, and his platelets held where they were Sunday. They are still quite a ways from normal, but it is our understanding that once they start holding on their own, it isn't long

63 Ibid., pg. 1103.

before they start building on their own. The white count and ANC both dropped but are still normal. The nurses said we should expect them to drop some since Billy isn't getting the shots to build them up.

Billy is feeling a little better this evening. We have stayed on top of the nausea, and that is helping. Things just don't taste right to him, and that still makes it hard to eat. He doesn't enjoy what he does eat, but he is working on it. He is doing really well with his drinking, and he is drinking some of the V8 V-Fusion drink each day. It has vitamins from fruits and vegetables and was recommended by the dietitian in Tulsa since Billy isn't big on vegetables. He did sleep really well last night, and that helps things too.

Thank you for checking in and for your prayers! We love you all!

Our prayers continue to be for no fever, for the counts to continue to rebound on their own, for no complications, for the nausea and appetite issues to resolve, and that this transplant does its job.

God is good, all the time!

—Dione

> Praise the Lord! Oh, give thanks to the Lord, for He is good! For His mercy endures forever.
>
> —Psalm 106:1

Saturday, December 12, 2009, 9:15 p.m.

> I will stand my watch and set myself on the rampart, and watch to see what He will say to me, and what I will answer when I am corrected.
>
> —Habakkuk 1:16

> Stand Watch—No amount of reasoning or problem solving can explain some of life's circumstances. Only a word from God can make things clear and bring peace to our hearts. The diligence with which we await that word will determine what we hear.[64]

Day +18: It has been a busy couple of days. Yesterday Faith, Levi, and Cassy helped me make some goodies, which we then took to my Sunday school Christmas party. We all went and really enjoyed our evening. Billy really enjoyed visiting, as did the rest of us. Kaylyn had to work, so she came over when she got off work. It was a wonderful evening with friends, fun, laughing, and of course, food! Kaylyn took Billy home at around 9:30, and the rest of us headed home at around 10:30. Billy and I then visited with the kids some, and everyone headed to bed at about 11:30. It was a wonderful evening!

This afternoon Max, Cassy, and I went into town to do some shopping and then drop Max off at church to go with the puppet team to Journey to Bethlehem. The puppet team is entertaining there this evening, so Kaylyn and Max will be home fairly late. Kaylyn went over right after work. After dropping Max off, Cassy and I did a little more shopping before coming home to relax for the evening.

Justin, Levi, and Faith stayed home with Billy today, and everything went well. Billy continues to take the nausea medication, and that is really helping. He ate a little better today, so hopefully he will keep improving on that. He has a long way to go to build up his strength, but he is at least starting to feel a little better. It is all just going to take time, but we are seeing improvement.

Thank you all for your continued prayers, messages, encouragement, and support. We love you all!

God is good, all the time!

—Dione

---

64 Ibid., pg. 1104

> Praise the Lord! Oh, give thanks to the Lord, for He is good! For His mercy endures forever.
>
> —Psalm 106:1

Sunday, December 13, 2009, 9:55 p.m.

> "What is man, that You should exalt him, that You should set Your heart on him, that You should visit him every morning, and test him every moment?"
>
> —Job 7:17-18

> What Is Man?—Almighty God watches over us and is aware of all we do. We matter to Him. Such interest from the Almighty is beyond comprehension.[65]

Day +19: We all enjoyed going to Sunday school and church this morning. It was really good to be back with our church family. Billy enjoyed the morning and made it through Sunday school and church. He napped pretty well this afternoon. He does seem to be feeling better, but he is still dealing with fatigue and just feeling weak. He ate some today but has a long way to go to be eating what he needs too. He continues to drink V8 V-Fusion drink, which is good for him, and he is staying well hydrated. It is just going to take time for him to get his appetite and strength back.

We go back to St. Louis for the checkup with Dr. G on Tuesday. If Billy's platelets are up enough, then he can have the catheter taken out. Hopefully that is the case because it will be nice to get rid of that thing. I am hoping the dressing on it will last until Tuesday. I have a dressing and everything needed to change it, so I can do it if need be.

Thank you for your prayers and checking in. We love you all and keep you in our prayers.

---

[65] Ibid., pg. 603

God is good, all the time!

—Dione

> Praise the Lord! Oh, give thanks to the Lord, for God is good! For His mercy endures forever.
> —Psalm 106:1

Tuesday, December 15, 2009, 9:17 p.m.

> If then you were raised with Christ, seek those things which are above, where Christ is, sitting at the right hand of God. Set your mind on things above, not on things on the earth. For you died, and your life is hidden with Christ in God.
>
> —Colossians 3:1-3

> Obscured by His Glory—We are to be where Christ is, therefore obscured by His glory. Christ will increase in our lives as we are hidden in Him, dead to self and alive to Christ. Never allow anything in your life to distract people from seeing Christ.[66]

Day +22 (oops, I was a day behind): We spent a good part of the day in St. Louis. Billy had a blood draw and then an appointment with Dr. G. The doctor working with Dr. G got rather concerned when Billy's heart rate was 150. Billy's blood pressure, temperature, and oxygen saturation were good, but the high heart rate seemed to concern the doctor. The doctor asked Billy if he was dizzy or if he could feel his heart beating. While listening to Billy's heart, the doctor said it was really pounding hard, and he was surprised that Billy couldn't feel it or didn't feel funny because of it.

---

66 Ibipg. 1424

Billy has had an issue with a high heart rate since this all started. In fact, it was the high heart rate that finally caused the doctor to do enough investigating for Billy to get him diagnosed. However, his heart rate has been more reasonable lately, down in the eighties and nineties. The doctor then talked to Dr. G, who came in and talked to us. They decided to do an EKG, draw blood cultures, and give Billy some fluids. Basically, they were checking several possible reasons for the high heart rate. The EKG came out fine, at least as far as we know, since they didn't keep Billy any longer and nothing was reported to us. The blood cultures are to check for a possible infection, and they gave him fluids because infection and dehydration are both possible reasons for a high heart rate. They went ahead and gave him some IV antibiotics, so if there is an infection, they will be on top of it. He wasn't dehydrated (we could have told them that), so the fluids made little to no difference in the heart rate. They will let us know if the blood cultures grow anything.

Billy's counts were good today. His white count and ANC are well within the normal range, and his hemoglobin and platelets have both come up, so he didn't need any blood or platelets. However, his platelets were not quite high enough to be able to take out the catheter. I will call Dr. V's office in the morning because Dr. G wants Billy to have a blood draw done on Friday, and he said Dr. V could do that. Then we will go back to St. Louis on Tuesday (December 22) for a blood draw and an appointment with Dr. G. Hopefully they will be able to take Billy's catheter out on that day.

Prayers:

Thank you for checking in and for your prayers! We love you all!

God is good, all the time!

—Dione

> Praise the Lord! Oh, give thanks to the Lord, for He is good! For His mercy endures forever.
>
> —Psalm 106:1

Thursday, December 17, 2009, 9:39 p.m.

> Teach me, Oh Lord, the way of Your statutes, and I shall keep it to the end. Give me understanding, and I shall keep Your law; indeed, I shall observe it with my whole heart. Make me walk in the path of Your commandments, for I delight in it. Incline my heart to Your testimonies, and not to covetousness. Turn away my eyes from looking at worthless things, and revive me in Your way. Establish Your word to Your servant, who is devoted to fearing You. Turn away my reproach which I dread, for Your judgments are good. Behold, I long for Your precepts; revive me in Your righteousness.
>
> —Psalm 119:33-40

Day +24: We have been staying busy with some excitement we could do without. I will get to that shortly. Yesterday Billy didn't feel up to going into church. Tuesday wore him out, and he decided to just take it easy for the day. I called Dr. V's office, and Billy will have a blood draw in Columba on Friday morning. Kaylyn had to work, so she stayed in town after work and went to church. I took the rest of the kids in and helped get the meal ready. We also had our Christmas celebration with the kitchen crew. Thank you, Sheri and Ruth! It was very sweet of you! Levi and I left church at about 4:30, picked up some milk, and came on home. Billy ate a little better yesterday. We are timing his meals within an hour of him taking his nausea medication, and that has really helped.

Billy seems to be feeling a bit better today. He isn't as tired and has eaten okay. He still has a long way to go to be eating what he needs to, but he is making progress. Right after lunch I took Cassy, Justin, and Levi into town to do their Christmas shopping. We had an enjoyable time getting their shopping done, and they did a good job. The kids draw names and buy presents for each other. Levi bought a present for Kaylyn, and he did a great job, I think she will be very pleased with his choice for her. Cassy had Max's name and has been having a hard time figuring out what to get him, but she also came up with a good present. Justin had Levi, which was easy for Justin since they like a lot of the same things. Anyway, it was a nice afternoon.

On our way home from shopping, we met Kaylyn on route C and waved to her. She was on her way into work. Then the extra excitement occurred. When we arrived home and walked into the house, Billy was on the phone with Kaylyn. She had just been in an accident. Some man ran a red light at C and Southwest and hit her. Thankfully (God is good!) Kaylyn is okay. She has several bruises and seatbelt burn on her neck and is a bit sore. She will probably be pretty stiff and sore in the morning, but she is okay. Her car, on the other hand, is totaled. Kaylyn was able to take a few pictures with her phone, and the wreck really did a number on her car. She will be driving Billy's truck until we can get her something else. We will have to wait for insurance to pay for it and then start looking.

The guy who hit Kaylyn told the police that his light was green and Kaylyn ran the red light. Of course, Kaylyn told them her light was green and his was red. When the police told her he was saying his light was green, Kaylyn told them that wasn't possible, and if that was the case, they had better get the lights checked because their timing is off. Kaylyn did have a witness who could not wait on the police but gave Kaylyn her name and number and told Kaylyn that she was in the right and the other guy ran the light. Since this lady was right behind the guy who hit Kaylyn, she would know whether his light was red or not. Kaylyn gave the police this lady's information and kept a copy for herself so we can give it to our insurance company. Kaylyn works with very sweet people, and one of them worked for her this evening so Robert could bring Kaylyn home. (Thank you, Robert!) They are also going to cover her morning shift for her tomorrow so she can sleep in. Everyone figures she will be pretty sore in the morning, and this way she won't have to go to work until 4:00 tomorrow afternoon.

I really hate that Kaylyn had to go through this, but I have to say we are so proud of her. She has handled it all beautifully and in a very grown-up way. She gave the police officer all of the information he needed, answered his questions over and over, and stood her ground when the other guy was trying to rattle her by saying she had the red light and his was green. She did not talk to the other driver. She thought it was best not to since he was mad. She figured if she tried talking to him, she would end up saying something she shouldn't or would just get upset. She waited for the police to get his name and insurance information and then just got it from the officerShe then pointed out her car and said that if there had been a passenger in her car, he or she could have been badly hurt, and then she would have been really mad. We are so thankful that she is okay. As we told her, the car isn't that big a deal. We will deal with it.

Prayers:

- That Billy's eating continues to improve
- That he regains his strength
- That the transplant puts the cancer into remission

I would also ask if the Lord brings her to mind that you would pray for Kaylyn—that she not be too sore and that she not be nervous about driving (not to mention that I am not too nervous about her driving).

Thank you for your prayers! We love you all!

God is good, all the time!

—Dione

> Praise the Lord! Oh, give thanks to the Lord, for He is good! For His mercy endures forever.
>
> —Psalm 106:1

Chapter 25

Saturday, December 19, 2009, 11:37 a.m.

> Let Your mercies come also to me, O Lord—Your salvation according to Your word. So shall I have an answer for him who reproaches me, for I trust in Your word. And take not the word of truth utterly out of my mouth, for I have hope in Your ordinances. So shall I keep Your law continually, forever and ever. And I will walk at liberty, for I seek Your precepts. I will speak of Your testimonies also before kings, and will not be ashamed. And I will delight myself in Your commandments, which I love. My hands also I will lift up to Your commandments, which I love, and I will meditate on Your statutes.
>
> —Psalm 119:41-48

Day +26: Yesterday ended up being a pretty busy day, and the appointment in Columbia took much longer than expected. We thought we were just going to Missouri Cancer Associates in Columbia for blood work. However, things got a little more complicated. They take vital signs before doing anything, and Billy's heart rate was 132 and his oxygen saturation was only 91, both of which concerned them a bit. We then waited for them to do the blood draw, and before doing it, the nurse checked Billy's oxygen and heart rate again. His heart rate remained in the 130s and his oxygen saturation was only at 85 percent. The nurse said, "That is not acceptable."

The nurse did the blood draw and then checked the oxygen again, giving Billy a chance to take some deep breaths and see if that made a difference.

When it was checked the third time, his heart rate still in the 130s and his oxygen 86. The nurse put him on oxygen and called Dr. V's nurse. At this point, we learned that Billy was supposed to have an appointment with Dr. V but the scheduler failed to schedule one. Dr. V worked Billy in anyway. Billy's blood work looks great! Dr. V was really pleased. He said that for this stage post-transplant, the blood work looks wonderful. However, he was concerned about the oxygen saturation and said, "That is not acceptable. You are going on oxygen today." They also did a chest X-ray to make sure there wasn't anything building in Billy's lungs. The X-ray looked good, so we were able to head home.

On our way home, we stopped and got the rest of the stuff out of Kaylyn's car. We are so thankful she is only bruised and sore. Her car is a mess! We will get the ball rolling on Monday for getting things taken care of through insurance. Billy wanted to give the officer a chance to get a hold of the witness and write the report first. Although Billy has talked to our insurance and given them the other guy's name and insurance information, as well as the witness's information, we just haven't opened the claim yet. Kaylyn is driving Billy's truck today. She will be driving it back and forth to work for now. She really likes driving the truck.

We ended up getting home at about 2:30, and Justin (Billy's supervisor) pulled in shortly after us. He came to visit with Billy for a little while and also brought a box of goodies from the Farm Bureau family. I don't know how many work places can be referred to as a family (maybe most?), but Farm Bureau truly is a family. They have been so good to us. Thank you! There were lots of goodies, and Billy has been eating a few of them. His sense of taste seems to be improving because he has not complained about things not tasting right—at least not as much as he had been. The nausea medicine is also working well, and he may even be getting past the nausea. It is going better either because of that or because we have figured out how to time the nausea medication and eating. Billy seems to be feeling a little better each day. Visitors are welcome, so feel free to stop in if you are in the neighborhood.

I was headed back into town to meet my brother at about 4:00 to take him shopping. Since Kaylyn had to be at work at 4:00 I took her to work, and then my dad brought her home when she finished. I was able to finish up my Christmas shopping while I was out with my brother, so now I just need to do the wrapping.

Billy's oxygen was delivered while I was gone. The doctor's order is for two liters of oxygen twenty-four hours a day. At first Billy was saying that he was not going to wear it all the time. He was not very happy about having it. He has now decided that he will keep it on all the time when he is at home but will not wear it at church. Maybe he decided it was a good idea to use the oxygen because I pointed out that the doctor put him on it for a reason, 85 percent oxygen saturation is fairly low, and his organs need the oxygen. At any rate, I was much happier with him deciding to use it all the time at home. I can live with him not wearing it at church. I was afraid I was going to have to nag and lecture him on why he needed to use it. I think the fact that he was not able to do deep breathing and bring the saturation up also helped him realize he might need the help for a little while. In the past, any time his oxygen saturation has been down (except when he was an inpatient in Tulsa), he was able to take some deep breaths and bring it up to an acceptable level. We will see what Dr. G has to say on Tuesday. It does look like Billy will be able to get his three-line lumen catheter out on Tuesday because his platelets were 53,000 and the doctor told us they just needed to be above 50,000 to take it out. It will be good to get rid of that thing.

Thank you all for checking in and most of all for your prayers! As I have said before, we have an amazing support system, and you have all blessed us in amazing ways. We love you all and keep you in our prayers.

Prayers:

- That Billy continues to improve
- That this oxygen issue resolves itself
- That his heart rate returns to a more acceptable rate
- That the transplant did its job

God is good, all the time!

—Dione

> Praise the Lord! Oh give thanks to the Lord, for He is good! For His mercy endures forever.
>
> **—Psalm 106:1 saSunday, December 20, 2009, 8:20 p.m.**

> He went a little farther and fell on His face, and prayed, saying, "Oh My Father, if it is possible, let this cup pass from Me; nevertheless, not as I will, but as You will."
>
> —Matthew 26:39

> Trusting God's Purpose—Trials will either make us more sinful or more holy, depending on our relationship to God. When testing comes, we either trust God's purposes and find peace, or we trust our own plans and develop bitter, cynical hearts. We may not like our situation, but we love God, and we must trust His will for our lives.[67]

Day +27: Billy is doing pretty well. He is wearing his oxygen, and we checked his heart rate last night. It had come down to a normal rate when we checked it. His nausea is quite a bit better. He only took his nausea pill once today, and he is eating better each day. It is good to see the improvements. His checkup in St. Louis with Dr. G is on Tuesday. He is hoping he will be able to give up the oxygen. I'm sure it will all depend on how he is doing.

While Billy is doing better, our concern and prayer request tonight is for Kaylyn. She did end up with an injury from her car accident. It didn't show up until yesterday afternoon. The right side of her back just above the kidney area began hurting her, and it just got worse and worse. She had a company Christmas party last night but came home early because she was hurting so much. She took both ibuprofen and Tylenol, but they didn't touch her pain. She could take the ibuprofen again at 10:00 last

67 Ibid., pg. 1177

night, so I gave her the maximum dose she could have and gave it some time to see if it would help.

At a little after 11:00, she was still in a lot of pain and could not get comfortable in any position, so she could not rest. Although Kaylyn didn't really want to, Billy and I decided it was best to take her to the ER. They got her right in, but we were still there for a while. They did a urinalysis because there are things they can look for to determine if there is a kidney injury. Everything looked good that way. The doctor checked her over and asked lots of questions. Of course, we did tell him about her accident on Thursday, and he had her explain what happened and how and where the car was hit. That helped him to understand what it had done to her.

The doctor determined that she has a muscle injury to the large muscle that runs next to her spine. He told us that muscle injuries usually take about two days to show up. Kaylyn told him about working yesterday morning and what she did, and he was sure that is the issue. The doctor told her she couldn't work today, Monday, and Tuesday. They gave her a dose of Vicodin and a prescription for Vicodin and a muscle relaxer, which we picked up at Walgreens before coming home. We made it home around 2:30 or a little after this morning.

The medications take a little of the edge off and make her sleepy, so she has been able to sleep, but they really don't help as much as we would like. The medications also both have a side effect of causing vomiting, and Kaylyn has had trouble with that all day. She has vomited five times, usually about an hour after taking the meds. At least she isn't throwing them up. She has tried eating something just before taking them, and she has been trying to take in fluids all day, but she continues to throw up. The ER doctor said that it would take some time for the muscle to heal, but he didn't say how much help the medication should be. (It's not much.) He also said if it wasn't any better in a week, to contact our primary doctor. Her throwing up is making us worry about dehydration, and the medications are only giving her a minimal amount of relief, so I am going to at least call and possibly take her in to see our regular doctor tomorrow. Surely there are other medications that will give her some relief and not cause her to vomit so much. Billy really feels for her.

We are praying Kaylyn will have a good night and if at all possible, that the medication will start doing more good and she will not have any more issues with vomiting. Kaylyn felt really bad about not being able to work over the next few days, but I don't think anyone will hold it against her. Everyone was concerned when she had the accident, and it isn't something she has any control over. The ER doctor did give her a doctor's note in case work needs it for her file or something. Kaylyn told him she works with really nice people and it would be okay. Kaylyn likes her job, and she really enjoys everyone she works with. She is thrilled to have a job where she likes going to work and enjoys being around her coworkers. There are many people who don't have that, and Kaylyn understands it is a blessing.

Thank you so much for all of your prayers, and if you are led to do so, please pray for Kaylyn tonight. While we are a bit skeptical when it comes to doctors in Jefferson City, the doctor's diagnosis does seem to fit the symptoms and makes sense. I am just thinking there might be some meds that would work better and not cause Kaylyn the issues with the vomiting. Thank you again, and we love you all!

God is good, all the time!

—Dione

> Praise the Lord! Oh, give thanks to the Lord, for He is good! For His mercy endures forever.
>
> —Psalm 106:1

MONDAY, DECEMBER 21, 2009, 8:11 A.M.

Thank you for your prayers. It looks like things are beginning to improve for Kaylyn. I know we tend to want things better right now, and it doesn't always work that way. We may just have to give things more time. The ER doctor did say, "If it is not any better in a week, contact your family doctor." I guess he didn't expect much improvement in twenty-four hours.

Billy and I just want her to be feeling better fast, and things don't always work the way we want.

Kaylyn did have a good night, and she has not done any more throwing up. She had been throwing up around an hour after she would take her pills. She has started taking them with ginger ale and has not thrown up since around 7:00 last night. She had meds at 10:00 p.m. and 2:00 a.m., and everything stayed down. Her pain med was due again at 6:00 this morning, and it was almost 7:00 before she woke up asking what she could take. She decided to try ibuprofen instead of the prescription pain med. We are hoping she can start transitioning to using ibuprofen and Tylenol since the doctor didn't write a prescription for very many of the Vicodin. She is using moist heat, and that is also helping some. It looks like I may not need to call the doctor. We will wait and see how the ibuprofen does. If it isn't helping enough, I may need to call for a refill of the pain meds, but I shouldn't need to take her in.

Billy only took one nausea pill first thing in the morning yesterday. He ate pretty well and didn't have any trouble with nausea all day, so he is going to try not taking any nausea meds today and see how it goes. Things are improving. God is good, all the time!

Thank you again for your prayers. We really appreciate them.

God is good, all the time!

—Dione

> Praise the Lord! Oh, give thanks to the Lord, for He is good! For His mercy endures forever.
>
> —Psalm 106:1

Tuesday, December 22, 2009, 9:21 p.m.

> I will praise You with my whole heart; before the gods I will sing praises to You. I will worship toward Your holy temple, and praise Your name for Your lovingkindness and Your truth; for You have magnified Your word above all Your name.
>
> —Psalm 138:1-2

> Magnified Your Word—The more we encounter God's word the greater meaning it has for us. God stands by His word, working it powerfully into our lives.[68]

Let's see where to start. I think I will start with Kaylyn. She is doing better. (Prayer works!) She does not need the prescription meds and is just taking ibuprofen and Tylenol as needed. She has been up and around more today. She said the pain is much better, but she is very tired and gets dizzy fairly easy. We figure that is because she has been flat on her back, for the most part, since about 2:45 on Sunday morning. Billy and Kaylyn both figure she will regain her energy as she gets up and around more.

Billy called the Jefferson City police department yesterday. They have finished their investigation, and the report is finished. They did find the other driver at fault and determined he ran the red light. We filled a claim with his insurance company, and they have called and taken Kaylyn's statement. They have also looked at her car and determined what they will pay for it. However, the lady who did that cannot cut the check until the insurance investigator finishes. The investigator had not gotten a copy of the police report or talked to the witness yet, so we figure it won't be too much longer before things are settled since the police report says the other driver did run the red light.

Day +29: It was a long day in St. Louis, but everything turned out good. Billy's counts look good, and he was able to get his three-lumen catheter out. Billy did wear his oxygen on the way down but did not take it in with

---

68 Ibid., pg. 731

him. He didn't want to pull it around. They checked his oxygen saturation a couple different times, once around noon and then again just before we were done around 4:00. It was running between 93 and 98. His blood pressure was good, but his heart rate was 130, which it has been off and on since March. Dr. G decided to do an ECO on Billy's heart, and it looked good. The gal who did it said that his heart was really getting with it, but everything looked fine. She said that if she had any concerns at all, he would not be going home; he would be seeing a cardiologist today. However, she sent us on our way. Billy has said all along that his heart is fine. It is just fast. Thankfully the EKG last week and the ECO this week confirm that.

Some more good news is that Dr. G does not need to see Billy again until January 26. We are to see Dr. V in two weeks for a checkup and to have blood work done. We actually have an appointment with him for Tuesday, but Billy wants me to call and change it to the following week to fit what Dr. G said. That shouldn't be a problem. Dr. G said that at the next appointment, he will do the blood work that gives them an idea of how things are with the cancer. Then a month later they will do the bone marrow biopsy and will then determine if the transplant worked or if they need to plan on a second transplant.

Prayers:

- That Billy continues to improve
- That this transplant works
- That Kaylyn continues to improve and starts getting her energy back

God is good, all the time!

—Dione

> Praise the Lord! Oh, give thanks to the Lord, for He is good! For His mercy endures forever.
>
> —Psalm 106:1

Wednesday, December 23, 2009, 10:35 p.m.

> Seek the Lord, all you meek of the earth, who have upheld His justice. Seek righteousness, seek humility. It may be that you will be hidden in the day of the Lord's anger.
>
> —Zephaniah 2:3

> It May Be—God's people make no demands upon their Lord. They have no right to exemption from suffering; God owes them nothing. Yet where else can they turn but to Him? They must therefore appeal to God's grace and mercy to save them.[69]

Day +30: We had an enjoyable day because we had Christmas with my side of the family. We went by where Kaylyn's car is and got the license plates and took some pictures. The tow truck driver who towed her car was there and glad to see her doing well. He was not surprised to learn that the other driver ran the red light and was in the wrong.

Billy has felt good today. He has eaten pretty well and seemed to enjoy the day, as did all of us. Billy went with his dad to check out a vehicle for Kaylyn, and they brought it to the house this morning for her to look at. She likes it, and it is a good deal. The dealer has agreed to hold on to it until things are settled with the insurance. As soon as the insurance settles things and cuts the check, Kaylyn will have a new (well, new to her) vehicle.

Kaylyn is doing much better today and is going to work tomorrow. She figures she will be moving a little slower and plans to be careful with her movements. She was definitely doing better today, so I will try not to worry too much tomorrow.

---

[69] Ibid., pg. 1110.

Thank you for checking in and for your prayers. They are being answered. We love you all, and Merry Christmas!

God is good, all the time!

—Dione

> Praise the Lord! Oh, give thanks to the Lord for He is good! For His mercy endures forever.
>
> —Psalm 106:1

Thursday, December 24, 2009, 8:36 p.m.

> Now the birth of Jesus Christ was as follows: After His mother Mary was betrothed to Joseph, before they came together, she was found with child of the Holy Spirit. Then Joseph her husband, being a just man, and not wanting to make her a public example, was minded to put her away secretly. But while he thought about these things, behold, an angel of the Lord appeared to him in a dream, saying "Joseph son of David, do not be afraid to take to you Mary your wife, for that which is conceived in her is of the Holy Spirit. And she will bring forth a Son, and you shall call His name JESUS, for He will save His people from their sins." So all this was done that it might be fulfilled which was spoken by the Lord through the prophet, saying: "Behold, the virgin shall be with child, and bear a Son, and they shall call His name Immanuel," which is translated, "God with us." Then Joseph, being aroused from sleep, did as the angel of the Lord commanded him and took to him his wife, and did not know her till she had brought forth her firstborn Son. And he called His name JESUS.
>
> —Matthew 1:18-25

> Fear Not—Life circumstances often appear out of control, but when God is involved there is no need to fear, God sized events will always take us out of our comfort zone and leave us totally dependent on His intervention.[70]

Day +31: Although we are all getting tired of the rain, it was a very nice day. We had Christmas with Billy's side of the family today, and I think everyone enjoyed the day. It was very relaxed and nice. We are also looking forward to our day tomorrow because we will be spending the day at home, all together, celebrating Jesus' birth and thanking the Lord that we are all home together.

Billy is feeling pretty well and eating okay, but he still needs his nausea medicine at least part of the day. He still tires fairly easy, but considering all he has been through this year and that his transplant was just a month ago, he seems to be doing quite well. He is still using his oxygen at night and some during the day when we are home. I ordered a pulse oximeter, which reads the pulse rate and oxygen saturation in the blood. I suggested it to Billy, and we discussed it. We decided it would be a good idea because we could keep track of Billy's oxygen level as well as heart rate. That way we will be able to determine if he needs oxygen on a regular basis or just sometimes or if he no longer needs it at all. I think it will be something helpful to have now as well as for the long term.

Kaylyn is doing pretty well, and she did work today, which went well. The muscles in her back were tight this evening but not truly hurting her. She used the heating pad to help loosen them up, and I rubbed her back some. That seems to have helped, and she only needs ibuprofen or Tylenol from time to time now. We are very thankful that she is doing so much better.

Merry Christmas! Thank you all for your continued support, encouragement, messages, and most of all, prayers. We have seen many prayers answered this year and are very thankful for that. You are all a blessing to us, and we love you all!

---

[70] Ibid., pg. 1141

God is good, all the time!

—Dione

> Praise the Lord! Oh give thanks to the Lord, for He is good! For His mercy endures forever.
>
> —Psalm 106:1

Chapter 26

FRIDAY, DECEMBER 25, 2009, 9:55 P.M.

> And it came to pass in those days that a decree went out from Caesar Augustus that all the world should be registered. This census first took place while Quirinius was governing Syria. So all went to be registered everyone to his own city. Joseph also went up from Galilee, out of the city of Nazareth, into Judea, to the city of David, which is called Bethlehem, because he was of the house and lineage of David, to be registered with Mary, his betrothed wife, who was with child. So it was, that while they were there, the days were completed for her to be delivered. And she brought forth her firstborn Son, and wrapped Him in swaddling cloths, and laid Him in a manger, because there was no room for them in the inn.
>
> —Luke 2:1-7

Merry Christmas!

Day +32: I hope everyone has had a good day. We have really enjoyed our Christmas. It has been a very relaxed day, and everyone is very happy we were all able to be home together. Billy is feeling pretty well. If the stem cell transplant date had not been moved up from the original date we were given, then Billy would not be feeling very good yet. This worked out really well because he is eating and feeling better, and we all really enjoyed our day.

As always on Christmas morning, we told the kids they could get up at around 5:30 if they woke up on their own. They are not to set alarms, and they can't get us up until 7:00. However, we usually wake up shortly after they get up and listen to them as they go through their stockings. They are fun to listen to as they have to check out each other's stuff as well as their own. There is usually a lot of giggling too. It was a typical Christmas morning, with lots of giggling and checking each other's stuff out and the older ones saying, "Shhh, don't wake up Mom and Dad." Then there is always the discussion as to who is going to come wake us up. That usually takes them a few minutes to decide. This morning Justin and Levi were elected.

Thank you for all of the prayers! Take care, and stay warm. We love you all!

God is good, all the time!

—Dione

> Praise the Lord! Oh, give thanks to the Lord, for He is good! For His mercy endures forever.
>
> —Psalm 106:1

Saturday, December 26, 2009, 9:50 p.m.

The following verses from Joshua contain a conversation between Joshua and the Israelites. It is very relevant to our lives because it speaks of serving other gods. We don't always realize that even though we don't have actual gold statues, we worship we do have other gods. Anything or anyone we put before God or think a little more of than we should is in a sense a god. Some of these gods are money, power, fame, sports, another person, a house, or a car. A god can be almost anything. We must remember that God is to be first in our lives, always!

> "Now therefore, fear the Lord, serve Him in sincerity and in truth, and put away the gods which your fathers served on the other side of the River and in Egypt. Serve the Lord! And if it seems evil to you to serve the Lord,

choose for yourselves this day whom you will serve, whether the gods which your fathers served that were on the other side of the River, or the gods of the Amorites, in whose land you dwell. But as for me and my house, we will serve the Lord." So the people answered and said: "Far be it from us that we should forsake the Lord to serve other gods; for the Lord our God is He who brought us and our fathers up out of the land of Egypt, from the house of bondage, who did those great signs in our sight, and preserved us in all the way that we went and among all the people through whom we passed. And the Lord drove out from before us all the people, including the Amorites who dwelt in the land. We also will serve the Lord, for He is our God." But Joshua said to the people, "You cannot serve the Lord, for He is a holy God. He is a jealous God; He will not forgive your transgressions nor your sins. If you forsake the Lord and serve foreign gods, then He will turn and do you harm and consume you, after He has done you good." And the people said to Joshua, "No, but we will serve the Lord!" So Joshua said to the people, "You are witnesses against yourselves that you have chosen the Lord for yourselves, to serve Him." And they said, "We are witnesses!" "Now therefore," he said, "put away the foreign gods which are among you, and incline your heart to the Lord God of Israel." And the people said to Joshua, "The Lord our God we will serve, and His voice we will obey!"

—Joshua 24:14-24

A Jealous God—God is divinely jealous of your affection and loyalty. He wants nothing less than all of your heart mind, and strength. He zealously protects His divine right to your life.[71]

[71] Ibid., pg. 283

Day +33: Billy is feeling pretty well. He only needed one nausea pill today and is eating a little better almost every day. We enjoyed a visit from our good friends Russ and Trish and their little boy, Christian. It was really good to see them, and we all enjoyed our visit. Billy really does enjoy company and visiting, so if you would like to stop in, we would be glad to see you.

Some of the kids and I went into town this afternoon to pick up milk and some other odds and ends. Levi and Faith also had gift cards burning holes in their pockets and just had to do some shopping. We got a call a little bit ago that church is canceled for tomorrow because the parking lot is too slick. Everyone is a little disappointed because we always enjoy going to church, but it is best not to take a chance. We don't want Billy to slip and fall. We will just hang out together and enjoy ourselves.

We hope you are all snug and warm. Thank you for checking in and for all of your prayers. We love you all!

God is good, all the time!

—Dione

> Praise the Lord! Oh, give thanks to the Lord, for He is good! For His mercy endures forever.
>
> —Psalm 106:1

Monday, December 28, 2009, 9:12 p.m.

> For we were saved in this hope, but hope that is seen is not hope; for why does one still hope for what he sees? But if we hope for what we do not see, we eagerly wait for it with perseverance.
>
> —Romans 8:24-25

Day +35: It has been a quiet couple of days. We are fine with quiet, since excitement around here seems to be the wrong kind of excitement. Billy has been feeling okay—not great but pretty good. He is still taking nausea medication once or twice a day, but it has been several days since he has vomited, so it continues to get better. He is eating okay, again not great, but it is gradually improving.

Kaylyn seems to be pretty well recovered. She worked today and didn't have any problems. She is working nine days straight, so she is glad she has recovered. We haven't heard any more from the insurance company yet, but hopefully they will get things squared away this week.

Billy had an appointment with Dr. V tomorrow, but since Dr. G said Billy didn't have to have blood work or see Dr. V until next week, I called and rescheduled. The pulse oxometer that I ordered for Billy came today. It is pretty cool. It is just like what they use at the hospital. You put it on your finger, and it reads your oxygen saturation and heart rate. We are going to keep a record of Billy's oxygen saturation and heart rate for a while just because. I will write it down four times a day or so. By the time we see Dr. V next week, we will know if Billy still needs to have the oxygen or not.

Billy's heart rate is rather odd because one time it will be around 86 and the next time it will be 120 or higher. There really doesn't seem to be any rhyme or reason for his heart rate. So far today it has ranged from 84 to 141. His oxygen was low only a couple of times today. The first time was just after he had been up moving around, and it came back up on its own after a couple of minutes. The second time was when he came in from outside. He went out to park the Suburban and truck under the car port. (Max and I can both do it, but he wanted to.) His oxygen was pretty low (in the upper seventies) when he came back in from the cold, so he used his oxygen a few minutes, and that brought it back up.

We did have a little excitement using the pulse oxometer just after getting it today. Billy had used it, and then we were putting it on all of the kids. Everyone's oxygen and heart rate were good until we came to Kaylyn, and she had us worried for a few minutes. The first time we put it on her, it said her oxygen was 72 and her heart rate was 41. We tried a different finger, and it really wasn't any better. Billy had her use his oxygen to see if that helped, and we were asking her all kinds of questions about how she was feeling. When the readings on her really weren't getting any better, Billy tried it on himself again and it read fine. Then we tried it on Levi, and it read fine. Then it occurred to us that Kaylyn was wearing fingernail polish. I checked the book, and sure enough, fingernail polish can cause a problem with how the oxometer reads. After she took the polish off of one of her fingers, the readings were much better, so all is good.

Thank you for your prayers, support, and encouragement. We love you all and keep you in our prayers.

God is good, all the time!

—Dione

> Praise the Lord! Oh, give thanks to the Lord, for He is good! For His mercy endures forever.
>
> —Psalm 106:1

Tuesday, December 29, 2009, 10:41 p.m.

This verse reminds me of something I learned while going through the *Experiencing God* classes years ago. I don't remember if it was in that material itself or if it was something the person leading the class pointed out. Anyway, it went something like this: God will accomplish His purposes with or without you. If God chooses you but you turn Him down and don't do what He asks, He will just find someone else to do His work, and you will miss out on the blessing. When God asks us to do something, we receive a great blessing when we obey.

> For if you remain completely silent at this time, relief and deliverance will arise for the Jews from another place, but you and your father's house will perish. Yet who knows

> whether you have come to the kingdom for such a time as this.
>
> —Esther 4:14

> Such a Time as This—God prepares you throughout your life for your next encounter with Him. Each step of faithfulness prepares you for His next assignment. Your current circumstances are the tools He will use for His next great work in and through your life.[72]

Day +36: Billy ate pretty well today and only needed nausea medication once. Well, I only gave it to him once; I'm not sure if he really needed it. I give him a nausea pill with his pain medication first thing in the morning. He might not need it, but the last time he started the day without taking it, things didn't go very well. We will try not giving him any nausea medication again in another day or two. Billy is doing pretty well but still has a long way to go as far as getting his strength back, even to get back to where he was just before the transplant.

For the most part things are going well here. The kids are doing well. I spent most of the day working on assignment sheets for the kids' school. We will start back to school on Monday. It will be good to get back into the school routine.

Thank you for checking in and for your prayers. We love you all!

Prayers:

- That Billy continues to improve
- That he has no complications or set backs
- That this transplant achieves remission

God is good, all the time!

—Dione

---

[72] Ibid.,pg. 591

> Praise the Lord! Oh, give thanks to the Lord, for He is good! For His mercy endures forever.
>
> —Psalm 106:1

Wednesday, December 30, 2009, 10:21 p.m.

> While he was still speaking, behold, a bright cloud overshadowed them; and suddenly a voice came out of the cloud, saying, "This is My beloved Son, in whom I am well pleased. Hear Him!"
>
> —Matthew 17:5

> Listen to Him—In great moments with the Lord, we need to do two things: be quiet and listen. In the midst of our constant chatter, the Father says, "Stop talking and listen to My Son. He knows My will for your life, if only you would listen." He is God; He doesn't need our suggestions. Learn to be quiet, meditate, and listen.[73]

Billy has not felt quite as well today, but I think it is mostly because he is more tired today. We didn't go to bed until late last night, and then he got up at 6:00 this morning when I got up. I took Kaylyn to work since the roads were pretty snow covered. We didn't have any trouble. I just drove pretty slowly. Hopefully the roads will be in good shape in the morning.

There was a sad occurrence at our house today. It hit Cassy the hardest, but she is doing better now. Cassy's rabbit, Thumper, died. We have no idea why, but she was found dead today. Cassy had her in the play house since the weather had been so wet and cold. Thumper seemed to be doing okay. She was more than five years old, and her sister, who was Kaylyn's rabbit, was killed by a critter quite some time ago, which left Thumper a little lonesome.

[73] Ibid., pg. 1163

Billy called the insurance company today about Kaylyn's car. They are just waiting on the police report to finish things up. The agent Billy talked to said that he had requested a copy of the police report, but it takes two to four weeks to get it. It has been about two weeks, so he said he could get it any time now.

I took Max and Levi to get their hair cut this afternoon. They were both getting pretty bushy. I think they both look good now.

Prayers:

- That Billy continues to improve
- That he regains his strength
- That the stem cell transplant does its thing

Thank you for checking in, for all of the prayers, and for all that you do for us. We love you all!

God is good, all the time!

—Dione

> Praise the Lord! Oh, give thanks to the Lord, for He is good! For His mercy endures forever.
>
> —Psalm 106:1

Thursday, December 31, 2009, 9:51 p.m.

> Therefore, as elect of God, holy and beloved, put on tender mercies, kindness, humility, meekness, longsuffering; bearing with one another, and forgiving one another, if anyone has a complaint against another, if anyone has a complaint against another; even as Christ forgave you, so you must do. But above all these things put on love, which is the bond of perfection. And let the peace of God

> rule in your hearts, to which also you were called in one body; and be thankful.
>
> —Colossians 3:12-15

Day +38: Billy slept in until almost 11:00 today. I knew he had gotten pretty tired over the last couple of days. He didn't sleep very well on Tuesday night after going to bed late, and then he got up early Wednesday morning. He still isn't feeling great, but he is doing okay. He is still eating. It is not as much as he really should but it is not too bad. Progress is just slow. He has been monitoring his oxygen and heart rate. For the most part, his oxygen has been doing pretty well, and the few times it has been a bit low, it comes up on its own pretty quickly. His heart rate continues to be up and down. One time it will be around 89 and the next time it will be around 115. His heart rate was running like that when we were in Tulsa as well, and Dr. R never got excited about it. The high heart rate appears to just be Billy, at least right now.

There was not too much excitement today. Kaylyn had to work, and I have been doing some cleaning and organizing in our closet and room. Our room and closet tend to be used partly for storage, and with Billy and I being gone so much this year, things just got dropped, stacked, and shoved out of the way until I could get to it later. Well, it is later. I have the assignment sheets done and things ready to start doing school again on Monday, so I decided it was time to tackle the other stuff. I sorted through everything in the closet, organized, restacked, and made it through some of the room. I will tackle the rest of the room tomorrow or Saturday.

Levi has a cold, with a stuffy nose, sneezing, and some coughing. He has not had a fever, and other than being a bit draggy and aggravated with his stuffy nose, he seems to feel okay. To round out the day, Max took Faith for a ride on the four-wheeler this afternoon, and due to her gloves causing her an issue with holding on, she fell off and sprained her ankle. Max checked it out at the time, and it seemed to be okay. When they first got home she was doing okay, but it wasn't long before she was complaining of it hurting and not wanting to put any weight on it. At first our thought was she was using it as an excuse to get out of helping clean up the kitchen after supper. However, when I took a look, I found that it is pretty swollen on the outside of the right ankle, and a bruise is starting to show. Faith got out of cleaning up the kitchen, and instead we put her on the couch with her ankle elevated and ice on it, and I helped Cassy clean the kitchen.

Happy New Year! Thank you all for sticking with us all year and for all of the prayers, support, gifts, visits, phone calls, messages, and everything you have all done this year. Cassy says, "2009 is the worst year ever." Billy told her that while it has been a tough year, we all know that the Lord has been with us every day and every step of the way. We have been very blessed through the year. He also told her that when you think about it, things could have been worse, and we have a lot to be thankful for.

I know I am very thankful for so many things and so very blessed! One of my biggest blessings is my amazing husband. He has been through so much this year, and in many ways he has had a lot taken from him, yet he does not complain, whine, feel sorry for himself, or get mad. He simply trusts that the Lord has a plan and a purpose and will use this for His good and glory.

I am also blessed with six amazing, strong, loving kids who have had a lot to deal with this year and have done so with a faith and maturity beyond their years. And of course, I have the blessing of all of you, all of our family, including our church and Farm Bureau families, our many friends, and even those we have never met but who pray for our family regularly. We truly are blessed, and the Lord has been very good to us and provided in many amazing ways.

We simply cannot thank you all enough! We feel your prayers daily, and we have seen so many answered this year. God is good, all the time! All the time God is good! We love you all and keep you in our prayers. Have a wonderful, blessed 2010! We know that no matter what 2010 brings, the Lord is there every day, every hour, and every step of the way, and we trust Him no matter what we face in the New Year. However, the biggest prayer I have for 2010 is that Billy will be in remission, gains strength through the year, and is able to get back to doing the things he enjoys and loves. I have other prayers as well, but that is at the top on the list.

God is good, all the time!

—Dione

> Praise the Lord! Oh, give thanks to the Lord, for He is good! For His mercy endures forever.
>
> —Psalm 106:1

Chapter 27

FRIDAY, JANUARY 1, 2010, 10:16 P.M.

> And whatever you do, do it heartily, as to the Lord and not to men, knowing that from the Lord you will receive the reward of the inheritance; for you serve the Lord Christ.
>
> —Colossians 3:23-24

> Labor of Love—There is no place for mediocrity and laziness in God's service. If you are a child of the King, everything you do is for His glory. Your labor is an expression of love to God.[74]

I think the above is a good reminder that we are to do everything to the best of our ability and for God's glory.

Day +39: This has not been one of Billy's better days. He just hasn't felt very well today, although he said a few minutes ago that he is feeling better this evening than he has felt all day. He has had more trouble with nausea the last couple of days and even vomited today. It is rather frustrating for him since he had several days of doing much better. He was really hoping he was past the nausea issue, but apparently not just yet.

On another note, his oxygen saturation has been good. It occurred to him last night that when he has had low oxygen readings, it was on his right hand. Because of the nerve issues in the right arm and hand, the readings

[74] Ibid., pg. 1425

are not always correct. Last night he was getting a reading of 86 (oxygen saturation) on his right hand, so he switched to his left and it was 94. That is when it occurred to him that the day they were getting the readings of 85 and 86 and put him on oxygen, they were using his right hand and we didn't think to have them try the left hand. Most likely his oxygen was okay on that day too; they were just getting a bad reading on the right hand. When we were in Tulsa, they didn't use the right hand very often, and when they did start using it, if they got an odd reading, then they would check things on the left. We are pretty sure his oxygen saturation is fine and most likely has been all along.

Faith's ankle is still rather swollen, and we made her keep it up quite a bit today and had ice on it some of the time. Staying put with her foot up is not the easiest thing for her to do. We have not had her try to walk on it today, but I did dig out my ankle brace from several years ago when I sprained my ankle, and Cassy dug out her crutches from when she broke her leg. Faith has been using the crutches to get around the house. We are going to put the ankle brace on her tomorrow and see how she gets along with it.

Thank you for checking in and most of all for your prayers. We love you all!

God is good, all the time

—Dione

> Praise the Lord! Oh, give thanks to the Lord, for He is good! For His mercy endures forever.
>
> —Psalm 107:1

Saturday, January 2, 2010, 10:25 p.m.

The following story about a missionary will make you think: Jonathan Goforth was born on February 10, 1859, on his father's farm outside

London, Ontario, in Canada. As young adults, he and his wife, Rosalind, sailed for China as Presbyterian missionaries. They planned to evangelize regions deep within China that were as yet unreached with the gospel. The Goforths suffered untold hardships: the deaths of five children, the repeated loss of all their possessions, threats on their lives, and numerous bouts with disease. Yet through their ministry, thousands of Chinese people came to Christ. Then God used Goforth to spark revival among Christians in China. There was great outpouring of God's Spirit upon His people. God worked powerfully through this dedicated couple. Someone asked Jonathon the secret to his success. He replied that when he was young, he made Zechariah 4:6 the theme of his life. This verse is inscribed on his tomb as a lasting tribute to the power of the Holy Spirit:

> So he answered and said to me: This is the word of the Lord to Zerubbabel: "Not by might nor by power, but by My Spirit," Says the Lord of hosts.

Day +40: Today is Billy's thirty-eighth birthday! It has been a quiet day. We usually don't do too much for Billy's or my birthday. We sometimes go out to dinner, but not every year. I asked Billy more than once what he would like for supper and if he would like a cake or something. His sense of taste still isn't quite right. Some things do taste like they should but not everything, so he opted not to request anything special since he just didn't know if things would taste like they should. He did eat okay today and felt better than the last couple of days. The nausea didn't seem to be as big of an issue today, so hopefully he will be getting past that soon.

Faith's ankle seems to be doing better today, and we have her walking on it some. She needs to be careful and she is moving a little slow, but I think she will do okay. It isn't aching or hurting as much, and while it is a little painful walking on it, she isn't doing too badly. The swelling is down quite a bit.

It was very cold today, and other then Kaylyn going to work and Max taking care of his dog, we all just stayed inside where it is nice and warm. Despite the cold, everyone is looking forward to Sunday school and church tomorrow. We all feel like it has been too long since we have been to church. With no meals or kids' classes, we did not go to church the last two Wednesdays, and then church was canceled last Sunday because the parking lot was slick. The week just doesn't feel right when we don't have church. We all really missed it and are looking forward to tomorrow.

Prayers:

- That Billy continues to improve
- That Billy regains his strength
- Most of all, that Billy is in remission

Thank you for your prayers and all that you do for us. We love you all and keep you in our prayers.

God is good, all the time!

—Dione

> Praise the Lord! Oh, give thanks to the Lord, for He is good! For His mercy endures forever.
>
> —Psalm 106:1

Sunday, January 3, 2010, 9:30 p.m.

> "For My thoughts are not your thoughts, nor are your ways My ways," says the Lord. "For as the heavens are higher than the earth, so are My ways higher than your ways and My thoughts than your thoughts."
>
> —Isaiah 55:8-9

> Aren't you glad God's ways and thought are higher than ours? I know I am.

Day +41: Billy is feeling better today. He has eaten better today and said that he feels pretty good. It shows too because he has been rather spunky and a bit ornery this evening. He and Cassy have been enjoying their bull riding. A new season has started, and they have both been quite entertaining because they have their favorites. We all enjoyed going to Sunday school and church today. It was so nice to see everyone and be where we belong on a Sunday morning. Even with snow on the ground and still falling, we had a pretty good turnout at church. While Billy is feeling better today, climbing the stairs at church was almost too much for him. He is still pretty weak and just doesn't have much stamina. We know that will come with time, but it can be rather frustrating for him.

We have still been doing a little reminiscing about 2009 and what a year it was. We continue to be amazed with the blessings we have been given, and we see God's hand in so many things, both big and little. Billy's diagnosis finally came about basically by accident when the doctor was actually looking for something else—or was it by accident? I have to say no, I don't think it was an accident. I think it was by God's prompting that Billy's cancer was found when it was. Why did it take three months of extreme and debilitating back pain for it to be found? I have no idea, but I do know that God was there all along.

God was obviously in control as things came together for us to go to Cancer Treatment Centers of America in Tulsa and again when the stem cell transplant worked out at Barnes. The Lord and I got very close during that first month in Tulsa. I know He was right there every minute because I felt Him, and at times He was the only thing that kept panic or total fear at bay. There were many nights during that first month in Tulsa when I spent quite some time on my knees by Billy's bed. Almost anyone who knows me knows I am a talker, and I can go on and on and over talk and over think things. Well, on those nights I had the Lord's ear, and I know He was listening. I made sure He was very clear on what I wanted, but I also agreed to accept His will no matter what it might be. I told Him that He would have to give me the strength to handle it and to help my children through if it was not what I desired. I agreed to do whatever I needed to in order to take care of Billy but asked that the Lord would keep me healthy, because that is important for multiple reasons. He continues to answer prayers, give strength, and walk with us day by day and even hour by hour. The Lord has blessed us with all of you and your support, encouragement, messages, and most of all, prayers. Wow, there have been so many prayers answered!

It occurred to me today that 2010 is going to be a big year, with quite a few milestones met in our household. Kaylyn will graduate high school; Cassy will graduate eighth grade and then start high school in the fall; Max will turn sixteen and get his driver's license and has every intention of getting a job; Justin will become a teenager and start eighth grade in the fall (that will give us four teenagers in the house); Levi will be eleven and start fifth grade; and Faith will be nine. We also intend for Billy to be in total remission. I am thinking of having a big remission party when we get the test results to confirm it. (I am thinking positive here!) I had told Billy we should have a party or do something special for his birthday, but he said not to. I said that when we get the test results to confirm it, then we need to have a big remission party. Billy really hasn't said anything about that. He isn't too sure about the idea, but the kids and I like it. Hmm, with a high school graduation, eighth-grade graduation, a sixteenth birthday, a thirteenth birthday, and Billy's remission (again positive thinking), it may just be a partying kind of year.

Prayers:

- First is thanks that Billy is feeling and eating better today (I know that has been in your prayers)
- That Billy will continue to feel better and regain his strength
- That he *will* be in remission

Once again, thank you all for your prayers and everything you are doing for us. There just are not enough words, and I have not found the exact words to tell you all how much you mean to us and how much you bless us! We love you all!

Thank you again for checking in.

God is good, all the time!

—Dione

> Praise the Lord! Oh, give thanks to the Lord, for He is good! For His mercy endures forever.
>
> —Psalm 106:1

Monday, January 4, 2010, 8:48 p.m.

> Let your conduct be without covetousness; be content with such things as you have. For He Himself has said, "I will never leave you nor forsake you."
>
> —Hebrews 13:5

Day +42: It is cold outside, but we are staying nice and warm inside. Billy is feeling pretty well, and he ate fairly well today. Hopefully each day will continue to be a little better. We are supposed to go to Columbia for blood work and see Dr. V on Thursday. It could be an interesting trip depending on how the snow ends up falling. We will see how it all works out.

We started back to school today, and that went well. Everyone just started in and got their work done with no complaining. Whether they will admit it or not, I think the kids are all glad to get back to doing school. It makes things seem more normal and gives us a more regular schedule. There has always been a routine at our house, with the days having a schedule of when we eat meals, when we start school, and so on. I think it is good to get back to that schedule.

Thank you all for checking in and for your prayers. We love you all!

God is good, all the time!

—Dione

> Praise the Lord! Oh, give thanks to the Lord for He is good! For His mercy endures forever.
>
> —Psalm 106:1

Tuesday, January 5, 2010, 8:44 p.m.

> Now He who searches the hearts knows what the mind of the Spirit is, because He makes intercession for the saints according to the will of God. And we know that all things work together for good to those who love God, to those who are the called according to His purpose.
>
> —Romans 8:27-28

Day +43: Billy seems to be feeling a little better each day. He ate well today, although he did find that his stomach is not ready for spicy food just yet. His lunch did not sit well, and since he ate something pretty spicy for lunch, we decided that must be the problem. Other than the issue with lunch, the day went well. My dad came out to visit this afternoon, and we enjoyed his visit. Billy enjoys having company and visiting, so if you are thinking of dropping in, that would be great. It helps him to pass the time and brightens his day.

Kaylyn is a pretty happy camper this evening. We got a call from the insurance company of the man who hit Kaylyn, and they will be settling the claim and paying for her car. We will meet with the insurance agent tomorrow to sign over the title and get the check for Kaylyn's car. We will then go get her new vehicle on Friday. She will be getting a 1994 four-wheel-drive Ford Explorer.

I took Levi to the dentist this morning. On Friday he had a tooth hurting him. His blood sugar readings ran pretty high on Thursday and were running high Friday as well. I took a look and saw he had a swollen spot on the gum next to the tooth, and it was obvious that it was hurting. I gave him some ibuprofen, and that helped. I was afraid he had an abscessed tooth.

Late in the day on Friday, he said that it wasn't hurting him anymore and I took another look. The puffiness had gone down, but it was still rather pink or a little red around the tooth. Thankfully the dentist found that it is a baby tooth (as I was hoping), and it is fairly loose but not loose enough that he could just pull it out. The dentist didn't feel it was worth putting Levi through what it would take to pull it. He told Levi to keep wiggling it and get it pulled as soon as he can and it will be fine. The adult tooth is right there. The problem is just that this baby tooth needs to come out and doesn't seem to want to turn loose.

We (which includes Kaylyn and Cassy) are always getting after Levi to brush really well and take care of his teeth. (He hasn't always done very well with that.) Since he has lows fairly often at night, he ends up getting milk or something in the night, and he is usually not awake enough to have him brush his teeth at that time. When I give him milk in the night, I usually have him rinse his mouth out with water when he finishes the milk. However, I don't think Max does that, and sometimes Levi is not awake enough to do it at all. That has always made me wonder about how his teeth are really doing, since he ends up with milk residue on his teeth for the rest of the night. His teeth seem to be in pretty good shape, and that was good to hear.

Some of the kids are really hoping for a decent amount of snow, but they do not want it to affect church. They are rather picky that way; they never want anything to keep them from going to church. I think that is a good thing. We will just have to wait and see what happens.

I hope everyone is staying warm and cozy. Thank you for your prayers, support, and encouragement. We love you all!

God is good, all the time!

—Dione

> Praise the Lord! Oh, give thanks to the Lord, for He is good! For His mercy endures forever.
>
> —Psalm 106:1

Thursday, January 7, 2010, 4:10 p.m.

> Behold, I set before you today a blessing and a curse: the blessing, if you obey the commandments of the Lord your God which I command you today; and the curse, if you do not obey the commandments of the Lord your God, but turn aside from the way which I command you today, to go after other gods which you have not known.
>
> —Deuteronomy 11:26-28

> No Excuse—God is just in all His ways, and He clearly defines the consequences of our actions. Every person has a choice between a blessing and a curse. The fact that many choose the curse reveals the blinding effect of sin; only God's word can bring light and lead us to choose the blessing.[75]

Day +45: The kids were all disappointed yesterday because the meal at church and classes were cancelled because of the weather. Billy, Kaylyn, and I went into town after lunch to meet the insurance agent, get the check for Kaylyn's car, and get the paperwork taken care of so she can get her new vehicle. Billy is planning on us going to get the Explorer tomorrow. Kaylyn was very pleased because her payments will be less than she thought they might be.

We are all staying in and keeping warm today. I made cinnamon rolls, which pleased everyone. We didn't try taking Kaylyn into work this morning. We had her call in. They had no problem with it. I was going to take her in to work this afternoon, but they let her know that things are very quiet and she didn't have to come in today. Billy and I also decided not to go to Columbia for Billy's doctor's appointment today. I called and rescheduled it for Tuesday. It is supposed to be warmer on Tuesday. Dr. G wanted Billy to have his blood counts checked in between our

---

75 Ibid., pg. 222

appointments in St. Louis. We don't go back to St. Louis until January 26, so Tuesday works out well because it is two weeks before we go back to St. Louis. Billy is feeling pretty well and has been eating much better. There isn't anything going on for us to be concerned about, so it should be fine to wait until Tuesday for his appointment.

Not much is going on. We are mostly just keeping warm and enjoying each other's company. We are all thankful Billy is eating and feeling better. He doesn't have much strength or stamina yet, but that should come with time.

Thank you all for your prayers, support, and encouragement. You are all a blessing to us, and we love you all.

God is good, all the time!

—Dione

> Praise the Lord! Oh, give thanks to the Lord, for He is good! For His mercy endures forever.
>
> —Psalm 106:1

Sunday, January 10, 2010, 8:25 p.m.

> And I set my heart to know wisdom and to know madness and folly. I perceived that this also is grasping for the wind. For in much wisdom is much grief, and he who increases knowledge increases sorrow.
>
> —Ecclesiastes 1:17-18

> Chasing After Wind—God's wisdom is not attainable except as He reveals it. All our attempts at enlightenment and our pursuit of knowledge fall far short of God's wisdom. We are God's creatures. When He reveals His

> wisdom and His ways to us, this is an act of love and grace toward us.[76]

Day + 48: Billy is doing pretty good. It is going to take a while for him to regain his strength, but he is eating and feeling better. This morning at church he said that he did better climbing the stairs today so he could tell there was some improvement from last week to this week. He has blood work and an appointment with Dr. V in Columbia on Tuesday. The blood work is to check his hemoglobin, platelets, white count and such. Should be an uneventful appointment.

We decided not to go get Kaylyn's new vehicle on Friday because it was so cold and some roads were still questionable. Billy just didn't feel like getting out in the cold. So we will go get it tomorrow. Kaylyn was okay with not getting it on Friday. She said that it might be better not to be driving a new vehicle that she is unfamiliar with when the roads are not in the best shape. A couple roads around here were still questionable on Friday, but everything is in good shape now.

I took Kaylyn to work on Friday morning because we were not sure what the road conditions might be. I had something rather interesting happen. In fact, I found it to be rather amazing. I dropped Kaylyn off at work and then headed over to my parents' house to visit for a little bit until Kaylyn was done. Because it was so cold that morning, I wore Billy's warm coat with a hood. As I pulled up to the stop light to turn right and go over to my parents' house (after dropping Kaylyn off), I turned my head to the left to check traffic and something poked me in the eye and popped my contact out. This was very concerning for me because I am pretty blind without my contacts. I can go without my right one but not without my left one. All the way to my parents' house I was saying (this may sound silly, but I did it), "Oh God, please let me find it, please let me find it." I was also trying to think of what to do if I could not find it because my glasses are still my old prescription, and I am not even sure where they are because I can't wear them without getting a really bad headache.

---

76 Ibid., pg. 778

When I got to Dad's house, I sat in the vehicle and moved very carefully, trying to see if I could find the contact. As I arrived, my dad was headed out to pick my brother up from work. I knew he would only be gone for about ten or fifteen minutes, and I was hoping I could find it. I did my best to find it before going in the house and didn't have any luck. I moved carefully and went into the house and to the bathroom to look the coat over and see if I could see the contact on the coat. I had no luck. I took the coat off very carefully and looked it over again, as well as checking my shirt over carefully since the coat was partly unzipped. I still saw nothing, so I put the coat back on and went back out to the Suburban and looked for it on the seat and the floor, but I still had no luck.

I went back into the house and took the coat off. My dad and brother came home, and I sat down at the kitchen table with a cup of coffee and was visiting with them. I was also thinking about whether I should try to get an appointment with the eye doctor after picking Kaylyn up from work. Kaylyn would have to drive home since I really couldn't see well enough to be driving. I was wondering if I should I go on home and tell Billy, try to find my glasses, and then get an appointment. It has been long enough since I had my eyes examined that I have to have a checkup again before I can order more contacts. I was already planning to make an appointment soon—just not that day.

As I am sitting there talking to Dad and John and had these thoughts running through my head as to what I should do, I put my hand down on my right leg and put my hand right on top of my contact! I could hardly believe it! I very carefully picked it up off my pants leg, went to the bathroom to rinse it off, and put it back in. Then I told my dad and John what had happened. Amazing! I had gone into the house, taken my coat off, put my coat back on, gone back out to the Suburban, came back in, and took my coat off again, yet there was my contact on my jeans! I was so very thankful and made sure to tell God so.

We all enjoyed Sunday school and church today, as we always do. It is so nice to be back with our church family on a regular basis again. The kids do not want weather to cancel church anymore this year.

Our prayers for Billy continue to be for his strength to return, for the cancer to be in remission, and that he will not need a second stem cell transplant. Billy continues to amaze me with how well he deals with all of this. He really is very special.

If you are in the area or just feel like dropping in, feel free to do so. Billy really enjoys the company and visiting.

Thank you for sticking with us and most of all for your prayers. We are grateful and blessed by all that you do for us. We love you all!

God is good, all the time!

—Dione

> Praise the Lord! Oh, give thanks to the Lord, for He is good! For His mercy endures forever.
>
> —Psalm 106:1

Monday, January 11, 2010, 7:20 p.m.

> Therefore I say to you, do not worry about your life, what you will eat or what you will drink; nor about your body, what you will put on. Is not life more than food and the body more than clothing? Look at the birds of the air, for they neither sow nor reap nor gather into barns; yet your heavenly Father feeds them. Are you not of more value than they? Which of you by worrying can add one cubit to his stature? So why do you worry about clothing? Consider the lilies of the field, how they grow: they neither toil nor spin; and yet I say to you that even Solomon in all his glory was not arrayed like one of these. Now if God so clothes the grass of the field, which today is, and tomorrow is thrown into the oven, will He not much more clothe you, O you of little faith?

> Therefore do not worry, saying, "What shall we eat?" or "What shall we wear?" For after all these things the Gentiles seek. For your heavenly Father knows that you need all these things. But seek first the kingdom of God and His righteousness, and all these things shall be added to you.
>
> —Matthew 6:25-33

> Kingdom Living—To seek the kingdom of God is to abide with the King. When we live in His presence and follow His purposes, He takes responsibility for our needs.[77]

Day +49: Billy continues to be improving and is only taking the nausea medicine once a day. It is going to take a while for him to get his strength back. He is hoping his bones will be hard enough soon so he can start working on building some muscle back up. Until further notice, they have only given the okay for him to walk. He isn't up to doing too much more than that just yet and will need to build up his stamina a bit.

Kaylyn, Billy, and I went to California this morning and picked up Kaylyn's new vehicle. She left for work a little while ago. I think she is pretty pleased with her new wheels. She hadn't planned on making a payment just yet, but it is a small one and she will do fine.

This afternoon Aaron dropped in while he was out and about. Billy really enjoyed the visit. We had not seen Aaron since him and Amy helped Mike and Heidi bring the kids to Tulsa to see us. I think Aaron was glad to see Billy doing better than when he saw him last, and I know Billy was glad to see Aaron and enjoyed passing the time with him. Like I have said before, feel free to stop in. We all enjoy the company, but it is really good for Billy. He greatly enjoys visitors.

I chose today's verses because the Lord has really provided for us in every way, and I am so very grateful. In many cases the Lord has used you all to provide for us in various ways. His timing always seems to be perfect,

---

[77] Ibid.,pg. 1147

and just when I start to worry about a bill or something happens like the water heater going out or when we needed a new air conditioner, the Lord provides. He really is amazing, and I am so glad I know Him. I am also very blessed that He has put all of you in our lives. Thank you for your prayers and all you do for us! We love you all!

Prayers:

- That Billy continues to feel well
- That he starts getting his strength back
- That he achieves remission and does not need a second transplant

God is good, all the time!

—Dione

> Praise the Lord! Oh, give thanks to the Lord, for He is good! For His mercy endures forever.
>
> —Psalm 106:1

Tuesday, January 12, 2010, 6:00 p.m.

> Bless the Lord, O my soul; and all that is within me, bless His holy name! Bless the Lord, O my soul, and forget not all His benefits: Who forgives all your iniquities, who heals all your diseases, who redeems your life from destruction, who crowns you with lovingkindness and tender mercies, who satisfies your mouth with good things, so that your youth is renewed like eagles.
>
> —Psalm 103:1-5

Day +50: We had a very good appointment with Dr. V today. Billy's counts look good, and Dr. V is just tickled (he really is; you would have to know him) with how Billy is doing and how things look. Billy got his bone-builder medication today, and we will see Dr. V again on February 10 for blood work, a checkup, and to get the bone builder again. Billy asked Dr. V if he thinks a second stem cell transplant will be needed right away. While we won't know for sure until the bone marrow biopsy is done around the end of February, Dr. V feels that everything is looking really good and at this point there is a good chance that one stem cell transplant will achieve remission. God is good, all the time

Billy also asked when he could start shooting his guns and get back on his motorcycle. Dr. V said that he can shoot anytime he would like as long as it does not cause pain. He said that he didn't recommend getting back on the motorcycle until more like June or July because Billy needs to regain some strength first. We are cutting Billy's pain meds in half to see how that goes. If it doesn't work, we will go back up on the dose, but Dr. V would like to see Billy get off some of the pain meds, so we are going to give it a try. The only other thing I can think of right now is we will see about doing something for Billy's back three to four months after he is found to be in remission. All in all, it was a good visit and a good day.

The kids have been having fun playing in the snow! Faith, Levi, Justin, and Cassy spent about three hours out in it today. Justin came in a little earlier than the others, and Cassy went out after the rest had been out a few minutes. They all had a great time!

Max, Kaylyn, and I have GROW at church tonight. GROW is an outreach program our church started almost three years ago. Kaylyn, Max, and I are supposed to go the second Tuesday of every month, but we did not make it most of last year. We plan to get back in the swing of it.

I have found that I am a little paranoid about things. When one of the kids is acting a little off, a little more tired than usual, doing something out of the ordinary like Justin laying on the couch all covered up in the middle of the day (Justin is almost never cold, but of course he had been playing in the snow), or just anything that seems off to me, I quiz them about how they are feeling. If they feel even a little warm to me, I take their temperature. Of course, I am always keeping a close eye on Billy. I guess with there being no history of diabetes in our family and Levi having it and then Billy being twenty-five to thirty years too young to have the cancer he has, I just don't want to overlook something. Anyway, the kids are so good about humoring me even though the way they smile at me as I take their temperature tells me they are thinking I have lost my mind, but it is best to just humor their crazy mother. They are so sweet!

Thank you for checking in and for your prayers. Prayer works! We love you all and keep you in our prayers.

God is good, all the time!

—Dione

> Praise the Lord! Oh, give thinks to the Lord, for He is good! For His mercy endures forever.
>
> —Psalm 106:1

Thursday, January 14, 2010, 10:18 p.m.

> For it is God which worketh in you both to will and to do of His good pleasure.
>
> —Philippians 2:13

Billy is a little tired today, but he is doing okay. I think he is tired because of the long day on Tuesday, and then yesterday was also pretty long for him since we went into church just after lunch to help with the meal and it was almost 9:00 before we got home last night. That made for a long day with no recliner to rest in. He was having trouble getting comfortable by the time the day was over. He slept in a little and took it easy today.

I dropped everyone off at church at around 1:00 yesterday afternoon, and then I went to Kmart to refill prescriptions. Our insurance changed at the first of the year, so I needed to give them the information for the new insurance company and then get all of Levi's diabetic stuff refilled, as well as a couple of Billy's. The new insurance does not pay for the strips for Levi's current glucose meter. Since the strips are $1.00 each and Levi usually tests five times or more a day, it really wasn't an option to pay for them out of pocket. The pharmacist recommended buying a new meter the insurance would pay for the strips for, so I got the new meter and the pharmacist went ahead and filled the prescription for the strips. Since I didn't actually have a prescription for those strips, he was pushing it through. I will just need to get a hold of Dr. B and get a prescription for the correct strips as well as for lancets for the new lancet device. We have a bunch of lancets still, so Levi is still using his old lancet device for now.

I had not thought of getting a new meter as being a big deal or exciting, but Levi was very excited about it. You would have thought we got him a new toy. When I told him I had to get him a new meter, he was very excited and wanted to see it right away. I suppose like with other things, using the same meter over and over every day gets mundane and it changes things up to get something new. We all like getting new things. It came with a case to hold everything, and it is a little different than his old one, so he thought that was pretty cool too.

Faith and I went to town after lunch today to do some grocery shopping. Faith has been asking and asking if she can go somewhere with me by herself. She still had some Christmas money, so she spent most of it. She seemed to enjoy herself. She told me on the way home it was one of the best days she ever had.

Things are fairly quiet and somewhat routine around here, which is nice. We have no doctor's appointments this next week. We go back to St. Louis to see Dr. G on the January 26. Thank you for your prayers, support, encouragement, and messages! We love you all!

God is good, all the time!

—Dione

> Praise the Lord! Oh, give thanks to the Lord, for He is good! For His mercy endures forever.
>
> —Psalm 106:1

Saturday, January 16, 2010, 8:56 p.m.

> But sanctify the Lord God in your hearts, and always be ready to give a defense to everyone who asks you a reason for the hope that is in you, with meekness and fear; having a good conscience, that when they defame you as evildoers, those who revile your good conduct in Christ may be ashamed. For it is better, if it is the will of God, to suffer for doing good than for doing evil.
>
> —1 Peter 3:15-17

Yesterday was just a quiet school day. Dad came out to visit in the afternoon, and Billy's parents came up on Thursday evening for a little while. It is always nice to have some company, and Billy enjoys the visits. Levi spent some extra time going back over two days' worth of math. He is into multiplication and working on memorizing his multiplication tables. A mistake here and there is expected, but this was just nuts. He was either just not paying any attention at all to what he was doing or his blood sugar was low when he was doing the math the first time. It has been proven that when his blood sugar is low, he cannot concentrate or think straight. Other than that, school has gone very well this week even though Max and Cassy both had math exams that they stressed over at first. Max is in Algebra 2 and Cassy is in Algebra ½. I found it rather funny that they were both worrying about the exams the day before and they hadn't even looked at them yet. When they got them out and actually looked at them, they discovered they were not as scary as they thought they would be.

Billy is doing okay this week. He is eating pretty well and has not had any trouble with nausea this week. Dr. V cut one of his pain medications in half. Billy has now been on the lower dose for four full days, and he is not sure it is going to work out. He isn't truly in pain, or at least not much, but he said that he just isn't as comfortable as he had been. He said that it may be partly in his head since he knows the pain medication was cut in half. He is going to give it another day or so and see how it goes to decide for sure.

Kaylyn worked today, so she dropped Max off at church to help Rick with the Sunday school rooms he is building. Kaylyn went back over to the church when she got off work at about 2:00 and ended up helping the guys. They made it home about 5:00. I was glad I had planned a big supper with fried chicken (and I had lots of chicken), mashed potatoes, gravy, and green beans, because Kaylyn and Max had not eaten all day, and they both came in very hungry! They both had a good day and were pleased with everything they got done.

I spent part of the day checking school work and doing some laundry. The boys are playing PlayStation back in the bedroom, and the rest of us are watching bull riding. We all like bull riding, but Cassy is a bull-riding fanatic. She has decided she will marry a PBR bull rider so she can go to all of the events. Her good friend Hannah has told her that isn't right because Cassy is just planning to use the poor guy and isn't really marring for the right reason. Cassy says, "So?" I asked her if she was going to be a good wife, and she hesitated and said, "I can cook." I guess that means she will be a good wife. I know she can be because she is a very good housekeeper and spoils her Daddy a bit. Anyway, Cassy keeps a list of all the bulls' names and keeps track of how well they do. She also knows almost all of the bull riders' names and how they are doing, but she doesn't keep a list of the guys.

Thank you all for checking in and for your messages, support, and prayers. Billy still has a long way to go, but thanks to the Lord and all the prayers, he has come a long way. We love you all and keep you in our prayers!

God is good, all the time!

—Dione

> Praise the Lord! Oh, give thanks to the Lord for He is good! For His mercy endures forever.
>
> —Psalm 106:1

Sunday, January 17, 2010, 10:16 p.m.

> O Lord, our Lord, how excellent is Your name in all the earth, who have set Your glory above the heavens! Out of the mouth of babes and nursing infants You have ordained strength, because of Your enemies, that You may silence the enemy and the avenger. When I consider Your heavens, the work of Your fingers, the moon and the stars, which You have ordained, what is man that You are mindful of him and the son of man that You visit him? For You have made him a little lower than the angels, and You have crowned him with glory and honor, You have made him to have dominion over the works of Your hands; You have put all things under his feet, all sheep and oxen—even the beasts of the field, the birds of the air, and the fish of the sea that pass through the paths of the seas. O Lord, our Lord how excellent is Your name in all the earth!
>
> —Psalm 8:1-9

> Why? Within the majestic expanse of the universe, we are insignificant specks. Yet God sees us, knows us intimately, and loves us ceaselessly. Such heavenly consideration is truly beyond our comprehension.[78]

We all enjoyed our Sunday school classes and church this morning. It is so nice to be back to our regular routine with church. The week just doesn't seem right when we miss church.

---

78 Blackaby, *Blackaby Study Bible*, pg.639

Billy is feeling okay today. I think he is feeling better after his nap this afternoon. He had trouble going to sleep last night and then kept waking up. I think part of the problem last night was because he had trouble sleeping the night before, so he slept in Saturday morning and then napped off and on through the day. Hopefully he will sleep well tonight and be back on schedule. Since he has not had any nausea for about a week or so, I am not going to give him his nausea pill first thing in the morning and see how that works out. He has not said anything about the lower dose of pain medication today, so maybe that is going to work out for him.

Some schools are off tomorrow, but not us. We don't have any doctor's appointments this week, which is nice. It should be a fairly quiet, uneventful week.

Thank you for checking in and most of all for your prayers. We love you all!

God is good, all the time!

—Dione

> Praise the Lord! Oh, give thanks to the Lord, for He is good! For His mercy endures forever.
>
> —Psalm 106:1

Monday, January 18, 2010, 10:44 p.m.

> Happy is he who has the God of Jacob for his help, whose hope is in the Lord his God, Who made heaven and earth, the sea, and all that is in them; Who keeps truth forever, Who expects justice for the oppressed, Who gives food to the hungry. The Lord gives freedom to the prisoners.
>
> —Psalm 146:5-7

> Happy Is He—Perfect circumstances do not bring joy. Hope in the Lord does. With God there is always hope, there is a reason to rejoice in every situation.[79]

There is not much to report today. Billy tried going all day without any nausea medicine, and it went pretty well. He is still debating on the pain medication but used the smaller dose today. Overall he has felt pretty good today.

Libby, our care manager from Tulsa, called today. She wanted to let us know that they are thinking about us and have received the information about the transplant and all that is going on. She said that Dr. River is very happy that Billy was able to get the stem cell transplant. Libby said she and Dr. River knew that was what Billy needed, but it wasn't something they could do, so they were very happy that it worked out so well. They would love for us to come visit them when we can. There is an aquarium, zoo, and other things to do in Tulsa, so we may just have to take the kids for a few days sometime, and we can include a visit at CTCA to see everyone.

Thank you for checking in and for your continued prayers. We love you all!

God is good, all the time!

—Dione

> Praise the Lord! Oh, give thanks to the Lord, for He is good! For His mercy endures forever.
>
> —Psalm 106:1

[79] Ibid., pg. 736

Tuesday, January 19, 2010, 9:56 p.m.

> What is man, that You should exalt him, that You should set Your heart on him, that You should visit him every morning, and test him every moment?
>
> —Job 7:17-18

> What Is Man?—Almighty God watches over us and is aware of all we do. We matter to Him. Such interest from the Almighty is beyond comprehension.[80]

It is day two of no nausea medication, and everything went well. Billy ate pretty well today, definitely better than yesterday, and did fine without the nausea medication. He has continued with the smaller dose of pain medication and so far is sticking with it. He has been making a habit of going to bed at about midnight and then sleeping late in the morning, but he decided to get up earlier this morning and try to start going to bed earlier. I think that will disappoint the older kids. Kaylyn, Max, and Cassy have been staying up with Billy since no one has told them to go to bed earlier. I am not sure what the draw is with teenagers to stay up late, but they sure do it every chance they get.

Kaylyn took Buddy (Levi's guinea pig) to work with her this morning so Stacey could take a look at him. He has just not been quite himself. I think a couple of the kids thought I was being a little paranoid, because he was eating, drinking, begging for treats, and has been very active, but I felt he had lost some weight. He was drinking a *lot,* and he was also squeaking a lot more than usual. Some of his squeaking didn't sound like his normal sounds but almost like he was in pain. It turns out he has a bladder infection, so he was sick. Kaylyn left him at work for the day and will bring him home after a while. She said that Stacey was giving him some antibiotics, but I am not sure if he will be coming home with antibiotics for us to give him. Justin said that I can give Buddy his medicine since I give everyone else in the house medicine when they need it.

---

80 Ibid.pg. 736

Kaylyn took Max and Cassy with her when she went to work this afternoon and dropped them off at my parents' house until she got off work. Then they were all going over to church to help Rick with priming the new Sunday school rooms. Hopefully they can get quite a bit done this evening. Kaylyn figured they wouldn't be home until 10:00 or later. They took Buddy's cage along so he would be comfortable hanging out at church until they can get home.

Kaylyn has tomorrow off and is ready for a day she can sleep in. We are going to go help cook at church tomorrow, but I need to be there fairly early (between 12:30 and 1:00). Last week was just too long a day for Billy, so Kaylyn is going to bring him in later in the afternoon. That way he doesn't have to spend all afternoon at church. I don't know if all of the other kids will go with me or if a couple of them will stay with Billy and Kaylyn and come in a little later.

Thank you checking in and for your prayers. We love you all!

God is good, all the time!

—Dione

> Praise the Lord! Oh, give thanks to the Lord, for God is good! For His mercy endures forever.
>
> —Psalm 106:1

Thursday, January 21, 2010 9:28 p.m.

> Therefore do not worry about tomorrow, for tomorrow will worry about itself. Each day has enough trouble of its own.
>
> —Matthew 6:34

Billy is feeling pretty well. He no longer needs nausea medication and is eating fairly well every day. He did decide to go back to the stronger dose of pain medication. He was just not as comfortable, and it seemed to be getting worse, not better. It worked out much better for Billy to come in to church later in the afternoon yesterday. He didn't get as tired or uncomfortable. Billy is planning to take Max in to church for a little while in the morning to help Rick. Billy said he isn't sure how much he can do, but he won't know until he tries. He isn't sure how long he will last or if he will do more sitting than working, but he will have Max there to help. When Billy gets tired, they will come home.

Buddy does have an antibiotic to take twice a day, but he takes it well and seems to be feeling better. I think he looks better, and he has quit doing some of the things he was doing that made me wonder if he was sick. Levi has been giving him his medicine. Other than Buddy, everyone is healthy and doing well, although, no one is real happy about all the rain, mostly because of the mud.

School is going well. Cassy has adopted a rather odd schedule for some of her work, but since she is homeschooled, she has that flexibility. As long as it is getting done and being done well, it really doesn't make that much difference when she does it. The older three have all been staying up until midnight with Billy. The younger three go to bed at 10:00, although Justin reads for an hour to an hour and a half before going to sleep. I have been going to bed at around 11:00. Billy was going to try and change his schedule, but this one seems to be working well for him as far as being able to go to bed, go to sleep, and sleep well. I think he kind of likes the time with the kids as well, and I know the kids like it.

Cassy has been getting her math out at around 11:00 to see what she is going to be doing the next day. Several nights recently she ended up getting started on the lesson and then was up until about 1:00 working on it. She seems to be doing fine with it. I had read years ago that you remember things better if you work on them just before going to sleep. When Kaylyn was six, she memorized the entire chapter of 1 Corinthians 13, and we usually worked on it just before she went to bed as part of our nightly routine. At any rate, maybe what Cassy learns will stick with her better if she does it just before going to sleep. You never know.

While I am on the subject of school, Levi really surprised me with a couple of history tests. He has had two history tests in the last two weeks. I have him read one subject a day to me to make sure he is doing well with his reading and not skipping over words or mispronouncing words. (Faith still reads most things to me as well.) He has been reading history on his own. He goes back to one of the bedrooms and reads it. I was not sure how this was going to go because he seems to read fast when he goes and reads to himself. I was afraid he was skipping over things and not really reading everything. However, the tests were twenty questions each for a total of forty questions, and they involved a lot of different people, so there were lots of names to remember, as well as what those people did. Out of forty questions, he only missed one, and he very seldom even hesitated before answering a question.

Thank you all for your support, encouragement, messages, and most of all, prayers. We love you all!

God is good, all the time!

—Dione

> Praise the Lord! Oh, give thanks to the Lord, for He is good! For His mercy endures forever.
>
> —Psalm 106:1

Saturday, January 23, 2010, 9:38 p.m.

> Finally, brethren, whatever things are true, whatever things are noble, whatever things are lovely, whatever things are of good report, if there is any virtue and if there is anything praiseworthy—meditate on these things. The things which you learned and received and heard and saw in me, these do, and the God of peace will be with you.
>
> —Philippians 4:8-9

Billy is still doing pretty well. He is taking the full-strength pain medication again and will just stick with that for now. Yesterday Max and Billy went into church for a few hours and helped Rick and Bob B. finish up the priming. He did pretty well. He did not do as well as he would have liked, but they were there for around four hours and he put primer on a wall or two. His back and neck were pretty tired when he got home, and he was ready for a nap, but I think it was good for him to get out and be able to do something. He slept in some this morning and napped quite a bit today. He is still eating pretty well.

Kaylyn, Max, Cassy, and Justin went in to church today and helped with painting the new rooms and two hallways. There was a pretty good crowd there to paint today, and they were able to get it all done. The kids thought it all went very well and were pleased with how much help there was and how much was done. The kids stayed and helped Rick clean up, and they made it home around 4:00, which Billy and I thought was pretty good.

Faith spent the day with Billy's mom and dad. She really enjoyed herself. She likes to go do something by herself once in a while (as do all the kids). That left Levi as the only kid at home. I worked on checking some school work, and Levi did some house cleaning. He cleaned the kids' bathroom, including sweeping and mopping it, and then he cleaned up the living room, dusted, and vacuumed the living room and hallway. After lunch I played a game of Clue with him, and he played the entire game and won!Since the kids made it home from working at church, they have taken turns getting their showers and visiting with us, as well as some cutting up and silliness. They are so much fun! It was the girls' turn to clean up after supper, but since Kaylyn and Cassy worked at church most of the day and Faith wasn't back from Grandma and Grandpa's yet, Levi helped me clean up after supper. Even though it was under protest, he still helped.

Thank you for checking in and for your prayers! We love you all!

God is good, all the time!

—Dione

> Praise the Lord! Oh, give thanks to the Lord, for He is good! For His mercy endures forever.
>
> —Psalm 106:1

Monday, January 25, 2010, 9:42 p.m.

> The four living creatures, each having six wings, were full of eyes around and within. And they do not rest day or night saying: "Holy, holy, holy, Lord God Almighty, Who was and is and is to come!" Whenever the living creatures give glory and honor and thanks to Him who sits on the throne, who lives forever and ever, the twenty-four elders fall down before Him who sits on the throne and worship Him who lives forever and ever, and cast their crowns before the throne, saying: "You are worthy, O Lord, to receive glory and honor and power; For You created all things, and by Your will they exist and were created."
>
> —Revelation 4:8-11

The last couple of days have been pretty quiet. We all enjoyed Sunday school and church, as always. With the sun shining yesterday, all of the kids spent most of the afternoon outside, although they were getting pretty chilly by the time they came in.

Billy seems to be doing pretty well. He has a long way to go to get his strength and stamina back. It will take some time. I keep forgetting to mention that at Billy's last appointment with Dr. V, it was discovered that his thyroid is a little low, so he is now on thyroid medication to help it out. Whether that will be something permanent or if it just needs some help for a little while, we won't know for a while. They will continue to check the thyroid levels at each appointment with Dr. V.

Tomorrow is the appointment in St. Louis for blood work and a check up with Dr. G. It looks like tomorrow may be the best day as far as weather to be going to St. Louis. They are going to do the blood work to check where things are with the cancer. I don't think we will have those results until later this week or sometime next week, but we will get the blood count results that tell us where things are with the white count, ANC (infection fighters), hemoglobin, and platelets.

Thank you all for checking in, for your prayers, and for your support. We love you all!

God is good, all the time!

—Dione

> Praise the Lord! Oh, give thanks to the Lord, for He is good! For His mercy endures forever.
>
> —Psalm 106:1

Chapter 28

Tuesday, January 26, 2010, 4:56 p.m.

> Praise the Lord! Praise the Lord from the heavens; Praise Him in the heights! Praise Him, all His angels; Praise Him all His hosts! Praise Him, sun and moon; Praise Him, all you stars of light! Praise Him, you heavens of heavens, and you waters above the heavens! Let them praise the name of the Lord, for He commanded and they were created. He also established them forever and ever; He made a decree which shall not pass away. Praise the Lord from the earth, you great sea creatures and all the depths; fire and hail, snow and clouds; stormy wind, fulfilling His word; mountains and all hills; fruitful trees and all cedars; beasts and all cattle; creeping things and flying fowl; kings of the earth and all peoples; princes and all judges of the earth; both young men and maidens; old men and children. Let them praise the name of the Lord, for His name alone is exalted; His glory is above the earth and heaven.
>
> —Psalm 148

God is good, all the time! The trip to St. Louis this morning went very well. Dr. G had gotten hung up in LA and was trying to get back. They didn't know if he would make it back today or not, so we saw Dr. W, who works with him. We met Dr. W at our first appointment at Barnes and have seen him a few times since then. He did not see Billy the last time we were in St. Louis, and he was very pleased to see how well Billy is doing. He asked Billy, "Do you feel as good as you look? Because you look good."

Billy's counts are looking pretty good, and they will have the results of the other blood tests the end of the week or first part of next week. Dr. W said that basically no news is good news. They will only call if they see something that concerns them, but we are welcome to call if we are curious. We currently do not have any more appointments in St. Louis. We will just be seeing Dr. V for checkups and to continue getting the bone builder.

Dr. W, like Dr. V expects Billy to be in remission when all of the test results come in. He said that Dr. V can do the bone marrow biopsy, so I will call his office and get that set up for February 10, which is when Billy is supposed to see him again. We have been told that with this particular cancer, it is not a matter of if it comes back but when. Regardless, we feel that is in God's hands, and if He chooses to use the transplant as a cure, then Billy will be cured! Billy asked Dr. W if he is in remission but the cancer then comes back in say to four years if they would be able to use the stem cells that are already frozen. Dr. W said they would.

He went on to explain that while they would do another stem cell transplant if the cancer returned in two years or more. They would not do it if it returned in six months or so. The reason for this is that if Billy has two years cancer free, it means the transplant was successful. However, if it returns in six months to a year, it means that the transplant is not truly effective with Billy's particular myeloma, and they would look at other options for treatment, such as various chemo drugs. I know this is a little confusing since if Billy is not in remission, they would plan a second transplant right away. It has to do with the difference between being in remission and then relapsing versus getting in remission in the first place. We will just pray for total remission and put it in God's hands as to how long that will be.

We continue to take it one day at a time and one step at a time. Once we know for sure if Billy is in remission, we will talk to a surgeon, most likely Dr. C, the surgeon we spoke to back in July, and see what can and should be done for Billy's back.

Prayers:

- That Billy is in remission
- That Billy continues to stay healthy and regain his strength

And praise the Lord for what He is doing!

Thank you so much for all of your prayers! We have seen so many prayers answered and are so very blessed! Thank you so much, we love you all!

> Praise the Lord! Oh, give thanks to the Lord, for He is good! For His mercy endures forever.
>
> —Psalm 106:1

Thursday, January 28, 2010, 9:59 p.m.

> And we know that all things work together for good to them that love God, to them who are the called according to His purpose.
>
> —Romans 8:28

We had a good day yesterday, as we always do on Wednesdays. The older three kids and I went in to church around 1:00 to help fix the meal for that evening. Billy brought the younger three in later in the afternoon. Everyone enjoyed the day, as well as classes and prayer meeting that evening.

Billy is feeling pretty good. He slept in pretty late yesterday. He doesn't sleep very well the night before going to St. Louis. We also had to be up early on Tuesday to make the trip to St. Louis, and it tends to wear him out. He didn't get up until 11:30 yesterday (hopefully I don't get in trouble for telling that), but he looked very rested when he got up. He has a couple of medications that he takes at 7:00, and after I gave them to him yesterday, he went right back to sleep and didn't wake up again until

11:30, so he was sleeping pretty well. At around 10:30, Cassy asked if I had checked on him. I said that I hadn't for a while, but he was sleeping. She thought I should check on him. She said, "Don't you think you should make sure he's sleeping? What if he's dead?" I don't think she actually thought he might have died, but she did think I needed to make sure he was okay, and since I hadn't done so, she was making sure I would. At about 11:00, I did check on him, and he was sleeping soundly and breathing fine.

Things are rather uneventful around here, and that is okay with us. We continue to pray that the bone marrow biopsy will show Billy is in remission. Although Billy still isn't sure, I still think a remission party is a good idea, and several others agree with me, so I am hoping to make that work out.

Thank you for your continued prayers, support, encouragement, and messages. They mean a lot to us, and we are very grateful! We love you all and keep you in our prayers!

God is good, all the time!

—Dione

> Praise the Lord! Oh, give thanks to the Lord, for He is good! For His mercy endures forever.
>
> —Psalm 106:1

SATURDAY, JANUARY 30, 2010, 8:29 P.M.

Billy was watching an Alan Jackson special the other day promoting his gospel CD. He sang the following song. He did a beautiful job, and it really spoke to me.

We have had a couple of good days. Billy is eating well and is feeling pretty good. He is trying to regain some strength. It will take some time, but he is doing a little more and trying to work on it.

Kaylyn and Cassy did a little shopping yesterday afternoon. Kaylyn has needed a new pair of shoes and had said something about staying in town one day last week and going shopping. When I asked her about it later, she said that she had decided she would wait and take Cassy with her. I thought that was very sweet of her. Yesterday in the early afternoon, Kaylyn and Cassy took Max in to town and dropped him off to stay with a friend, and then they went shopping. Cassy stayed at Mom and Dad's while Kaylyn worked her evening shift. It was snowing and very slick when they came home in the evening. Kaylyn took it really slow and used her four-wheel drive most of the way home. She likes having four-wheel drive.

My sister and her boys came out to visit this afternoon. I think everyone enjoyed the visit. The kids played outside some. There wasn't enough snow for sledding, so I think they just wandered around, but they were happy to be able to go outside.

Thank you for checking in and for all of your prayers. We love you all.

God is good, all the time!

—Dione

> Praise the Lord! Oh, give thanks to the Lord, for He is good! For His mercy endures forever.
>
> —Psalm 106:1

Sunday, January 31, 2010, 9:22 p.m.

> The righteous man walks in his integrity; His children are blessed after him.
>
> —Proverbs 20:7

> Better is the poor who walks in his integrity than one who is perverse in his lips, and is a fool.
>
> —Proverbs 19:1

> Character Before Riches—Seeking personal gain at the expense of integrity is never worth the cost. God places high value on good character and personal integrity. Resist the temptation to compromise godly, moral values in the pursuit of worldly comforts. Be assured that the Lord watches and blesses according to the purity of your heart.[81]

At our house, Billy talks about character and integrity a lot! The kids have heard some of the sermons . . . umm, I mean talks quite often. When an opportunity arises and Billy brings up the subject, the kids all shake their heads, roll their eyes, smile a knowing smile, and then once again listen to Dad talk about the importance of character and integrity. What I think is really neat and makes the biggest impression on the kids is the fact that Billy is a man of integrity. He has not just talked or preached at them; he also lives it, and they know that.

Billy is doing well. I have really seen it over the last few days. He is not as sleepy during the day, and he is just getting up and doing things for himself. He is eating well, and things taste good to him again. He is looking for things he can do and wants to start getting back into the swing of things. He is on some committees with our church association, and he is ready to start going to those meetings again as well as his RRJ (Road Riders for Jesus) meetings and his GROW night at church. It is good to

81 Blackaby, *Blackaby Study Bible,* pg. 760

see him feeling good enough that his interests are returning. He is also planning to visit Farm Bureau before long to say hi to everyone.

Billy would really like to get back to work as soon as he can. He is feeling good enough that he is thinking about how soon he might be able to make it through a full week of work. However, we have talked about it, and while he would really like to get back to work, we need to talk to the surgeon about his back first. We need to know what kind of surgery is required and what we will be looking at as far as recovery before he goes back to work.

I e-mailed Dr. Choma, the surgeon we saw back in July, and let him know that we just need the bone marrow results to know if Billy is in remission or not. I asked him if he would be willing to see Billy again. He e-mailed me back the same day and said that he would be happy to see Billy again and see what he can do, but he agreed that we needed to wait until Billy is released by the transplant doctors. Technically, he has been released by them since we do not currently have any more appointments in St. Louis. However, we need to have the official word that Billy is in remission before pursuing any kind of back surgery. Once we get the bone marrow results, we will then make the appointment with Dr. C and see what he thinks as far as what he can do and how soon. Of course, the bones will have to be recovered enough, and we already know Dr. C will not do anything unless he is confident the bones can handle it.

As always, everyone enjoyed Sunday school and church. We all love our church family, and it is always so good to see everyone. It has been really nice getting back into our regular weekly routine and not having so many doctors' appointments. We won't see Dr. V again until February 10, and then, as long as all continues to go well, we will only see him once a month.

Thank you for checking in to read my ramblings. Thank you so much for all of your prayers, support, encouragement, messages, and love! We love you all!

God is good, all the time!

—Dione

> Praise the Lord! Oh, give thanks to the Lord, for He is good! For His mercy endures forever.
>
> —Psalm 106:1

Thursday, February 4, 2010, 7:31 p.m.

> But when the kindness and the love of God our Savior toward man appeared, not by works of righteousness which we have done, but according to His mercy He saved us, through the washing of regeneration and renewing of the Holy Spirit, whom He poured out on us abundantly through Jesus Christ our Savior.
>
> —Titus 3:4-6

There isn't much to report. Everything continues to go well. We went to church and cooked for our Wednesday-evening meal yesterday. We all enjoyed the day, and everyone seemed to enjoy the meal. School continues to go well. We are all curious to see what the weather does. We have had some snow and sleet so far. It hasn't amounted to much, but it sounds like we may be getting snow through the day tomorrow and into Saturday. We have our winter Bible study at church this weekend, and the kitchen crew is supposed to fix a meal for tomorrow evening. We will just have to see how things go.

We enjoyed a visit with Joe this morning. Billy really enjoyed having the company, and we all enjoyed visiting. Kaylyn, Cassy, and I cooked for a mission trip with our association's building team during the summer of 2008. Joe was part of the building team, and Kaylyn and Cassy not only helped cook but were also entertainment and comedy relief. Unfortunately for Joe, he ended up being at the receiving end of some of their antics. Joe took it well and it was all in fun, but he knows to keep an eye on those two.

As I said, there just isn't much going on, so there is not much to talk about. We are very thankful Billy is feeling so much better and that things are going well. Billy and Max are planning to help put the suspended ceiling in the new Sunday school rooms at church on Saturday. Billy is looking forward to helping. He isn't very sure what he will do, but I'm sure there will be something for him to do.

Thank you for your prayers! We have come a long way in a year. Last year at this time Billy was in incredible pain and was going to bed at around 6:30 in the evening because it was the only way he could get away from the pain. In fact, on February 4, 2009, Billy was supposed to start physical therapy, but we had to call and cancel for that day. When Billy tried to get up that morning, he was having muscle spasms in his back that were so bad he couldn't even stand up. He was in unbelievable pain. When I called the physical therapist to cancel for the day and told him what was going on, he said to get Billy in to see his doctor. I called the doctor, and he could not see Billy that day but made an appointment for February 5. That actually worked out for the best because there was no way we could get him into the vehicle and to the doctor's office on February 4.

Getting Billy to the doctor's office the next day was a bit of a trick. On February 5 a year ago, the muscle spasms were not as bad, but the pain was still incredible. Billy could stand up (with a lot of effort) and take just a few steps before he would *need* to sit down. To get him into the Suburban and to the doctor's office, I parked the Suburban as close to the deck as I could with the passenger door open. Billy stood up, and I walked in front of him with him holding on to my shoulders and using me for support and balance while Kaylyn and Max followed close behind him with the office chair on wheels so he could sit down if needed. If I remember right, as we went across the living room and deck, he did need to sit down a couple of times. It was slow and very painful. I am so grateful he is no longer in pain. He has been through a lot in a year, but thankfully he is not hurting. That truly is a blessing.

God is good, all the time!

—Dione

> Praise the Lord! Oh, give thanks to the Lord, for God is good! For his mercy endures forever.
>
> —Psalm 106:1

Saturday, February 6, 2010, 11:06 p.m.

> Finally, my brethren, be strong in the Lord and in the power of His might.
>
> —Ephesians 6:10

Our winter Bible study was canceled last night due to the weather, so we did not go in to cook for the evening meal. However, the kids had a ball playing in the snow! We have three huge snowmen in the yard, and Billy and I laughed and laughed watching the kids build them. The snowmen started with Levi and Faith rolling balls of snow almost as tall as they are. We were watching them out the window and saw that they couldn't move them anymore. That is when the other kids decided it looked like fun and that Faith and Levi needed help, so they headed out. Shadow (Max's dog) had a great time playing with the kids as well, although Faith wasn't too happy with Shadow when she stole the carrot that was doubling as the nose for her snowman. Cassy was able to get the carrot back, but Shadow ate part of it, so the snowman's nose is a bit shorter.

Billy and Max went to church this morning to help put the suspended ceiling in the new Sunday school rooms. It is nice to have Billy feeling well enough to get out and do something. We have our winter Bible study tonight, so Billy is only planning to work until noon so he will be able to rest this afternoon. While he is feeling better, he does get worn out pretty quickly, and it takes him a little while to recover.

Looking Back

During the week of February 6, 2009, Billy started sleeping on a mattress on the floor in the living room. When we saw the doctor on

February 5, he recommended Billy try sleeping on the floor to give him a very firm surface, which works with some back issues. Billy had also been prescribed pain pills and muscle relaxers. However, because the pain was not from a muscle strain (which, of course, we didn't know at the time), they did little to no good. I was giving Billy the medications around the clock as often as he could have them, hoping that would help them work better. Since Billy was sleeping on the floor in the living room and getting up off the floor was a real challenge and incredibly painful for him, I slept on the couch so I was close if he needed something.

Even though Billy was in so much pain, he continued to get up and go to work almost every day. He had to get up earlier because it took him longer to get ready for work, and I would help him get dressed because he was hurting so badly. I really don't know how he managed to keep going to work. He is amazing. Billy started physical therapy, and thankfully the physical therapists were very concerned about his pain, so they had him exercise in the therapy pool. God was definitely watching over Billy. The exercises he did in the pool helped him maintain his muscle and didn't hurt him because the water supported his weight. I went with him to therapy to help him change his clothes. We are so thankful Billy is no longer in pain, even if it does mean he is taking quite a bit of pain medication.

Praise:

- That Billy is feeling better
- That he has avoided illness (colds, flu)

Prayers:

- That Billy continues to gain strength
- That he stays healthy
- That he is in full remission

Thank you for your continued support and prayers. We are very blessed by all of you! We love you all, and you are in our prayers.

God is good, all the time!

—Dione

> Praise the Lord! Oh, give thanks to the Lord, for He is good! For His mercy endures forever.
>
> —Psalm 106:1

MONDAY, FEBRUARY 8, 2010, 7:48 P.M.

> For God gives wisdom and knowledge and joy to a man who is good in His sight; but to the sinner He gives the work of gathering and collecting that he may give to him who is good before God. This also is vanity and grasping for the wind.
>
> —Ecclesiastes 2:26

> God Rewards Good—The Lord will give wisdom, knowledge and joy to those who love Him and serve Him. Those who lack these things should humbly seek them from God.[82]

Billy and Max made it home at around 2:30 on Saturday. They stayed for a while longer than Billy had planned, but everything went well. Billy ended up working on the computers in the offices at church while Max helped with other things. We then had our winter Bible study later that evening, as well as after church on Sunday. I thought Billy would be pretty wiped out, but while he was tired, he really did pretty well.

There has not been much excitement here. The kids played out in the snow again today and came in very wet. Even though all the schools in the area cancelled today, the kids did their school work. Justin and Faith

---

82 Ibid., pg. 780

have colds. They are nothing major but are just mainly annoying for them because their noses are stuffed up and their sinuses are draining. Kaylyn didn't go to work this morning, but she was able to go in this afternoon and made it to work and home with no problem. She crawled back into bed when she didn't have to go into work and enjoyed sleeping in. It worked out well for her since she stayed up until midnight last night with Billy, Cassy, and Max. They were having a good time being silly and cutting up. Kaylyn has tomorrow off as well, so I expect the older three and Billy to have another late night. That seems to have become their pattern, and they really enjoy it.

The appointment with Dr. V in Columbia is on Wednesday. Billy will get his IV bone builder, and Dr. V will do the bone marrow biopsy. We are praying that it will show Billy is in remission, as the doctors expect. Thank you for your prayers! We love you all!

God is good, all the time!

—Dione

> Praise the Lord! Oh, give thanks to the Lord, for He is good! For His mercy endures forever.
>
> —Psalm 106:1

Thursday, February 11, 2010, 10:02 p.m.

> But now the righteousness of God apart from the law is revealed, being witnessed by the Law and the Prophets, even the righteousness of God, through faith in Jesus Christ, to all and on all who believe. For there is no difference; for all have sinned and fall short of the glory of God, being justified freely by His grace through the redemption that is in Christ Jesus, whom God set forth as a propitiation by His blood, through faith, to demonstrate His righteousness, because in His forbearance God had passed over the sins that were

> previously committed, to demonstrate at the present time His righteousness, that He might be just and the justifier of the one who has faith in Jesus.
>
> —Romans 3:21-26

Billy's appointment yesterday went well. Dr. V is very pleased with how everything is going and how Billy's blood counts look. The counts are all in the normal range, or at least so close that they can be counted as normal. The bone marrow biopsy was a little bit rougher this time. Billy did feel it some, but that may partially be because Dr. V had to try two places. In the first place he tried he couldn't get any bone marrow, so he tried another spot and then had no problem getting it. Billy said the spots where Dr. V went in are a little sore but not too bad.

After the bone marrow biopsy, Billy got his two-hour infusion of bone builder, so he took a nap during most of that time. I used the time he was napping to run to Sam's and pick some things up. The kids love it when I go to Sam's because there are a few things that I only buy at Sam's, just because they are more affordable. Whenever I go to Sam's, there are a few treats we don't otherwise get, and everyone enjoys that.

If we don't hear anything about the bone marrow by Wednesday, we will give them a call and see how it looked. Dr. V expects it to look good, so there is a chance we won't hear anything from them if all looks good. However, we would like official word, so will give them a call if need be. Once we know for sure that the bone marrow looks as we expect, I will make the appointment with Dr. Choma to see what he can do about Billy's back. I am sure he will have to do several tests like MRIs, X-rays, and so on to see how things are looking now. One day at a time is our new motto. We are doing our best to stick with it and not think too far ahead.

Billy is feeling quite good. After his doctor's appointment, bone builder, and everything else we did in Columbia yesterday, we went to church to help finish fixing the meal. Billy did really well and was even able to stay for business meeting after the meal. He is starting to regain some strength and isn't getting worn out as easyWe still have a cold going through the house. Faith and Justin are almost over it, but Cassy got up with it this morning. Max has already had it, and Kaylyn is hoping to avoid it. Thankfully it is more of an annoyance than anything, and no one is getting very sick with it. Kaylyn is off this weekend, so she is planning to help work at church, along with Cassy, Justin, Max, and Billy. Billy is planning to take the boys in for the men's breakfast on Saturday morning before they start working at church, and Kaylyn and Cassy will go in a little later. That way they won't have to get up as early. Billy is also planning to take the boys to the men's and boys' wild game supper on Monday. Our church association holds this event once a year, and it is always a big hit. Billy was not able to go last year because his back was hurting so much. He is really looking forward to going this year, as are the boys. It is so good to see him feeling good enough that he wants to go do things and actually feels like doing them.

Thank you so much for your prayers! We are very blessed to have so many people praying for our family, and we love you all!

God is good, all the time!

—Dione

> Praise the Lord! Oh, give thanks to the Lord, for He is good! For His mercy endures forever.
>
> —Psalm 106:1

Saturday, February 13, 2010, 7:08 p.m.

> Walk in wisdom toward those who are outside, redeeming the time. Let your speech always be with grace, seasoned with salt, that you may know how you ought to answer each one.
>
> —Colossians 4:5-6

> Say It Out Loud—God has given us a powerful tool to bless others—our tongue. Godly speech is the result of our unity with Him. Our relationships in this life are opportunities to bless others with God's kindness.[83]

The kids are all hoping (and I think there is a little praying) that there won't be enough snow overnight to cancel church in the morning. The kids really hate to have church cancelled; it messes up the entire week. We tell them not to get too excited about it since we have no control over it and there is a pretty good chance it won't really amount to that much, but they still worry about it a little. It is good that church is so important to all of them that they don't want to miss it for any reason.

Billy, Max, and Justin went to the men's breakfast this morning and then over to help with the work day at church. Kaylyn and Cassy headed in a little later to meet them at church. It sounds like there were several people helping today, and quite a bit was done. Billy came home at about 1:30. He did pretty well, but his back and neck were tired and had enough for one day. He said, "My neck and back are done." I asked him if they were hurting, and he said that it wasn't really that they hurt; They were just tired. He has been taking it easy in the recliner since getting home. While his back and neck were really tired and had enough for one day, he did quite well otherwise. He was not completely wiped out, which he has been before after attempting to do some work. Until we are able to get his back and neck checked out, they probably won't be able to take too much. I am just hoping that his bones are getting hard enough that the surgeon will be able to do what is needed soon.

The kids made it home a little after 5:00. They had picked a few things up for me at Wal-Mart after finishing at church. I think they are all a little tired, but they had a good day, and it sounds like they did a good day's work.

There is not too much excitement around here (and that's okay with us). Thank you for your support, encouragement, messages, and prayers. We love you all!

---

83 Ibid., pg. 1425

God is good, all the time!

—Dione

> Praise the Lord! Oh, give thanks to the Lord, for He is good! For His mercy endures forever.
>
> —Psalm 106:1

Sunday, February 14, 2010, 4:31 p.m.

> Though I speak with the tongues of men and of angels, but have not love, I have become sounding brass or a clanging cymbal. And though I have the gift of prophecy, and understand all mysteries and all knowledge, and though I have all faith so that I could remove mountains, but have not love, I am nothing. And though I bestow all my goods to feed the poor, and though I give my body to be burned, but have not love, it profits me nothing. Love suffers long and is kind; love does not envy; love does not parade itself, is not puffed up; does not behave rudely, does not seek its own, is not provoked, thinks no evil; does not rejoice in iniquity, but rejoices in the truth; bears all things, believes all things, hopes all things, endures all things. Love never fails. But whether there are prophecies, they will fail; whether there are tongues, they will cease; whether there is knowledge, it will vanish away. For we know in part and we prophesy in part. But when that which is perfect has come, then that which is in part will be done away. When I was a child, I spoke as a child, I understood as a child, I thought as a child; but when I became a man, I put away childish things. For now we see in a mirror, dimly, but then face to face. Now I know in part, but then I shall know just as I also am

> known. And now abide faith, hope, and love, these three; but the greatest of these is love.
>
> —1 Corinthians 13
>
> Christ's Love—We can do all the right things, but unless they emanate from the love of Christ they are dead works. When God's Spirit loves others through us, these people experience God's love firsthand.[84]

Well, the kids got their wish, and the snow did not come, so Sunday school and church went on as usual. It was a good morning. Everyone enjoyed their Sunday school classes, and Bro. Brian had a very good Valentine's Day message.

Then my dear, sweet husband surprised me. When the service was over, Bro. Brian asked us all to sit back down. As we sat down, he said that Bill Campbell wanted to say something, and Billy was making his way to the front. Billy then gave the church an update on his health, telling everyone that while we are waiting for the final word, it appears that he is in remission. He also told everyone how he and I know that the Lord brought the two of us together since I was born in Colorado and grew up in Nebraska before making my way to Russellville, Missouri. (He left out that I came to Russellville via a short stay in Wichita, Kansas, but that's okay.) He asked me to come to the front of the church with him. He knew I didn't really want to do that, but I did it anyway. He continued by telling everyone very nice things about me and what I mean to him. It was very sweet! Bro. Brian then had us stay at the front, and the church members came around and hugged us. We have an incredible church family! They have supported us in many ways and pray for us faithfully. We couldn't love them any more if we tired. I know several Cornerstone family members read this, so thank you for all you do for our family! We are so blessed!

While today is Valentine's Day, it is also my thirty-ninth birthday. The kids no longer find it cute when we are in a store just before Valentine's

---

84 Ibid., pg. 1375

Day and I say, "Oh look, isn't it nice of them to go to all of this trouble just for my birthday!" They seemed to find it funny the first couple of years I did it, but not anymore. I am now older than Billy again, or at least that is how the kids see it. When they first discovered I was older than Billy, they seemed to think that was strange. They thought the guy should be older. However, they then found a way to try and use it to their advantage. When there is something they want to do, they often ask me first. They know they will have to ask Billy or that I will talk it over with him, but they have a plan. They ask me first and feel me out to see if it is something I would let them do, and then when they ask Billy, they will say, "Mom thinks it is okay," or they will ask me to tell Billy that it is okay with me. There have been a few times when something was okay with me but Billy was leaning toward telling them no. In that case they will say, "Well, you always tell us we have to obey our elders. Mom is older than you, and she thinks it's okay." Of course, they only do that when it fits the mood. Otherwise it could backfire.

Thank you all for checking in and for your continued prayers and support. We love you all!

Happy Valentine's Day!

God is good, all the time!

—Dione

> Praise the Lord! Oh, give thanks to the Lord, for He is good! For His mercy endures forever.
>
> —Psalm 106:1

Monday, February 15, 2010, 9:20 p.m.

Complete remission! God is good, all the time! Our prayers have been answered! Thank you for your prayers!

Dr. V's office called late this afternoon to let us know they had the final word on the bone marrow, and Billy is in complete remission! While we knew this was most likely the case, it is still good to get the official word.

Billy and the boys are at the wild game supper. I am curious to hear about their night because I know they were planning to honor Billy tonight, and he knew nothing about it. The girls and I have been hanging out watching a girly movie and playing Clue. We have had a lot of fun this evening just being silly.

Thank you all for your support, encouragement, messages, and most of all, prayers! Our prayers have been answered in a huge way! We love you all and keep you in our prayers!

God is good, all the time!

—Dione

> Praise the Lord! Oh, give thanks to the Lord, for he is good! For his mercy endures forever.
>
> —Psalm 106:1

Chapter 29

Wrapping Up 2010

After Billy was found to be in complete remission, the year progressed nicely, with us at home all year, which we were all very thankful for. Billy was not able to have any back surgery, however. We met with Dr. C in Columbia after learning that Billy was in remission. Dr. C did some MRIs to get a good look at the bones in Billy's back. His recommendation was to not try any surgery and just leave things as they are. There are many compression fractures in Billy's back, and Dr. C said that it is amazing how they collapsed upon themselves and did not pinch the spinal cord. He even called it a miracle that Billy had not been paralyzed.

The neck where things are really bad is the main area Dr. C was looking at since that is where the nerves to Billy's right hand are being pinched. He said that the spinal cord is compromised because there is less fluid there and not much room between the bone and the spinal cord, but things have hardened and are stable. He was concerned that trying to go in to fix that area could make things worse. He has no idea how working on that area would affect the rest of Billy's back, and he felt the chance of paralyzing Billy was quite high. He then said that it is up to us, and if we really wanted him to do it, he would. His understanding was that we wanted his opinion on whether surgery was a good idea, and he was giving us his opinion that he did not feel it was a good or safe idea. In the end, Billy had no surgery. Billy remains on his two pain medications, but he is doing well with them.

In March we decided that with Billy being in remission and since all of the kids were old enough to get something out of it, it was time to take a vacation to Washington DC. We have talked about it for years and told the kids that when they were all old enough to understand the history, we would go. Kaylyn was working now, and Max was turning sixteen in July and then would also be working, so we felt there wasn't a better time. The kids were thrilled with the idea and we were all super-excited because we had not taken a vacation in a long time.

Our original plan was to stay with my aunt Margaret, who lived in Maryland and was only about forty-five minutes from DC. I called her in mid-March to talk to her about the dates we planned to be there (the end of April into May). She was thrilled with the idea of us being there, but she also told me she had been sick and had recently been diagnosed with a cancer of the lymph nodes. She still wanted us to come and was very excited about seeing us. However, this was not to be because she passed away ten days later. This was a surprise, but Aunt Margaret knew and loved the Lord. I have no doubt that she is now praising Him in heaven.

Since we were no longer going to be able to stay at Aunt Margaret's, we decided to shorten our vacation by a few days (we had originally planned for two weeks). Billy found a hotel that was only a few miles from the metro, and we made plans to ride the metro on most days.

We had an awesome trip to DC! The kids all loved it, as did Billy and I! We took two days to drive out and went through Cumberland Gap. The kids loved walking up and being able to see three states from the top of the gap. The drive itself was very enjoyable, and we had so much fun with the kids. Billy did well driving but was very tired by the end of the day.

On the way to DC, we made a list of all the places everyone wanted to see and then put them in order with all of the places everyone wanted to see first and then everything else. On the first night we arrived at the hotel, we just relaxed and made plans for what we would try to see the next day. Each day we parked at the metro parking lot and rode the metro into DC, getting off at the station closest to what we wanted to see for that day. Because the metro prices were higher in the evening, we would get back to the hotel between 3:00 and 4:00. This worked out really well because Billy was worn out by then, and his back was pretty much done for the day. At the hotel, we had connecting rooms and would leave the door open between them. It worked out great. We took a lot of our own snack food and then picked up some sandwich stuff and other food at the grocery store once we arrived since there was a little refrigerator and microwave in each room. We would spend the evening visiting about the day, planning where to go for the next day, and just hanging out watching some TV or being silly.

On the day we went to Arlington, we drove into DC so we could park at Arlington. It was incredible! Everyone was amazed, and the changing of the guard was one of everyone's favorite things. Max was able to film the changing of the guard. We left Arlington on foot, walked across the Potomac, and then walked around the Lincoln Memorial, the Korean Memorial, and the World War II and Vietnam Memorial. Then we walked back to the Suburban at Arlington. Before we crossed back over the Potomac, Billy needed to rest for a while because it was really more than he could do for the day. He took some extra pain medication, and we all got something to drink and rested. While we were resting, we discussed the day, as well as the previous days. (This was close to the last day.) We all agreed that Arlington was everyone's favorite, and Max spoke for everyone when he said, "Today has been the most walking, but I think it is my favorite day."

We had gone to Arlington on Friday, so we decided to take it easy on Saturday and get the laundry done. I can't remember if the metro didn't run on Saturday or if it was just more expensive to ride. It worked out really well that we let everyone sleep in on Saturday. Of course, Levi and I got up so he could get his shot and breakfast, and then he helped me take the laundry down and get it started. The older kids and Billy slept in very late, and it was obvious Billy really needed the extra rest. Later in the day, after I had the laundry done, we decided to get out of the hotel for a little while, so we went to Wal-Mart and the Dollar Tree and had supper at Arby's. (I had promised we would have a meal at Arby's at least one time while on vacation.) We then went back to the room and watched movies. The kids played some games, and we took turns messing around on the computer.

On Sunday we went to the National Air and Space Museum and the Bull Run battlefield. Billy felt so much better on Sunday after taking it easy on Saturday that we were all glad we had not tried to do any sightseeing on

Saturday. The Air and Space Museum and the Bull Run battlefield were a big hit. Everyone really enjoyed both. Levi was very excited to see a real cannon. One thing he talked about during the entire trip was getting to see a real cannon.

We drove home in one day. It was a long day—fifteen hours of driving—but it was a pretty drive, and everyone rode really well. It was a wonderful vacation, and we were all very glad we made the trip. It is something everyone will always remember.

Max turned sixteen in July. He got his driver's license on his first try, and within about three weeks of getting his license, he got a job at Wal-Mart as a cart pusher. He likes the job and the people he works with and has proven to be a good worker. They seem to be very pleased with him.

Kaylyn turned seventeen, graduated high school, and started working as the groom at Southwest Animal Hospital, where she had been the kennel help. She is proving to be a very good groom, and her clientele is growing. She had been told that the grooming would drop off to nothing as winter arrived, but Kaylyn continues to stay very busy. She started out by grooming on Mondays, Tuesdays, and Fridays, but she has done some grooms on Thursdays and will be adding every other Saturday as a groom day after the first of the year. She also helps out where needed otherwise and has done reception work and assisted with surgeries. She really likes where she works as well as everyone she works with, and I think they are pretty happy with her too.

Billy tried to go back to work in August. However, it did not work out, and he has had to remain on disability. Because he was not able to go back to work, I have had to find a job and am now working at Wal-Mart in HBA (health and beauty aids). I continue to home school the kids and generally work a 2:00 to 11:00 shift and have been getting thirty-two to thirty-four hours a week. I like the department I am working in, and it is going well.

Since I am now working, Cassy and the other kids are doing more around the house. Cassy has become the cook, and she often does laundry. She is really handy to have around and has taken on the extra responsibility with no complaint.

While Kaylyn finished high school this year, Cassy graduated the eighth grade. The girls wanted to have a graduation party, and they really wanted to have a hayride, so we had their party on the first Saturday in November. We had a hayride. We grilled hotdogs, and they hung out and played games in the yard. We had about twelve youth come to the party and a few adults who were the transportation for the youth. I think everyone enjoyed it.

I think that pretty much wraps up the year. Billy is still in remission and enjoying the time he spends with our family and friends. He took a seminary class this fall and will be taking the second half of it beginning in January. He really enjoyed the class and is looking forward to the next one. He has struggled some because of the things he can no longer do and his lack of stamina with the things he can do. The fact that I have had to go to work bothers him at times because he has always been and planned to be the provider. While these things bother him and get him down from time to time, for the most part he handles it all very well and accepts it as just being what it is. We just have to make the best of it. He continues to look for the Lord's plan in his life and ways that the Lord can use him.

We have been blessed in so many ways and by so many people. It is truly amazing. The Lord has been very good to us, and He continues to provide and make Himself known in our lives. We will continue to trust Him and do our best to live our lives in the way He would have us to.

April 2011

So far 2011 is not as good a year as 2010. Billy's multiple myeloma has relapsed, and he is on chemo once again. This time unless something else is discovered, Billy will continue on chemo permanently. While each person is different and the doctor does not have a true life expectancy for each individual, the average life expectancy for someone with multiple myeloma is three to five years. We know the Lord has the final say. Only

He knows how many days Billy has. We continue to trust the Lord and know that His will is perfect, even if we are not very fond of it.

I continue to update Billy's Caringbridge page. If you would like to continue following Billy and our family on this journey, you are welcome to check out www.caringbridge.org/visit/billcampbell.

Epilogue

October 2011

I had already finished this book, but because of events that have happened over the last couple of months, I decided I needed to add this. Billy had been receiving chemo once a month since May when in September, the doctor told us the numbers were not looking very good anymore and we needed to go back to getting chemo once a week for two weeks in a row and then taking one week off. However, this did not happen as planned. Billy received the first dose of chemo for his first two weeks on, one week off cycle on September 27. He was unable to receive the second dose the next week because his platelets and red cell counts were too low. He was given a couple extra weeks off of chemo, hoping his counts would come up and was supposed to return to the doctor for chemo on October 21. This was not to be. On Monday, October 10, Billy was not feeling well, and he did not feel well most of the week.

Friday, October 14, began our lay ministry weekend at church. Billy had organized and planned this weekend, and it was very important to him. Teams from several states came in to lead our weekend, which was to happen on Friday evening, Saturday morning, early afternoon, and evening, and Sunday morning and early afternoon. It was an amazing weekend! Billy did not feel well at all through the weekend and was completely exhausted. Many of us were worried about him, but he would not allow anyone to take over his responsibilities because it was just too important to him.

We made it home from the weekend at around 3:00 on Sunday afternoon on October 16, and Billy went right to bed. I checked on him several times and gave him his pills, and then at around midnight on Sunday night, he was running a low fever, so I started him on an antibiotic the doctor had given us for just an occasion. I called the doctor first thing Monday morning, and he wanted to see Billy. They drew blood and started IV fluids. Billy was not feeling well at all, and it showed. After seeing the blood work, the doctor told us that we had reached the point where chemo was now doing more harm than good because it was dropping Billy's platelet count, red cell count, and white count way too low. Billy needed blood and was scheduled to get it the next day. His platelets were at 33,000 when normal is 130,000 or more. We discussed the fact that it was time to quit trying to fight the cancer and just focus on how Billy was feeling. The doctor was hoping that Billy had an infection going on that we could treat and get him feeling better, at least for a little while. Again, it was not meant to be.

After Billy finished getting his IV fluids and antibiotic, we headed home to explain things to the kids and our other family and friends. This was a very tough day but only one of several to come. At a little after 7:00 that evening, I received a phone call from the doctor on call to let us know that Billy's calcium level had come back critically high and Billy needed to be in the hospital as soon as I could get him there. I loaded Billy up and headed for the hospital in Columbia, Missouri, which is an hour from our house. Billy's calcium level had been eighteen when they drew his blood that morning. They drew it again when we got to the ER, and it was up to twenty-one. The reading of eighteen was critically high, and the ER doctor was surprised Billy was not in a coma.

The hospital admitted Billy and ran fluids all night. They gave him literally gallons of fluids trying to flush the calcium from his system. By morning his calcium had come down less than two points, his platelets had dropped to 16,000, and his kidneys were shutting down. Dr. V came in and told us that unfortunately, as he had feared, the cancer had simply taken off like wildfire and there was nothing more they could do. He asked us if we wanted hospice to come in that night or the next morning. We agreed on the next morning because we wanted to have some time to talk to our kids, family, and friends.

Things moved unbelievably fast after that. Billy was released from the hospital just after noon on Tuesday, October 18 (Levi's twelfth birthday).

We went home and talked to the kids and our families, and I made many, many calls to our friends and church family. It was a very tough and emotional day. Hospice came to our house first thing on Wednesday morning, October 19, and Billy was able to sign the paperwork and walk for them. He was having some trouble staying focused. He was falling asleep easily and often and was dealing with muscle spasms.

Billy had many visitors through the day Wednesday. All our visitors were gone by just after 8:00 in the evening, and the kids and I then spent some time taking turns hugging and loving on Billy and telling him how much we love him. We had seen a lot of deterioration through the day and were not sure what the night and next day would bring. By midnight we were very concerned by how fast things were moving and called the hospice nurse to come assess Billy. I also called our good friend Aaron, who had grown up with Billy. He had wanted to come see Billy but had not been able to get here during the day Wednesday. Aaron is also a paramedic, and I wanted his assessment as well. Aaron arrived before the hospice nurse and was able to visit with Billy for a few minutes. Billy recognized him and was able to visit a little. Aaron's assessment was that Billy would only be with us for about twenty-four to forty-eight hours. The hospice nurse arrived after that and did her assessment as well. She was in agreement with Aaron. We discussed liquid pain meds and other things that would be needed for Billy, and she said she would put the order in for first thing in the morning.

Thursday, October 20, found Billy unable to walk and only able to wake up and know people part of the time. We had hospice get us a hospital bed so we could move Billy to the living room and keep him there. They delivered the bed by 10:00 in the morning, and I called Aaron to help us move Billy since he knows how to move people without hurting them. Doris and Jim brought up a wheelchair to help with the move, and Aaron was able to tell Max what he needed him to do. They did a great job, and the move was very smooth. Billy had his last visitors just after lunch on Thursday. He did seem to recognize them but was unable to stay awake for more than a few seconds. After that Billy was no longer able to open his eyes or talk to us. However, he did manage to communicate by raising his eyebrows and squeezing our hands. Just after supper, Jim had me go lay down for a little while since I knew I would be up all night with Billy. I was able to get a couple hours of sleep, and then Doris and Jim went home to rest for a while. The kids all went to sleep either in their beds or on the floor and couches in the living room.

Doris and Jim came back at about 4:30 in the morning on Friday, October 21. Jim sent me for another nap as soon as he arrived. I only intended to get a twenty-minute power nap but ended up sleeping a couple of hours. The kids slept fairly well and longer than they expected. We spent the majority of the day gathered around Billy's bed, holding his hands and talking to him. He would raise his eyebrows to let us know he was hearing us. Around mid to late afternoon when we were gathered around him, Kaylyn noticed he was mouthing something. As we watched, we were able to read his lips and found that he was saying, "I love you." Then he named every one of us. It was amazing, just as he was. At about 8:00 that evening I was swabbing his mouth. He liked the moisture but did not like the texture of the little sponge. While I was running it around in his mouth, he bit down on the stick and held on. I laughed at him and told him he was being a pill. He raised both eyebrows at me, and then Kaylyn said, "Well, you know he doesn't like that." When Kaylyn spoke, Billy cocked one eyebrow toward her and tried to grin.

I don't remember what time it was—8:30 or so maybe—when Billy's parents went home to rest for a little while. They called about 10:00 or so and there really had not been any change, so they planned to come back again at about 3:00 a.m. unless we called earlier. About twenty minutes later, Billy's breathing changed, and we knew it would not be much longer, so we called Billy's parents to come back. We were all gathered around Billy, and we all spoke to him. We let him know how much we love him, how proud we are of him, and that it was okay to go. He had completed his work and earned his reward, and we wanted him to know it was okay to go. Shortly before he took his last breath at 11:50 p.m., a tear rolled down his cheek.

We miss him more than I can even say, but we know where he is and know the Lord welcomed him with open arms. The Lord has granted the kids and me a peace we did not expect, and we are very grateful for that. We will do our best to live our lives as Billy did—for the Lord.

Max, our oldest son, has written something as if it were written by Billy. He titled it, "A Message from Heaven," and I will end with that letter. Max knew his dad very well, and it sounds just like what Billy would have said.

A Message t from Heaven

Back in 2009, I was diagnosed with cancer. I was in a lot of pain before I even found out I had cancer. The doctor just told me I had strained my back, and after some therapy, I would be as good as new. After going through this therapy, I did not seem to be getting any better. The pain in my back continued to intensify, along with back spasms and a few other things. The pain was excruciating. After many more tests and very long weeks of pain, in March of 2009, the doctors finally diagnosed me with multiple myeloma, a form of this nasty disease we hear so much about, cancer.

My wife, Dione, and I now had to go home and begin telling my six kids, my parents, my sister, my wife's family, and the rest of my family and friends. This was a very hard thing for everyone to hear, including myself. However, we were all hopeful that I would pull through. My parents saw an advertisement on TV for Cancer Treatment Centers of America. The nearest location they had was Tulsa, Oklahoma. My parents immediately called them, and the people at CTCA seemed very hopeful that they would be able to help me and especially get me out of the horrible pain I was in. After my wife made a call to them, we found out that our insurance was accepted. After my wife began informing them of my condition and how I was doing, they said we needed to get down to Tulsa as soon as possible. Dione immediately began packing and getting everything together. We said good-bye to our children, family, and friends and began our journey to Tulsa, Oklahoma.

The center very quickly took me into care and began getting my pain under control. Because of my condition, there are many things I do not really remember about this time. Dione said she was quite worried about me, but she managed to keep it all together, stay strong, and do everything that need to be done, just like she has always done.

We were in Tulsa from March until June. In this time, I received many visitors. Many friends and my family came to see me multiple times, which was a big help, because my family has always meant a great deal to me.

In June I was finally able to come home and be with my family again. This was wonderful for all of us because we have always been very close. Being separated for three months was hard for all of us. After more treatment, including a stem cell transplant at Barnes in St. Louis in February of 2010, I was declared to be in remission, although the cancer had done some permanent damage. The cancer had caused multiple vertebrae compression fractures in my neck and back, which caused me to be about four to five inches shorter than I was before this all began. It also caused a few pinched nerves, which caused my right hand and arm to become very weak. I would be able to build some of the strength back, but I would never regain the strength I once had. This was very hard for me to accept, but after a long time of praying and reading my Bible, I realized that even though this was not what I wanted, God had a purpose for this. I knew I needed to use this to glorify God. This brought me to a kind of contentment with what I had been through and what I would go through in the future.

The year 2010 was a brand new year. It was a good year because I was able to spend a lot of time with my family and stay very active in church and with my church family. My family and I were able to take a vacation to Washington DC as well. We all had a wonderful time just being together, enjoying each other's company, and learning a lot in all of the museums and memorials. It was time we all needed—time to just be with family.

In February of 2011, Dione and I went to the doctor for just another checkup, like we had done dozens of times before. This time we were informed that it appeared the cancer had returned. This was not news we wanted to hear, but we were hopeful that chemo would help.

It was around the October 10, a Monday, when I came down with a nasty cold. I fought this cold all week because I had a lay renewal at my church. A lay renewal is a weekend journey where a team of people from all around the country come to a specific church to revive the church and help the church get back into the habit of living for God and letting everything they do show God in their lives. I was the state coordinator for lay renewal, and I had put this one together for our church.

I rested up until Friday and was feeling a bit better, but after a long Friday of getting prepared and beginning the first day of lay renewal, I was feeling extremely run down. I went home and rested up because Saturday was yet another very full day of lay renewal. After getting up on Saturday morning, I still felt rather tired, but I pressed on because I knew the Lord wanted me to be at church and finish what I began.

I went on through the weekend, and while the lay renewal was an amazing experience, I became more and more run down. God gave me the strength to push through the weekend, and on Sunday afternoon after everything was over, I went home and slept for hours, hoping to feel better when I awoke. My wonderful wife was watching me very closely because she was worried that since the cancer had my blood counts down, this cold I had was not going to go away on its own. She checked my temperature in the middle of the night on Sunday and found I now had a low fever, so early the next morning she took me to the doctor to find out what we needed to do.

We got to the doctor's office, and they immediately began running a few tests. Little did we know the devastating news we were about to receive. The doctor quietly came in, sat down, and just sat there in silence for a few minutes. He finally began to speak in a slightly shaky voice. The cancer was so aggressive that chemo was no longer helping. It was only making things worse. After speaking with him for a few minutes, we found out there was nothing left for the doctors to do. They did not know how long it would take before the cancer began taking over.

They sent us home, and we had to tell this devastating news to the kids and the rest of our family. It was one of the hardest things I've ever had to do. It was that night when the hospital called and said I had critically high calcium and needed to get to the emergency room as soon as possible. They attempted to bring the calcium number down as much as they could, but it only came down a little. They sent me home. This time they told us we could expect me to live anywhere from a couple of days to maybe a few weeks. My family and I told each other how much we loved each other and said our good-byes.

The next few days were especially tough. The cancer began destroying my body. It caused involuntary muscle twitches, and it also affected my memory and my ability to comprehend things. I began losing control of my body. Within a couple of days, I could not walk, I could not open my eyes, and I could not even speak, but I could hear things going on around me. God gave me enough strength to give my family little signs, like a smile or the raise of an eyebrow, to show my family I could still hear what they had to say.

On Friday, October 21, I lay in bed, unable to control my body and unable to move. God still gave me the strength to gently squeeze the hands of my wife and children. I began to breathe strangely. My time was drawing near. God gave me the chance to say one last good-bye. He gave me the strength to mouth the words "I love you," and the names my wife, my kids, my sister, and my parents. This was a miracle in itself because before

I did not have the strength to do any of these things. Within a few hours, with all of my family at my side, I took my last breath here on earth.

The final breath is not the end. It is merely leaving this sinful world and entering a world of peace and pure perfection. It is a place where cancer cannot show its ugly face, a place of only happiness and rejoicing. Right now I'm sitting up in heaven, cancer free, pain free, and once again six feet tall. I am happy, I am at peace, and I am with our Lord and Savior, Jesus Christ. It was incredibly hard to leave my friends and family, but I am rejoicing in the fact that one day all of my family and friends will be in this perfect place with me, celebrating, worshiping our Creator, and never having to deal with a single ache, pain, sickness, or even sad thought.

I don't want you to be sad for me. I want you to strive to be the best Christian you can be and one day join me in this wonderful place. I want you to have the peace of mind that I had, knowing that after leaving this earth, you will reach the most wonderful place you have ever seen.

I want you to do me a favor. Think of the most wonderful place on this earth—the place that you love or want to see more than anything. Now think of the most horrifying, deepest, darkest place on this earth you can think of. Now if you had the choice, which place would you go? No brainer, right? When we die, we spend eternity in one of those two places—that amazing place you love or want to see (heaven) or that deep, dark, horrifying place you wish to never see (hell). Heaven is so amazing that we can't even fathom how wonderful it is. Hell is so deep, dark, and painful that we can't even imagine how horrifying it is. Which sounds nicer to you?

Here is the cool part. You have the choice right now to decide where you will go when you leave this earth. You can go to that wonderful place, and the best part is that there isn't a catch. It's as easy as ABC. All you have to do is pray to God and admit to Him that you're a sinner.

Believe that Jesus came years and years ago and died on the cross for you and me, and confess that Jesus is your Savior. That is it. Anyone can do it.

Perhaps this still sounds strange to you, or perhaps you are skeptical. Let me bring this to your attention. Let's say, for argument's sake, that I am wrong. You wasted five minutes of your time saying this prayer. Now, let's say you're wrong and you chose not to say this prayer and follow Jesus. When you reach the end of your life, you will end up spending eternity in a horrible place full of pain and suffering, with no escape. Is the fact that you're not sure if this can be true or that you're a little skeptical worth that risk? I want you to spend eternity up here in heaven with me, and so does Jesus Christ. The choice is yours. Where do you wanna be for the rest of eternity: a place more beautiful and perfect than you can imagine or a place more terrifying, dark, and painful than you can imagine? The choice is yours. Choose wisely.

I hope to see you here.

—Bill Campbell